EARLY HISTORIES

of

BELFAST MAINE

ANNALS OF BELFAST FOR HALF A CENTURY
by
William George Crosby

SKETCHES OF THE EARLY HISTORY OF BELFAST
by
John Lymburner Locke

HISTORY OF BELFAST
From its First Settlement to 1825
by
Herman Abbot

A HISTORY OF BELFAST
with Introductory Remarks on Acadia
by
William White

PICTON PRESS
CAMDEN, MAINE
1989

Annals of Belfast for Half a Century by William George Crosby (1805-1881) was originally published in fifty-two installments in the Belfast, Maine newspaper *The Republican Journal*, 1874-75

Sketches of the Early History of Belfast by John Lymburner Locke (1832-1876) was originally published in serialized form in the Belfast, Maine newspaper *The Progressive Age* in sixteen issues beginning 10 April 1856.

History of Belfast From its First Settlement to 1825 by Herman Abbot (1783-1825) remained in manuscript form at the time of his death and for many years was feared lost. When the manuscript was finally rediscovered it was published in serial form in four issues of *The Republican Journal* of Belfast beginning 25 Jan 1900, and was then published in Belfast, also in 1900, by Miss Grace E. Burgess.

A History of Belfast with Introductory Remarks on Acadia by William White (1783-1831) was first published in Belfast, Maine in 1827, and was the first bound book published in that town.

Transcription of all four histories above was done for this volume by Elizabeth M. Mosher, RFD 2 Box 825, City Point, Belfast, Maine 04915

Available from:

Picton Press
P. O. Box 1111
Camden, Maine 04843
Manufactured in the United States of America
using acid-free paper

TABLE OF CONTENTS

NOTE TO THE READER

All four of the histories contained in this volume were transcribed, with her usual meticulous care, by Elizabeth M. Mosher of City Point, Belfast, Maine. It was at her suggestion and initiative that the two much older histories, Abbot (1825) and White (1827) were included in this volume. Both Abbot and White are exceedingly scarce books, while Crosby and Locke have never been published in book form before. Researchers both historical and genealogical will find this volume an excellent source of information on Belfast and its environs; a source made even more valuable and useful by the inclusion of a consolidated Every-Name index and by the use of acid-free paper in printing.

The Introduction to Crosby's *Annals* and Locke's *Sketches* written by Alan Taylor of the Department of History, Boston University, which follows on pages v through xiv, adds significantly to our understanding of Belfast's growth. An Editor's Note on Abbot's *History of Belfast* and White's *A History of Belfast* will be found on page 229.

"SPRUNG UP IN A DAY"

BELFAST, MAINE EMERGES AS A

MARKET TOWN

In 1801 William Crosby was a young and ambitious lawyer chafing at the limited career prospects offered by his small, long-settled hometown: Billerica, Massachusetts. That summer he traveled to the Maine frontier in search of a new residence where he could prosper. He sought a particular sort of community: a commercial town, a place where merchants congregated to sell imported goods to the gathered loggers and farmers from the hinterland. This commerce inevitably produced debts and disputes, from which a lawyer profited. Crosby pressed northeastward beyond relatively well-settled York, Cumberland, Kennebec, and Lincoln counties in south central Maine. He bypassed their well-established market towns -- Kittery, York, Kennebunk, Saco, Portland, Brunswick, Bath, Hallowell, Augusta, Wiscasset, Waldoborough, and Thomaston; they were either well-stocked with lawyers or unlikely to grow rapidly in the future. Crosby sought an emerging commercial town, a community that had left behind the hardships of initial settlement, that was well-situated to draw in the commerce of an extensive hinterland, but that had yet to attract a surfeit of lawyers. He sought a community that had itself left behind the frontier stage and stood to reap the trade of an adjacent backcountry that was just starting to develop, a town that was not yet substantial but that promised to become so rapidly. Crosby meant to be that town's entrenched lawyer when its growth took off.[1]

By 1801 the northeastward flow of Maine's settlement had brought the Penobscot valley to the point of development most attractive to an ambitious young lawyer. Crosby had heard that Bangor was "a central point which would rise to eminence" because it lay at the head of the river's maritime navigation. He directed his horse "Robin" along the frontier's stump-ridden and mirey roads until he reached Bangor. It proved far too new and rough for Crosby's tastes; "I was so disappointed and mortified that I made up my mind to return home in the most direct way immediately." On the Fourth of July his return route down the west bank of the Penobscot River and Penobscot Bay brought Crosby to Belfast, then a slightly older and more impressive town than Bangor. Crosby was sufficiently intrigued by the "considerable appearance of business and activity" to return in the fall. He then found five or six new stores under construction and but a single lawyer in residence. Moreover, that lawyer, a newcomer named Bohan P. Field, recognized that there was already more business than he could handle alone; he and Crosby "entered into a league of amity." The latter hastened back to Billerica to wrap up his remaining business and close his law office there. In January 1802 he settled in Belfast. Two years later he married Sally Davis of Billerica who on September 10, 1805 gave birth to their eldest son and the author of the "Annals of Belfast for Half a Century," William George Crosby. The elder Crosby chose his new residence well for both he and his son prospered in Belfast, primarily as lawyers, but also as traders, land speculators, and political figures.[2]

William Crosby's timing was perfect. Belfast was poised for its takeoff because, of the towns on Penobscot Bay's west bank, it was best positioned to capture the trade of the backcountry towns to the northwest that were just then receiving their first permanent white settlers. Had he visited a decade earlier he would have found more hardship than opportunity; a decade later he would have come to a commercial village well-stocked with entrenched lawyers. In 1790 Belfast was less than twenty-years old and had been severely disrupted by the Revolutionary War and subsequent depression. That year the Federal census taker found that Belfast had only 245 inhabitants. Over the next two decades Belfast's population increased five-fold, reaching 1274 in the 1810 Federal census.[3]

During the same period Belfast's commercial wealth also grew dramatically. In 1790 most of the inhabitants dwelled in crude log cabins, and they lacked the capital for commercial enterprise: to construct stores, wharves, shipping, and mills. In 1789 the inhabitants explained to the Massachusetts General Court, "Wee have nothing to sell but cord wood or a trifle of lumber and that will fetch no money for we own no vessels in the town and are Dependent on those that sail transiently for a market." According to its tax valuation, in 1792 Belfast possessed no shops, only fourteen frame dwelling houses (the rest were log cabins), two mills, no wharfage, and but 150 tons of shipping (the equivalent of one ocean-going ship, or two coasters). At $1771.83 in aggregate valuation, Belfast ranked a mediocre eleventh out of Hancock County's eighteen assessed communities (until 1827 Hancock County included Belfast and most of the rest of what is now Waldo County). By 1811 this assessed wealth had grown four-fold to $7493.76 and Belfast ranked an impressive seventh among the sprawling county's forty-nine communities. That year Belfast had 161 frame dwelling houses, twenty-one shops, three tanneries, a potash works, three warehouses, three grist mills, three carding machines, two fulling mills, nine saw mills, 8375 feet of wharfage, and 576 tons of shipping. Five lawyers had come to live off that commerce and its disputes: Crosby, Field, John Wilson, Phineas Ashmun, and Oakes Angier. Benefitting from their earlier arrival, Crosby and Field were the town's preeminent lawyers in both status and wealth.[4]

Most of this impressive growth occurred after 1800. During the decade 1790-1800 the population grew by 429 compared to an increase of 600 during the following ten years. Similarly, aggregate assessed wealth grew by $619.97 during the decade 1792-1801 versus $5101.96 during the subsequent decade. In short, William Crosby's January 1802 arrival came just as Belfast's demographic and commercial growth took off.[5]

At the turn of the century visitors described Belfast as an emerging boom town: equally rough-hewn and dynamic. In 1793 William West arrived from Kingston, New Hampshire to find only two frame buildings in the town's village located beside Sandy Beach; indeed much of the emerging village's ground was still smoking from recent fires set to clear the underbrush. Three years later Belfast's village consisted of twelve frame buildings, only one of which stood taller than one story. At that time, the visiting Rev. Paul Coffin of Buxton noted "we came to the view of the harbor directly from thick woods. The settlements round the harbor go back but little from the water." In 1802 Crosby erected his law office "in the midst of large hemlock logs and stumps" but took cheer from ten new stores and dwelling houses then under construction in the village. Four years later the visiting Leverett Saltonstall noted, "Belfast is a very pretty town, handsomely situated on the bay. The houses are generally painted which gives it a sprightly appearance....This town has more the appearance of having sprung up in a day than any I have seen. The gardens, yards, and sides of the streets are ornamented with stumps and half-burnt trees."[6]

Belfast attests that not all towns on the Maine coast became equally populous or equally prosperous. A select few emerged as trade and service centers for most of the other, smaller, and poorer hinterland towns. As Crosby had anticipated, by 1810 Belfast had assumed its place in the middle of New England's three-tier hierarchy of towns. At the bottom were the many hinterland communities and lesser coastal villages whose many small farmers and fishermen produced small surpluses of lumber, crafts, produce, or fish. Roads, navigable rivers, or the coast funnelled their surpluses toward the most convenient nearby market town, usually located at the head of a bay or river where deep-water navigation began. The market towns sat atop the local pecking order and represented the median tier. There the rural farmer, artisan, or fisherman found traders, warehouses, stores, wharves and shipping. The trader connected the small producer with the Atlantic economy. At the market town he could exchange his surplus for the trader's imports from the far corners of the globe. The trader, in turn, exported the small producer's surplus to pay for the European manufactures and tropical staples that filled his shelves.[7]

Sometimes the market town merchants traded directly with foreign ports, dispatching their own deep-water vessels to England, France, Holland, and the West Indies. More commonly, these traders assembled small cargoes on "coasters" small vessels of less than 100 tons that proceeded to the region's preeminent cities: Portland, Portsmouth, Newburyport, or, overshadowing all, Boston. Perched atop the hierarchy of places, these cities housed the wholesalers who put together large cargoes drawn from the retail merchants in the market towns; in return they broke up and dispersed large lots of foreign imports. In this manner the shingles produced by a settler in Unity, Maine passed through the hands of a Belfast trader and a Boston merchant before reaching the West Indies. There the shingles procured the rum that ended up warming the Unity farmer through the long cold winter of shingle-making.[8]

To emerge and prosper as a market town a community needed to capture as much of the hinterland trade as possible. The process was cumulative; the more country trade a particular town could draw, the more attractive it appeared to those newcomers - such as William Crosby - with the capital necessary to finance wharves, stores, warehouses, and mills. As a town acquired an edge in these improvements it drew in more trade and an ever larger share of ambitious newcomers. Initially, new coastal or riverine settlements that were near neighbors competed with each other. A favorable combination of a superior harbor with good access to the newer settlements in the immediate interior generally determined which town emerged preeminent in its vicinity. Lacking a decent harbor and hemmed in by rough terrain in its interior, Northport could not compete with Belfast as a mercantile center.[9]

Belfast had other important advantages over its near neighbors: it was settled by a relatively homogeneous group committed to civic improvement and possessed of clear title to their individual land holdings. In 1768-1769 a group of prosperous Scotch-Irish farmers from Londonderry, New Hampshire purchased the site of Belfast from the Waldo heirs for £1500. Over the next thirty years, the proprietors or their assigns subdivided the township into individual homesteads. Many were settled either by the proprietors or, more commonly, their sons. Consequently Belfast's settlers had, by Maine standards, a relatively high degree of group identity and that they owned their land outright, which meant a greater readiness to develop their lands and buildings and to bear taxes to support schools and the ministry. Belfast stood in marked contrast to the neighboring coastal towns of Lincolnville, Northport, and Prospect which were settled by diverse groups of squatters in defiance of the absentee Waldo heirs. Fearing possible ejectment, the squatters were slow to make permanent improvements in their homesteads. Instead they lived by lumbering and fishing, pursuits that lifted few of them out of their poverty. Poor and drawn from different places, they were slow to develop the means and cohesion necessary to establish community schools and churches. In 1794 the French traveler the Duc de La Rochefoucauld-Liancourt noted the dramatic difference as he passed across Little River from Northport into Belfast:

> The houses are better, and are, even in some instances, painted. The lands have been brought into a better condition. This territory was sold thirty years ago, by the family of Waldo, and its present state of superior improvement seems to evince, that the uncertainty of the possession of those who have settled in other townships, must be the chief reason that occasions them to leave their lands destitute of culture.

Naturally, men of property interested in settling along Penobscot Bay were drawn to Belfast, rather than its immediate neighbors, because it offered them secure land titles and established civic institutions. Consequently, capital accumulated in Belfast rather than in its immediate neighbors.[10]

INTRODUCTION

By 1800 Belfast (rather than Northport), Castine (not Penobscot), Bucksport (rather than Orland), Frankfort (but not Prospect), Camden (rather than Lincolnville), Thomaston (not Cushing), Waldoborough (instead of Friendship), Wiscasset (rather than Edgecombe), Augusta (not Vassalborough), and Hallowell (instead of Pittston) emerged in their locales as the prime contenders for shares of the surplus produced by the country folk dwelling between the Kennebec and the Penobscot rivers. The more successful coastal towns of each cluster then strove against one another to extend their sway over more of the hinterland. Again superior location largely decided the contest. Possessed of the larger, deeper harbor and a river that reached into a relatively level portion of the backcountry, Belfast eclipsed its southern rival Camden with its small harbors and its interior barrier of rugged mountains. Most of the settlers in Searsmont, Belmont, Morrill, Lincolnville, Liberty, Montville, and Northport found it easier and cheaper to take their commodities to market in Belfast rather than Camden.[11]

Given the period's primitive technology of transportation, two other geographic factors also favored Belfast in her competition for the country trade. First, its hinterland towns to the northwest - Thorndike, Unity, Jackson, Knox, Dixmont, and Troy were well-timbered with hardwoods and were relatively fertile by Maine's standards. This meant that the settlers there could produce somewhat larger surpluses than could those dwelling in the interior behind Castine and Wiscasset. After initially superior growth in the 1790s, those two market towns stagnated while Belfast continued to grow, outstripping both by the mid nineteenth century. A harbor that was ice-free for the entire winter was the second consideration that favored Belfast. Given Maine's rough terrain and the primitive state of its stump-, stone-, and mud-filled roads, bulky commodities produced in the interior moved best on large sleds and sleighs when a layer of snow covered the ground. Winter, then, was the season when the country folk did most of their marketing. But it did the farmer little good to haul his lumber or hay to a market town whose river or harbor was jammed with ice until the spring. For this reason the aptly named Winterport (then a part of Frankfort) wrested from ice-clogged Bangor much of the commerce from the upper Penobscot towns. Similarly, although Unity, Benton, Troy, and Freedom lay closer to the Kennebec River than to the Penobscot, their trade generally flowed to Belfast rather than to Hallowell or Augusta because ice closed the Kennebec to navigation during much of the winter.[12]

An important human factor came into play on the margins of geographic advantage; by "boosterism" - aggressive, competitive promotion - a particular market town's entrepreneurs could best their rivals. In 1827 Moses Greenleaf, Maine's astute geographer and a resident of the Penobscot Valley, explained,

> It will be obvious that superior enterprize, and skill in its direction, on the part of the inhabitants of one market-town, in improving the natural, or creating artificial, means of communication with the interior, which otherwise would naturally be connected with some other market; and thus would increase their own wealth and importance, at the expense of some of their neighbors.

In part promotion meant convincing migrants, ship-captains, and farmers of the superior advantages to be found in the entrepreneurs' particular community. Boosters also strove to relay word of the inconvenience, backwardness, perversity, and extraordinary immorality that prevailed in competing market towns. To entice merchant vessels entering the Penobscot River into their ports - Winterport and Bucksport - the lower river inhabitants rowed out to inform the sea captains of the allegedly dangerous conditions upriver that rendered proceeding on to rival Bangor exceedingly foolish. Naturally, Bangor's inhabitants regarded this ploy as the ultimate outrage. When Searsport (then split between Belfast and Prospect) began to grow at

INTRODUCTION

Belfast village's expense, the Belfasters labeled their emerging rival "Sodom." The "Sodomites" returned the favor by calling Belfast "Gomorrah."[13]

Boosterism also meant competing to improve access to the interior. In 1800, Belfast's principal inhabitants petitioned the General Court to incorporate them as a toll-bridge company. At their own expense they meant to erect a bridge across the Passagassawaukeag (or Belfast) River, in return for the subsequent income from tolls. More importantly, by improving back-country access to Belfast, a new bridge promised to boost the town's economy. Competing towns lobbied against the act of incorporation as "inconvenient" for the backcountry inhabitants. This lobbying delayed incorporation until March 14, 1805, but construction then proceeded rapidly with completion in 1806. In 1824 Belfast's leading men shrewdly strengthened their commercial ties to the hinterland by organizing the Hancock County Agricultural Society and hosting the first county fair in October of that year. According to William G. Crosby the fair drew "a large concourse of spectators" to do some trading on the side and spend their pence and shillings on the Belfasters' sweet cider, pumpkin pies, doughnuts, and hard-boiled eggs.[14]

Creating an environment attractive to properous men was important to a town's efforts to attract and retain capital. Recognizing that propertied men were more likely to settle and remain where their sons could receive the education necessary to make them gentlemen, in 1808 Belfast's town fathers secured incorporation of the Belfast Academy. In the early 1820s the leading entrepreneurs erected impressive new brick structures - the Eagle Hotel, a new town hall, a brick distillery, Phoenix Row, and the Bean and Derby block - that attested to the town's sense of prosperous maturity. In 1823 the town fathers described their impressive new town hall, then in the planning stage, as "a durable monument of the taste, foresight, and judgment of its founders, a lasting ornament and honor to the town." Because so many of the leading entrepreneurs who governed the town and principally financed the building were members of the Masonic Order, the town voted "to accommodate the Masonic Society by permitting the upper story or garret of the town-house to be finished for their use." During the 1820s the villagers strove to beautify the town by straightening crooked streets, planting ornamental trees, laying out sidewalks, fencing in yards, and improving the public square. Their sense of beauty stressed orderliness. In 1827 the town's leading citizens took offence at the disorderly spectacle of boys sledding on the public streets; they formed a mutual association devoted to demolishing the sleds of "any boy found coasting in the streets or high ways." All these efforts sought to create a controlled landscape that attested to the leading inhabitants' successful and profitable mastery over nature.[15]

Finally, boosters aggressively lobbied the state government in order to attract public institutions to their town and away from rivals. Market towns especially lusted to become their county's shire town, the seat of county government. The semi-annual court sessions attracted many rural folk who generally transacted business during their visit; and the judges and court officers settled in the community, pumping their comfortable incomes from court fees into the town's economy. In other words, the county courts were one more way by which a market town captured the surplus produced in the hinterland. The Belfasters invested in such an impressive town hall in order to strengthen their efforts to persuade the state government to remove Hancock County's courts from Castine to Belfast. The new town hall enabled the Belfasters to argue that they could house the courts in appropriate style. By wresting away the county courts, Belfast's boosters meant to administer a final blow to stagnating Castine, cementing Belfast's preeminence in the Penobscot Bay area. Castine's political resistance forestalled removal in favor of a compromise: in 1827 the state legislature divided Hancock County, setting off the western half as Waldo County with Belfast as the shire town. As expected, Belfasters received most of the appointments as court officers. [16]

As a result of geographic advantage and aggressive boosterism, by 1830 Belfast had become a highly successful market town, preeminent in Waldo County. Postage sold by a town's post office was a good measure of commercial activity. During the fiscal year 1 March 1825 - 28 February 1826 Waldo County's 22 post offices sold $1336.93 in postage. Belfast's post office sold $555.34 or almost half the county total. By contrast, Belfast's two eclipsed commercial rivals in the county - Camden and Frankfort - sold $197.21 and $167.66, respectively. The other nineteen post offices did an indifferent business, selling a combined $416.72, for an average of $21.93 per post office (one twenty-fifth of Belfast's sales). In sum, Belfast served as Waldo County's economic portal to the outside world.[17]

In the countryside as far west as Palermo, Freedom, Unity, Benton, and Troy a network of rough roads directed the farmers' ox- or horse-drawn sleds, sleighs, and wagons southeastward toward Belfast's stores and wharves. Rising before dawn, the farmers bore their shingles, clapboards, staves, cordwood, ship's timber, spruce spars, hay, potatoes, oats, butter, and livestock to market. Arriving in the early afternoon, they delivered their commodities to the town's traders in return for some mixture of store goods and diminution of their debt for items advanced on credit at an earlier time. The farmers spent some time idling, bargaining, gossiping, joking, and drinking in the local taverns. In late afternoon they set their course for home with a return cargo of salt fish, flour, cloth, tools, molasses, and rum. A farmer would make several such trips to Belfast during the course of the year.[18]

Generally the country folk found their ties to Belfast's merchants necessary and useful. But it was obvious that most of the profits from the trade accumulated in Belfast. Brick or white-clapboard mansions built by merchants and lawyers proliferated on Belfast's hills overlooking the harbor; log cabins or one-story frame houses unpainted on the outside and unplastered on the inside were the norm in the countryside. Many rural farmers felt aggrieved that their payments made so little dent in their debts to Belfast's traders and that they so frequently confronted an impatient creditor's suit for payment. The records of the Hancock and Lincoln County Courts of Common Pleas reveal that during the ten years 1796-1805 residents of coastal, commercial Belfast and the inhabitants of backcountry towns confronted each other in 134 debt cases. In nine out of ten cases (119 of 134) the Belfast resident was the plaintiff and the back-country inhabitant the defendant. Moreover, those suits tended to pit plaintiffs of superior wealth and status against poorer defendants of lesser standing. In two-thirds (78 of 119) of the debt cases brought by Belfast residents against backcountry folk a gentleman or his status equivalent - a trader, merchant, Esquire, or physician - sued a yeoman or laborer. The plaintiffs won every one of those cases. In contrast, on only one occasion did a backcountry yeoman or laborer sue a Belfast gentleman, and that suit failed. The suits added heavy court costs to the farmer's debt and they led to forcible executions where his livestock or land went on the auction block. The country folk periodically grumbled that the economic structure and judicial system existed to fleece the common folk and profit the "parasites": the lawyers and merchants. It often seemed to the country folk that Belfast grew rich at their expense.[19]

Debt suits were not the farmers' only legal problem. Many were squatters unwilling or unable to pay the land prices demanded by their absentee proprietors. The proprietors' lawsuits meant additional profitable unpopularity for Belfast. William G. Crosby explained, "The lawyers who brought these suits of ejectment for proprietors, and the officers employed to serve them, resided in this place, and it was not strange that they were regarded by the squatters as in league with the proprietors who were adopting measures which in their view were unjust and oppressive; neither was it strange under the circumstances that there should exist to some extent a feeling of hostility against Belfast." Serving the proprietors was one more mechanism by which another piece of the backcountry surplus was redistributed into the hands of Belfast's traders and lawyers. Finally, the smug tone of moral superiority assumed by Belfast's town fathers added insult to the dirt farmers' injury.[20]

During the decade 1800-1810 the backcountry settlers were most vulnerable to debt and ejectment suits; the farmers intermittently organized themselves by neighborhood to forcibly resist deputy sheriffs bearing writs from creditors or proprietors. The country folk set up a watch system where sentries who spied an approaching deputy sounded the alarm on tin horns. The nearby settlers then donned Indian disguises, grabbed their muskets, and gathered around the interloper. Most deputies promptly fled. Those reckless few who pressed on had their writs confiscated and destroyed; occasionally they were roughly handled. On at least two occasions surveyors for the proprietors were shot and wounded when they attempted to run survey lines in Thorndike.[21]

Occasionally posses ventured forth from Belfast to arrest and carry away suspected "White Indians." These raids led to backcountry threats to descend on Belfast in force and set the village ablaze. In late June 1801 some "White Indians" did appear outside Belfast, but the town's militia turned out in force to prevent any further trouble. A more comical alarm occurred in late October 1807. The "White Indians" of Greene Plantation (now Searsmont, Morrill, and Belmont) ambushed a persistent deputy sheriff, killing his horse, seizing his papers, and putting the man to flight back toward Belfast. A posse arrested a suspected "Greene Indian" and brought him to Belfast. That night rumors of an impending counterattack, followed by the ominous sound of gunshots on the approaches to town, led to a general alarm; Belfast's men tumbled out of bed, took up arms, and mustered in defense of their town. They spent a sleepless night starting at every noise until it dawned on them that they were the butt of a practical joke; some young pranksters had spread the rumor and fired the shots. In fact, as William G. Crosby explains, "every Greene Indian in the Plantation had been sleeping quietly under his own roof, never dreaming of any invasion of Belfast save with a goad-stick in his hand and a horse or ox drawing a load of cordwood or shingles, with no thought of plunder beyond the market value of his load in salt-fish, pork, and 'New England [rum].'" Delighted by the Belfasters' embarrassment, Joseph Dolliff, the "squatter poet" of Greene Plantation, composed a mock epic entitled "The Greene Indian War," which lampooned the greed and folly displayed by Belfast's town fathers.[22]

This then was the Belfast made by William Crosby's generation and inherited by William G. Crosby's generation: successful and proud but not particularly well-liked for that smug propriety. The second generation strove to memorialize as well as ornament their fathers' accomplishments. Histories of Belfast's ascent began to appear in the 1820s, at the same time and for many of the same reasons that the streets were straightened and purged of sledding boys. During the nineteenth century an impressive succession of town histories carefully documented Belfast to a degree unparalleled elsewhere in the county. Successful market towns took better care of their town and family records and secured them from fires in the vaults of brick town halls. Successful market towns had the concentration of prosperous and well-educated men who could write and patronize historical works. So we now know much about Belfast but next to nothing about the origins of Waldo County's backcountry communities. Hence, this differential historical knowledge is one more legacy of the redistribution from hinterland to seaport effected by William Crosby's generation; they created the aggregations of wealth that sustained the memorializing efforts of their offspring. In his *Annals of Belfast for Half a Century* William G. Crosby styles himself an "Old Settler" when of course he was nothing of the sort. He was, instead, a successful and well-educated lawyer who grew up in the comfort of a well-established commercial town. The real "Old Settlers" of the interior rarely possessed the education or the means to record their reminiscences. William G. Crosby's *Annals of Belfast for Half a Century* and John Lymburner Locke's *Sketches of the Early History of Belfast* are two testimonies to - as well as descriptions of - their fathers' successful struggle to economically yoke the Waldo County backcountry to the wharves and stores they build beside Belfast's Sandy Beach.[23]

Of the two authors we know far more about William G. Crosby. He attended Bowdoin College, graduating in 1823. He read law and was admitted to the Hancock County bar. In 1831 he married Anne Patterson, the daughter of another of Belfast's properous makers: the sea captain Robert Patterson the Fourth. William G. Crosby inherited his father's conservative politics as well as his wealth. His father had been a rather passive Federalist; the son became an active Whig, successfully winning Maine's governorship in 1852 and 1854. When that party collapsed over the sectional crisis Crosby miscalculated, casting his lot with the Democrats (then the more conservative of the two parties) rather than with the newly emergent Republicans who rapidly rose to statewide dominance. This meant that in the 1860s and 1870s William G. Crosby had plenty of time for his private law practice, for attending to his duties as Belfast's customs collector, and for collecting the historical materials that went into his *Annals*. His work covers the first fifty years of his life, 1805-1855, and was first published in fifty-two installments by Belfast's leading newspaper *The Republican Journal*, 1874-1875. Crosby died in Belfast March 21, 1881, aged seventy-five.[24]

Rather less is known about the Rev. John Lymburner Locke. He was the son of Samuel Locke, a relative newcomer to Belfast, arriving in the 1820s, and of Jannet Lymburner. John L. Locke was named for his maternal grandfather Captain John Lymburner, one of Belfast's earliest inhabitants. John L. Locke inherited and dwelled in the house that his grandfather had built in the village in 1803 during its first surge to prosperity. That house lay on the same block as the fine mansion that William Crosby built with the profits from his legal career. John L. Locke studied for the ministry and served the Methodist ministry. He early demonstrated an interest in and flair for historical writing. In 1856 the Belfast newspaper, *The Progressive Age*, serialized his *Sketches*. In 1863 he published a pamphlet history of Belfast's Phoenix (Masonic) Lodge, to which he belonged. He also published a brief history of Belfast's Methodist Church and a longer history of the town of Camden, one of the coastal communities that lost out to Belfast in the struggle for the country trade. Locke died in Belfast on February 18, 1876 aged only forty-three.[25]

Both works are full of delightful vignettes that add to our picture of the social world of a market town. I confess to a slight preference for Locke's work. Crosby periodically lapses into long lists: the information is valuable but it breaks up the narrative flow. More importantly, Locke has a more colorful sense of the past and records images of Belfast's public character that are available nowhere else: the religious pamphlet that sets everyone to talking and divides the town, speculation about the haunted hulks by the shore, and the public reading of news from the War of 1812. These all conjure up a world where people daily shaped their understanding of their place and the outside world through street encounters: bantering in a tavern, gossiping before and after church, stopping to talk on an errand to an artisan's shop, or conversing on the way to a Fourth of July celebration in a local town. It was both a very busy place and yet small enough for everyone to have a good fix on everyone else's character and business. Crosby illuminates the same world but not quite as vividly as Locke does. Read together they add greatly to the rich picture we have of life in early Belfast.

Alan Taylor   Department of History   Boston University

INTRODUCTION

1. Joseph Williamson, *History of the City of Belfast in the State of Maine* (Portland, Me., 1877), Vol. 1:199-200; and Edward Augustus Kendall, *Travels Through the Northern Parts of the United States in the Years 1807 and 1808* (New York, 1809), Vol. 3:33-34.

2. William Crosby's autobiography quoted in Williamson, *Belfast*, Vol. I:199-201.

3. Bureau of the Census, *Heads of Families at the First Census of the United States Taken in the Year 1790: Maine* (Washington, D.C., 1908), p. 9.

4. Belfast Aggregate Valuation, 1792 in the Volume of Aggregate Valuations for 1792, Massachusetts State Library (MSL hereafter). The 1792 assessment was for £531.11.8 which has been converted at 6s = $1. Belfast Aggregate Valuation, 1811 in the Hancock County Valuation Aggregates, Vault, MSL. Massachusetts General Court, *Abstract of the Report of the Committee on the Valuation* (Boston, 1793, Evans # 25771), p. 12; Massachusetts General Court, *Report of the Committee of Valuation* (Boston, 1811, Shaw-Shoemaker # 23322), pp. 12-13; and (for Belfast's lawyers) *The Massachusetts Register and United States Calendar for the Year of Our Lord 1810...* (Boston, 1809).

5. Massachusetts General Court, *Report of the Committee of Valuation* (Boston, 1802, Shaw-Shoemaker # 2625), p. 13; Bureau of the Census, *Return of the Whole Number of Persons within the Several Districts of the United States* (Washington, D.C., 1801).

6. On Belfast's slow growth prior to 1800 see William White, *A History of Belfast with Introductory Remarks on Acadia* (Belfast, Me., 1827), p. 50. William West's testimony is in Williamson, *Belfast*, I: 197. Belfast village's buildings in 1796 are described in Jonathan Greenleaf, *Sketches of the Ecclesiastical History of the State of Maine* (Portsmouth, N.H., 1821), p. 167. William Crosby's autobiography is quoted in Williamson, *Belfast*, p. 201. William G. Crosby, *Annals of Belfast for Half a Century*, Chapter V. Leverett Saltonstall's travel journal, August 17, 1806 entry, in Robert E. Moody, ed., *The Saltonstall Papers, 1607-1815, Volume II: 1791-1815* (Massachusetts Historical Society, *Publications* Volume 81, Boston, Ma., 1974), p. 329.

7. William Tudor, *Letters on the Eastern States* (Boston, 1821), pp. 121-122; and Edwin M. Cook, Jr., *The Fathers of the Towns; Leadership and Community Structure in Eighteenth-Century New England* (Baltimore, Md., 1976), pp. 76-79.

8. On Maine's wood coasters see Alexander Baring to Hope & Company, December 3, 1796 in Frederick S. Allis, Jr., ed., *William Bingham's Maine Lands, 1790-1820* (Volumes 36 and 37 of *Publications of the Colonial Society of Massachusetts*, Boston, 1954) Vol. 37: 787; Moses Greenleaf, *A Survey of the State of Maine, in Reference to its Geographic Features, Statistics, and Political Economy* (Portland, Me., 1829), p. 247; Francois Alexandre Frederic Duc de La Rochefoucauld-Liancourt, *Travels Through the United States of North America...* (London, 1799), vol. 1: 419; James B. Vickery, III, *A History of the Town of Unity, Maine* (Manchester, Me., 1954), p. 127; and White, *Belfast*, p. 63.

9. White, *Belfast*, p. 83. Similarly, prior to the advent of the railroad in the 1830s, Hallowell overshadowed Augusta because the latter had a steep ridge, "Burnt Hill," that obstructed the access of the farmers in western Kennebec County. See James W. North, *The History of Augusta From the Earliest Settlement to the Present Time* (Augusta, Me., 1870), p. 302.

10. Williamson, *Belfast*, pp. 65, 87, 187; White, *Belfast*, p. 33; La Rochefoucauld-Liancourt, *Travels*, Vol. I: 434-435; and John Lymburner Locke, "Sketches of the Early History of Belfast, Number 10," *The Progressive Age* (Belfast, Me.), June 12, 1856. See also the Rev. Daniel Little's "Journal," September 29, 1774 entry, pp. 141-142, Kennebunk Unitarian Church.

11. White, *Belfast*, p. 83.

12. Joseph Whipple, *A Geographical View of the District of Maine with Particular Reference to its Internal Resources...* (Bangor, Mr., 1816), pp. 10-12, 37; Leverett Saltonstall's travel journal, August 10, 1806 entry, in Moody, *Saltonstall Papers*, Vol. 2: 328; Williamson, *Belfast*, I:369; White, *Belfast*, pp. 83-85; M. Greenleaf, *Survey*, p. 127.

13. M. Greenleaf, *Survey*, p. 125; "Mercator," *Bangor Weekly Register*, July 20, 1816; and Crosby, *Annals*, Chapter 4. For explorations of the booster ethos see Robert R. Dykstra, *The Cattle Towns* (Lincoln, Neb., 1968); and Don Harrison Doyle, *The Social Order of a Frontier Community; Jacksonville, Illinois, 1825-1870* (Chicago, Ill., 1983).

14. Crosby, *Annals*, Chapters 6 and 18. For counter-lobbying see George Ulmer to Henry Knox, April 19, 1800, Henry Knox Papers Vol. 43: 31, Massachusetts Historical Society (MHS hereafter).

15. Chapter LXV (February 29, 1808) in Massachusetts, *Acts of the General Court of Massachusetts, 1808* (Boston, 1808, Shaw-Shoemaker # 15525), pp. 270-272; White, *Belfast*, pp. 48-50; Williamson, *Belfast*, I:142-143, 215; Crosby, "Annals," Chapters 18, 20. For a similar picture see Doyle, *The Social Order*, pp. 34-36.

16. Williamson, *Belfast*, I:143-144, 369-371; and Crosby, "Annals," Chapters 18, 20.

17. M. Greenleaf, *Survey*, p. 466.

18. Timothy W. Robinson, *History of the Town of Morrill in the County of Waldo and State of Maine* (Belfast, Me., 1944), pp. 118-119; White, *Belfast*, pp. 50, 63, 85; Vickery, *Unity*, p. 127; M. Greenleaf, *Survey*, p. 249; and Allen Goodwin, "The Early Settlers of Montville," *The Republican Journal* (Belfast, Me.), February 5, 1885.

19. For this manner of thought among the settlers see Alan Taylor, "'Stopping the Progres of Rogues and Deceivers:' A White Indian Recruiting Notice of 1808," *William and Mary Quarterly* Third Series Vol. 42 (January 1985): 90-103. The court records for Hancock County and Lincoln County are at the Maine State Archives in Augusta.

20. Crosby, "Annals," Chapter 7. For an example of the indifference of the Belfasters' sense of superiority see the petition quoted in Williamson, *Belfast*, I:187-188.

21. "The Early History of Monroe," *The Republican Journal* (Belfast, Me.), February 16, 1882. See also Taylor, "Stopping the Progres," p. 94.

22. George Ulmer to Henry Knox, June 28, 1801, Henry Knox Papers Vol. 44:14, MHS; John Wilson to Benjamin Joy, November 2, 1807, Box 7 William King Papers, Maine Historical Society (Portland, Me.); and Crosby, "Annals," Chapter 7. Robinson, *Morrill*, p. 51 and Locke, "Sketches...Number 11," present garbled versions of the events leading up to the scare in Belfast.

23. In addition to the works of White and Williamson see Herman Abbot, *History of Belfast, Maine to 1825, with an Introduction and Notes by Joseph Williamson* (Belfast, Me., 1900).

24. Williamson, *Belfast*, Vol. 2: 124-127.

25. Williamson, *Belfast*, Vol. 1:100, 208-209, 304-305, Vol. 2:389.

Annals of Belfast

for

Half a Century

by

William George Crosby

PICTON PRESS

CAMDEN, MAINE
1989

Annals of Belfast for Half a Century by William George Crosby (1805-1881) was originally published in fifty-two installments in the Belfast, Maine newspaper *The Republican Journal*, 1874-75

Sketches of the Early History of Belfast by John Lymburner Locke (1832-1876) was originally published in serialized form in the Belfast, Maine newspaper *The Progressive Age* in sixteen issues beginning 10 April 1856.

History of Belfast From its First Settlement to 1825 by Herman Abbot (1783-1825) remained in manuscript form at the time of his death and for many years was feared lost. When the manuscript was finally rediscovered it was published in serial form in four issues of *The Republican Journal* of Belfast beginning 25 Jan 1900, and was then published in Belfast, also in 1900, by Miss Grace E. Burgess.

A History of Belfast with Introductory Remarks on Acadia by William White (1783-1831) was first published in Belfast, Maine in 1827, and was the first bound book published in that town.

Transcription of all four histories above was done for this volume by Elizabeth M. Mosher, RFD 2 Box 825, City Point, Belfast, Maine 04915

Available from:

Picton Press
P. O. Box 1111
Camden, Maine 04843
Manufactured in the United States of America
using acid-free paper

ANNALS OF BELFAST FOR HALF A CENTURY.

BY AN OLD SETTLER

(Hon. Wm. G. Crosby.)

CHAPTER I. (1805.)

In 1827, William White, Esq., then residing in Belfast, who died in 1831, published a small duodecimo volume of one hundred and nineteen pages entitled "A History of Belfast, with Introductory Remarks on Acadia." That portion of the volume relating to the history of Belfast occupied forty-two pages. In his preface to this little volume the author remarks that "should this sketch preserve a single incident, or material, suitable to be used hereafter when the history of the State shall be written, this essay will not have been altogether in vain." The compiler of these annals has no higher object in view.

The history of Belfast is yet to be written. The preparation of that work is already in able hands; its appearance is anxiously awaited by all who cherish a laudable pride in the past and present of the home of their nativity or adoption. The History of Maine, from the date of its discovery, A. D. 1602, to the date of its separation from Massachusetts, A. D. 1820, written by Hon. William D. Williamson, published in 1832, has stood the test of criticism for forty years, and is still recognized in as authority, and as one, to say the least, of the ablest and most accurate State Histories that have ever issued from the press; we are fortunate in having for the future historian of Belfast the nephew of the historian of Maine.

The compiler of these annals was born in Belfast in 1805, and with the exception of occasional temporary absences this has always been his home. He thinks that under this state of facts he may, without subjecting himself to the imputation of vanity, rightfully make claim to the title he assumes, that of "An Old Settler." There are but few left who can show better title to the appellation. The generation to which he belongs is rapidly joining

"The innumerable caravan which moves
To that mysterious realm, where each shall take
His chamber in the silent halls of death."

In a few years there will be few left who can write or speak from personal recollection of the events that transpired in this place during the first two decades of the current century; that those events may become matter of local history, not left to float in fragments on the dim, misty sea of tradition, is the ruling motive of the compiler in undertaking this work. To the generation now immersed in the business cares of life, and the generation not yet entered upon them, the object may seem hardly worth the trouble. It will be otherwise with both as the time draws near when the curtain shall fall that hides forever from mental vision the shadowy Past, and the sad consciousness comes on that when it next rises it will be upon the limitless Future.

The compiler will not undertake to speak with entire confidence, from personal recollection, of the condition of things or the events that occurred in Belfast during the year 1805; for during the portion of that year that elapsed after he assumed the burthen and responsibilities of citizenship the larger portion of his time was devoted to cultivating the acquaintance of his mother and making the best use he could for his physical development of the "weapons which God and nature had put into his hands. Even of that year, however, he does not speak without authority; for he is able to call to his aid the memory of his earliest friend--next to his father and mother--our own highly esteemed and venerable fellow-citizen, Mr. William Quimby, who still hale and vigorous, in mind and body, although he has lived through his four score years does not find "their strength, labor and sorrow," notwithstanding the prediction of the Psalmist to the contrary. He was born in Lebanon, N. H., in 1792, came to Belfast in 1804, and during all that time his home has been here.

In 1805, the year after Mr. Quimby came to Belfast, the year with which these annals commence, the entire population of the town was about 900; it was 245 in 1790, 679 in 1800, and 1259 in 1810, according to the census taken in those several years. The whole number of buildings houses, barns, shops included, within the limits of the village, was 42; of this number 30 were dwelling houses. By the term village is meant the territory bounded by Field's Hill on the north, the Miller, or Frothingham lot on the south, Wilson's Hill on the west, and the river on the east. With the exception of the cleared land in the vicinity of the corner, Nesmith's Corner it was called, the point where High and Main streets intersect, and the further exception of a strip of land bordering on the river on its eastern side, and an occasional "clearing" of a few acres on the roads leading through and from the village, the entire territory of the town was covered by the original, unbroken forest. On that portion through which Church street now passes and on a strip of land lying on each side of Main street as far westerly as Wilson's Hill, although the forest trees had been felled and the land partially cleared up, the stumps of the trees were still remaining. On that portion through which Cedar, Congress, Miller, indeed all the streets lying southerly of Main street and westerly of Court street now run, the forest was untouched save here and there where a little firewood had been cut. The stumps were still standing on the premises now occupied by the Post Office, the Unitarian and Universalist churches, the brick schoolhouses, and the buildings standing in their vicinity; and indeed the list might be enlarged so as to embrace the front or back yard of nearly every dwelling-house in the village. It was no unusual occurrence for the good men, and women also, of those days to sit up o'nights to watch the burning stumps in their door-yards, regarding it essential for the safety of their dwellings so to do.

Mention has been made of Nesmith's corner. It is the corner where the wooden store occupied by Mr. David Lancaster stands. It derived its name from James Nesmith, Esq., who erected a large two story building upon the premises now occupied by Mr. Lancaster and Mr. J. C. Thompson adjoining, and occupied it as a dwelling and store. He was the first trader--there were no merchants then--who opened a store in Belfast; it was in 1799. The building erected by him was destroyed by fire on the night of December 29th, 1854. The Insurance Company made good the loss sustained by the owner of the building, but were so well satisfied that it was a case of spontaneous combustion on the part of the tenant that they delined to make good to him the loss sustained in the destruction of his goods. He never ventured on a suit to enforce his claim.

On the easterly side of Main street, opposite Nesmith's corner, on the site now covered by a portion of McClintock's Block, there stood in 1805 a one story wooden building occupied as a hatter's shop; it was removed soon afterwards. Adjoining it was a one story dwelling house which after passing through divers changes and being occupied for divers purposes, some of them of rather questionable character, was finally burned in January 1850.

On the opposite side of High street on the side now occupied by the Messrs. Howes, stood a dwelling house built of George Hopkins; some years later it was occupied as a Tavern; mention will be made of it hereafter. The building now occupied by the Messrs. H. is part of the original dwelling house. When built it stood on a high bank; some ten or fifteen feet higher than the level of the street in front; the bank was taken away and the building let down to its present place several years ago. While it occupied its original position, and the bank on which it stood afforded a comfortable reclining place for the loafers and lookers on and the boys who were always ready to "keep tally," the street in front of it was the favorite battle-ground of the ball-players of that day; not the players of base ball; that game compared with the game played by the boys of 1805, is a "modern invention;" not an improvement on the old one those boys would say were they here to speak for themselves; but one after another they have reached the home-goal and counted one on Death's tally; with them the game of life was long since finished.

CHAPTER II. (1805).

Our last chapter left us at the corner now occupied by the Messrs. Howes. On the corner opposite, where the Telegraph building so called stands; there was a building occupied as a store by Brown and McDonald; Edmund Brown and Simon D. McDonald. Mr. Brown was the brother of the late John G. Brown, and of Mrs. Haraden, widow of the late John Haraden; no descendant of his is living here. Mr. McDonald was the father of Mr. George McDonald, grandfather of the McDonalds now living in our midst, and discharging the duties of their various occupations with credit to themselves and the place of their nativity. This building now constitutes a part of the Telegraph building; the part nearest High street. This as well as the Hopkins house stood on elevated ground; the underpinning on the northerly and easterly sides remains where it was originally placed. Many years afterwards the bank on the High street side was taken away and the cellar converted into a grocery store. In no long process of time it became the favorite resort of a portion of the population whose stomachs struck the hours of 11 A. M. and 4 P. M. as regularly as the clocks did; if there ever was any perceptible difference of time it was generally ascertained that the clock had lost a few minutes.

There were many queer incidents connected with this ancient locality, remembered, doubtless, by many still living. It was here that the logical butcher "agreed' to the argument of his adversary, and in proof of it knocked him down; it was here that the bluff old sea-captain declared that, "by Kyst--there never was a time when he had more liquor aboard him than he could carry," to which startling assertion a brother of the craft replied that it might be so, but that he had seen him many a time when he would have made better headway if he had gone twice for it; it was here that for many a year the hat was "thumped," the book "cut," and the copper "flipped;" it was here that the Yorick of those days "a fellow of infinite jest, of most excellent fancy," was wont to "set the table on a roar;" it was here that the courteous request was so often made, "Wait a moment, if you please; the Captain's coming"; and it was here that once upon a time a worthy citizen, yielding to the influences of good fellowship, imbibed a sufficient quantity of motive power to carry him home, and through his wife's loom, carrying away the web with him, and in reply to the reproachful intimation of the good woman that he was drunk, apologized for himself and attempted to pacify her by saying, "don't say a word, wife; it didn't cost me a cent!" But time would fail to recount, or even allude to a tithe of the reminiscences that cluster around the locality; once the scene of so much wit and merriment--now--a meat shop! "To what base uses we may return, Horatio!"

Next westwardly from the Telegraph building, on the same side of Main street, stood a one story dwelling-house built by Dr. John S. Osborn, father of the late Alonzo Osborn, in 1795; it was the first framed house erected on Main street; it stood there until 1824 when it was removed after passing through many vicissitudes, and the Eagle Hotel, now the American House, was erected on its site. It is now standing, a portion of it at least, occupied as a wheelwright shop on the street running from Hayford block to High street.

The next building on Main street westerly from the Osborn house, on the same side of the street, was the house formerly owned and occupied by Judge Crosby; now occupied by his son, Wm. G. Crosby. It was erected in 1803 by John Milliken, who sold it before it was finished and removed to Davistown; it was first occupied as a dwelling in the spring of 1805.

The next to that on the same side of the road, was a log house on the farm now owned by Mr. Josiah Mitchell, formerly known as the Hartshorn place; it was the last survivor of the log houses that stood in the vicinity of the village. On the western side of Main street there was no building between the Hopkins house, now the Howes store, and a log house on the farm now owned by Mr. Franklin Banks; formerly the Campbell place; distance about one mile.

Returning to Nesmith's Corner, next below it on the same side of Main street stood two stores, one owned by Thaddeus Hubbard, and occupied by Mr. Derby as a store and dwelling, the other by James Cassin; Cassin remained here but a short time; Hubbard, better known in later days as Doctor Hubbard, remained here a long time; finally went to Norridgewock, in 1846 and died there not far from 1853. The warfare of life finished, it is to be hoped that he has found a good neighborhood; for it was his frequent complaint in life that he had always had the misfortune to live in a bad one. The stores occupied by Samuel S. Hersey and E. & L. Robbins stand where these stores stood; they were both destroyed by fire in the winter of 1829. At the time of the fire they were occupied by Frederic A. Lewis and James B. Norris; in the chambers were the law offices of Judge Crosby and his son, whose libraries were entirely consumed.

Next below the Cassin store stood a large two-story building, used for the twofold purpose of store and dwelling, erected by Capt. Samuel Pierce of the Belfast militia, of whose military career mention may be made hereafter. Some years later it was occupied by Ladd & Morrill, a firm which existed for many years and was dissolved in 1822; during their occupancy, in January 1821, it was burned, as well as a small building adjoining, which in 1805 was occupied by the late Stephen Longfellow. The stores now occupied by Messrs. Albert C. Burgess and E. C. Hilton nearly cover the ground on which these buildings stood. Next came a one story dwelling house known as the Weeks house, and just below it another called the Coburn house. The site of both was not far from where the Railroad Store, so called, now stands; both were burned in the great fire of October 12, 1865. Next came the Merriam house, which stood about where the store of Martin P. White stands. It was removed from the original site to Front street, converted into a store and occupied for several years by P. & E. T. Morrill; it was burned in the fire of 1865. Next below, and at the foot of Main street stood the building afterwards known as the Farmer's Inn; on the site of the store now occupied by Messrs. Knowlton & Hazeltine. Its first landlord was Mr. John Huzzey, now deceased; afterward Mr. Josiah N. White, now of the Phoenix House; it was burned April 27, 1850.

On the western side of the street opposite the house last described stood the Hobbs house; occupied as a tavern in 1805 and for a few years afterwards. In 1810 it became the property of one Cremer, who lived here two or three years, and then left in a brig of which he was the owner for a port in some one of the West India Islands. Neither Cremer or his brig ever returned. The rumor of the day ran that after arriving at his port of destination, disposing of his cargo and taking in a new one, and when all ready for sea he became "involved in a little onpleasantness" growing out of the discovery of a stolen "nigger" or two in the hold of his brig, and that thereupon without any particular regard to the forms of law, he was arrested and hung up by the heels until, like Abner Dean in Bret Hart's "Society upon the Stanislaus"--

"The subsequent proceedings interested him no more."

The Cremer house subsequently came into the possession of Jonathan Wilson, Esq., father of the late Purser Nathaniel Wilson, the generous benefactor of this the place of his nativity. There was a large hall in the building known for many years as Wilson's Hall, in which the worthy town-folk of those days were accustomed to imbibe their punch and blow off their patriotic steam on the "Glorious Fourth": the last celebration of the day in that hall was on the fifth day of July, 1824, the fourth being Sunday.

Next above the Cremer house and in close proximity stood the Libby house. Next the Badger house, which stood very near if not on the site of the Sanborn House. Next the Furber house, just above the Shoe Factory.

Next, the Anderson and Russ houses, standing close together; these were removed a small distance from their original site just before the Morrison block was built.   Next, the Hubbard house, where the store of Mr. F. M. Lancaster now stands.   All these buildings, Cremer house included, were destroyed by the fire of 1865.

Crossing Washington street, the next building was a small two story dwelling owned by Reuben Kimball, one of the wags of the day, known as "Honest Kimball"; he subsequently converted the lower story into a store; it was the first store in town recognized as a grocery: the only sign on it, over the door, was "Groceries:"   a word which was for some time a sad puzzler to the uninitiated, who pronounced it   as if spelled Grockeries.   He and his horse "Pelter" were notabilities in their day.   His humor did not desert him to the last; during his last sickness he was often visited by a pious friend who labored to impress on his mind the importance of a "change of heart" before he exchanged this life for the next, and drew from him the promise that if he became conscious of any change he should be sent for.   During the night when he died the watchers discovered and frankly told him that the last great change was near at hand.   "Send for Moulton!" he exclaimed; Moulton came, "I promised you," said he, "that if there was any change in me I would send for you; these men say that there is and I have sent for you according to promise.   Now, what have you got to say about it?" Rousing a few moments afterwards from the death-slumber into which he was rapidly falling, he exclaimed, "Tell Goddard," an old friend who had been lying for some time at death's door, "Tell Goddard to take Pelter and hurry up or I shall get there before him!"--and   so   Honest Kimball passed on.   His friend Goddard, without the   aid of Pelter, soon overtook him.   Who shall presume to say what place Honest Kimball, doubter as he was, heretic perhaps, now occupies in the Father's house which hath many mansions.

The Kimball house was demolished to stop the progress of the fire that consumed the "Babel," so called, in 1846; it stood on the site of the store now occupied by Mr. Edward Perry.   Between it and the corner where McClintock's Block stands, there was one building only; a small one occupied as a tailor's shop.   This shop was subsequently removed to the premises on Bridge street formerly owned by Nicholas Phillips, now by Dr. L. W. Pendleton, and converted into a painter's shop.   It is a noticeable fact that, with the exception of this shop and the Kimball house, demolished as before stated, every building that stood on Main street between High street and the beach, in 1805, has at one time and another been destroyed by fire; the lesson taught by the fact is worthy of practical remembrance.

CHAPTER III. (1805.)

Having completed in the preceding chapter a description of the buildings standing on Main street in 1805, the same course will now be pursued with High street.

From McClintock's corner there was no building on the northerly side of the street so far as the eye could reach in the direction of the Upper Bridge, except the hatter's shop and the building adjoining hereinbefore mentioned, and a barn standing on the same premises. On the southerly side, the building next to the Hopkins house, on Howes' corner, was the office of William Crosby, Esq., on the site now occupied by the brick store of Mr. Arnold Harris. This office was built in 1802, and it was necessary to remove the fallen trees to make room for it; it was burned in 1866. Next beyond it was the dwelling house of John Angier, Esq., the same house occupied by his widow at the time of her recent decease. A short distance beyond this house the travelled portion of the road diverged a little to the south leaving on the left a one story dwelling owned and occupied by Doctor Osborn, standing on the site of the Court House, and thence wound its way up the hill, passing the next building, which was the house of Thomas Whittier, Esq., or, as he was called in those days, Squire Whitcher; the same house occupied by the late Alfred W. Johnson, Esq., at the time of his dicease. While Squire W. lived there it was kept as a tavern and was regarded as in every sense the model tavern of eastern Maine. He removed to Searsmont some ten years later, entered extensively into the manufacture of lumber, built the large house still standing, subsequently occupied by Harry Hazeltine, Esq., and continued to reside there until his decease. While he lived here, the land now occupied by the buildings of Ex-Gov. Anderson was his garden plot, filled every summer with a luxuriant growth of flowers and vegetables, over which Madam W. was the presiding genius. She was the "Lady Bountiful" of the day; when she left, many, old and young, who had been the receipents of her charaties and kindly favors. always profusely bestowed, felt that they had sustained a personal loss; a feeling with which the community at large sympathized.

Next beyond the Whittier house, on the premises now occupied by Mr. Charles B. Hazeltine, stood a two story dwelling owned by another Thomas Whittier who was called "red-headed Tommy" to distinguish him from still another of the same name. He sold the premises in the fall of 1805 to Captain Robert Patterson, then the fourth of the name, who was lost at sea on his passage to Cuba, where he was in business, in December 1830, aged fifty-four. He was the son of James Patterson, one of the original settlers who came here in 1770, the husband of Mrs. Margaret Patterson who died in September, 1872, aged nearly ninety-five, and the grandfather of Capt. Edward P. Williams, who was in command of the Oneida when she was sunk by collision with a British steamer not far from Yokohama in 1870, and sank with her. The house referred to remained on the premises until 1859, when it was taken down by Mr. Hazeltine, who had then become its owner.

From the spot where this house stood there was no building within sight beyond it on the road to the Upper Bridge. Some idea of the estimated value of real estate in that section of the town in 1805 may be gathered from the fact that the price then paid for the house lot, with the house and barn on it, finished and in good condition, and twenty acres of land in the rear of it, the lot next northerly from Grove Cemetery, a portion of which is now within the Cemetery, was one thousand dollars; the same property was sold in 1855, just half a century later, for twenty-four hundred.

On that portion of High street lying southerly of Main street the next building to the Nesmith store, on the same side of the street, was a one story dwelling owned and occupied by John Durham, who died in 1823, aged seventy-four. It stood on the site now occupied by McClintock's Block of brick dwellings; when they were built it was removed to the rear, and was burned in the great fire of 1865. Next to this, on the spot where Mr. L. R. Palmer's house stands, was the blacksmith's shop of Mr. Jonathan Quimby; his dwelling house was on the opposite side of the street; it is now occupied by Mr. Anson E. Durham. The shop was removed, some years later, to the opposite side of the street to ground now covered by the buildings occupied by the Belfast Library Company.

Mr. Quimby came here to reside in 1804 from Lebanon, N. H.; the residue of his days were passed here; he died in 1827, aged sixty-two. He was a skillful workman and therefore a valuable acquisition to the community, a man of large muscular development and great physical power. The writer well remembers him and the many times he has lingered at the shop door on his way to and from school, wondering at the might of the arm that wielded that heavy sledge, and watching the

--"burning sparks that fly
Like chaff from a threshing floor."

He never to this day reads Longfellow's "Village Blacksmith," from which the above quotation is made, without thinking of Jonathan Quimby, and the old shop:

"Under a spreading chestnut tree
The village smithy stands;
The smith a mighty man is he
   With large and sinewy hands;
And the muscles of his brawny arms
   Are strong as iron bands."

The next building to the blacksmith's shop was the Miller house, known lately as the Frothingham house. It was built by Mr. James Miller in 1791: it was the first house of two stories built in the town, and at the time of its destruction in the great fire of August last was the oldest dwelling house standing on the western side of the river.

There was a plot of ground lying between the blacksmith shop and the Miller house, just southerly of the Baptist meeting house, which in this enumeration has been inadvertently overlooked. It contained a small cluster of very lowly dwellings, their roofs covered with green turf, with here and there a head-stone on which was inscribed the name of the tenant and the date when the tenancy commenced. It was a very quiet neighborhood. There were no heart-burnings there, no back-bitings, no jealousies, no envy, no struggle for wealth, no strife for office, no ambition to be called great. There was no hum of business there, no click of hammer, no crowd of thoughtless idlers; now and then a few visitors came, but they walked slowly in and out, and spoke only in low tones half-smothered words. It might well be named the "City of Silent." Its first tenant was the grandmother of the compiler of these annals: she came there in 1791: and there she and those who followed her from time to time remained, disturbing none and undisturbed, until they were reverently removed in 1851 to the place known as Grove Cemetery; whither their children and children's children already have followed them, or will ere long.

Crossing High street from the Miller house, there stood, where it still stands, the McFarland house, built and owned by Captain Ephraim McFarland, who for more than a score of years ran a "coaster" between this place and Boston, carrying usually a hold full and a deck-load of cordwood, and as many passengers in her cabin as had the temerity or disposition to run the hazard. A passage to Boston in her, with the privilege of breathing foul air through the night, sleeping two in a berth, squeezing and being squeezed, having enough to eat whenever hungry and an "eye-opener" every morning before breakfast time, cost three dollars! Taking into consideration all the privileges and luxuries enumerated, was it not cheap enough? Some time before his dicease, which was at a very advanced age, Capt. McFarland went to reside with a daughter living in Penobscot county, it is believed: the date of his decease is not remembered.

Next to the McFarland house, on the return to Nesmith's corner, and on the premises recently occupied by Hon. Joseph Williamson, stood the Meeting House, and near to it, and nearer the highway, stood the schoolhouse. The Meeting House was built in 1792; one was built on the eastern side of the river the same year, the one last named was taken down about 1830; the first named was sold to the Baptist Society in 1822, was removed to Bridge street and occupied for public worship until about 1837, when it was sold; the purchaser converted it into a stable, for which purpose it has since been used. It is still standing in the rear of the house on Bridge street owned and occupied by Mr. Benjamin Brown at the time of his decease.

The schoolhouse was a marvel in its day: it was painted: the front and sides white, the rear red. It was removed, date not remembered, to the land opposite the Court House where the Langworthy brick building stands, and the town school kept in it until it was removed to Front street, in the vicinity of the Foundry; it was burned in some one of the fires which have devastated that section.

Next to the schoolhouse, opposite to James Miller's house, stood his barn. There was no building between that and the house of Robert Miller, son of James, still in existence and now occupied by Mr. Judson Condon. According to the most reliable information thus far obtained, it is the oldest dwelling house now standing on the westerly side of the river. Next to that stood the Quimby house, of which mention has been made, and next to that, on land now covered by buildings occupied by the Belfast Livery Company, stood Moor's blacksmith's shop.

John Moor, the owner of the shop, subsequently removed to Montville where he died, and where some of his descendants still live. He was a man of genial temperament, always ready for a skirmish of wit. There are many amusing reminiscences connected with his name; we have space but for one of them. He had contracted the habit, when in earnest conversation or when excited by sudden impulse, of prefacing his sentences with the word "but," several times repeated. He was sitting in his front door about noon of a very hot day in July, when he discovered one of his neighbors, who was using both sides of the highway, his legs terribly tangled up by his morning potations, passing by homeward bound. It occurred to Moor that it would be an act of kindness to his neighbor and family to get him out of sight as soon as possible. How was it to be done, was the question, for the neighbor happened to belong to that class of men who are apt to believe themselves soberest when they are the least so, and indignantly resent the slightest intimation that they are not fully competent to take care of themselves. Moor knew well that to effect his object resort must be had to strategy; there was no time to lose; stepping out on to the bank in front of his house, where if need be he could lend a helping hand, "Squire," said he, "but--but-hadn't you better come in and warm yourself?" The Squire accepted the invitation and warmed himself until sunset, when he left for home, a soberer if not a wiser man.

The next building to Moor's shop was the Telegraph building; and here terminates the enumeration and description of the buildings standing on Main and High streets in 1805. The streets, their history and topography, will be the subject of the next chapter.

CHAPTER IV. (1805.)

For several years before 1805 the cows had been laying out streets in different directions through the village, but up to that time only one of them had been formally accepted by their owners, namely, Market street; the street leading from Main street near the house of Mr. Alden D. Chase, passing the Phenix House and down the hill to Puddle Dock. Its name was derived, probably, from the fact that it led to a parcel of land in that locality which was granted to the town for the purpose of a market; it was located by the cows belonging to the people of that neighborhood, probably, who in making the location did not overlook the fine spring that gushed from its side near the foot of the hill.

There were but two roads passing through the village; the road leading from Little River to the Narrows, a portion of which had been laid out and accepted as High street, and the road leading from Sandy Beach to Greene Plantation and thence to Davistown, a portion of which had been laid out and accepted as Main street. They were the same roads now known as the Northport and Belmont roads, save that the innumerable "kinks" in them have been taken out from time to time, and the decidedly crooked made comparatively straight.

For illustration take a portion of the Belmont road; it ran very nearly on its present course from the village until it reached Hemlock Hill, where Mr. John Whitmore now lives; the hill derived its name from the immense growth of hemlocks upon it. At the foot of the hill the road diverged to the south and wound around a portion of the southern base of Hayford's Hill, then changing to a northerly course crossed the road as now travelled not far from the schoolhouse, and thence winding around the northerly portion of the hill returned to the road as now travelled not far from the place occupied by the late Benjamin Monroe. That such a circuitous route was ever adopted, seems, at first blush, inexplicable. The explanation is this: the earliest settlers came in advance of roads, they selected their locations according to their fancy, and built their log houses and hovels; roads followed them. That was the golden age when every man claimed the right to have a road to his own barn door, a right readily conceded, without any great sacrifice on the part of the public, for the construction of a road involved no expenditure of money or labor beyond felling the trees on a narrow strip through the forest, grubbing up the largest stumps, and building here and there in low swampy localities a "gridiron bridge"; such bridge consisting simply of logs of suitable length laid across the road; the size of them was a secondary consideration. Beyond the point now known as Belmont Corner, the roads were but little more than "bushed out," passable in the summer for travellers on foot or horseback only, but in the winter, after snow fell, for sleighs--pungs, rather--and sleds.

On the easterly side of the river there was a road from Half-way-creek, the former dividing line between Belfast and Prospect, extending as far westwardly as the Wescott Stream, passing Fish Cove on the way, the greater portion of which came up to the statute requirements; that is it was "safe and convenient for travellers." That the road on the eastern side was in a more advanced stage than those on the western will not seem strange when it is remembered that it was on that side that the large majority of the early settlers located and made improvements; there, in their judgment, was the site of the city then in embryo. Travellers from this place to Bangor, as late as 1817, went over this road as the most eligible route, crossing the Ferry at Bucksport and thence to Bangor on the eastern bank of the Penobscot.

Having given the termini, as anciently designated, of the two roads passing thro' this village, it may not be amiss to add a few words in the way of interpretation or definition. Greene Plantation was the name by which the territory embracing the towns of Belmont, Morrill and Searsmont was known; Davistown is now Montville. The Narrows was the name by which the locality where the Upper Bridge now crosses the

river was known; the first bridge was built there in 1801. Sandy Beach
is the low flat of land at the foot of Main street where the Railroad
depots and buildings stand; known at a later date as Puddle Dock.

At the date of which we are now treating there were several buildings
on the westerly side of the Beach. At the foot of the hill, on Market
street, stood and still stands the Washington Webster house; next to
that a small building containing three rooms; known as the Smith house,
this house is still standing. Next came the Mansur house, standing
on the site of the two story building just northwesterly from the engine
house. Next a two story building which was occupied as a store, dwelling
house, and still later as a junk-shop, subsequently removed. Next a
building occupied successively as store and dwelling, known as the Russ
house. On the other side of the Beach, not far from where the freight
depot now is, stood a small building called the Ferry house, occupied
by the Ferryman, who at that time was Daniel Hibbard. There was a road
running from the foot of Main street to the foot of Market street, and
on that street, on the site now occupied by Mr. Henry Wyman, stood a
blacksmith shop occupied by Mr. Ansel Lothrop, who subsequently removed
to Searsmont village, where he resided many years and died in 1834,
aged fifty-four.

For more than thirty years prior to the erection of the East Bridge
in 1806, there had been a public ferry across the river, the starting
point on the west side of the river being just westerly of Lewis' wharf,
a portion of the time just easterly of it, nearly opposite the foot
of Main street. On the easterly side the starting point was a little
down the river from the spot where the eastern end of the bridge now
stands. From that point the travellers bound eastward wound their way
up the bank to the road leading to Searsport village; which locality,
by the way, was then known as Sodom; the Sodomites sometimes returned
the compliment by hurling Scripture at Sandy Beach, calling it Gomorrah.
There were three wharves on the Beach; Russ', just northwesterly from
Lewis' wharf, Nesmith's, just southerly from it, and Mansur's, near
the Washington Webster house, a portion of which is still standing;
these, with a wharf built by "old Major Cunningham," near the westerly
end of the Upper Bridge, constituted the wharf accommodations of the
place in 1805.

There are few, probably, of those who now designate the Beach as
Puddle Dock who are aware that a portion of the premises was once used
for dockage purposes. That portion lying at the foot of the upland was
lower than that portion nearer the river, and in the spring, and at
high tides always, was covered with water. There was for many years
prior to 1805--the remains of it then visible--a dam at the westerly
side of the Beach, between the Smith and Mansur houses before described,
near where the Engine House now stands, for the purpose of letting in
the water at high tide and keeping it in when the tide fell. Through
that dam there was a sluice-way through which ship and other timber
cut up the river and rafted down was floated into the dock, where it
lay safe from storm and freshet until needed for use. After the dam
went down the water still continued to come in as before, and on that
locality the boys of 1805, and for years after, found their best skating
ground.

Belfast was not, like Rome, built on seven hills, but she came
within two of it. There were in 1805, and for years after, five points
in the village of such elevation that they were called hills. On Main
street, there were Wilson's Hill, not called by that name until Mr.
Wilson erected his house in 1806, Crosby's Hill, on the summit of which
Mr. Crosby's house stood, and the Hobbs or Cremer Hill, where the Hobbs
or Cremer house stood, the location of which was given in a previous
chapter. There was not then the gradual descent that there now is,
from Wilson's Hill to the foot of Main street. At the foot of that
hill, which, steep as it now is, was then terribly steeper, after passing
some thirty rods of gradually descending ground, came Crosby's Hill;

some idea of the height of it may be gathered from the inspection of the underpinning of the house which remains where it was sixty-eight years ago, and, which when laid was about five feet above the level of the street.   From that point there was a rapidly descending grade until the Hobbs house was reached, and thence a steep descent to the beach.   The boys of 1874, who think that the coasting down the Wilson Hill is "first-rate," have but little conception of the luxury of coasting as enjoyed by the boys of 1805, who started their sleds on the top of Wilson's Hill, and with but slight diminution of speed brought up on Sandy Beach; sometimes in the dock.   "Clear the coast!" in those days meant something worth looking out for.

On High street was Field's Hill, so called after Mr. Field erected his house in 1807, which has now become almost obliterated from the catalogue of hills, and Quimby's Hill, at the summit of which stood, and still stands the Quimby house, which hill has ceased to exist; yet in 1805, and for some years later, it was so much of an elevation that a person standing midway between the foot of it and Nesmith's corner, could barely discern the top of a man's hat sitting on horseback in front of the house occupied by Captain James Miller, deceased.   So late as 1814 it was so much of a hill that people gathered there for better observation of the British frigate as she hove in sight on her way from Castine to Belfast.   For the few still left who can remember those hills as they were more than sixty years ago, whose eyes have watched them crumbling away year after year before the onward stride of improvement, until they are nearly lost to mortal vision, there is a melancholy satisfaction in the reflection that there are other hills to which they can still "lift up their eyes--the hills from whence cometh their help."

With a brief allusion to two other notable localities on Main street this chapter will close, and with it all further mention of the streets and buildings standing on them in 1805, unless it be incidentally. The land at the corner of Main and Church streets, where the store of Mr. Alden D. Chase stands, and for several rods in the rear of it, and half, at least, of the width of that portion of Church street, was then a quagmire; on the site of The Republican Journal building, in which this goes to press, grew flags, of the species producing cat-tails. The water from this quagmire oozed off through a gridiron bridge across Main street, the eastern end of which was not far from the store now occupied by Doctor Sylvester.   In 1859, when gas pipes were laid down in the streets of Belfast, the pine logs that formed this bridge were uncovered, at the depth of four feet.   The author of these annals said "good morning" to them, as old acquaintances.   Main street from that point as far up as the brick building now owned by the Belfast Savings Bank, was so springy and soft in the spring of the year and fall that it was no unusual occurrence for heavily laden teams to get stuck in the attempt to pass over it.   There is hardly room for doubt that some of the logs originally placed in that locality may still be found at the depth of four or five feet below the present surface of the street.

A few years prior to 1805, John Milliken, a tanner by trade, sunk a few vats on that part of the premises occupied by the late Dr. Monroe, which lies between the house and driveway on the eastern side of it. They were subsequently taken up and in their place there was, as late as 1812, quite a large pond fed by the numerous springs on the hillside; the surplus water from it passed across the street under a log bridge, discharging itself on the land now occupied by Mr. Chase, about midway between his house and Waldo Avenue.   It was a famous frogpond in its day, and the Paradise of Polliwogs.

CHAPTER V. (1805-6.)

Marvellous tales are told of the wealth of forest and stream by those who were old enough to wield fowling-piece and fishing-rod in the years with which we are now dealing, and the years that followed them.   Duck, pigeons, partridges, wild fowl of various species, were abundant on the shores of the river and bay, and in the forest; the streams everywhere were alive with speckled beauties. The more adventurous hunter brought down his deer, and now and then a wildcat, within a short distance of the village; and the trapper found ample use for his traps in the capture of otter, beaver, mink, musquash, rabbits and woodchuck in whatever direction he roamed.   Musquash, cleaned and laid on a stump for three or four days in the blaze of a summer's sun, although rather strong for an unsophisticated stomach, was regarded a delicious tit-bit by the hereditary trapper.

The writer remembers that as late as 1815 a five minutes walk from his father's back-door carried him so far into the forest that a plenty of game was visible, but not a building in the village was within sight. So late as 1819 a party of anglers could pass a very pleasant day on the margin of Wilson's stream, filling their baskets with trout, so remote from civilization that they had no apprehension that any one would interfere to "mar the festivities of the occasion."

A row of fifteen minutes from the mouth of Little River brought the fisherman onto good ground for cod and haddock. Salmond were plenty at six cents per pound, shad six cents each, halibut at one cent per pound, haddock from two to five cents each, and alewives were so abundant and cheap that they were hardly regarded worth taking into account. Lobsters--not the miniature specimens now hawked about our streets--but of heroic dimensions, scrambled over our shores; and clams--Belfast clams--immortalized in the doggeral so often repeated:

"Northport for beauty
   Camden for pride.
Had it not been for clams
   Belfast would have died."

were so large, luscious, juicy, that the mere mention of them brings a sparkle to the eye and a muscular quiver to the lip of the old settler who was then old enough to dig for himself; the second quality then were superior to the first now so famous; in fact, they were "better nor Gilson's." Oysters were planted on the eastern side of the river, but the contrast in size and flavor between them and the clams was so apparent that they died of mortification. There was another side, however, to this picture, so full of beauty to the lover of good cheer; there were few chickens and turkeys; there were no smelts; or if there were the angler had not smelt them out.

The following Price Current, compiled from the day-books of traders in the village, may not be uninteresting. The prices, it must be remembered are those charged at retail for merchandize delivered over the counter. The charges were made in pounds, shillings and pence; reduced to Federal currency they are as follows: Flour, per bbl. $8.00; Rye, per bushel, $1.17; White Beans, 1.34; Salt, $1.50, Corn, $1.08; Coffee per lb., 42 cts.; Sugar, 20; Tea, Bohea, 50, Souchong, 83, Hyson, $1.68 to $2.00; Cheese, 12 1-2; Lamb and Mutton, 6 1-4; Salt fish, 6; Salt Mackerel, 6 1-4; Salt Pork, 20; Molasses per gall., 67 to 75; N. E. Rum, 75; W.I. Rum, $1.25 to $1.50; Brandy, $1.50; Gin, $1.50; Cider, 32; Tobacco per lb., 50; Candles, 25; Eggs per doz., 12 1-2; Cordwood delivered at the wharf brought $2.00 per cord; it sold in Boston from $4.00 to $5.00 per cord. Butter, beef, potatoes, meal, seem not to have been commodities dealt in by the traders of those days; unless they are embraced in the charges very frequently found of glasses, gills, half-pints, &c.

The leading traders in the place were John Angier, father of Mr. Oakes Angier, Edmund Brown and Simon D. McDonald, father of Mr. George McDonald, James Cassin, Reuben Derby, James Nesmith, Benjamin Palmer, father of Charles Palmer, Esq., and Francis Anderson, uncle of Ex-Gov. Anderson; Brown, Cassin and Derby did not remain here long; Derby was succeeded by his brother Andrew, who will be remembered by many now living.

The lawyers were Bohan P. Field, who came in 1801, William Crosby in 1802, and John Wilson in 1803. The Physicians were John S. Osborn, who came prior to 1795, Chauncey C. Chandler and Thaddeus Hubbard, who came after the beginning of the present century. The Blacksmiths were Jonathan Quimby, father of Mr. Wm. Quimby, Ansel Lothrop, father of Mr. Thomas W. Lothrop, John Moore, and on the eastern side of the river Walter Hatch. Housewrights, John Haraden, father of Mr. Daniel Haraden, Thomas Bartlett, Benjamin Joy, Reuben Kimball and George W. Webster. Shoemakers, Jonathan Basford, Stephen Longfellow and Wiggins Merrill. Masons, James Bicknell, grandfather of Mr. Stephen G. Bicknell. Tanner, William Durham, father of Mr. Anson E. Durham. Cabinet-maker, Samuel Peck. Hatter, a Mr. Rowse. Tailors, Abel Baker and Mr. Cole. Painter, Mr. Mitchell. Innholders, Thomas Whittier and --Hobbs. There were five Justices of the Peace; Bohan P. Field, W. Crosby, James Nesmith, Robert Houston and Benjamin Poor; two Deputy Sheriffs, John Huse and Francis Anderson; one Notary Public, James Nesmith. The foregoing list contains the names of thirty-six individuals; children of thirteen of them are still living here.

Belfast was then in Hancock county. Three terms of the court of Common Pleas and one Term of the Supreme Court were held annually at Castine; there were three Judges on the Bench of the Common Pleas; neither of them of the legal profession.

The first ship ever built here, the ship Fox, her tonnage less than one half of one of the three-masted schooners of these days, was built in 1805 by Major Wm. Cunningham, near the Upper Bridge. The Jenny Miller, a schooner, was built some years previous, near the spot where the railroad turn-table stands. There is a tradition that a sloop was built in 1791, near where the Upper Bridge stands; her name is not remembered, but she was known by the nickname of the "Pizenwater;" so named because she leaked so badly that she poisoned all the water she passed through. Unless the tradition that assumes to fix the time and place of her being built is authentic, the Jenny Miller was probably the first vessel built here. There was a sloop Mary which ran between this place and Boston several years prior and subsequent to 1805, but the better impression is that although owned she was not built here. The next vessel in order of time after the Fox was the schooner Superb. She was built in 1807 on the site of Condon's wharf, by Messrs. Whites and Pattersons, and commanded for a time by Capt. Robert Patterson, 4th. She was launched at midnight, and there is a bit of romance connected with the event, to the effect that a "lady fair," who had never witnessed the launching of a vessel, and who was bound not to die without the sight, mounted her horse and arrived just in season to see the Superb glide, not into her native element, but into the element on which she was destined to float until she went where all old schooners go. The Superb was still plying between this port and Boston, as late as 1824.

On the twenty-second of December of that year, 1807, Congress laid an embargo on all the shipping in the ports and harbors of the United States, the effect of which was to suspend the building of vessels here and elsewhere. The embargo was partially repealed by the non-intercourse act of March 1, 1809, which permitted the departure of our merchant vessels to all other ports than in Great Britain and France. Under the provisions of this act commerce revived and our coasting trade was almost entirely relieved from embarrassment. The ship Belfast was built on the eastern side of the river, near Goose River, by Walter Hatch, for western parties, and the brig Illuminator on the western side, on the same site where the Superb was built, for the Whites, Pattersons, John Angier of this place and James A. Allen, of Boston. The war with Great Britain, which followed the next year, put an end to this species

of enterprise for a while.   After the close of the war the energies
of our people began to recuperate and ship building recommenced.

In September of this year (Sept. 25th, 1805) the Rev. Alfred Johnson
was installed as Pastor of the First Congregational Parish, at a salary
of seven hundred dollars.   His predecessor was the Rev. Ebenezer Price,
whose connection with the Parish terminated in 1802.   In 1812 Mr. Johnson,
in view of the great depression in business, the result of the war,
voluntarily relinquished all claim for his salary during its continuance,
and on the second day of October, 1815, dissolved his connection with
the Parish.   He was the father of the late Judge Johnson and of our
venerable and highly esteemed fellow citizen, Hon. Ralph C. Johnson.
A biographical sketch of Rev. Mr. Johnson will be given hereafter.

Belfast was not represented in the Legislature of 1805; as the
law then was it was optional with towns to send a representative or
not; Belfast voted "not to send."   The next year John Wilson, Esqr.,
was elected.   The municipal officers for 1805 were, William Crosby,
Tolford Durham, and Reuben Derby, Selectmen; Jonathan Wilson, Town Clerk;
two from each side of the river.   James Nesmith was Postmaster, and
the office was kept in the counting room in his store at the corner.
There was then but one mail per week from the West; it was brought,
via Camden, on horseback.   The postage on a single letter from Boston
was seventeen cents: from New York twenty cents; two sheets or pieces
of paper constituted a double letter and on such the rates were double
those before named.   Thomas Whittier, Esq., succeeded Mr. Nesmith, and
while he continued to be Postmaster the office was kept at his house;
Madam W., named in a previous chapter, having the principal charge of
the mails.   Thomas Whittier was succeeded by his son Benjamin; during
his term of office the Post office was kept successively in the basement
of the Major Chase house, next northerly from the North Church, in the
northerly end of the building now the Phoenix House and in the store
which stood where the store of Mr. F. M. Lancaster now stands.   Mr.
Whittier held the office until his death in 1822; Joseph Williamson,
Esq., was his successor.

There is no single particular, probably, in which the great changes
wrought in the lapse of three score years and ten is more apparent than
in the increased facilities of postal communication.   Then, a solitary
rider on horseback, his advent announced by the tooting of his horn,
brought here once a week all the mail matter from the West for this
place and the vast territory lying east of us; now, the rushing locomotive
heralded by the shriek of the steam-whistle, brings us twice in every
secular day the same matter multiplied a hundred fold.   The letter which
was then a week on its way from Boston at a cost of seventeen cents
for transportation, reaches its destination now in eleven hours, at
a cost of three cents!   Our evening paper, instead of bringing to us
news a week old, is damp from the press when it comes to hand!   Time
and space are not annihilated, it is true; but what miracles, wrought
in the meantime, the annalist of seventy years hence may have to record,
is beyond the grasp of the most fervid imagination.

CHAPTER VI. (1806-7.)

This year, 1806, was long remembered as the year of the Great Eclipse. It was an eclipse of the sun, and occurred June 16th. It was "total at Philadelphia and other cities in the Union," as the almanac predicted. Belfast, although not a city, was not overlooked on the occasion. It was so dark, of course, that the father of the family couldn't see to read in the almanac at four P. M., the period of the "greatest obscuration," The cows came home in advance of milking time, the hens went to roost, and the roosters began to crow as the eclipse began to close; the number of "digits" eclipsed varied with the locality and the kind of glass used for observation.

In this year the East Bridge was built; it was one hundred and twenty-two rods in length, and cost about eighteen thousand dollars; a major part of the stock was taken and paid for by non-residents. The act incorporating Jonathan Wilson and his associates under the name of "The Proprietors of the East Bridge in Belfast," was passed March 14th, 1805. The first meeting of the Corporation was held at "the house of Thomas Whittier, innholder" on the 10th day of December of that year; at which meeting Francis Anderson was elected Clerk, Jonathan Wilson, Thomas Knowlton and Tolford Durham, Managers, Samuel Houston, Samuel Prescott and Jonathan White, Assessors; and Thomas Whittier, Treasurer.

At a meeting held soon afterwards it was voted "that nine shillings per day be allowed to each man that works on the bridge, and that ten hours make a day."

The bridge as originally built was from a point on the western side of the river near the house now occupied by Captain W. O. Alden; the terminus on the eastern side was near that of the present bridge. The remains of some of the spiling of the original bridge may still be seen at low water. In 1830, the bridge having become very much out of repair, a portion of it was carried away by a violent gale and storm, and the proprietors decided not to repair but to build anew where the bridge is now located. The new bridge was accordingly built under a contract with James McCrillis, Esq., and in August 1832 a few carriages passed it for the first time; it was not then completed, however; there was no sidewalk for foot passengers, nor railing on it.

By the terms of the act of incorporation the charter was to continue for the term of sixty years from the day of the "opening of the bridge for passengers." The bridge was first opened for that purpose January 1st, 1807; at the expiration of the sixty years, December 31st, 1866, the bridge was surrendered by the proprietors, and it became, as it now is, a free bridge, sustained by and at the cost of the city.

Jonathan Wilson, the party most active in starting and carrying out the enterprise, was the first toll gatherer. His successor was Tolford Durham. After him came James McCrillis, who held the office for a long series of years with occasional breaks. It was during his administration, when the toll gate was at the eastern end, that the old bridge became a favorite evening promenade for the girls and boys who found the walk a pleasant one, doubtless, but derived full as much pleasure perhaps, from watching the shade of disappointment that stole over the visage of the toll-gatherer as he came out for their pennies just as they came within reaching distance of the toll-house and wheeled to the right-about-face. If the old bridge was in existence now, and had a tongue, it could tell of a "Bridge of Sighs" elsewhere than in Venice. It was a famous place too for catching flounders and lobsters in nets made of hoops and rope yard: the saddest Saturday afternoon the compiler of these annals ever knew was the one when he dropped his new fish-line overboard before his sinker had touched bottom.

For many years after the first bridge was built the annual meeting of the proprietors was quite an event in the village. According to tradition it was an event that furnished occasion for a larger amount of hilarity than would be deemed becoming in these days of the stringent enforcement of the Maine Law; but the tradition is not well founded.

The annual meeting, always held in December, was strictly a business meeting. As a faithful annalist, however, it is our duty to record the fact that our progenitors, the bridge proprietors, were not unmindful of creature comforts; to their credit be it added, they paid for them out of their own pockets, not from the treasury of the corporation.

At the annual meeting held Dec. 1st, 1807, the following vote was passed, as appears of record: "That the members of this corporation with their officers and such gentlemen as the directors may invite, sup together on the first day of January, unless that day shall happen to be Sunday--in that event on the succeeding day--at such time and place as the directors shall appoint, and give notice thereof by their Clerk."

It is a well authenticated fact, although it does not appear on record, that these "sups" were sometimes of a rather exuberant character, as the following incident serves to show. At the close of one of them, after the party had risen from the table and were about to separate, a member made a motion "that we all take a night-cap and adjourn to the first Monday in next January." Whereupon a worthy deacon, who was embracing one of the door posts at the time, suggested that it would be well before acting on the motion to look at the almanac and make sure that the day named didn't come on Sunday. The question was divided; the night-cap was taken, but the consultation of the almanac was indefinitely postponed.

The military strength of the town was composed of two Companies of Militia, locally known as the East side and West side Militia, a Company of Artillery, organized in 1803, and a Company of Cavalry organized in 1804. They were all attached to the Second Regiment, First Brigade, tenth division of the Militia of Massachusetts. Alexander Campbell of Steuben was Major General, John Crosby of Hampden, Brigadier General, and Thomas Knowlton of Northport, Lieut. Colonel. The Military Rosters of those days embrace no such officer as Colonel.

The east side militia was commanded by Capt. Robert Kelsey; the west side, prior to 1806, had been commanded by Capt. Samuel Pierce, then pronounced Pairce; he left here in the fall of 1805, and the company was for some time commanded by the Lieutenant. Capt. "Pairce" was a man of a decidedly "military turn," but too much of the "fuss and feathers" order to command the respect or suit the fancy of the rough-hewn and boisterous wags whose names were borne on his roll, or, to use the language of a looker-on, "who trained under him, and round him, and over him."
"Training-day," while he was in command began the night before.   It was the custom to "salute" the Captain, as it was styled, by a fusilade made up of the discharge of muskets loaded, half-loaded, squibs, and flashes in the pan, beginning about midnight, around the Captain's domicile, and kept up until the parties concerned were "invited in," and then followed a scene that

"Frighted the reign of Chaos and old Night."

It annoyed exceedingly the staid and sleepy villagers, but the Captain was delighted with the attention paid to him.

Morning came in due time, and with it came the Captain, gorgeously arrayed in military costume, and his soldiers armed and equipped in the most fantastic manner that human ingenuity, in those days, could devise; one with a shoe on one foot, his trousers leg cut off at the knee, an old boot on the other foot; another with a black earthern jug slung over his shoulder canteen fashion; another with a large stone jug on his back in lieu of a knapsack; another with gigantic epaulettes made of burdocks, and another with a strip of birch bark round his hat, a cow's tail stuck in for a feather; these are but specimens only, from which some idea may be formed of the general military air and costume of the company when drawn up for parade.

Capt. "Pairce's" military career culminated at the Fall Training in 1805. He was drilling his Company in Miller's field, marching at

their head, wheeling occasionally to survey them, marching backwards
as was the military usage in those days, when he found himself, unconscious
of its proximity, brought up against a board fence in his rear and the
bayonets of the front rank who were pressing him hard sticking into
the boards on each side of him.   To resent the indignity he put four
of the ring-leaders under arrest, and ordered them to be confined in
Miller's "back chamber."   One of them, Ben. Joy, who was the very soul
of humor, and prince of wags, took a bullet from his pocket and dropping
it into the muzzle of his gun, declared that the first man who attempted
to put him into the back chamber would do so at the peril of his life.
The Captain began to feel his "valor oozing out as it were at the palm
of his hands," as Bob Acres in the play did, and the matter was compromised
by sending the offenders under guard to Whittier's Tavern, the place
of their own selection.   When the military labors of the day were concluded,
the captain marched his company to the square in front of the tavern;
the place where they were usually dismissed for the day, and gave the
order "Front face!"   The yell of laughter that broke forth aroused him
from his military reverie.   There, in the front windows of the bar-room,
the sashes thrown up, their heads bowed nearly to the floor, their backs
to the streets, bare of clothing as Adam was before Eve took up the tailor-
ing trade, sat the four prisoners under guard!   The captain evaporated
without giving the word of command, "company dismissed!"   When the company
next turned out it was in command of the Lieutenant; the Captain was
not here to be "saluted."

The artillery was commanded by Capt. Thomas Cunningham, who lived
at or near the Head of the Tide; Capt. Ephraim McFarland was Lieutenant.
The gun-house stood on the McFarland lot, a short distance from the
spot where the house occupied by Capt. Henry McGilvery stands, and the
usual place of parade for many years was the green plot between the
McFarland house and the road.   There were two brass field pieces attached
to the company, which were retained for many years, and passed through
many and varied experiences.   In the war of 1812 they were removed beyond
the reach of the British when they landed here; subsequently one of
them became the prey of domestic invasion.   The field-pieces now here
were substituted for those above named.

Capt. Cunningham was the first to introduce here a military manoeuvre
called "whipping the snake."   It was never omitted on the training-days
and was a never failing source of amusement and wonderment to the non-comba-
tants.   It consisted in throwing nis men into apparently inextricable
confusion and bringing them out of it with as much accuracy and precision
as if they were a mere piece of mechanism.

Abel Baker, by trade a tailor, was Captain of the Cavalry.   He
was for one or more years collector of taxes; became a defaulter--a
rare bird in those days--and took wing and flew from this latitude some
time about 1809, clothed, as rumor said, in plumage very like that worn
by the President of the Confederate States at the time of his capture
by the Federal forces.   Rumor further said that at the time of his flight
he was mis-mated with another strange bird.   Robert Miller was one of
the sureties on his collector's bond and was compelled to make good
the deficiency to the town.   The land on which the Custom House and
Peirce's block stand and the land in the vicinity which is now on Church
street was taken in payment.   Subsequently an exchange of land was made
and out of that came the "acre" on which the Unitarian meeting-house
stands.   It was one of the stipulations in the negotiation between the
town and the parish that the seats in the gallery, or a portion of them,
should forever be free to the public for public worship on the Sabbath.
It is believed that they have never been so crowded but that, like an
omnibus, there was "room for one more."

CHAPTER VII. (1807.)

"The Fourth of July," says a letter under date of July 7th, 1807, "was attended with much bluster and stir. The Company of Artillery and Cavalry turned out, and there was a public dinner at the Hall of T. Whittier, Esq. General Ulmer and Major Jona. Wilson made their appearance in uniform!"--Generals, Colonels and Majors were not as plenty as in these days. All the territory embraced in the present counties of Waldo, Hancock, Penobscot, and Washington was within the limits of the Tenth Division of the Militia of Massachusetts, and General George Ulmer was the first of that rank, probably, who ever made an appearance in uniform before the eyes of the good people of the place. Gen. Ulmer was a man of note in his day. He resided in Lincolnville and represented that town in the Legislature. He was a Senator from Hancock before the Separation, and in the first Legislature that convened after Maine became a State. He was once Sheriff of the county, and early in the war of 1812 he resigned his office as Major General on being appointed by President Madison to the command of the troops at Fort Sullivan, Eastport, with the title of Colonel-commandant. He was succeeded as Major General by Gen. David Cobb of Revolutionary fame.

For some years prior to 1807 considerable antagonism had existed between the Proprietors of the wild lands, as they were termed, lying between the Penobscot and Kennebec rivers and the settlers on those lands. Some of those settlers had gone into possession under conveyances from individuals who assumed to be the owners of the soil, but in reality were not; others, under verbal license, or contracts to purchase, the conditions of which they found themselves unable to perform; others had taken up lots and made improvements not knowing what parties held the title, acting on the belief that when the rightful owners did appear they should be able to procure title to their land at a fair price; the last named class were denominated "squatters." It was not always an easy matter for the settler to decide, in the multitude of conflicting claims, what party really held the title, with whom he might safely negotiate. In many instances the proprietors of lands were not disposed to trade with parties who had taken up lots and made improvements on terms which were regarded fair and reasonable. Next in course of time followed suits at law brought by proprietors to eject settlers from their lands; and next, opposition and in some instances organized resistance to the service of legal process, and to the exercise of the ordinary acts of ownership by proprietors. Surveyors sent on by them to make surveys of lots, officers attempting to execute legal process, were resisted and in some instances assaulted by parties disguised as Indians. Some of the earlier settlers of Greene Plantation were of one or the other of the classes before named, and were known as "Greene Indians." An agent of some of the proprietors was assaulted by parties thus disguised and severely beaten; the horse of an officer who was attempting to serve legal process was shot under him. The lawyers who brought these suits of ejectment for proprietors, and the officers employed to serve them, resided in this place, and it was not strange that they were regarded by the squatters as in league with the proprietors who were adopting measures which in their view were unjust and oppressive; neither was it strange under the circumstances that there should exist to some extent a feeling of hostility against Belfast. This very brief and imperfect statement is necessary in explanation of the local excitement which pervaded the little community here for the greater part of a night and which is still referred to occasionally as the "Greene Indian War;" it might, with much greater propriety be styled the "Greene Indian Scare." There is some slight difference in the recollection of our oldest inhabitants as to the time when it occurred; the conclusion arrived at is that it was in 1807.

One of the most prominent of the settlers in the Plantation had been arrested by an officer residing here for an alleged breach of the peace, or violation of the law, and brought here on his way to the jail

at Castine.   It was late in the day and the wind being unfavorable for
the packet to cross the Bay, he was placed in charge of keepers for
the night.   Such an event was not of frequent occurrence and of itself
created some little excitement; that excitement was increased by a report
which began to circulate about sunset that men disguised as Indians
had been seen skulking in the woods and stealing across the road just
beyond Wilson's Hill.   Fuel was added to the fire by still another report,
purporting to come from "out back," that the Greene Indians were coming
in to rescue the prisoner and burn the village.   A remark from the prisoner
to the effect that his keepers wouldn't keep him more than fifteen minutes
after midnight, fanned the fire; and when soon after dark the report
of a gun here and there in the woods, or among the stumps on the side-hill
was heard, the whole village was ablaze.   The fighting men turned out
fully armed and equipped, pickets were sent out, guards stationed, and
every precautionary measure taken to guard against a surprise and to
repel any attack that might be made.   One highly excited individual
intent on rallying to the front every available man, came upon another
of more phlegmatic temperament who was very deliberately mixing his
glass of toddy; seizing the glass he poured forth a torrent of abuse
on the head of the offender, whom he denounced as reckless of duty in
the hour of peril, poured the contents of the glass down his own throat
and started on the search for other delinquents.   Another one, of equally
nervous temperament, was observed to start whenever a report louder
or nearer than ordinary reached his ears, and load his gun.   On examination
the following morning it was found to contain seven charges; farther
examination disclosed that there was no flint in the lock!

As the night wore on, some of the cooler and clearer-headed discovering
that "mirth and fun grew fast and furious" among the mirth-loving portion
of their younger townsmen, began like Hudibras to "smell a rat," and
stole quietly off to their homes.   Others, however, of more ardent temperament continued to maintain their stations and stand to their arms; and
it was not until day dawned that the suspicion began to dawn on their
minds that somebody had been terriby hoaxed!   Such was the fact; for
during the whole of that eventful night every Greene Indian in the Plantation had been sleeping quietly under his own roof, never dreaming of
any invasion of Belfast save with a goad-stick in his hand and a horse
or oxen drawing a load of cordwood or shingles, with no thought of plunder
beyond the market value of his load in salt fish, pork and "New England."
The wild wags of the day had their joke, however, and Jo. Dolliff immortalized the event in rhymes of which the following is the opening stanza:

Good people all, both great and small,
  Give ear to what I write.
I'll tell you what a dreadful war
  Took place the other night."

The whole poem, (?) or that portion of it which has been rescued
from the clutches of oblivion, was published in The Republican Journal
of December 29, 1870.

And who was Jo. Dolliff, the first white man, probably, who ever
"waked to ecstacy the living lyre" on the banks of the Passagassawaukeag?
An old settler here who claims to remember him says, that he was "a
harmless, inoffensive man, who lived at or near the place called Belmont
Lower Corner, who sometimes had a few shingles to sell which he brought
to Belfast for market."   Another, who claims an equally early acquaintance
with him says that he "was a man of quick wit, rich humor and wonderful
facility in stringing together verses in which there was apt to be more
reason than rhyme, and but little to spare of either; and that he usually
found in this locality ampler field for the development of muse and
muscle than he did at home."   His poetical effusions, like those of
Homer, were not reduced to writing in their day, but have been transmitted
orally from generation to generation.

Among them is one denominated "Dolliff's Prayer;" it had its origin in the following circumstances. He, with other, were employed one day in cutting the grass in the mowing field of a neighbor. According to the custom of the times, when 11 o'clock a. m. came, the grog for the mowers was brought to them in the field. All partook of course, and all detected a very peculiar and not very agreeable flavor in the beverage. Having gone through the ceremony, all, with the exception of Dolliff, commenced on their next swarth. Returning to their starting point they found him still there, cup in hand, tasting and meditating. In answer to the inquiry what he made of it, Dolliff took off his straw hat, drew his shirt-sleeve across his forehead, took another taste, and with great solemnity exclaimed.

"O Lord of love, look from above
    On us poor mortals here!
And send old--to hell with speed,
    For mixing rum with beer!"

He had solved the problem; by accident, the rum had been poured into a jug in which there was a small quantity of beer.

"Doliff's Blessing" has also come down to us. He with other had been employed during the forenoon in reaping; at noon the laborers were called to dinner. Their employer, his family, and some friends who had called unexpectedly had dined, and the table presented a beggarly account of empty dishes for a lot of hungry men fresh from the field. However, they seated themselves, and while glancing their eyes in hungry despair over the fragments before them, one of them remarked that it would be "hard work to make a dinner out of that without a blessing." Dolliff began to remove the remnants of meat from the platter to his own plate very deliberately, exclaiming while doing so,

"Lord from on high, cast down thine eye,
    Also a knife, or sickle,
To cut the throat of the gentlefolk
That ate up all the vitual!"

Remarking at the conclusion, "Men, you can make a dinner out of the potatoes and the blessing; I prefer the meat." The sentiment of the "blessing" was bad, the rhyme worse; but the whole bears the impress of the genuine Dolliffian inspiration.

A mere accident brought to the hands of the writer, some twenty years ago, an old volume which bore internal evidence of having once been the property of Dolliff or some one of his immediate neighbors. From the various handwriting on its fly-leaves it appeared to have been the property of four different individuals, who had successively inscribed their names and the fact of their ownership in such language as indicated that they had imbibed to some extent the inspiration, if they had not in fact adopted the words of their neighbor poet. One of them under date of Nov. 1, 1800, writes:

"This book belongs to me, my friend,
It wasn't made to borry nor lend,
To let you known from whence it came
Underneath I write my name."

Under date of 1804, no month or day, as supplementary to the foregoing, probably, the owner next in order writes:

"Steal not this book, I pray
Lest in the awful judgment day,
The Lord should up and say,
Where is the book you stole away."

It seemed to have passed next into the hands of one of the gentler sex, who writes under date of Nov. 20, 1809:

"Hannah Bryant Hur Book.
God give Hur grace therein to Look,
And when the Bells for her doth Toll,
The Lord have Marcy on her sole."

To which very devout aspiration she adds the following lines from good Dr. Watts, slightly changed:

"Life is the Time that God hath given
To skeep from Hell and flea to Heven."

If the foregoing were not improvisations from the lips of Dolliff, there is good reason for the supposition that they were inspired by his genius.

Learned scholars have learnedly discussed the question whether any such men as Homer and Ossian, whose poetry has stirred men's hearts like the sound of a trumpet for centuries, ever lived. Who shall venture to say that the name of Jo. Dolliff, the reputed Squatter-Poet of Greene Plantation, in whose verse is embalmed the memory of the heroic men of Belfast in the "Greene Indian War" may not be found a century hence in the catalogue of myths!

CHAPTER VIII. (1808-9)

The three years prior to this, 1808, were years of prosperity. During those years there had been a large influx of population and of the right class; men who did not come to spy out the leanness of the land nor squeeze out its fatness, but to lay the foundation of homes for a lifetime. Their energy, enterprise and industry contributed largely to building up the place, developing its resources, and carrying it through the dark period in its history upon which it was now to enter.

Among them came one who deserves something more than a passing notice, Nathan Read; better known to those who remember him, as Judge Read. Of those who came here contemporaneously with him there were many, doubtless, energetic business men, who contributed more largely than he did to the material wealth of the place; but no one of them who labored so earnestly and persistently to promote the moral and intellectual welfare of its people; no one who felt a deeper interest or was a more active worker in every cause which had for its object the advancement of the public welfare.

Judge Read was born in Warren, Mass., 1759, graduated at Harvard University in 1781, and was for nearly four years a member of its Board of Instruction. After resigning that position he commenced the study of medicine; but soon abandoned it for pursuits more congeniel to his taste, agriculture and the mechanic arts. While residing at Danvers, where he owned and carried on a large farm, he invented and obtained letters patent for the nail machine, since that time extensively used for cutting and heading nails at one operation. He was the inventor of several valuable improvements in agricultural implements, and it is claimed that he was the inventor of the multi-tubular boiler and portable high-pressure engine, and the discoverer of the true mode of applying steam-power to navigation and railways. The mass of facts and testimony collected in the biography of him compiled by his nephew, David Read, seem to establish conclusively the justice of the claim.

It was while he resided in Danvers that he represented Essex South District in Congress. He was a member of the House at the time of the contest for the Presidency between Jefferson and Burr. In 1802 he was apppointed by Gov. Strong a Special Justice of the Court of Common Pleas for the county of Essex, and after his removal to this place he presided for several years as Chief Justice of that Court for the county of Hancock.

Attracted by the glowing accounts, then rife in Massachusetts, of "Down East," the beauty of its scenery, the wealth of its forests, the fertility of its soil, he came here on a tour of exploration in the fall of 1805, and was so favorably impressed that he made a large investment, for those days, in land, purchasing at that time and in the year following four hundred acres lying on each side of the road leading from Nesmith's Corner to Little River. In 1807 he came here with his family to reside, and here he passed the remainder of his days, devoting them to agricultural pursuits, experiments and inventions in the mechanic arts, and the study of the natural sciences, always taking, as his biographer well remarks, "a lively interest in all matters of a public character, especially such as were designed to improve the moral condition and advance the intellectual and social improvement of the people among whom he lived." He died Jan. 20, 1849, in his ninetieth year, in the full possession of his intellectual powers until within a few days of his decease; enjoying during his long and somewhat chequered life, the respect and esteem of all who knew him best.

The laying of the Embargo by Congress, Dec. 22, 1807, was the first dark cloud that gathered on the horizon. The people of our town in that day were eminently a commercial people; the principal business of the place was buying, selling and shipping cord wood to Boston and other western ports, and lumber to the West Indies. It was in reality the only business that yielded money, or its equivalent, in return. Under the restrictive policy adopted by Congress this class of business was almost paralyzed. Shipping and sailors, who constituted a very respectable portion of the population here and elsewhere on the coast of Maine, were thrown out of employment. This state of things continued, with the exception of a brief interval immediately following the passage of the Non-intercourse Act, until the close of the war in 1815. During all this time, however, a new field of labor was opening in the improvement and cultivation of the lands lying in the interior. Loss of profit from commercial enterprise, although a heavy blow, did not dishearten the men of that day. They accepted it as an inevitable necessity; if they could not plough the sea they could plough the land, and they went into the work manfully.

During the years before named a large number of dwelling houses, stores and mechanics shops were built. Many, if not most of them, have from time to time fallen a prey to fire or the demand for improvement; few of those that remain would now be recognized by the original owners, through so many changes have they passed. An enumeration of the few still remaining may not be uninteresting: among them are the following. The house now occupied by Mr. B. F. Field, built by his father, Bohan P. Field, Esq. The Major Chase House, so called, standing just north of the North Church, built by John Russ, Esq., uncle of the editor of the Progressive age, The Leach House, at the corner of Church and Bridge streets, now owned by Mr. Oakes Angier, built by Andrew Leach, Esq. The basements of the two buildings last named were finished for stores, and occupied for some time as such; the upper stories for dwellings. The house occupied by Capt. W. O. Alden, built by his father, Apollos Alden. The Edmunds' House, formerly so called, on Main street, next easterly from the house of Mr. Asa Howes, now occupied by Messrs. W. McFarland and S. A. Blodgett, built by Mr. Alvin Edmunds. The house next easterly, now occupied by Messrs. Riley Kittridge and S. G. Howard, also built by Mr. Edmunds; the lower story of which was occupied for some years as a store by William Avery, Esq., father of Mrs. Daniel Lane, the upper story as a saddle and harness-marker's shop by Mr. Edmunds. The house now owned and occupied by Mr. A. D. Chase, built by Mr. John B. Durham. The house now occupied by Mr. Moses W. Rich, built by Wiggin Merrill, who carried on the business of boot and shoe-making quite extensively for some years in a portion of it and occupied the residue as a dwelling. The house now occupied by Mr. John N. Stewart, built by Mr. Samuel Peck, the first cabinet-maker in the place. The Lymburner house, formerly so called, on High street, built by Capt. Lymburner, now occupied by Mr. Horatio J. Locke. The house now occupied by Rev. Wooster Parker, built by Doctor C. C. Chandler. The house occupied by the late James Miller at the time of his decease, built by Col. Thomas Cunningham and occupied by him for several years as a tavern. The Moor house, built by Mr. John Moor, blacksmith, now occupied by Mr. J. C. Thompson; the same into which a certain Squire was invited "to warm himself," as narrated in a previous chapter. The Ben. Eells house, built by Mr. Eells, which now constitutes part of the New England House. The foregoing enumeration is not intended to embrace any buildings erected prior to 1805, or subsequent to 1808, nor any building erected during the years intervening which has ceased to exist.

One of the events of this year, 1808, was the erection by Simon Watson of a large two story building on Hayford's Hill, as it is now called, which he opened as a tavern and which continued to be occupied for that purpose six or seven years; the same building became the property of Mr. Hayford many years afterward, and was burned in 1860. It was a notable tavern in its day; the inevitable stopping-place of the yeomanry on their way to and from market, and in winter the terminus of all sleigh-rides from "the Beach." A short ride for a pleasure-party it would be accounted now; but in those days, before the hills had bowed their heads to the plough and scraper, and when fur coats and buffalo robes were "unknown quantities," it was long enough for comfort. The best of cheer and a rousing fire in an open fireplace--no air-tights then--always awaited the coming guests, and many a time and oft did those stout old

rafters vibrate to the music of the dancer's feet and the old, old song,
"We won't go home till morning." All gone now; the house and its keeper--
the dancing feet at rest--the merry voices silent!

In the fall of this year Mr. Nesmith retired from business as a
trader and leased his store (Nesmith's Corner) to a young man, then
only eighteen years of age, who had been his clerk for nearly three
years preceding, and so commenced business, to use his own words, "by
offering at retail a small stock of groceries &c." He continued to
occupy that store until 1816, when he removed to the building now the
Phoenix House. He represented Belfast in the first Legislature convened
after Maine became a State, and was her first Mayor after she became
a city. It is hardly necessary to add that the young man is now our
honored fellow citizen, Ralph C. Johnson.

The year 1809 was not marked by any notable event of local interest.
After the passage of the Non-intercourse Act, March 1, business partially
revived, and the coasting trade became again lively; it was not of long
duration, however; there was a rift in the cloud but it did not long
remain open. Preliminary measures were taken for the organization of
a Methodist and Baptist Society, and for the first time in this locality
the religious creed of the denomination known as Universalists was presented
to the people in a discourse by a preacher of that faith at the house
of Benjamin Joy; the same house subsequently occupied as a tavern which
stood on the site where the store occupied by Francis Whitmore now stands,
next northerly from the New England house; it was destroyed by fire
in December 1854.

CHAPTER IX. (1810-11)

The population of Belfast according to the census of this year, 1810, was twelve hundred and seventy-four. The town officers elected at the annual spring meeting were Samuel Houston, Jr., John Merriam, Henry Goddard, Selectmen; Jonathan Wilson, Clerk; John Wilson, Treasurer; three of them residing on the east side of the river, two on the west.

The nineteenth day of January was long remembered as the "Cold Friday"; in the almanacs and newspapers for several years succeeding mention was made of it by that name. Williamson in his History of Maine speaks of it as the coldest day known in this locality since the cold winter of 1784; yet the mercury in the thermometer stood at only 15 deg. or 16 deg. below zero. The day preceding was unusually mild; so warm that persons engaged in chopping wood, and other manual labor in the open air, found it uncomfortable to work with their coats on. Just before night the wind began to blow from the north with snow squalls which increased in severity as the night wore on. In the morning of the 19th, and during that day, the cold was so intense that all out-door work was suspended; piling on wood in the old-fashioned fire-places furnished sufficient employment to keep all hands out of idleness.

During the night preceding a schooner at anchor off Knowlton's cove in Northport broke from her moorings, was driven across and stranded at a place then known as Grinnell's Point, on Long Island. She was discovered in the morning by the islanders, who boarded her as soon as they were able so to do and found all the crew insensible, apparently frozen to death; the captain was not on board. They got them on shore, however, as soon as possible, and to the nearest house. One of them, who was the best clad of them all, and who proved to be the mate, was laid aside as dead beyond question. The others exhibiting some signs of vitality a messenger was immediately despatched to this place for a physician, this being the nearest point at which one could be found. Before he reached the Island the dead mate had come to life, and it is a singular fact that he was the only one of the number who proved not to be frost-bitten in any of his limbs. The others were so badly frozen that amputation of one or more of their limbs became necessary to save their lives; one of them lost both legs. As soon as it could be done with safety they were brought across to Northport where medical aid could be more readily and conveniently afforded. Their suffering appealed loudly to the sympathy and charity of the good people of this place, and received a prompt and most liberal response. Many years afterwards the sailor who lost both his legs made his appearance here; he did not come, he said to hunt up his legs, but to see once more the people who were so kind to him when he lost them.

This year the Belfast Academy was built. A brief history of this institution, which has lived nearly up to its three-score years and ten, may not be out of place here. It was incorporated by the General Court of Massachusetts in February, 1808. The act of incorporation embraced a grant of one half township of land six miles square in the county of Washington, now Aroostook, on condition that within three years from the passage of the act the sum of three thousand dollars should be raised for the endowment of the academy and appropriated to that use. The meeting of the Trustees for organization was held on the thirtieth day of March following, and before the twenty-seventh day of July, then next, the amount required was raised by subscription. The largest portion of the funds was raised here; there were some liberal donations, however, from non-residents owning lands in the vicinity. The general depression in business and various other causes combined to delay active operations for a while, and it was not until this year that the erection of the building was completed. It was of about the same dimensions and model as the present brick building, with a tasteful portico; it stood nearer High street, the front of it being but a few feet westerly of the westerly line of what is now Church street, which was not located until many years afterwards; the approach to it was

by an avenue leading from High street.   It was the habit of the boys
of those days who attended the Academy to utilize High street, when
school was dismissed, during the summer time, by playing "leap-frog"
from in front of it to Nesmith's Corner.
   It was formally dedicated on the eighteenth of May, A. D. 1811.
The character of the services on that occasion may be gathered from
the following votes passed by the Trustees as a meeting held on that
day.   "Voted, that the thanks of the Trustees be presented to Mr. Porter
for his elegant and appropriate oration delivered at the dedication
of Belfast Academy, this day, and that a copy be requested for the press."
"Voted, that the thanks of the Trustees be presented to William Moody
and the other musicians for their appropriate and highly gratifying
performances on this occasion."   What those "performances" were does
not appear of record; possibly the "Ode on Science" and the "Dying Christian;"
those being about the only anthems known to the sweet singers of those
days, and let off on all occasions, Fourth of July only excepted, and
that only so far as the last named was concerned.
   The Academy went into operation immediately under the charge of
Mr. James Porter, the orator referred to above.   He was a brother of
Zaccheus Porter, Esq., Counsellor at law, who came here to reside in
1813, and died in 1824; and who was the father of Mrs. Conner, widow
of our highly esteemed and lately deceased fellow citizen, William H.
Conner.   Mr. Porter did not long continue as Preceptor; he became a
clergyman, and afterwards resided in Pomfret, Conn., where he died.
He was succeeded by George Downes, afterwards Hon. George Downes of
Calais; he also is dead.   His successor was John Bulfinch, Esq., who
is still living in Waldoborough.
   It was the original design of the Trustees to preserve the square
near the center of which the building was erected as a public park,
to be ornamented with trees, in due time, perhaps, with statuary, making
it in appearance at least an "academic grove."   To that design they
adhered with laudable pertinacity; it is to be regretted that they were
not permitted to carry it out.   When Church street was located, in 1819,
its southern terminus was north of the Academy Square, the intention
being to connect it ultimately with High street by a street running
at a right angle, leaving the square intact; but the aesthetic was doomed
to yield to the practical, and at a later date Church street was located
as it now runs, through the square to High street.   At the town-meeting
called to act on the matter the trustees presented a very elaborate
protest, replete with arguments against the proposed continuation, which
in these days would have been regarded conclusive; it was of no avail,
and the street was accepted and built.   A suit was subsequently brought
by the trustees to test the legality of the proceedings, but the decision
of the Court was adverse to them.   With that event commenced the decadence
of the institution as an academy.
   While the British were in possession of this place in 1814, it
was occupied as a barrack by a portion of their troops.   After that
time and before the Unitarian meeting-house was built, it was occupied
occasionally for public religious services.   In the summer of 1829 it
was occupied for awhile by a troop of strolling play-actors; who succeeded
admirably well in murdering Shakspeare and victimizing all who were
indiscreet enough to give them credit.   For a while after that, until
1836, it was left to take care of itself; its door open day and night,
tantamount to an invitation to all tramps and night-walkers to enter
and take possession; the haunt of the muses was no longer "classic ground."
After that it was occupied from time to time by public and private schools
until December 17, 1842, when it was destroyed by fire.   A vote was
passed December 24, 1845, to rebuild, and to raise the funds for that
purpose by mortgage or sale of the lands granted by the Commonwealth;
and in 1846-47 the present brick building was erected.

In 1811 the Baptist Society, which had been for some years gradually increasing in numbers and strength, was incorporated. The old Court of Common Pleas was abolished, and the Circuit Court of Common Pleas was established; the counties of Hancock and Washington constituted the Third Eastern Circuit, and Hon. William Crosby of this place was appointed Chief Justice. Under the last census there had been a new apportionment of Representatives to Congress; by this apportionment seven were allowed to Maine, and Hon. John Wilson of this place was elected to represent the Fifth District, embracing the counties of Hancock and Washington. This year the Durham house, on Wilson's Hill, opposite the house then occupied by Mr. Wilson, more recently by Hon. A. G. Jewett, was built.

On the fourth day of March, died James Nesmith, Esq., in the forty-seventh year of his age. He was one of the most prominent and worthy members of this little community, and his death was deeply deplored. He had been for many years the only Notary Public, and was emphatically the magistrate of the place; the one before whom all actions within the jurisdiction of a Justice of the Peace were brought. He possessed in a remarkable degree the confidence of the entire community, and his decisions were almost uniformly acquiesced in. He was the first one who opened a store in town for the sale of merchandise. Commencing trade at Little River, he subsequently removed to the village where, after trading for awhile in a building that stood on the site of McClintock's block, he built on the opposite side of the street, long known as Nesmith's Corner, and continued to trade there until the fall of 1808, when he was compelled by failing health to retire from active business. He was for several years Postmaster, succeeding Tolford Durham, who first held the office in this place, and was succeeded by Thomas Whittier, Esq. He was the father of James Nesmith of the old firm of Nesmith and Leeds, formerly doing an extensive business in New York, well known to our merchants and ship owners of twenty years ago. A daughter of his became the wife of the late William Cunningham, Esq., of Montville; she and her children are the only descendants of Mr. Nesmith living in this vicinity.

CHAPTER X. (1812-13.)

Since the publication of our last chapter it has been suggested that a description of the forms and ceremonies on funeral occasions at the period of which we are now treating would be acceptable. It was before the day of rosewood, black-walnut and metallic caskets, or of hearses. The coffin was usually of pine, stained black, and a bier was the vehicle on which it was carried to the grave. At the funeral of an adult there was a gathering of almost the entire adult population in the neighborhood. The religious services at the house of the deceased consisted of selections from the Scriptures and prayer; on rare occasions there was singing and a brief discourse. Those services completed, the coffin was taken from the house, placed on the bier, and a pall thrown over it. The relatives of the deceased were then escorted by the master of ceremonies, hat in hand, to their positions in rear of the bier; until within a few years of this time the master wore a sword and a cocked hat such as were worn by military men in the days of the Revolution. Next after the relatives followed the friends and neighbors of the deceased, two by two; usually a long procession.

At the signal from the master, always given by the waving of a white handkerchief, four of the bearers, there were always eight of them, took the bier on their shoulders, the other four taking their positions in front in readiness to relieve the four bearing the bier should they become weary under their burthen; the pall-bearers, there were usually six, walked by the side of the bier, three on each side, taking hold of the hem of the pall. Arrived at the graveyard the coffin was deposited in the grave, a few shovels-full of earth were thrown upon it--there was none of the modern filigree parade then about "dust to dust, ashes to ashes" &c.--the bereaved husband, or father, in other cases the officiating clergyman, expressed to the bearers and pall-bearers thanks for the kindly service they had rendered, and the procession returned in the same order to the house. Arriving there, the relatives having passed in, the pall-bearers and bearers were invited by the master to a room where refreshments in the form of wine and, sometimes, other kinds of liquor were provided for them; all partook and then separated. There was no excess; a simple glass sufficed; there was no merriment, but everything was conducted with the solemnity befitting the occasion.

This custom continued until a public sentiment adverse to the use of intoxicating liquors on any occasion was awakened, and then this came to be looked upon as "a custom more honored in the breach then the observance." In these days it would be so in conflict with the conventionalities of society that it would hardly be tolerated. Let us not be too harsh in condemnation of our fathers in this particular. In the days when it was regarded as right, almost a religious duty, to drink "standing and in silence," to the "Memory of Washington" and of the "Heroes of the Revolution," it was but another phase of the same sentiment to drink to the memory of the departed friend and neighbor. At the funeral of a small child no bier was used, and there were no pall-bearers. A white handkerchief was tied around each end of the little coffin and it was carried to the grave by four boys, a few years older than the deceased, two walking on each side, each taking hold of one side of the handkerchiefs.

It became apparent early in this year, 1812, that a war with Great Britain was inevitable. On the fourth day of April Congress laid an embargo for ninety days "on all vessels in the harbors of the United States;" this was followed by a declaration on the eighteenth of June following that "war exists between Great Britain and the United States." Intelligence of the event reached here by due course of mail on the same day that the frame of the house now occupied by Hon. R. C. Johnson was raised. The blow was not unanticipated, but it fell with stunning effect on the good people here. A panic pervaded the community; almost every possible evil was predicted, and the opinion freely expressed that it would soon become necessary for all living on the coast of Maine

to abandon their possessions and remove beyond reach of the enemy.
Taking into consideration the fact that the prosperity of the place
was so entirely dependent on navigation and commerce it is not strange
that the prospect for the immediate future was any thing but bright;
nothwithstanding it was a war undertaken for "Free trade and sailors'
rights."

The allusion to the raising of the frame of Mr. Johnson's house
furnishes the fitting occasion for calling to mind another custom of
"ye olden times."   It was regarded then just as much out of the question
to raise a frame as it was to go through haying-time without rum; both
were occasions when the use of that article for "mechanical purposes"
was considered indispensible.   If the building to be raised was a small
one, a gallon of "Old Whiteface" answered the purpose, at a pinch.
If it was a two-story dwelling-house the quantity was duplicated; unless
the raising was in a time of drouth, when a still larger quantity was
required.   If the owner was reputed to be wealthy, or the building was
of a public character, it was always found necessary to substitute for
"Whiteface" a mixture called "rum-punch."   Half a dozen pailfuls would
raise a dwelling-house, ell and barn; nothing less than a barrel full,
per diem, would raise a meeting-house; as late as 1818 it required two
barrels-full to raise the Unitarian meeting-house; the compiler had
to use two pailfuls to raise his barn; but that was in a very dry season.

After the frame was raised it was the custom to "name it," as the
performance was styled.   Two of the parties engaged would bestride
the ridge-pole, one at each end.   One of them would say

> "Here is a fine frame,
> Without any name,
> And what shall we call it?"

To which the other would reply in equally poetical language, but without
answering the main question.   After passing numerous questions and answers
of the same character the frame would be "named."   Three cheers were
then given, a parting cup taken, and that was the end of the ceremony.
In the raising of a frame all services were rendered gratuitously.
The approved recipe for the mixture above referred to was "One sour,
Two sweet, Four strong, Eight weak;" the art of compounding it is now,
probably, one of the "Lost Arts."

Soon after war was declared the brig Illuminator, built here the
year preceding, the major part of her owned by parties residing here,
commanded by Capt. Robert Patterson and manned by a crew the most of
whom belonged in Belfast, was captured by a British frigate, sent to
Halifax and condemned.   Her officers were liberated in a few days and
sent home on a cartel-ship; her crew remained in prison about four months
and were then exchanged.   She was on her voyage from Liverpool to New
Orleans, was spoken by the frigate and the inquiry made if war had been
declared between Great Britain and the United States; the master of
the brig replied, of course, that he had not heard of any such declaration.
The frigate left, but soon after fell in with a British merchantman
who reported that she had been fired into by an American cruiser; of
course the frigate "bout ship" and captured the Illuminator.   Such was
the story told, for the accuracy of which the compiler does not assume
to vouch.

This event, involving as it did the total loss of property belonging
to parties residing here, served to impress the minds of all more deeply
with a sense of the uncertain tenure by which they held what remained
to them.   Shipping deteriorated in value at least fifty per cent; vessels
were hauled up and stripped.   The hazard attending foreign voyages put
an end to all enterprize in that direction; even the coasting business,
light as it had become, was still farther checked by the presence of
British privateers hovering on our coast.   The sloops Mary and Washington,
both owned here, were captured and burned, and another brig, principally
owned here, laden with spars and beef, was captured early in 1813, sent

to Halifax and condemned.   Extravagant prices were demanded for most articles of foreign production.   Flour and other bread stuffs commanded very high prices, and in consequent of the unfavorable season for crops there was much suffering among the poor here and in the surrounding region.   Coffee which before the war sold for eighteen cents per pound ran up to thirty-five cents; carrots, beets, barley, and rye were roasted and used as substitutes very extensively; indeed there were very few families in which one or the other was not used.   Tea advanced from one dollar and eighty cents to three dollars per pound; as an almost absolute necessity there were myriads of families in which the use of it was entirely abandoned; in others it became the occasion luxury in lieu of the daily beverage.   Molasses advanced from sixty cents per gallon to one dollar and fifty cents; other articles of domestic consumption in the same proportion.

The year 1813 dragged slowly, gloomily along, unmarked by any local event that left any impression on the memory of the compiler. He remembers it only as a season of general despondency and acrimonious bickerings between the supporters and opponents of the national administration and its measures.   There was but a small numerical difference in this section between the two political parties.   At the gubernatorial election the vote in this county (Hancock) was for Varnum (Democrat) 1,643; for Strong (Federalist) 1,443; the majority for Varnum in the District was only 1,070. The organs of the two parties which circulated most extensively in the locality were the "Boston Patriot," Democratic, and the "Columbian Centinel," Federal; both published in Boston, weekly, at $4.00 per year. During the year Congress levied a direct tax on lands; never a popular measure, it was at this period regarded as particularly onerous by those who depended for their daily bread on the products of the soil; a soil, too, which was yielding but a niggardly return for the labor expended on it.

As the year drew towards its close, however, a better and more harmonious feeling began to prevail.   The brilliant and repeated successes of our little navy on the ocean, the signal victories of Commodore Perry on Lake Erie, and of General Harrison over General Proctor near "old Moravian town," thrilled the hearts of the people, awakening them to a consciousness that as partakers in common in the nation's glory they had a common interest in maintaining its supremacy.   The capture of the British brig Boxer off Portland on the fifth of September, by the Enterprise, was a matter of universal joy among the inhabitants on this coast, for during the year she had been a greater annoyance to our coasters than all the other cruisers combined.

Every new country has its "Leather-stocking" or Daniel Boone; men who seem to have been born with an instinctive aversion to civilization; natural born hunters.   Two men of that class were found at an early period in this region; Michael Davis, and Hodgdon, whose Christian name is not remembered.   It is not known what became of the first named; Hodgdon baited his trap for the last time this year.   He would not be regarded, were he now living, as a very eminent "Son of Temperance" or a model in dress for a fashionable tailor.   Amusing anecdotes are told of him; one must suffice for our purpose.

Col. K. who resided in a neighboring town, was at one time very much annoyed by bears who made inroads on his corn field. Meeting Hodgdon one day he represented to him the extent of his annoyance and asked his advice as to the best mode of relief.   "Colonel," said H., "bears is awful fond of molasses, now you just make a little trough and fill it with molasses and rum, and put it where they come into your field, and they'll just drink it for the sake of the molasses; and the rum'll just make 'em so drunk that you can go out in the morning and knock 'em on the head just as if they were sheep." The Colonel followed the advice and went to his field early the next morning to knock the bears on the head.   The only bear he found there was Hodgdon, drunk as he had predicted the bears would be!

CHAPTER XI. (1814)

Early in the morning of September first the British fleet made
its appearance at Castine and took possession of the place. Its appearance
was not unexpected there, and the people here were on the look-out for
it. Very soon three of the vessels belonging to the fleet--which proved
to be a frigate and two transports--were seen to be heading in this
direction, and several others in the direction of the mouth of the Penobscot;
the latter, as afterwards learned, in pursuit of the United States corvette,
Adams, which was then up the river for repairs, having been on shore
at Isle au Haut a few days before; she was burned by order of her commander,
Capt. Morris, on the third of the month, to prevent her capture by the
enemy.

The wind being light the vessels bound for this place did not arrive
until afternoon, when they came to anchor not far southerly from where
the monument now stands. Somewhat later in the day a barge was seen
to put off from the frigate and lay its course for this shore; it landed
just northerly from the upper steamboat wharf, rather from where the
wharf now is. The officer in command of the barge, bearing a flag of
truce, requested an interview with the Chief Magistrate of the place.
There was quite a crowd assembled at the point where the barge landed,
and the compiler well remembers the anxious interest with which he and
others saw an individual, long since deceased, brimful of rum and patriotism
hustled back out of sight and hearing through fear that the terrible
British might hear his muttered curses against "the d--d redcoats."

The officer was conducted to Huse's tavern, the building now occupied
by the Messrs. Howes, and introduced to Asa Edmunds, Esq., as the chief
magistrate of the place, he being Chairman of the Board of Selectmen.
The chief magistrate was thereupon informed that a body of His Majesty's
forces proposed to take and hold possession of the place for a few days,
peaceably if possible, if not, forcibly; that if they were permitted
so to do without molestation, the persons and property of the inhabitants
would be respected, and that for all supplies required an adequate compensation should be made. The reply of the chief magistrate was in effect
that if His Majesty's troops saw fit to take possession of the place
they would not be molested by any of its inhabitants--that our means
for furnishing supplies were limited, but that they should be furnished
to the extent of those means--adding that "if we had received earlier
notice of your coming, we should have been prepared to give you a different
reception." This somewhat equivocal remark occasioned no slight merriment
on the quarter deck of the frigate when reported by the officer to whom
it was addressed.

Sometime in the night preceding the brass field-pieces belonging
to the artillery company had been removed beyond reach of the enemy,
and during the day many of the towns people removed their families and
most valuable household goods; most of them but a few miles out of the
village; some of them as far as Searsmont.

Shortly after dusk the troops began to disembark, and when the
sun rose the next morning the good people of the place, whose slumbers
had been but slightly disturbed by the military movements, so quietly
were they conducted, awoke to find themselves in possession of the redcoats,
and guards stationed on the roads leading to Northport and Belmont,
and at the westerly end of the bridge. The number of troops landed
was about seven hundred. General Gosselin, commanding the forces, made
his headquarters at the McFarland house; the old meeting-house, the
academy and the gun-house were used as barracks, and the town-pond;
standing on the easterly side of High street, a little southerly from
the academy, was converted into a battery. The troops remained here
unmolested and molesting no one for four days, when they re-embarked
and returned to Castine. No requisitions were made for supplies, but
while they remained here quite a lively retail trade was going on in
the articles of milk, bread, butter, eggs, potatoes and all kinds of
garden vegetables. Our people, who had a surplus of those commodities,

faithfully obeyed the Scriptural injunction, "if thine enemy hunger feed him," and were not unmindful of the other clause, which does not appear in the common version, "and make him pay double what the feed is worth." Ten cents a quart for milk, fifty cents for a brown loaf, twenty cents a pound for butter, seventeen cents per dozen for eggs, and fifty cents for the smallest sized basket full of potatoes or vegetables were the ruling prices.

The next day after the British left, the military, who had been gathering from the interior and were encamped near Simon Watson's tavern on Hayford's Hill, marched into town; they remained but a day and left, very much to the relief of the proprietors of gardens, potato-patches and hen-roosts. The military companies in this place, the artillery under command of Capt. Alfred Johnson, and the militia under command of Capt. Nathan Swan, were called out to reinforce the troops collected up the river to resist the British force which had gone to capture the Adams, and were ordered to rendezvous at Searsport, then Prospect. On arriving there information was received that the Adams had been burned and our forces dispersed; their further services were not required of course, and they immediately returned. The artillery company did not bring back their field-pieces to the village, but concealed them on the eastern side of the river, where they remained until the close of the war.

As a truthful annalist it becomes the duty of the compiler to record the fact that after the British took possession of the eastern section of the State, and Castine especially, the patriotism of the people here and in the surrounding region was not in all cases proof against the temptation to furnish fat beef to the enemy at good fat prices, or to import goods of foreign manufacture without rendering "to Ceasar the things that are Ceasar's," in other words without payment of duties. The hazard attending the importation by vessels from abroad added to the high duties, had so far enhanced the market value of foreign merchandise as to place it beyond the pecuniary ability of most of the people to purchase even those articles which had come to be regarded as necessaries. The long stretch of territory in this section necessarily left unguarded by revenue officers afforded great facilities for smuggling, and the high prices paid by the enemy for our products, beef especially, constituted an inducement to supply them, although at the hazard of seizure and condemnation, which many were not strong enough to resist.

During this fall and the winter succeeding, especially after the Penobscot was closed by ice, a brisk contraband trade was carried on between Castine and the western side of the river. All sorts of devices were resorted to to elude the vigilance of the revenue officers. Wagons with double bottoms constituted one of those devices and a very successful one, until it was detected, and in this wise: Moses Adams, Esq., Sheriff of the county, residing in Ellsworth, on his way to Boston chanced to stop for the night at Wiscasset. There was something about the construction of his wagon that attracted the attention of a loafer in the stable-yard and upon examination it was found to have two bottoms between which was concealed a quantity of valuable English merchandise; it was seized and condemned. Occupying the high official position he did, and being a prominent member of the Federal, or anti-war party, he was regarded as a shining mark and the following shot was fired at him in the Boston Patriot of Nov. 9, 1814: "THE DOUBLE BOTTOMED WAGON. The next trip Mr. Sheriff Adams takes to Castine, we would advise him to make use of an Air-Balloon as there appears to be no safety in travelling on the land. The doubled bottomed wagons are not safe from the gripe of James Madison's sentinels; but in an Air Balloon there will be perfect safety as the officers of Government are not permitted to travel in the air, nor to make seizures there."

After sleighing commenced, sleighs with false backs and fronts, pungs with false bottoms, became favorite vehicles with the smuggling community. It was not unusual to see a large, portly gentleman drive up to the tavern door just at dusk, order his horse to be "put up," and taking supper retire for the night leaving orders to be called early in the morning; he invariably came from the east. A rigid examination of him and his surroundings would have led to the discovery, probably, that the plump saddle on his horse's back was stuffed with sewing silk, that silks and satins were hidden between the two backs and fronts of his sleigh; that the false crown in his hat concealed a pound or more of needles, and that his trunk contained nothing but his comb and tooth-brush and lot of old newspapers. The lean, lank, shad-like guest who appeared in the early morning would hardly be recognized as the portly gentleman of the night preceding, and the increase in the weight of his trunk during the night was truly miraculous. It was a singular fact that all travellers of this character when they left here took the back route for the west; all the revenue officers were stationed on the shore route.

Large quantities of foreign merchandise were smuggled across the river at and near Bucksport. About three miles this side of the Ferry was Shute's tavern, where a nice supper could be had at any time on call. An invitation to a revenue officer at this place to take a ride to Shute's behind a span of spanking bays was irresistible. While he and the owner of the bays were enjoying their supper the bays were harnessed to another sleigh and the unsuspecting officer rode back with a cargo of merchandise under his feet which had never paid tribute to "Uncle Sam," his presence was a guaranty to all other officers, that no search was necessary. Gill--the "generous, whole-souled Gill"--and his span of bays enjoyed a refreshing season here until peace was declared and then disappeared as mysteriously as they came.

One more incident of the smuggling era, which will be remembered by a few who were not indifferent spectators on the occasion, must be recorded. A prominent trader, whom we will call Mr. P., occupied the old telegraph building, keeping, as the sign indicated, a "Variety Store." Two of his friends came in great haste one afternoon and informed him that the revenue officer was coming to search his premises. There was time only for a few words between them before the officer came in and informed P. that he had come to search his cellar for smuggled goods. P. flew at once into a towering passion, apparently, denounced in most violent language all spies, informers and revenue officers, concluding with the assertion that any man who attempted to search his cellar would do so at the peril of his life; all which only served to satisfy the officer that he was on the right track. At the same moment that he began to raise the trap-door leading to the cellar, P. rushed to the front door of the store, threw it wide open, then to the fire-place from which he seized a large brand, and screaming at the top of his voice, "Powder! every man to look out for himself!" flung it through the opened trap into the cellar and rushed into the street, the officer at his heels. Several individuals who were standing in front of the store alarmed by the outcry joined the stampede, which did not terminate until all engaged in it, P. on the lead, had nearly reached the old tan-yard opposite the Court House. There all came to a halt and stood momentarily expecting the explosion which was to send the "Variety Store" and contents on an aerial excursion. After a while the officer began to suspect, from the tittering about him, that he had been victimized and deliberately retracing his steps he re-entered the store and proceeded to make a thorough search through the cellar, but found nothing liable to seizure. It was not long afterwards that he learned, indirectly, that while he was running for dear life and waiting for the explosion, P.'s friends had adroitly removed through the back cellar door quite a number of suspicious looking packages and deposited them elsewhere; but it was a long time before he ceased to be reminded of the "Power Plot" and his "race for life."

CHAPTER XII. (1815-18.)

In the winter of this year, for the first time since 1780, the Bay was frozen so that travellers on foot passed from the main to the head of Long Island. On the 11th of February the British sloop of war Favorite arrived at New York bringing the Treaty of Peace concluded at Ghent on the 24th of December previous and ratified by Great Britain on the 27th. It was forwarded without delay to Washington and ratified by Congress. Intelligence of the joyful event was transmitted to New York by express messengers, thence to Boston, and reached this place by due course of mail early in March. The news was hailed with all the demonstrations of joy which the place and people had the capacity to express. The field-pieces were brought from their hiding-place, a salute fired at the junction of Main and High streets, a respectable quantity of window-glass broken, and a still larger quantity of still thicker glass subjected to manipulations which would be entirely unintelligible to many of the people of these days. The dark clouds had passed away and once more the sun shone out. Business began again to flow in its wonted channels; lumbering and ship-building revived and the fisheries were resumed. Belfast brought out her working-clothes, which had been laid aside for two and a half years, dusted them, and with sleeves rolled up went to work. The heart heavily laden threw off the old burden and cheerfully took up the new; the dark, gloomy winter was at last "made glorious summer."

It proved, however, not to be a cloudless summer; "grim visaged war had smoothed his wrinkled front," but the fact of Nature scowled on the labors of the husbandman. The season of planting was cold, wet, discouraging; autumn made but a lean return for the outlay of summer. The "Ohio Fever," which had attacked individuals here and there predisposed to it in the early spring, began to be more prevalent; it was not, however, until the next year that it became epidemic.

This year, 1816, was long remembered by the farmers of New England as the "Year eighteen hundred and starved-to-death"; throughout Europe and America as the "year without a summer." In this latitude the spring was wet, cold, and unusually backward. The month of April, although at its commencement mild as ordinarily, terminated with snow and ice. In May ice made an inch think. June was the "coldest ever known;" on the tenth there was severe frost and snow fell. July the fifth ice made of the thickness of window-glass. August was still more cheerless; corn was so frozen that it was cut for fodder, and almost all field and garden vegetation was cut off. For about two weeks in September we had the mildest weather of the season; but before the month closed we had ice a quarter of an inch think. October was abundant in its products of frost and ice, and early in November we had good sleighing.

It was not then matter of wonder--it would not be now under the same combination of circumstances--that the captivating stories told of the rich lands in Ohio and Kentucky, where the climate was represented to be mild, the soil fertile, the summers long, articles of food abundant and cheap, should add fuel to the fever-fire which carried off many from this place and from the territory adjacent who really constituted part of the wealth of our population. It is true that many of them returned after the fever left them, but they returned financially weak and exhausted. It was estimated that this feverish excitement carried off some ten or fifteen thousand of the population of Maine.

As indicative of the financial condition at this time of the people in the towns back of us the following anecdote from the lips of a gentleman then engaged in business in this place will not be inappropriate. A very respectable and apparently well-to-do resident in Beaver Hill Plantation, now the town of Freedom, happened into the store of the gentleman referred to one day when the "hard times" was the topic of conversation. "How is it out at Beaver Hill?" was the inquiry made. "Bad enough," was the reply; "just as much as we can do to keep from starving." "All poor? not one rich man among you?"--"Wall--yes; there is one rich man--very

rich;--Squire S."   "What do you mean by very rich?" was the inquiry.
"Wall," was the reply, "Squire S. can afford to have pork with his beans
every day in the year."

This year Mr. Johnson (R. C.) erected the large wooden building,
since that time surrounded by a brick wall and now the Phoenix House.
When built the lower story was finished for stores; Mr. Johnson occupied
the southwardly and Benjamin Whittier the northwardly store; in the
latter the Post Office was kept for awhile.   Judge Johnson's office
was in the second story; he continued to occupy the same room until
1829, when he removed to "Williamson's Fire-proof Block;" the same building,
although materially changed since that time, in which Hon. Joseph Williamson
now has his office.

This year, for the first time, a movement was made looking to the
separation of the District of Maine from Massachusetts and the organization
of Maine as a sovereign State.   The question of separation was submitted
to the people of the District, and the result was adverse to the proposition.
The vote in this place was, in favor of separation ninety-five, against
it sixty-five; total vote, one hundred and sixty!   Alfred Johnson Jr.,
and John Merriam were elected delegates to attend a Convention at Brunswick
for the purpose of forming a Constitution should the decision prove
to be in favor of separation.

The winter of 1816-17 was the severest which had been experienced
for many years in this locality; the spring succeeding was cold and
backward.   Fears of a coming famine in the land were prevalent and strong
indications that the "Ohio Fever" would break out with more than former
virulence.   The month of July, however, brought the long-looked for
showers and sunshine; the face of Nature was once more wreathed in smiles.
The rich yield of Autumn furnished fresh assurance that the Good God
in the manifold distribution of his blessings had not forgotten this
portion of his foot-stool.   ·New courage was infused into the hearts
of the people and a new impulse given to business of every description.

This year, 1817, for the first time in this place, religious services
were held by members of the denomination known as Friends, or Quakers.
Most prominent among those whom the Spirit moved to speak on the occasion
was Anna Almy, from Providence, R. I., a young lady who won all hearts
by her personal charms, by the pure, almost divine spirituality of her
utterances, and who left behind her many warm friends "almost persuaded
to be Christians" according to her pure, peaceful, simple faith.   All
were not brought, however, within the influence of her teachings, for
this was the year of the "Smuggler's Fight."

The leaven which had leavened the whole lump during the late war
had not lost its virtue.   Importations from the British Provinces in
violation of the revenue laws still continued, although in smaller quantities and at greater hazard of seizure.   Information was communicated
to the revenue officer at Castine--this was before we had a Custom House
here--that a quantity of rum in hogsheads, imported without payment
of duties, was concealed in certain premises near Puddle Dock, not far
from the spot where the railroad turn-table is now located.   An officer
of the Customs, in company with some two or three stout, resolute men
as aids--men to whom a fight was as good as a feast--made their appearance
at one of our wharves one afternoon in a chebacco-boat.   Their information
was so definite as to the place where the rum was deposited, that there
was no difficulty or delay in finding it; they found but one hogshead,
however, and that was forthwith seized and deposited in the hold of
the vessel.   The wind having died away there was no movement made for
a return to Castine.

Soon after dark a half-dozen men might have been seen wending their
way in different directions towards the wharf where the vessel laid.
All was quiet on board when they arrived at the spot, and the natural
inference was that the crew had gone up-street.   The hatches were quietly
removed and some of the stragglers got into the hold while the others
were occupied in making preparations for hoisting out the contraband

hogshead.   To all appearance everything favored the proposed movement
when a sliding door between the hold and the cuddy was suddenly opened
and enter the aids to the revenue armed with fish-picks.   There was
no parley, no terms of peace proposed, no quarter asked or given; it
was'nt "war to the knife," but war to the fish-picks and any other weapon
that could be grasped; hand-spikes and marline-spikes took a hand.
It was a short, sharp, bloody fight, in which the aids being better
armed and better informed as to the lay of the land, were of course
successful.   The spoils were valueless to the victors, however, for
the hogshead lost one of its heads in the fray and "wasted its sweetness
on the desert air."   Some of our fellow townsmen were reported on the
sick-list the day following, having fallen on the ice or in some other
way injured themselves, and were confined to their houses for some two
or three weeks.   An indictment was subsequently found by the Grand Jury
at a term of the U. S. Court at Wiscasset against certain parties resident
here, charged with an attempt to rescue property seized by a revenue
officer.   It was said that when the case came on for trial the medical
gentlemen from this place were exceedingly oblivious of the nature of
their professional engagements about the time of the fray; some of them
were afflicted with conscientious scruples in the matter of an oath,
and were willing to "affirm" only.   One of the parties indicted, who
was so unfortunate as not to have required medical aid, was convicted
and imprisoned for a year in the county jail; another one was acquitted
on the ground of a misnomer in his Christian name; the others escaped
through some mesh in the legal net, or in some other mode.   Such is
the brief history of the locally famous "Smuggler's Fight."
    The prominent local events of the year 1818 were the opening of
Church street, the erection of the Unitarian meeting-house, and the
creation of a new and extensive Collection District, of which Belfast
was made the Port of Entry.
    The first movement toward opening Church street was in the year
preceding, when an informal   location was made; in November of this
year it was accepted from Main to Spring street; it was not accepted
through to Academy Square until 1824.   The first building erected on
the street was the dwelling-house next south from Peirce's Block, now
occupied by Mr. Edwin Salmond.   It was built in 1817 by Hon. John S.
Kimball, then a prominent trader here, subsequently our Representative
in the Legislature, a member of the Executive Council and of the Senate;
he removed from this place many years ago; none of his descendants are
now residing in this vicinity.   After occupying the dwelling referred
to for awhile, he built and occupied the house now occupied by Mrs.
H. G. O. Washburn; still later the brick house now occupied by Hon.
Wm. H. McLellan.   During the latter portion of his residence here he
was in business with his son-in-law, Mr. Charles Miller, now residing
in Salem, Mass., on Lewis' wharf, then known as Kimball and Miller's
wharf.   Mr. Kimball was born in Plaistow, N. H., Dec. 27, 1783, and
died at Salem, Mass., Aug. 28, 1867; his remains were brought here and
interred in Grove Cemetery.
    The next building erected on the street was the one standing at
the corner of Church and Spring streets, now occupied by Dr. Flanders,
built by Manasseh Sleeper, Esq., in 1818.   All the territory lying between
the southerly side of Spring street and the northerly line of Academy
Square was then pasture-land.   The great event of the year, however,
in the way of building, was the raising of the meeting-house; Samuel
French was the master-builder; two days were consumed in the operation.
A large number of stout, able-bodied men from the interior--most of
them practically familiar with handling heavy timber--came in and lent
a helping hand on the occasion; they were received with welcome and
entertained according to the "best skill and judgment" of all interested
in the work; open doors, well spread tables--not forgetting "the ingredients"
--were the order of the day. The house was completed and formally dedicated

on the 15th of November.   The pews had been sold prior to that time,
February 16th, at public auction; there were sixty-six on the ground
floor.   The highest price paid was $201, for the pew located about where
Hon. P. R. Hazeltine's now is; Mr. Chas. K. Tilden, then a leading trader
here, was the purchaser.   Pews about one-third of the way to the door
from the desk, on the broad aisle, brought from $150 to $190.   The corner
pew now occupied by Hon. James P. White sold for $160, and the one now
occupied by Hon. William C. Marshall sold for $150.   Hon. Ralph C. Johnson
is the only one of the original proprietors of pews who is now living.

CHAPTER XIII. (1818-19.)

Col. Daniel Lane, father of our fellow citizen Mr. Daniel Lane, was the first Collector of Customs at this Port. At the time of his appointment he resided in Portland. He came here early in the summer of this year, 1818, with his family and commenced house-keeping in the house on High street occupied by Capt. James Miller at the time of his decease. He afterwards purchased the Whittier place, the same premises occupied by the late Alfred W. Johnson, where he resided while he remained here. Nathaniel H. Bradbury, whom we all remember as the upright, excellent Cashier of the Belfast Bank for many years, was the first Deputy Collector and continued to hold the office until Col. Lane's successor was appointed. Noah Miller, of Northport, was the first Inspector in charge of the Revenue Boat. He was the Major Miller who in 1814 left Lincolnville in a barge well armed, and three leagues from shore captured a British sloop bound from Halifax to Castine with a cargo of merchandise on board valued at forty thousand dollars. Compelled by failing health to resign the position, Capt. James Douglas was appointed to succeed him. The other officers attached to the office were an Inspector at Bangor, Frankfort and Camden.

The Custom House was first kept in the second story of a wooden building erected by George W. Webster in 1817 which stood at the intersection of Market and High streets, opposite the present Phoenix House, the same building erected by Hon. Ralph C. Johnson the year previous. This building was subsequently purchased by Mr. John Haraden and removed by him in 1831 to the corner where the building now occupied by the Belfast Savings Bank stands. It was again removed in 1849 and converted into a dwelling house; the same now occupied by Mr. E. C. Hilton. In November 1821 the Custom House was removed to a room over the store of F. Tinkham & Co., in the brick block on Main street erected by Ladd and Morrill. In April 1822 it was moved back to the room where it was first kept, and continued there until June 1824 when it was removed to rooms in the brick block before named, and thence, in January 1829, to the office on High street previously occupied by Judge Crosby, on the site of the brick building now occupied as a store by Mr. Arnold Harris. In November 1834 it was removed to the rooms over the store on Main street now occupied by Mr. H. H. Forbes, erected that year; it was not again removed until a new Collector was appointed, in 1838. During this term of time it might have been denominated, not inappropriately, a Custom House on wheels.

Col. Lane was a native of Buxton in this State. In the war of 1812 he held a commission as Lieutenant Colonel in the regular army, but was in command of his Regiment during a large part of the time. He was stationed for a short time at Fort Independence in Boston Harbor; afterwards at Fort Preble, Portland, from which station he went to the frontier. He was in the battle of Plattsburgh, Sept. 5, 1814, and at several minor engagements prior to that date. When the office of Collector at this port was created his meritorious services were remembered and he received the appointment. He continued to hold the office, discharging its duties to the entire acceptance of the mercantile and seafaring portion of the community, until 1838 when Nathaniel M. Lowney, Esq., of this place, was appointed to succeed him. He soon after removed to Boston and was engaged for a short time in business as a Commission Merchant; from which business he retired on receiving an appointment in the Boston Custom House. He did not engage in any active business after the expiration of his official term but devoted a large portion of his remaining days to horticulture and kindred occupations, of which he was passionately fond. He is well remembered here as an ardent, not boisterous politician, a courteous gentleman, a faithful officer, a valuable member of society. He died at Newtonville, Mass., June 8, 1873, in the ninetieth year of his age; his remains were brought here and interred in Grove cemetery.

Mr. Bradbury was born in the town of York in this State, Sept. 16, 1795, and resided in that place at the time of his appointment. Prior to that time he had held the office of Deputy Collector in the Custom House at that port. He came to this place in 1818, with Col. Lane, and after his marriage, July 16, 1820, commenced house-keeping in the Ryan house, then so called, on Front street; it was burned in the fire of October 1865. In 1824 he erected the house on Church street now occupied by his widow. He was elected Town Clerk in 1825 to fill the vacancy created by the death of Dr. Herman Abbott and was reelected for several successive years. After the expiration of his official term as Deputy Collector he was for three successive years Chairman of the Board of Selectmen, and in 1840 was elected Cashier of the Belfast Bank, which office he held for nineteen years. On account of failing health he then retired from business and his son, Mr. A. H. Bradbury, the present Cashier of the Belfast National Bank, was elected to fill the vacancy. Mr. Bradbury died at his residence on Church street, December 2, 1861. He is still remembered in this community as a quiet, unobtrusive estimable fellow citizen, a faithful officer and a man of sterling integrity He was one of the few who have passed away from our midst of whom it may be said truthfully that he left behind him no one who would sow thistles on his grave.

With the opening of the year 1819 the question of separation from Massachusetts was re-opened: it was again submitted to the people and their decision this time was decidedly in the affirmative. The number of ballots cast in favor of separation was 17,091; against it 7,132. The vote in this county (Hancock) was 802 in favor against 761; the vote in this place was 145 in favor against 26. A Convention was held for the purpose of framing a Constitution and taking the necessary measures for the admission of Maine into the National Union. The Convention was held at Portland, commencing October 11th, terminating on the 30th. Alfred Johnson Jr., Esq., was the delegate from this place.

An analysis of the vote thrown in this county shows that of the 820 in favor of Separation, 662 were thrown in that portion of the county now embraced in Waldo; of the 761 against Separation, only 167 were thrown within the same territory. The separation was understood to be a democratic measure; it is quite apparent where Waldo stood politically at that time. "Stands Scotland where it did?"

Considerable alarm was occasioned early in the spring of this year by the appearance of small-pox in our midst. The story ran that a resident on the eastern side of the river found a pair of pantaloons on the shore and supposing them to have been lost from some vessel took them to his home where they were washed. The party who washed them was soon after attacked with the small pox. Various rumours were in circulation; among them that the garment had belonged to a man who died of that disease on board a vessel in the harbor. Every precaution was adopted to prevent the spread of the disease but, notwithstanding, quite a number were attacked by it; several cases proved fatal. There was a rush, of course, for vaccination. Unfortunately for the reputation of some of our medical gentlemen it proved that the virus used in numerous cases was the genuine small-pox instead of the kine. No little indignation was aroused; a legal investigation was had but nothing was developed tending to show any intention on the part of any one to practice deception in the matter. It was probably one of those accidents which will now and then occur without subjecting any one to the imputation of criminal intent or reprehensible negligence. It is not remembered that any one who was inoculated with the spurious virus died or suffered any serious detriment.

Another event of this spring was the purchase of the bell which still does duty in the belfry of the Unitarian meeting-house. By the terms of the contract for its purchase it was to be not less than twelve hundred pounds in weight; when cast it was found to be of somewhat lighter weight and smaller size than contemplated but was nevertheless accepted. From the Records of the Parish it is inferred that it was hung in the latter part of April or early in May; it was the first

"Church-going bell
These valleys and rocks ever heard."

In the month of February, died, Capt. Samuel Houston, aged ninety-two. He came here to reside in 1774, and was the second Town Clerk, in order of time, John Mitchell being his predecessor. He was a member of the "Committee of Safety" elected by the inhabitants of the place in 1776, and was the first captain of the militia company organized here after the Declaration of Independence. His successor in that office was his son, Samuel Houston, Jr., who was a member of "Washington's Body-guard" in the war of the Revolution.

On the 21st of July, Rev. William Frothingham was installed as pastor of the First Congregational Parish, popularly known now as the Unitarian Society, with a salary of six hundred dollars. This was not done in concurrence with the wishes of that portion of the parish denominated "the Church;" Mr. Frothingham's religious creed did not in all respects harmonize with theirs. As a consequence they took no part in the services of installation, which were conducted by an Ecclesiastical Council appointed by the parish committee. The church adhered to its original distinct organization, and became the nucleus of the present First Congregational Society, popularly known as the North Church. The sermon at the Installation was preached by Rev. Ezra Ripley, D. D., of Concord, Mass., Rev. John Allyn, D. D., of Duxbury, Mass., father of the late Rufus B. Allyn of this place, gave the Charge to the Pastor, Rev. Hezekiah Packard, D. D., of Wiscasset, the address to the people, and Rev. Silas Warren of Jackson, the Right-hand of Fellowship. The reverend clergy were escorted to the meeting-house by a procession of the parishoners; there was no drum and fife; the absence of which usual accompaniment of a public procession in those days led a jocose individual to remark that if it wasn't for the name of Installation he should think he was going to a funeral.

Many of the excellent good fathers and mothers of the day thought, doubtless, that the settlement of a minister without the concurrence of the church in matters of religious faith, was tantamount to a funeral of the staunch old doctrines to which their fathers and grandfathers held, and which they had been taught to regard as essential to salvation from the consequences of sin; their children and grandchildren, were they this day to learn for the first time the religious sentiments propounded in the exercises on that occasion, would marvel that such rigid views of man's moral and religious accountability and final destiny were entertained and taught only half a century ago; verily, the world moves.

It is not rephrehensible, in the judgment of the compiler, to mingle the gay with the grave, and therefore he records the following anecdote. While the procession before referred to was waiting to perform its escort duty, one of our townsmen, an honest and upright man in dealings but a little "mixed" in his notions of church organizations, doctrinal creeds &c., growing a little impatient at the delay walked up the hill on High Street where the procession was formed, and accosting one of the marshals inquired, why the procession did not move. "Some hitch between the Church and the Council," was the reply; "the Church isn't exactly satisfied with Mr. Frothingham's creed." "The Church!" said he, "let the Church go to ----! Why don't you make a new one, a respectable one; I and my wife'll join!"

The town officers for this year were Manasseh Sleeper, James McCrillis, John S. Kimball, Selectmen; Benjamin Whittier, Town Clerk. An amateur census taken in the fall shows that there were then one hundred and thirty-seven families residing within the radius of a mile from Nesmith's Corner. The amount of money raised for parochial purposes was $677 98; number of polls in the Parish 283; poll tax 40 cts.; per centum on the valuation of estates, real and personal, five cents. The largest tax against any parishioner was $11.90. The number of deaths in town during the year was twenty-eight.

CHAPTER XIV. (1820)

From and after the fifteenth day of March in this year, Maine became one of the "United States of America." At this point of time Belfast, in common with the residue of Maine, may be regarded as having taken "a new departure." Her population according to the census of this year, was 2,026; an increase of 752 from the year 1810. The selectmen elected at the annual spring meeting were John Merriam, James McCrillis and Nathan Swan; Benjamin Whittier, Town Clerk. The prominent physicians at this date were John S. Osborn, Herman Abbott, Ebenezer Poor, Hollis Monroe, Chauncey C. Chandler, Charles Hall, a comparatively young and promising physician died this year. The lawyers were Bohan P. Field, John Wilson, Alfred Johnson, Jr., Zaccheus Porter, William White, Joseph Williamson and Rufus B. Allyne. Benjamin Whittier was the Postmaster, Dudley Griffin the "fashionable tailor" and Job White the axe-maker and indispensable fiddler at all private parties.

The population of Belfast was the largest of any town in the county (Hancock) save Frankfort; her population was 2127. Efforts were made early in the year to have the towns of Frankfort and Monroe set off to the county of Penobscot; also to have Belfast made a half-shire town; both efforts were unsuccessful, and the last named succeeded, the creation of the county of Waldo might have been indefinitely postponed, or deferred for many years at least.

On the seventh day of May died Andrew Leach, who was born at Glencoe, Scotland, February 11, 1753, and came here to reside in 1805. He erected the building still standing at the intersection of High and Bridge streets; now owned by Mr. Oakes Angier, and occupied it for many years as a store and dwelling. One of his daughters became the wife of Hon. John Wilson, another of George Watson, Esq., who was sheriff of the county at the time of the Separation. It was the uniform custom in those days to toll the bell--where there was one--at the funeral of an adult while the funeral procession was on its way to the graveyard; the funeral of Mr. Leach was the first one at which the new bell was tolled.

The Fourth of July was duly celebrated; "ushered in," to quote the language of the Gazette of the sixth, "by the roaring of cannon"--two small field-pieces were all we had--"and the ringing of bells"--we had only one to ring--excluding the cow bells and the belles of the village. Joseph Williamson, Esq., was the orator of the day. There was a public dinner at the Sun Tavern, "served up in Cunningham's best manner." "Toasts were drank, accompanied by the discharge of cannon and enlivening airs of music." The following, given by Hon. John Wilson who presided at the table, is a fair specimen of the sentiment to which the occasion, and its accompaniments, gave birth: "Maine an independent State. May her Legislators possess the patriotism of Fox and the intelligence of Pitt; her Judges the science of Mansfield and decision of Holt; her Orators the lightning of Cicero and the thunder of Demosthenes." The people of Belfast, and of Maine generally, to use a slang phrase, were "feeling big" about that time. The "fair sex" were reminded, of course, that they were "Heaven's last, best gift to man."

On the sixth day of July the first number of the Hancock Gazette, the first newspaper started within the limits of the present county of Waldo, made its appearance. Fellowes and Simpson were its publishers; Mr. Fellowes died some years ago; Mr. Simpson is still living, residing in Penobscot county. It was published weekly, at two dollars per annum; the dimensions of the printed matter being about eleven by seventeen inches; about one page was filled with advertisements, which were inserted at the rate of "one dollar per square for three insertions and seventeen cents for every subsequent insertion." With the fourteenth number the success of the paper encouraging the expenditure, it was enlarged one inch in its dimensions! With its twenty-fourth number its title was enlarged by adding the words "Penobscot Patriot;" the object being to secure the patronage in Penobscot county, which was expected to follow the discontinuance of the Bangor Weekly Register, a newspaper which

had been published in Bangor since 1815.   Mr. Simpson transferred his
interest in the paper to Mr. Fellowes February 22, 1826, and Mr. F.
continued to publish it under the title of the Hancock Gazette and Penobscot
Patriot until the close of its sixth volume, when its old title was
dropped and that of the "Belfast Gazette" substituted.

It continued to be published under its new title until the 37th
number of its second volume issued when, unexpectedly to the community
at large, its publication was suspended; but a week afterwards the "Waldo
Democrat," in charge of the same publisher, appeared to take its place.
The leading editorial in the first number of the Democrat announced
that the paper was thenceforth to be, as its name purported, "heartily
and entirely democratic;" it advocated the re-election of John Quincy
Adams as President!   The Democrat died in less than a year, as might
have been anticipated; the office, press and material were sold by Mr.
Fellowes to Messrs. Robert White and Cyrus Rowe, and on the sixth day
of February, 1829, the "Republican Journal," the exponent of the democratic
creed according to Andrew Jackson, commenced its career as a political
missionary.

Messrs. White and Rowe were fellow apprentices in the office of
Mr. Fellowes.   Mr. White sold his interest in the Journal to Mr. Benjamin
Griffin about 1841, and engaged in mercantile business.   He held the
office of Register of Deeds and County Treasurer for several years and
subsequently was largely interested in ship-building.   He died Dec.
31, 1866.   In the fall of 1848 Mr. Rowe finally disposed of all his
interest in the Journal to Messrs. Moore and Wing.   Not long afterwards
he removed from this place to California and subsequently to Nevada;
he died at Nevada City, Dec. 12, 1858.

Prominent among the advertising patrons of the Hancock Gazette
in the first year of its publication were the following named traders:
Ladd and Morrill, John Angier, Franklin Tinkham, Benj. Hazeltine, Francis
Hathaway, John S. Kimball, Peter H. Smith, Oshea Page, all dead; Ralph
C. Johnson, John Clark, Hugh J. Anderson still living.   Innholders,
Samuel Jackson, who kept a public house on the site of the premises
now covered by the store of Francis Whitmore, John Huse, who kept the
house at the intersection of Main and High streets, and Thos. Cunningham
who kept the "Sun Tavern," the house occupied by the late Capt. James
Miller at the time of his decease; it was for some time called the "Pumpkin
Tavern"; especially by the democrats of the day, who could not forget
that Col. Cunningham during the war was a violent Federalist and firmly
believed to have secretly rendered aid and comfort to the enemy.

The origin of that belief was simply this.   While the British were
at Castine, and before they took possession of Belfast, a young man
then, an old man now, sportively arrayed himself one evening in a military
garb, antique as the days of the Revolution, for the purpose of surprising
a young lady on whom he was a little "tender."   While perambulating
Main street he happened to attract the attention of one of the "Paul
Prys" of the day--there were such animals around then as well as now--who
followed him for some time at a very cautious distance.   The young man
did not deem it judicious under the circumstances to go directly to
his home--perhaps the idea occurred to him that he would play a joke
on "Paul"--and on arriving in front of the Sun Tavern he turned in at
the gate, stole round the house and waited quietly until "Paul" fully
charged, took himself out of the way.   It was currently reported the
next day that a British officer was seen stealing in at the back door
of the Sun Tavern the night before; poor Cunningham had to suffer the
consequences.

Among the merchandise advertised for sale by the traders of that
day the following were almost uniformly to be found: "W. I. and N.
E. Run, Holland Gin, Cognac and French Brandy, Madeira, Lisbon and Malaga
Wines, and Cordials."   One of the craft a little in advance of his neighbors
advertised "13 puncheons of high proof Jamaica spirits."   It was no
more disreputable then to offer this species of merchandise for sale

than it was to offer pork, flour, sugar, tea, &c. It was not disreputable to drink intoxicating liquors; the few who did not, occasionally at least, were exceptions to the rule. A wonderful change has been wrought since then; the conventionalities of society now do not call for nor approve of the use of them as a beverage; what was then a majority, so far as the habitual use is involved, is now a minority.

There were "hard drinkers" in those days; if the history of man is to be relied on there always have been; it is a matter of fear and regret that there always may be. Looking back, the concession must be made, although reluctantly, that the number of victims to the inordinate appetite for intoxicating drinks, nor forgetting the increase in population, was less then than now. By the term "victims" is meant not those captured by the enemy but those slain on the field. How happens it? The question is left to be answered by those who have made the subject matter for moral and scientific investigation. We contribute our mite to the mass of facts already before them by simply suggesting that the intoxicating liquors used by the men of fifty years ago, temperately or intemporately, were what they purported to be; the juice of the vine, or of the still, pure and unadulterated. "American Gin," "American Brandy," and still worse, the villainous compounds now known and sold as "whiskey," were unknown. The men of those days knew, or were not indifferent as to what they were drinking; the simpletons of these days know not, or are indifferent as to what they drink provided it stimulates. Poor idiots! Still greater idiots they who close their eyes against the light that is streaming and has streamed from the throne of Godhead and illuminated humanity's pathway for centuries.

On the night of July 9th, the place was visited by a severe thunder storm; the house now occupied by Captain W. O. Alden was struck by lightning and set on fire; the fire was extinguished, however, with but little detriment to the building. There were two families occupying the house at the time, but none of its inmates were materially injured.

Under the Constitution of the new State, Belfast and Northport constituted one Representative District; Ralph C. Johnson, Esq., was elected Representative. At the same meeting at which he was elected the election of a member of Congress and of Presidential electors came off; the whole number of ballots thrown in this place was 107; in Northport 40. The two towns, however, were in different Congressional Districts; Northport being in the Third, Belfast in the Fourth.

On the 25th of September, a "Marine Bible Society" was organized, the sole object of the Society being, as expressed in its Constitution, "to circulate the Holy Scriptures without note or comment among seaman." The payment of seventy-five cents annually constituted any one a member of the Society; the payment of five dollars at one time constituted the donor a life-member. Col. Daniel Lane was elected President, Dr. Ebenezer Poor, and John S. Kimball, Esq., Vice President, Ralph C. Johnson Esq., Treasurer, Rev. Wm. Frothingham, Corresponding, and Bohan P. Field, Esq., Recording Secretaries. There was also a Board of Directors and a Committee to solicit subscriptions. The entire official board consisted of thirty individuals; the only one now surviving is the Treasurer. The exigencies of the day demanded such an association, doubtless, in the estimation of those who took an active part in it, and it was productive of good to the class for whose benefit it was organized; but like too many other schemes of a philanthropic nature it was spasmodic in birth and short-lived as a natural consequence.

The number of entries at the Custom House in this place from foreign ports during the year as 78; clearances to foreign ports 79. The value of exports to foreign countries was $83,894.36; being all of domestic product or manufacutre except $2,800.00. The number of deaths during the year was twenty-three. The town voted at its annual spring meeting to raise $125.00 for the purchase of a hearse; it was the first one owned here.

The market value of leading articles of trade, as embraced in a Price Current of Dec. 27th, was as follows: merch. boards per M. $7 to 8; shingles, $1 to 2.50; clapboards, $10 to 14; wheat per bushel, 84 to $1; rye, 67 to 75 cents; corn, 67 cents; beans, 84 to $1; butter per lb., 12 1-2 to 17 cents; cheese, 8 to 10; beef, 3 to 4; poultry 4 to 6; potatoes, per bushel, 25 cents; cider, per bbl. $1.75 to $2; Jamaica rum, per gallon, $1.10 to 1.20; molasses, 32 to 34 cents; tea, Souchong, per lb., 58 to 60; Turk's Island salt per hogshead $5.

CHAPTER XV. (1820-1.)

On the 30th of September, 1820, died John Huse, Esq., aged forty-nine. Mr. Huse came here to reside in 1802 or 3. He was by trade a house-carpenter. Soon after coming here he was appointed a deputy under Thomas Phillips, Esq., Sheriff of the county; and it is as deputy sheriff and landlord for many years of the public house at the intersection of Main and High streets--long known as the "Huse Tavern"--that he is especially remembered. He was a man of commanding presence, of rather brusk manner, of quick wit, and a general favorite. Many amusing anecdotes might be told of him; a few must suffice.

Shortly after his appointment as a deputy sheriff a writ was placed in his hands with orders to attach property of a debtor residing in Greene Plantation who was as destitute of legally attachable property as a Nova Scotia crow. It was a hard ride in those days from the Beach to the residence of the debtor. On arriving there H. informed him what his orders were. "Now," said he, "turn out your property." "But I haven't got any," said the debtor. "How in ---- then" was the reply, "can I serve the writ?" Don't you see what the orders are, "Attach property"? If I can't attach property I can't serve the writ. Haven't you got some oats? "Well--yes--" said the debtor. "I've got a few bushels." "Very well," replied H.; "I would just as soon have oats as money for my fees; put a bagful on my horse and I'll serve the writ." The proposition seemed fair enough; the bag was filled, put on the horse' back and the writ served. The inhabitants of "Greene Plantation" have learned a good deal since then; they know better now than to pay an officer in advance for serving a writ on them. "Landlord," said a pert, pompous young man, with his boots well blacked and his hair "pomatumed," as he drove up to the door of the Huse Tavern, "If you've got anything decent give my horse a bating; I havn't seen a thing fit for a horse to eat since I left Boston." "Perkins!" said H,., calling to his son, "Perkins! take this gentleman's horse round to the stable and give him a pint of beech-nuts and as many seed cowcumbers as he will eat; we don't give nice feed like that to common people's horses, Sir." A long, lank customer from the interior sold him a quarter of lamb one day; price fifty cents; remarking as an inducement to the trade that he would dine at the house. When the dinner-bell rang he was on hand in advance of the regular boarders, and by the time they arrived he had pretty effectually cleared one end of the table. Having finished his dinner he went to the office--bar-room it was then--and handed a dollar to H. with the remark that he wanted to pay for his dinner. H. quitely put the dollar in his pocket and went about his business. "I guess, Mr. Huse," said the guest, after waiting for awhile, "you've forgot to give me my change." "What change?" asked Huse. "Why I gave you a dollar," was the reply, "you only charge a man twenty-five cents for a dinner don't you?" "No," said H.; "that's all; twenty-five cents for a man--a dollar for a hog!"

The funeral services of Mr. Huse were at the "new meeting-house" on Sunday, the day after his decease. The sermon on the occasion was preached by Rev. Silas Warren, of Jackson; the choir sang that well known hymn by Dr. Watts, so full of comfort and consolation to surviving friends, commencing with,

"Hark from the tombs a doleful sound."

The remains of the deceased were followed to the grave by the Brethren of Belfast Lodge, of which he was a member, and by a large concourse of people from this and neighboring towns.

In the fall of this year an event occurred which may be remembered by many now living, certainly by one of our oldest inhabitants, himself the sole survivor of twenty-one passengers who left this place for Boston on board the schooner Superb, McFarland master, on the 27th of November. Most of those passengers belonged here and were heads of families. The schooner was not heard from for seventeen days; the families of the missing ones were in a state of great anxiety and the sympathies of their fellow-townsmen were deeply stirred. News came at last of her arrival in Provincetown. She had been blown off, compelled to lay to for five days, lost her deckload and boats, and on the tenth day after leaving here succeeded in getting into Provincetown, the nearest port she could make. For five days they were without water except a small quantity of rain they were fortunate enough to catch, and for the larger part of the time without food. When they reached Provincetown many of the passengers were so exhausted that they could not walk from the landing to the nearest house. Their tongues were badly swollen and their vital energy so reduced that they were not permitted to take any nourishment for some days, except the simplest and most easily digestible kind. It was a narrow escape they had from actual starvation, aside from the perils of the sea. Great was the joy of their friends and neighbors when news came of their safety. The sole survivor above referred to is our venerable friend and fellow citizen Mr. William Quimby.

During the winter of 1820-1 the weather up to the early part of February was excessively severe; at one time the Bay was frozen entirely across to Castine; which afforded occasion at the time for the very sage remark that "had such a severe frost happened while the enemy was in possession of Castine during the late war, great facilities would have been afforded for his dislodgement from that maritime stronghold of the State;" for "dislodgement" substitute "smuggling" and the remark quoted would be a sensible one; one which, probably, would have been practically illustrated.

This year, 1821, Belfast had her first notable experience in the matter of conflagration; it was quite a matter for the day, but was the merest "sprinkling" compared with the "baptism of fire" through which she has since been passed. On the night of January 2d a fire broke out in a large two story wooden building situated on Main street where the stores now occupied by Messrs. Albert C. Burgess and Blodgett and Co. stand; the first story was occupied by Ladd and Morrill, traders and two of the chambers by Rufus B. Allyne, Esq. Attorney at Law, and Sylvanus Gallison, tailor; this building and a dwelling house adjoining, were entirely consumed. A wooden building standing four feet easterly from the one in which the fire began was saved by suspending sails from the roof and keeping them drenched with water carried up on ladders, in pails. The Gazette of the 4th in giving an account of the event attributed the limited extent of the conflagration to "the exemplary alacrity with which the citizens assembled" and to the fact that "the town pump was in good order." The "town pump" was on the westwardly side of High street in front of the building now occupied by the Belfast Livery Company. A double line was formed from the pump to the scene of the fire for the purpose of passing water and re-passing empty buckets. That was the day when "woman's rights" were recognized; among them the right to take her place in the line and pass the empty buckets; and nobly did she exercise the right on that cold, bleak night in January; and no man scoffed at her. Before the close of the year Ladd and Morrill had covered the burned district with a two story brick block containing three stores; it was the first brick building erected in town; the brick block on Main street with granite front now covers the same ground.

The good people of the village accepted the fire as a "Providential intimation of the duty they owed to themselves," and took immediate measures to give effect to the intimation by forming a Fire Club and providing ways and means for the purchase of an engine, fire-hooks, ladders, &c. An engine was purchased at the cost of $500 and an engine company organized; the same engine was afterwards called the "Vigilance." It did good duty in its day, but was at last thrown aside to make room for others of greater power and improved mechanism. After its place was thus supplied it was used for several years for "watering vessels;" it was burned in the great fire of 1873; a charred fragment of one of its brakes is in possession of the compiler, the only tangible memento

of the first fire-engine ever owned in Belfast, or which he ever saw.
A house for the hearse and engine was built; its dimensions "20 by 12
feet on the ground, 8 feet high, shingled on the outside, with a plank
floor." It was erected on ground now covered by Johnson's Block, stood
there many years until was removed to Franklin street near the southwesterly
corner of the lot now owned by the United States; it was demolished
about the time the Custom House was built.

The Fire Club, styled the Belfast Fire Club, was originally composed
of twenty-four of the most prominent residents in the village. Col.
Daniel Lane was President, George Watson, Esq., Vice President, Hon.
John S. Kimball, Treasurer, Col. Phillip Morrill, Clerk: Col. Lane
who died in 1873, was the last surviving member. Its Constitution provided
that "every citizen of Belfast who shall furnish himself with two good
substantial leather buckets, 12 inches in length and 8 inches in diameter,
marked with his name, and a good substantial bag, 4 feet in length and
2 feet 3 inches in breadth, marked with his name, may become a member
of the Club on subscribing to its rules and regulations and paying twenty-
five cents." It is very apparent that the founders of the Club did
not intend there should be any shirking of obligations assumed; for
its regulations required "the President and Clerk to visit each member
of the Club quarterly and examine the situation of his buckets and bag
and report the condition of them to the next meeting." They also required
"every member of the Club to constantly keep his buckets in some conspicuous
and accessible part of his house, with his bag in one of them, where
he may lay his hand upon them as well by night as by day." Provision
was also made for the expulsion of any member who should be negligent
in the performance of his duty. It was the almost uniform custom of
the members to keep their buckets suspended in the front hall of their
houses, near the front door; one or more of them may yet be found occasionally in the lumber-room of some of our old mansions. An improved organization of our fire department was regarded as rendering the continuance
of the Club unnecessary and after awhile it ceased to exist. It was
a useful and effective organization in its day: a similar one might
render essential service in these days; especially in the event of an
extensive conflagration like that of 1873.

March 21st, George Watson, Esq., sheriff of the county, being of
the Federal persuasion politically, was removed from office and Leonard
Jarvis, Esq., of Ellsworth appointed; the deputies under Sheriff Jarvis
in this place were Nathan Swan, William Salmond and Stephen Longfellow.

On the 29th of March a store exclusively for the sale of cabinet
furniture was opened in a wooden building on Main St., which stood about
on the site of Dodge's Saloon; it was the first store of that description
in the place. Sinkler (Samuel) and Varney (Loring) "having removed
from Portland," were the proprietors. They were followed in May by
Bridgham (Derrick) and Howard (Daniel,) "late of Hallowell," who opened
a Furniture Store at the "head of Main street nearly opposite the new
meeting-house." The locality "nearly opposite the new meeting-house"
is the same on which the brick store now occupied by H. H. Forbes stands;
there was no building then to obstruct the view from the front door
of one to the front door of the other, except the house now occupied
by Edwin Salmond. They offered for sale, among other articles, a complete
assortment of elegant gilt and tortoise-shell chairs; some of those
chairs, now more than half a century old, are still in existence, the
"gilt" terriby tarnished and the "tortoise shell" scarcely distinguishable
in form and color from a dilapidated clam-shell. Mr. Bridgham died
young; Mr. Howard at his residence on Miller street in 1866, aged sixty-five.

Among the additions to our business community this year were Shaw
and Sawyer, saddle, harness and trunk makers, Heard Milliken, baker,
Gershom F. Cox, dealer in drugs, paints and dye-stuffs, and James Langworthy.
Mr. Cox's was the first store established in the place exclusively for
the sale of the merchandise above named. After retiring from trade
he became a preacher of considerable eminence in the Methodist denomination;

he is still living, but by reason of physical infirmity has ceased to labor in his profession.   Mr. Langworthy, who upon coming here announced himself as "recently from Portland," commenced trade in the brick block on Main street erected that year.   He afterwards erected the brick building on Church street opposite the Court House and for some time kept a store in the basement, occupying the upper portion as a dwelling.   He died Nov. 22, 1853, aged seventy-five.   Mr. Milliken carried on the business of baker for some years quite extensively.   His biscuit, stamped with his initials, "H.M.", sometimes translated "His Majesty," became quite a celebrity.   He removed from this place many years ago and died about two years ago at East Bridgewater, Mass.

There was no public celebration of "Independence day" in the place this year; but Manasseh Sleeper, Esq., having taken possession of the old "Huse Tavern" raised his sign on that day, bearing upon it the Coat of Arms of the new State; it was saluted with "three times three" and was thenceforth designated the "Maine Hotel."   There was a large gathering at Searsmont on the same day, at which many of our people were present, "for the purpose of taking into consideration the subject of a new county on the westerly side of Penobscot Bay and river and southerly of the county of Penobscot."   This was the entering wedge which finally split the old county of Hancock.

At the annual Fall meeting the whole number of ballots thrown was 160.   Doctor Ebenezer Poor of this place was elected Senator; James McCrillis, Representative.   At the annual meeting in the spring John Merriam, James McCrillis and Nathan Swan were elected Selectmen, Benjamin Whittier, Town Clerk.   The whole number of deaths in town during the year was twenty-six.

CHAPTER XVI. (1821-2)

On the 25th of July of this year, 1821, died Laughlin McDonald, the oldest person in town; his age was not accurately known, but from his own story of his life and what could be learned from his relatives he must have been nearly one hundred and ten years old at the time of his death.   He remembered to have seen the Duke of Marlboro, who died ninety-nine years before he did.   He was born in Scotland and entered the British service when very young.   He was in General Wolfe's army in 1759 and engaged in the memorable battle of the "Plains of Abraham." After the capture of Quebec he managed to dissolve his connection with the British army and eventually found himself located on the banks of the Penobscot not far from where the village of Bucksport now is; there were then but a few scattered settlers in that region.   He was residing there in 1779 when a party of British soldiers visited the locality and burned a saw-mill, vessel, and five dwellings; the list of their owners embraces the name of McDonald; one of the dwellings burned belonging to him, probably, or some relative.   After that event he removed to this place.   He was a hale, vigorous, and to the last a cheerful man. He resided on the east side of the river.   About the last time he came to the village an old friend met him with the salutation, "Why Mac! you alive yet?"   "Alive?" was the cheery answer, "Yes; and the Lord only knows but I'll live a hundred years longer!"

The "Press" of Hancock county which, so far as it had a local habitation within the territory now constituting the county of Waldo, up to this date had spoken only through the columns of the Gazette and the advertising show bills of public spirited individuals who were interested in the improvement of the breed of horses, gave utterance this year in the form of a pamphlet a "Communion Sermon, delivered by Rev. William Frothingham; published by request of hearers: printed by Fellowes and Simpson."   It was followed the next year by the publication in pamphlet form of a very learned discourse by Rev. Alfred Johnson, "published by request of hearers," on the Divinity of Christ consistent with the Unity of God."   Embodied in the same pamphlet is a discourse by the same author on the "Humanity of Christ."

Belfast had now become of such commercial importance that the right to have three mails per week had been conceded to her; accordingly the Western mail arrived on Monday, Wednesday and Saturday of each week at 1 p. m., and left on its return on the evening of same days; the mail from the East, via Bucksport, also came and left tri-weekly; the mail route from this place to Bangor was by the way of Bucksport.

There was at this time, and for several years before had been a library, owned in shares, denominated the Belfast Social Library.   It contained several hundred volumes, judiciously selected, and was largely patronized.   As its shareholders, one after another died, or removed, and private libraries increased, the interest in maintaining the institution gradually diminished until it died; where it was buried is as unknown as the grave of Moses.   Now and then one of its dry bones, in the shape of a volume substantially covered with sheepskin and dust is turned up by some bookworm--or Bridget--prowling among the heaps of rubbish in lumberroom or garret.

On the 13th day of December, Paul Giles, one of our most active businessmen was drowned on his passage from St. Johns to Eastport. The vessel on which he was a passenger struck a ledge near Campobello in a thick snow storm early in the evening, but in a few minutes slid off into deep water without sustaining any material injury.   The Captain, who was well acquainted with the locality, ordered the man at the helm to steer a certain course which would carry them clear of the ledges in the vicinity; on going aft he discovered that the card of the compass was unshipped, and at almost the same moment the vessel struck another ledge.   She remained on this ledge until after midnight, the sea breaking over her, during which time Mr. Giles, the captain and one of her crew were washed from the wreck and drowned.   His body was found about the

last of January, on the shore of Casco Bay Island, near the spot where
he was drowned, was carried to Eastport and buried by the Masonic Fraternity,
of which he was a member.

Mr. Giles came here to reside about 1800. He was a native of Gilmanton,
N. H., and by occupation a tanner. He was the founder of the old tan-yard
on the road to the Upper Bridge, now occupied by Nathan F. Houston,
Esq. He carried on for many years the business of tanning and manufacturing
boots and shoes, employing quite a number of operatives for those days.
Subsequently he engaged in the business of purchasing and shipping lumber
to the British Provinces. Soon after coming here, in 1802, he built
the house on High street, opposite the store of Mr. Oakes Angier, to
whose father he sold it in 1804, and then built a house which stood
on the site of the North Church, which was removed many years afterwards
to premises now occupied by Hon. W. H. McLellan, and was still later
destroyed by fire; this house was his family residence at the time of
his death. He was the father of Mr. Charles Giles, for many years publisher
of the Waldo Signal, and the maternal grandfather of the present editor
of The Republican Journal.

He was an active, energetic business man. Had he lived in this
day he would have been among the foremost in promoting the new local
enterprises of our city. He was of that class of man who seem to be
designed by nature to be the pioneers in a newly settled country; not
always of cool, deliberate judgment, but of earnest, ardent impulse,
empractically "go ahead" men. There were many of that class left here,
it is true, when those cold December waves broke over him, but no one
fuller of life and energy than Paul Giles.

The Belfast Light Infantry was organized this year, 1822, and the
following officers elected; Oshea Page, Captain, Joel Hills, Lieutenant
and Dudley Griffin, the 'fashional tailor' referred to in a previous
chapter, ensign. Mr. Page was one of the numerous proteges of Samuel
Upton and carried on business here for some years under his auspices;
his business light was extinguished with that of the luminary around
which he revolved. He removed from this place about 1858 and died at
Springfield, Mass., about two years ago; his remains were brought here
for interment. Mr. Hills, was deputy under Joseph Williamson, Esq.
Postmaster, during his whole term of office. He removed from this place
to Bangor, afterwards to Boston, where he died some years ago. Mr.
Griffin died in this place in 1825, aged thirty. He and Mr. Page both
married daughters of Dr. John S. Osborn. The company was composed entirely
of young men who manifested a laudable desire to improve in military
discipline and to qualify themselves for active service should occasion
call for it. It was their custom for some time to hold regular weekly
drills in Academy Hall.

The month of May brought with it a breeze that created quite a
ripple on the then ordinarily calm surface of society in this locality;
arousing the good people to a realizing sense that the crime of murder
might be, perhaps had been, committed at their very thresholds. Some
children who were strolling through a field in the vicinity of the village
in search of May flowers--which seldom bloom in this climate until June--
found a shirt with stains of blood on it, a jacket which appeared to
have been perforated by a bullet, and a hat in a very dilapidated condition
all lying together on the ground. The news spread through the village
with more than usual rapidity. Numerous parties, officials included,
visited the locality and critically examined the clothing. That a murder
had been committed was unquestionable; at least such was the adjudication
of all lovers of the marvellous, the horrible, and of gossip. When
the fever of excitement had raged about twenty-four hours some cool
head suggested that a murdered man would not be very apt to strip off
his own shirt and jacket, and that his murderer would not be apt to
do it for him. The result of the matter was that Dame Rumor came to
the conclusion, reluctantly, that a raid had been made on somebody's
clothes-line, on the principal that "exchange is no robbery," and that
somebody was minus a hat better, probably, than the one found.

There was no Fourth of July celebration this year, but the editor of the Gazette glorified the place by the announcement that on the Saturday preceding the fourth there was "hauled into the village on teams; as by actual survey, 136,086 feet of boards, 35 thousand of shingles, 3,789 staves, 1515 feet of oars;" a very good show for one days work fifty-two years ago.

On the 30th of August, at his residence on Main street, now occupied by Mr. A. D. Chase, died Benjamin Whittier, Esq., aged thirty-nine. He was the son of Thomas Whittier, Esq., of whom mention was made in one of our earliest chapters. He succeeded his father as Postmaster about 1813 and continued to hold the office to the time of his decease. In December following Joseph Williamson, Esq., was appointed to fill the vacancy, and removed the office to a wooden building standing on the site of the store now occupied by Mr. H. H. Forbes; that building was burned Jan. 22, 1834. Mr. Whittier was the fifth town clerk in order of time. He had held the office for several successive years prior to his decease. Dr. Herman Abbott was his successor, elected at a town meeting held ten days after the vacancy occurred.

In November the office of the Gazette was removed from Johnson's Building, now the Phoenix House, to a wooden building which stood where the building occupied by Clark & Fernald, Marble Workers, now stands, at the intersection of High and Market streets, and its publishers, Fellowes & Simpson, opened a book store in the room fronting on High street, where they "offered for sale an extensive assortment of school books, bibles, and miscellaneous works at the sign of the Bible." It was the first store opened in the place exclusively for the sale of books and stationery.

Among the notable events of the year was the visit of the celebrated Dr. Nathan Smith of New Hampshire, Professor of the Theory and Practice of medicine in the Medical School at Brunswick. The announcement of his advent brought hither from the region roundabout "a multitude of impotent folk, of blind, halt, and withered." The coming at this day of Dr. Brown-Sequard would not be the occasion of greater excitement among invalids. Dr. Smith was not a traveling empiric, such as have been seen here occasionally since his day, but was eminent in his profession and visited this section of the country at the call of patients residing here and at the east. There is an anecdote of him truly illustrative of the frankness with which he dealt with those who came to him for medical aid "Madam," said he to a lady who had been for a long time ailing and "spent all her living upon physicians, neither could be healed of any"--"I cannot cure you; but you can cure yourself. Empty all those phials into your slop-pail--stop making an apothecary's shop of your stomach--don't say a word to any living soul about your aches and pains for six months; at the end of that time you'll feet better; follow the same rule six months longer and you'll be well." The invalid, who fortunately for herself had as much faith in the doctor as her predecessors of nearly nineteen hundred years ago had in the angel who troubled the Pool of Bethesda, adopted and carried out the suggestion and lived until 1872, when she died aged ninety-two.

The brig Ospray of about 180 tons burthen, owned by Greenleaf Porter and John Clark, traders residing here, and the schooner Harriet and Eliza of 138 tons owned by John Angier and Salathiel Nickerson, residing here, were built this year and launched in the month of September; the Ospray from the ship-yard just northerly from the car-house of the Railroad, the Harriet & Eliza at the upper bridge. The first voyage of both was from this place to Port-au-Prince; Capt. Henry B. Eells, father of Mrs. Moses W. Rich, was master of the Ospray; Capt. Josiah Simpson, paternal grandfather of the Editor of the Journal, was master of the Harriet & Eliza. On the night of Feb. 20, 1829, the Harriet & Eliza, two days from this port bound to New York, went ashore at Eastham, Mass., in a violent gale which strewed the coast with wrecks, and was totally lost; the hull and such of the spars as remained were sold for the benefit of all concerned for the sum of $35; at the time of her loss she was commanded by the late Capt. Jeremiah Merithew of Searsport. The Osprey was sold to parties residing at the West; her fate unknown to the compiler.

At the annual Spring meeting the selectmen and clerk of the year previous were re-elected. At the annual Fall meeting James McCrillis, Esq., was reelected representative. The number of ballots cast was 110. The meeting was held at the old Meeting-house on the east side of the river and the attendance was small. It was the last town meeting held on that side; up to the time the annual town meetings had been held on both sides alternately. The meetings on the west side had been held for several years at the old Meeting-house which had been sold to the Baptist Society; the same building now standing in rear of the Phoenix House.

The erection of the Conference Room, as it was then called, was one of the events of the year. It stood on land just northerly of the dwelling house of Hon. R. C. Johnson. It was occupied as a place of public worship by the religious society now known as the North Church until their present Meeting-house was built. It was afterwards sold and removed to Front street near if not actually on a portion of the site of the Belfast Foundry; it was afterwards burned.

The number of families residing within a mile from Nesmith's Corner at this date was 162; of this number ninety were resident within the same limits in 1816. The number of deaths in town during the year was twenty-eight.

CHAPTER XVII. (1822-3.)

On the first day of December, died, very suddenly, Col. Thomas
Cunningham, aged forty-three, a native of Peterboro, N. H., who came
here to reside in 1803. He held the office of deputy for many years
under several successive sheriffs, various military offices, and was
the landlord, in succession, of the Huse Tavern, the Sun Tavern, the
Whittier Tavern, and the Washington Hotel, better remembered perhaps
as Cunningham's Hotel, which stood next westerly from the New England
House; he was occupying it at the time of his death. Mention has been
made of him more than once in preceeding chapters; something more is
due to his memory. He was a gentleman of fine personal address, a prompt
and energetic officer, an exceedingly affable and popular landlord.
He was thoroughly identified with the movements of the day which had
for their object the advancement of our local interests, and the general
feeling pervading the community on the occasion of his death was that
we had lost one of our most active, geniel, gentlemanly fellow-townsmen.
He left a son and several daughters, all of whom who are now living
reside in Baltimore.
     Later in the month Hiram Emery, a young man aged about twenty-two
uncle of our fellow-citizen Mr. Hiram Emery Peirce, was suffocated in
the cabin of the schooner Hope then lying at one of our wharves. It
was inferred by the inquest held on the occasion, from the position
in which he was found in the morning, at the foot of the companionway,
and from the general appearance of things in the cabin, that his bed
clothes caught fire, from a candle probably, while he was asleep, and
that on awaking and attempting to find his way out he was suffocated
and fell where he was found.
     Prominent among the business men who came to the place this year
were Samuel A. Moulton, Hutson Bishop and Frederic A. Lewis. Mr. Moulton
in connection with William I. Cross, under the firm name of Cross and
Moulton, opened a shop on Main street just below its junction with Washington street, where they carried on the business of "tin plate and sheet
iron working;" it was the first shop of the kind in town. The firm
was dissolved in 1824 and Mr. Cross returned to Portland. In 1844 Mr.
Moulton removed to Boston, but in 1853 returned and resumed his former
business in the brick store on Church street now occupied by Cates and
Stickney. He died suddenly, of paralysis, in February 1867, aged sixty-six.
He was a very quiet, unassuming, worthy citizen and most incorrigible
old bachelor. Mr. Bishop was a sea captain, retired from that vocation
on account of ill health. He opened a store for the sale of West India
goods and ship-chandlery, at wholesale, on the wharf now known as Lewis'
succeeding Oshea Page. He built the brick house on Church street now
owned by Ex-Gov. Anderson about 1824, and in 1823 the ship Alfred of
about 320 tons; she was the first copper-fastened vessel built here.
He was the husband of the late Mrs. Jane Bishop; the "Aunt Jane" of
a large circle in our community embracing members of three generations.
Captain Bishop died in August 1834, aged forty-three. Mr. Lewis commenced
business as a trader in a wooden building on Main street on the site
of the brick building now occupied by the Messrs. Robbins; he was occupying
it at the time it was burned, in the winter of 1829. Sometime afterwards
he opened an office as an attorney at law. He built in 1827 the house
on Church street now occupied by Wm. O. Poor, and in 1845 the brick
house on High street now occupied by Capt. Lymburner, and was residing
there when he died of paralysis in December 1867, aged sixty-nine; he
left several children none of whom are now residing here.
     The brick block on Main street now occupied by Woods, Matthews
& Baker and A. J. Harriman & Co., was built this year by Capt. David
Whittier and Captain, now Admiral Joseph Smith; Captain Whittier died
here in 1849; Admiral Smith is now and has been for many years resident
in Washington, D. C. The block was finished for two stores and dwellings
over them. The northerly store was first occupied by Whittier and Smith,
the southerly by John Clark, who is still living, residing in China,

Michigan.   The dwellings were first occupied by Messrs. Whittier and
Clark.

On the evening of May-day, 1823, Miss Plimpton, "the young Columbian
vocalist from Boston," gave a "Concert of Vocal and Instrumental Music,
assisted by her father and brother, with music on the violin, French
horn, and patent six-keyed bugle at the Hall of Dr. Hubbard": so ran
the hand-bills.   It was the first concert ever given here by professional
musicians.   The actual relationship existing between the artists was
a question which very much disturbed the gossips of the day. "Dr. Hubbard's
Hall" was in the second story of the dwelling-house now occupied by
Mr. Asa A. Howes.

The Anniversary of the nativity of John the Baptist, June 24th,
was duly observed by the Ancient fraternity of Free and Accepted Masons.
The Belfast Lodge and members of other Lodges present were escorted
to the Meeting-house by the Belfast Light Infantry under command of
Captain Hills, where an address was delivered by Manasseh Sleeper, Esq.;
prayer by Bro. Gershom F. Cox.   Masons Hall was then in a wooden building
on Main street called the Babel.   At the conclusion of the public ceremonies
the brethren repaired to Wilson's Hall where a bountiful repast was
provided and toasts were drank in conformity with the usages of the
day.   The officers of the Lodge were Jonathan P. Alden; W. M.; Samuel
Tyler, S. W.; Oshea Page, J. W.; John Clark, Sec.; Elijah Torrey, Treas.;
Samuel Jackson, Jr., S. D.; George Adams, J. D.; Job White, Nathan Swan,
and Otho Abbott were the committee of arrangements; it is hardly necessary
to add, such is the tenure of this life, that they, their orator, and
all but a very small number of those who participated in the celebration
were long since "summoned to the Grand Lodge above."

    "What is so rare as a day in June?
        Then, if ever, come perfect days;
    Then Heaven tries the earth if it be in tune,
        And over it softly her warm ear lays."

So sings the poet; he would have sung a different song had he been
here in June of this year.   On the afternoon of the fifth we were visited
by a severe thunder storm; a barn owned by Robert Miller, located near
the house on High street now occupied by Mr. Judson Condon, was struck
by lightning and one of its corner posts shivered to pieces; hail fell
copiously; some globular pieces measured three inches in circumference,
and others nearly square measured an inch and a half from corner to
corner diagonally.   They made sad havoc with the window glass in this
and neighboring towns.   On the night of the ninth there was a heavy
frost; ice formed on the northerly side of buildings of the thickness
of ordinary window-glass; and about noon of the tenth we were treated
to a very respectable earthquake for this latitude.   Heaven's "warm
ear," of which the poet sings, could not have been particularly charmed
with the tune which earth was playing in those "perfect days."

A "Grand Caravan of Living Animals" was exhibited here on the 5th
of July, and the day following; the place of exhibition was on Spring
street, between Church and High streets, on the premises now owned by
Major Chase; "doors open from 9 a. m. until 7 p. m.; admittance twenty-five
cents; children under twelve years of age half price."   The animals
constituting the Grand Caravan, were a full grown lion and two young
ones, "playful and active," a catamount, two lamas, two buffalos, a
leopard, a jackal, a black wolf, two ichneumons, and "Dandy Jack and
his pony who rides with that degree of horsemanship which was never
equaled in New England by any of his kind!"   It was the first exhibition
here of a large collection of wild beasts; although five or six years
before an elephant and a lion were here on exhibition for several days;
the elephant in the stable of the Huse Tavern, the lion in a barn which
stood on the site of the store now occupied by H. H. Johnson & Co.
They did not attract much attention outside the village; but "Dandy
Jack and his pony" carried the whole country by storm.   The business

manager and factotum of the "Grand Caravan" was one Macomber; a man of much humor as well as business capacity. He was standing one day at the entrance to the canvas tent officiating as ticket-master, when an inside customer, rather a rough specimen of the female persuasion, terriby dilapidated in dress and with a face which did not indicate any very familiar acquaintance with soap and water, presented herself saying, "Mister, I'm going out to get some refreshments and I want you to look at me so you'll know me when I come back. Do you think you will?" "Know you!" replied M.; "if you don't wash your face I shall know you for sure." The elephant above mentioned was a female and the largest animal of the kind which has ever been exhibited in this place. On her return to the west while passing through York county she was fired at by a miserable miscreant and killed.

The early part of September was a season of extreme and in many instances in this and neighboring localities of distressing drought. Vegetation presented the appearance of having been seared and large streams shrank to rivulets. It was difficult in some localities to procure a sufficient supply of water for domestic purposes; many families were compelled to procure the needed supply from a mile distant; cattle were driven two miles to water. The forests all around us were here and there on fire and the village was literally enveloped in smoke. The engine company and people generally were called out several times to protect buildings from the flames. Rain came, however, about the twentieth of the month and stayed the ravages of fire but too late to repair the damage done to vegetation by the drought.

The rain was followed by cold weather of unusual severity for that season of the year. On the night of the 29th there was quite a fall of snow; in some of the towns in the interior to the depth of three or four inches. It was an event unprecedented in the memory of our oldest inhabitants. The greatest amount of suffering and loss of property from the fires which were prevailing at this time was in the towns of Wiscasset and Alna. A large number of houses, barns, and their contents were destroyed. So great was the destitution which followed that an appeal was made for charitable relief throughout the State.

At the annual commencement at Bowdoin College, Sept. 3rd, two young men graduated who were residents in this town; one was William Jeffrey Read, son of Judge Read, who was born in Danvers, Mass., and died at his father's residence in this town in 1829--six years after he graduated, two years after he was admitted to the bar--aged twenty-nine. He was a young man of brilliant talent, and had his life been spared would have been an ornament to society and the pride of this the home of his adoption. The other young man was the compiler of these annals; who in charity may be excused for taking pride in the fact--the only one in a long life over which he has ever claimed to glorify himself--that he was the first native born of Belfast who ever graduated at a Collegiate Institution.

Early in the morning of November 12th a fire broke out in the boarding house of Samuel Jackson, then undergoing repairs preparatory to converting it into a hotel, on High street. His daughter, a very interesting girl about fifteen years of age, who had been watching through the night at the bedside of a sick relative and who had retired to rest in an upper room of the house only an hour or two before the fire broke out, perished in the flames. The dwelling house of George Watson, Esq., a store owned by him, occupied by Samuel B. Morril as a shoe store, and two or more barns standing southerly, and the store of John Angier, Esq., standing northerly from the building in which the fire commenced were burned. Within two months afterwards Mr. Watson had erected and finished so far as was necessary to make it tenantable a dwelling house on the site of his former one. It is the same building now occupied by by N. G. Prescott & Company and George G. Wells as stores. The store now occupied by Mr. Calvin Hervey stands on the site of the one occupied by Samuel B. Morrill. The residue of the burned district is covered by Phoenix Row.

John Durham, son of one of the original Proprietors of the township, died in October, aged seventy-four. He was one of the Highway Surveyors elected at the first meeting held under the act incorporating the town at the house of John Mitchell on the 11th of November, 1773. He was married in 1780, and commenced housekeeping in a log house which stood about on the same site of the New England House stable. He afterwards removed to a one-story frame house which he built and which stood about midway on High street between the New England House and the dwelling house of James Y. McClintock, Esq.; the bars to his pasture were about where the front door of Mr. McClintock's house now is. In 1811 he removed to the house which he built that year on Wilson's Hill, known as the Avery House, now in occupation of Messrs. Gilkey and Swift. He was the owner of Lot 36, one of the two lots on which the principal business portion of our city is located. Its southern boundary is Main street on the course it runs from Wilson's Hill to Custom-house Square and on the same course to the shore; its northern boundary is forty rods northerly from its southerly line. Lot 37, the other lot of the two referred to, known to the men of the last generation and some of the present as the Miller Lot, through which a portion of High, Church, Court, Cedar and Congress streets run, was "drawn," in the division of Lots among the original proprietors by Robert Patterson, who thought so poorly of it that he "dropped" it and "pitched" on a lot not far from the upper bridge in preference. Looking at his choice through the financial spectacles of this day he made a mistake; although in making the change he brought himself more immediately in contact, it is true, with salmon, shad, mink and musquash, the most practically available currency of the day. Mr. Durham left several children, sons and daughters; the only survivor resident here is Mrs. Charles Treadwell, wife of our universally respected Commodore of the Chowder Fleet.

At the Spring meeting, Philip Morrill, James McCrillis and William Avery were elected Selectmen, Herman Abbott, Clerk, Samuel French, Treasurer and among the other town officers William Crosby, Asa Edmunds and Calvin Pitcher, Tythingmen; an office which has a name and place on the Statute-book, but not elsewhere; at least so far as this locality is concerned. A faithful discharge of the duties originally attached to the office would furnish full employment now-a-day for one day in the week to the persons holding it and interfere seriously with the movements of the numerous class in our community who hold practically, if not theoretically, to the belief that "the groves were God's first temples." The time may come when the office will re-assume its pristine vigor: when it does, Wo to the Sabbath-breaking disciples of the Apostle who said "I go a fishing!"

At the foregoing meeting an election of members of Congress for this District came off; the whole number of votes thrown in this place was 285. At the annual Fall meeting, there having been no choice at the previous trial, another vote was taken; whole number of votes 179. There was very little interest felt in the result and there was, of course, a small attendance of voters. George Watson, Esq., was elected Representative to the Legislature. The whole number of deaths in this year was eighteen.

CHAPTER XVIII. (1824.)

This was a year of unusual business activity; unparalleled in the history of the town. A large number of buildings were erected; among them the house on High street now occupied by Mr. George F. White, built by his father-in-law Mr. Benj. Hazeltine; the brick house on Church St. now owned by Ex-Gov. Anderson, built by Capt. Hutson Bishop; the house on the same street now occupied by Mrs. Bradbury, built by her husband, Nathaniel H. Bradbury; the Bean and Derby brick block on Main street, the Town Hall, the Eagle Hotel, Phoenix Row and the distillery.

The Town Hall is the brick building on the Common standing next southerly from the meeting-house. The room on the ground floor was used for town meetings until we became a city; the first meeting held in it was on March 28, 1825. When the county of Waldo was established the room on the second floor was finished for a Court room and continued to be occupied for that purpose until the new Court House was built in 1853. The attic was finished for a Masonic Hall.

The Eagle Hotel, now the American House, was built by Otis Little of Castine, and Thomas Pickard of this place. It has been so much enlarged and modified, especially in its interior construction, that a brief description of it as it was originally may not be uninteresting. The westerly front room on Main street was the parlor; the room in rear of it, twenty-three feet in length, was the "spacious dining-room;" the two were thrown into one on great occasions by means of folding doors between them. The easterly front room as the Bar-room; the room in rear of it the sitting-room; the Bar was on the side of the bar-room fronting the door on the easterly end of the building which opens on the drive-way leading from Main street to the stable. On the second floor were a hall over the parlor and dining-room, and five sleeping rooms; the hall was used for balls and dancing schools and occasionally for lectures. On the third floor there were twelve sleeping-rooms in four of which there were fire-places. Above these there were, to use the language of the proprietors, "many apartment of circumambient construction where may be placed ten or twelve beds." There was a "projection" or ell, from the main building, eighteen by twenty feet, containing two kitchens and two bed-rooms over them. There was no piazza in front as there now is. When the ridge-pole was put in place a swivel made fast to it was discharged to announce the important event; there were other forms and ceremonies on the occasion the character of which must be left to the imagination of our readers. The building was ready for occupancy on the first of November but was not opened as a public house until the February following. John W. Appleton, from Portland, was its first landlord.

Phoenix Row, erected on a portion of the territory burned over in November previous, was completed in the fall of the year and the larger portion of it immediately occupied. The first occupants of the six stores, commencing at the easterly end, were as follows: John Angier, Foss & Lothrop, Benjamin Hazeltine, Peter H. Smith, John S. Kimball and James Langworthy; the only one of the number now living is Mr. Lothrop, who has for many years resided in New York. Mr. Angier was the father of Mr. Oakes Angier, Mr. Hazeltine of Mr. Charles B. Hazeltine, and Mr. Smith of Mrs. William Winslow; no descendant of either of the other tenants is residing here. In the third story of the store now occupied by Miss Wetherbee there was a large hall, called Phoenix hall, which was for many years the largest and principal hall in the place. It was used for balls and political assemblages. It was the gathering place of the Whigs during the 'log-cabin and hard-cider' Presidential campaign in 1840, and resounded night after night, until the contest was ended, with the rallying cry of "Tippecanoe and Tyler too." A few of the voices which then and there stirred the hearts of the people like the sound of a trumpet are still heard occasionally in feeble tones; but the eloquent lips of Webster Kelley, of George W. Cooley, which held all hearts spell-bound by the words they uttered, long ago put on the purple hue of death.

The distillery stood on the bank in the rear of the premises now occupied occupied by A. K. P. Moore and Thomas P. Logan, near the water, just northerly of an old brick-yard the remains of which, as well as a portion of the distillery wharf, are still visible.   It was built by John Slade & Son of Boston for Alfred Curtis of that city and Capt. William Barns of this place, who constituted one of the numerous firms over which Samuel Upton was the presiding genius.   It was built of brick and was one hundred feet in length by fifty in width.   It contained forty-two thousand gallon cisterns, with heaters, condensers and stills of sufficient power and capacity to manufacture five hundred gallons of rum per day.   The article manufactured, to use the language of a distinguished jurist of Maine recently deceased, was "bad stuff but good rum."   It had a high reputation, and from the method of manufacture and the superior quality of the water used was regarded as worth more per gallon than any other rum then manufactured in New England.   It was supplied with water from three reservoirs on the hill-side just above it.   Parties making an excavation last fall near the road which runs westerly of its site came across a reservoir about fifteen feet square, substantially built, the origin of which was unknown to the owner of the premises and was the occasion of no little wonderment to those whose attention was called to it; it was one of the reservoirs which supplied the old distillery.

Connected with the distillery was a large store-house of capacity sufficient to hold five hundred hogsheads; it was used for storing molasses. There was a solid, substantially built wharf, as is apparent from what remains of it, connected with the establishment; the best "tomcod" fishing of the day was to be found at the end of it.

"A jolly place it was in times of old!
But something ails it now; the spot is cursed."

The manufacture of rum in the distillery commenced in February 1825.   In the spring of 1827 it was sold by the original proprietors to Col. Daniel Lane, and was continued, in operation most of the time, until about 1838.   During a portion of this time an apartment was fitted up in it for bathing purposes; but the number of those who believed, practically, that cleanliness was next akin to godliness, did not afford patronage sufficient to warrant its continuance as an institution. In 1838 the property passed into the hands of Rufus B. Allyne, Esq., and was used for storage purposes until 1843, when the machinery was taken out and the buildings were subsequently demolished and the material sold.

During the time the distillery was in operation it was in charge of Mr. Freeman C. Raymond as superintendent and foreman.   He came to this place about 1825; in 1834 he commenced business here as a watch-maker and jeweller; and in 1840 he removed to Boston where he still resides engaged in the same occupation.   He is kindly remembered here by all who knew him.

The Bean and Derby brick block on Main street, consisting of two stores and a dwelling house, was built by Mess. Lewis Bean, father of our fellow-citizens Mess. Joseph and Lewis Bean, and Andrew Derby; Mr. Bean died in this place Aug. 1, 1834, aged 55; Mr. Derby, who came here early in this century, having become very infirm in health removed to Alfred, where he died many years since.   Mr. Bean was the first occupant of the dwelling house, Washburn and Eastman of the southerly and Joshua Pickard of the northerly store.   Mr. Pickard died here about 1850. Mess. Washburn and Eastman are still living; the former in China in this State, the latter in some one of the Western States.   The entire block was consumed in the fire of 1865.   On the site of the southerly store now stands the store occupied by Conant & Co.; the land covered by the residue of the block is vacant.   A wooden building, situated just southerly from the brick block, containing two stores, built by Mess. Bean & Derby in 1810 was consumed in the same fire; the stores now occupied by E. C. Hilton and Carle & Morrison and a portion of the store occupied by Sidney Kalish stand on its site.

The cellar walls of the Hazeltine and Bishop houses, the Eagle Hotel, Phoenix Row and the Distillery were all laid under the superintendence of our venerable fellow citizen, Major Chase, who understood then how to use the crow-bar and stone-hammer as skilfully as for many years after he did the minuter instruments required in this vocation of watchmaker and jeweller.

Early in this year a religious society under the style of the "Christian Society of Universalists in Belfast" was organized; its name was subsequently changed to that of the "First Universalist Society in Belfast." The meeting for organization was held at the Academy, March 4th; this was the origin of the present Universalist Society.

The 22d of May was a "white day" in our calendar. The Steamboat Maine, the first whose paddle-wheels ruffled the waters of the Penobscot, arrived here. There was a rush to the wharf to take a look at her, and a large party went on board soon after noon on an excursion to Castine. There are a few yet living who have a vivid remembrance of the somewhat troubled passage over--the "Sampson," strong in beauty, who landed at Castine--the "tender passages" on the return--and the midnight lectures which followed.

The steamer was of about a hundred tons burthen. The project of her owners was to run her regularly as a packet between Portland and Eastport, touching at this and other ports on the coast, connecting with a line which had been established between Bath and Hallowell. She continued to ply rather irregularly between Portland, Bath and Eastport, touching at this port, during the season, under the command of Capt. Smith Cram, who had been for many years previously a resident in Montville, who was born in New Hampshire and died in California. She went to Bangor occasionally, diverging from her regular route. It will amuse the steamboat patrons of this day, perhaps, to learn that by the advertised notice of the arrival and departure of the boat "passengers wishing to go in her are requested to leave their names at the store of Haraden and French, where they will find the boat's book."

She was followed, June 3d, by the steam-brig New York, Thomas Rogers, master. She was advertised to leave Boston on the 10th, 20th and 30th of every month, for Portland, Owls Head, Belfast and Eastport, inside the islands. Persons wishing to take passage from this place were "requested to leave their names at the Maine Hotel (Sleeper's), for as the boat would wait but a short time it was necessary for passengers to make some arrangement for being called." Passengers could be landed at any intermediate point on the coast or rivers by previous agreement. Compared with the steamers of this day both of them might appropriately be denominated "Accommodation Steamer." Both of them did a fair business; at any rate there was sufficient to keep them on the route until into October. The Marine List of July 18th noticed the arrival of the New York from Eastport with forty-three passengers; landed twenty and sailed for Boston.

On the 30th of June Rev. Charles Soule was ordained pastor of the First Congregational Church and Society; the services were held at the Unitarian Meeting-house and were as follows: Introductory prayer by Rev. Mr. Cummings of North Yarmouth, Sermon by Rev. Mr. Merrill of Freeport, Ordaining prayer by Rev. Mr. Gillett of Hallowell, Charge by Rev. Mr. Blood of Bucksport, Right hand of Fellowship by Rev. Mr. Ingraham of Thomaston, Address to the church and people by Rev. Mr. Tappan of Augusta, Concluding prayer by Rev. Mr. Mitchell of Waldoborough.

The Fourth of July was celebrated on the fifth--the fourth being Sunday--under the auspices of the Belfast Light Infantry. The forenoon was devoted to military evolutions, and in the afternoon the members of the company with a large number of invited guests dined at Wilson's Hall. Many toasts were given and an Ode written for the occasion by a young man of this place was sung to the old-time tune of "Adams and Liberty." The Presidential campaign, which resulted in the election of John Quincy Adams, was just beginning to wax warm. A toast given by Hon. Alfred Johnson, Jr., which went the rounds of the newspapers at the time, may be regarded as an expressive of the general political sentiment in this locality: "John Quincy Adams. The universal Yankee Nation will unite to make him our next President; should he fail of his election no more can be said of us that of the whole human race before--"In Adams fall we sinned all."

Some idea of the condition of trade in our village at this time may be gathered from the quantity of lumber and wood hauled in on wheels, according to actual survey, on the 17th of this month; Boards 110,778 feet; shingles 87 M.; joist 5000 feet; cordwood 8 cords; hemlock bark 36 cords. Total market value $1218.83.

The Hancock County Agricultural Society held its annual meeting and fair at this place on the 13th of October; it was the first one ever held here and attracted a large concourse of spectators. The show was held in a vacant lot next southerly from the old Frothingham place; the road thence to the old Gun-house, where Captain McGilvery's house now stands, was "garlanded" with the vehicles and tents of the sweet-cider, pumpkin-pie, doughnut and hard-boiled-egg merchants. An address was delivered by George Watson, Esq., at the meeting-house, and at its conclusion a large number of farmers, merchants, and members of the several learned professions partook of a dinner at the Maine Hotel. The thirteen regular toasts were announced from the chair and a large number of sentiments appropriate to the occasion were volunteered by gentlemen present. Everything connected with the meeting passed off pleasantly and harmoniously, and it was pronounced a decided success. Premiums were awarded to the amount of $80.25; the largest being $15.00, the smallest seventy-five cents.

This year Belfast achieved its first suicide; so far at least as appears of record. Nathaniel Holden, alias "Old Holden" as he was generally called, although only about thirty-three years old, relieved himself from the burthen of the life that now is, and the community from a useless member, by hanging himself. "My God! what a spectacle!" was the exclamation of the bereaved widow, who was not "like Niobe, all tears," when she saw him cut down. The scene of the performance was a house, afterward burned, which stood on Bridge street on the site of the house now occupied by Mr. Isaac Prince.

CHAPTER XIX. (1824-5.)

On the 18th of February, 1824, died James Patterson, aged eighty. He with three brothers, Nathaniel, Robert, and William, came here from Saco about 1770; they were among the first white men who ever wintered here.   Nathaniel, who died in 1826 aged 79, was the grandfather of our fellow citizens Alfred, Cyrus, and the late Judge Patterson.   Robert, who died in 1829 aged 87, was the father of Capt. Robert Patterson and Mr. George Patterson now residing on the east side of the river, and grandfather of Mrs. Alden D. Chase.   William, who died in 1828 aged 79, was the father of David Patterson now residing on the east side of the river.   James was the maternal grandfather of Messrs. James P., John W., William B., George F. and Martin P. White, residing here, and of Mr. Jonathan White who resides in Rockland; one of his daughters having married Mr. Jonathan White and another Mr. Robert White, brothers, deceased.   His son Robert was lost at sea in 1830; his son James, husband of Mrs. Nancy Patterson, who is still living, died in this place in 1816; he had another son, Martin who died abroad in 1802, leaving no children.   Mr. Patterson was one of the first Board of Selectmen, chosen at the first town meeting held Nov. 11, 1773, and of the Committee of Safety elected in 1776.   Among the early settlers of the town there was no one whose judgment was more respected or who exercised a wider or better influence; he died as he had lived, respected and beloved by all who knew him well.

On the third of May died Robert Houston, Esq., aged sixty-one. He was the son of the venerable Samuel Houston who came here in 1771, nor 1774 as stated in a previous chapter, and who died in 1819, aged ninety-two, and was the grandfather of our fellow citizen, Nathan F. Houston, Esq.   Mr. Houston was for a long series of years the principal surveyor of land in this locality.   "According to survey and plan of Robert Houston" and "according to Houston's survey" are familiar as households words to those who have had occasion to trace titles in the Registry of Deeds in this and Hancock county; there is no name found more frequently than his on the records of the last quarter of the last century and the first of this, unless it be the name of Noah Prescott. He was often elected to offices of trust by his fellow townsmen and never failed to perform the duties devolved upon him faithfully and acceptably.

Zaccheus Porter, Esq., a lawyer by profession, who came here to reside in 1813, died in November this year, aged forty-four.   He was a native of Danvers, Mass.   Soon after coming here he formed a co-partnership with Hon. John Wilson, under the style of Wilson and Porter, which continued while he lived.   He built in 1822 the house on High street now occupied by Dr. Lewis W. Pendleton.   He was a man of indefatigable industry in the practice of his profession and of unflinching fidelity to his clients.   One of his two daughters became the wife of Hon. Albert Pilsbury, the Democratic candidate for the office of Governor of the State in 1853, now deceased, the other the wife of our late fellow citizen William H. Conner.

At the annual Spring meeting, held at the Conference Room, George Watson, James McCrillis and Salathiel Nickerson were chosen Selectmen, Herman Abbott, Clerk, Thomas Marshall, Treasurer.

The annual Fall meeting was held at the Academy.   The number of ballots thrown on the gubernatorial ticket was 180; all but two of them were for Governor Parris.   James McCrillis was elected Representative.

Church street was accepted this year from Spring street to Academy Square.   The number of deaths in the town during the year was fifty-seven; of this number twenty-eight were young children; the prevailing disease which occasioned this unusual mortality was dysentery.

In February, 1825, the Eagle Hotel was opened by John W. Appleton, who came to this place from Portland.   He was a very attentive, gentlemanly landlord.   While he kept the house he made repeated attempts to establish a reading-room in one of its apartments but without success.   He left here in the fall of 1827 to take charge of the Elm Hotel at Portland.

There was a tavern kept at this time, and had been for several years, by Col. Nathan Stanley, in the valley between Hemlock and Hayford's Hill on the premises now occupied by Mr. Rufus P. Hill; it was then known as Stanley's Tavern; after it came into the occupation of the owner, Mr. Joseph P. Ladd, it was known as "the Spa." It was a famous place in its day for "Shooting Matches;" where a sportsman, as he was then designated, was permitted for an adequate consideration to fire at a turkey, goose, or some other feathered biped placed at a stipulated distance; if he hit he won the bird, if he missed he lost his money. The fashion of that day has passed away; at least in this locality. It was, for awhile, a place where "young men saw visions and old men dreamed dreams." It was not always that "the vision was made plain upon tables that he may run who readeth," nor that the dream failed of interpretation for lack of "Joseph." In December of this year Col. Stanley became landlord of the Maine Hotel, Mr. Sleeper who had been landlord having left it the month previous and removed to his house at the corner of Church and Spring streets.

The comparative quiet of our little village was interrupted several times during the season by the steam whistle. On the 8th of May the steamboat Maine, under command of Captain Daniel Lunt, made her re-appearance. She continued to ply during the summer between Bath and Eastport touching at this and other ports on the route. The steam brig New York, Capt. Rogers, touched here one or more times on her passage to Eastport, the steamboat Patent, Capt. Porter, the Eagle, Capt. Peirce, bound to the same port, and once at least the Waterville, under command of our friend of the year preceding, Capt. Cram.

This year for the first time a store was opened here devoted exclusively to the sale of "dry goods." Francis A. Bowers was the proprietor; the store was in No. 1 Pickard's Building, now occupied by Mr. Lucius F. McDonald. Mr. Bowers died of consumption a few years after he commenced business.

On the 30th of May another "Grand Caravan of Living animals, the largest that ever travelled the United States," accompanied by a "Museum of Wax Figures," made its appearance and exhibited in the rear of the Eagle Hotel; its coming was heralded by any quantity of trumpeting and show-bills. The "Grand Caravan" was a humbug with larger wings than any ever seen flying in this latitute, except the "Museum." "General Washington," who might have done service as a scare-crow in a corn-field, the "Goddess of Liberty," with a terrible lurch to port and a bust worthy the mother of triplets, "Lafayette," with a grin on his face like a baboon, half a dozen naval heroes, Queen Caroline, Bergami, and several celebrated pirates made up the contents of the "Museum." The whole affair was an imposition of such ridiculous dimensions that our good people and their cousins from the country, who might well have been justified in feeling indignant, could only laugh and make the most fun possible out of it. Hence the mirthful chaos that ran rampant through our streets for two days and nights.

There was no celebration of the Fourth of July at this place but there was at Lincolnville, in which a large number of our townsmen participated. It was estimated that there were fifteen hundred persons present. The oration was delivered by William J. Farley, Esq. of Thomaston, who will be remembered by many as one of the most eloquent advocates who ever addressed a jury in this county. This was the year when Lafayette visited Maine; he came no farther than Portland and was there in the latter part of June. Among the sentiments given at the dinner table on the above occasion was the following: "Lafayette: although too far north to see him, not too cold to love him."

One of our old landmarks, which had for a long time been precious in the sight of those who go down to the sea in ships, "went by the board," to use their own phraseology, in the night of July seventeenth. During a very severe gale the two tall pine trees which stood near the easterly end of the bridge and had been for many years a landmark for seamen entering the harbor were blown down.

There was a mail stage running weekly this year between this place and Augusta, leaving Augusta every Wednesday morning and arriving here at evening of the same day, and returning the next day. The tri-weekly stage from Portland was running, leaving Portland at 4 o'clock a. m. of one day and arriving here at 10 a. m. of the next; the stage fare between the two places was $5.62 1-2.

At the annual Spring meeting, March 28th, held at the Town Hall, the first meeting held there, Rufus B. Allyne, Joseph Smith and Samuel Gordon were chosen Selectmen, Herman Abbott, Town Clerk, and Thomas Marshall, Treasurer. At the annual Fall meeting the largest number of ballots thrown for any candidate was 132. Ralph C. Johnson, Esq., was elected Representative. A census of the inhabitants was taken in December; whole number 2,839, showing an increase of 813 within the preceding five years. There were then 171 dwelling houses within half a mile of the lower bridge.

The number of deaths in town during this year was seventy-six; forty-five of those who died were children under four years of age. This unusual mortality was caused by the prevalence of a flux and fever, or dysentery. Nearly one-half of our population were attacked by the disease within six weeks. Among the adults to whom it proved fatal was Doctor Herman Abbott, who died at the Eagle Hotel July 24th in the forty-second year of his age. He was a native of Wilton, N. H., and had been a practising physician in this place for fifteen years. He was a man of extensive scientific research and of skill in his profession, of unquestioned integrity and unaffected piety. No man ever lived and died here who was more respected by his fellow townsmen. He was one of the few of whom it might be truthfully said that by precept and the example of a pure life

"He taught us how to live and (Oh! too high
The price of knowledge) taught us how to die."

In his last hour he remarked to a friend that he looked on "death as the inevitable lot of man, but to the Christian not an evil." Doctor Abbott had been for several years collecting material for a history of the town; Mr. White in his History acknowledges his indebtedness to the Doctor's manuscript for many important facts; it is a matter of regret that that manuscript cannot now be found. At the time of his decease Doctor Abbott was Town Clerk, having held the office several successive years. Nathaniel H. Bradbury was his successor, elected in August following.

There was a good amount of activity this year in trade and commerce, especially in the articles of cordwood and lumber, which were two important elements of wealth in and around this section of the county. In one day in March there were hauled into the village 171 cords of wood on one road; as much or more, probably, on all the other roads. In this avalanche of cord-wood the reverend clergy were not permitted to escape a visitation; two loads, each containing five cords, were deposited in the back yards of two of them; they were graceless enough to make mention of the visitation in the Gazette as cause for gratitude!

The Custom House records show that during the year twenty-five vessels, principally brigs, loaded at this port for foreign ports, most of them for the West India islands. The cargoes consisted of the products of this and neighboring towns. Some of the principal articles were boards, shingles, staves, sugar-box and hogshead shooks, spars, pickled fish, dried cod fish and potatoes.

This year also is memorable for its forest fires. Many valuable wood lots in the vicinity of the village were much injured by the fire and nothing but a copious fall of rain prevented their total destruction. The loss of property in wood, lumber, houses and barns, oxen, cows, sheep and swine in the town of Ripley and vicinity in the county of Somerset was very large, but in Miramichi it may well be said that it was immense; the calamity was aggravated there by the loss of life which accompanied it.   One hundred and thirty were burned, ten drowned, and twenty, in addition, died from injuries received.   Some of our townsmen were sufferers in the loss of property and some who had previously resided here perished by fire or water.

On the 12th of December the Sloop Syren, commanded by our highly respected fellow-citizen Capt. Ezekiel Burgess, left this port for Boston, and early the next morning, owing to the thick vapor occasioned by the severe cold, struck on a ledge off Richmond's island, and immediately bilged.   The master, crew and the only passenger Mr., now the Hon. Jacob Sleeper of Boston, took the boat and landed on the island.   She had on board an assorted cargo comprising 7 pipes of Holland gin, 3 bags of pepper, 18 bars of iron, 24 barrels of shad, 9 of fish oil, 15 barrels of beans, 15 cords of wood, &c.   The sloop afterwards drifted off and went ashore near Townsend; the sails and rigging and a portion of the cargo was saved.

CHAPTER XX. (1826-7.

The earliest local event of the year, 1826, of a public character
was the public Installation of the officers-elect of Belfast Lodge at
the Unitarian Meeting-house on the 15th of February.   An address was
delivered by Hiram O. Alden, Esq., five hundred copies of which were
printed for distribution among the Fraternity.   The officers installed
were Samuel Tyler, W. M., Benj. Kelley, S. W., Oshea Page, G. W., Robert
Emery, Treasurer, Simeon Foss, Sec., Samuel Haynes, S. D., J. T. Quimby,
J. D., Luther Gannett, S. S., Joseph Bray, J. S., William Holt, Tyler,
Manasseh Sleeper, Marshal.   The orator on the occasion is the sole survivor
of the parties most immediately connected with it.
       The first fire of the year occurred on the first day of the same
month; at 8 o'clock in the morning the mercury was at twenty four degrees
below zero.   Mr. Luther Gannett, living on the east side of the river,
during the night preceding became the happy proprietor of a large litter
of pigs.   To protect them from the extreme cold a number of bricks were
heated and placed in the stye; the straw in it took fire, the fire was
communicated to the barn, the barn and a horse and cow in it were burned,
and there was a very perceptible odor of roast pig about the premises.
       On the 21st of June the last number of the Hancock Gazette and
Penobscot Patriot was issued, it being the completion of its sixth volume,
and on the 28th it reappeared as the Belfast Gazette.
       The anniversary of John the Baptist, the 24th, was celebrated by
the Masonic Fraternity.   Delegations from the several Lodges in the
county were present and an Address was delivered by Rev. William A.
Drew, now of Augusta, who was at that time pastor of the Universalist
society in this place.
       "Fourth of July" was ushered in with the usual bell-ringing, accompan-
ied by tin horns and India-crackers, and a party, not large but hilarious,
dined at the Eagle Hotel; the other services of the day were of rather
a unique character.   At eight o'clock in the morning a sermon was preached
at the Methodist Chapel by Bishop George of the Methodist Episcoal Connection.   At 10 an oration was delivered at the Unitarian meeting-house
by Mr. Wales of the Bangor Theological Seminary, at the conclusion of
which a contribution was taken in aid of the American Colonization Society.
In the afternoon a sermon was preached at the Conference-room.
       There was a public celebration at Searsmont which was numerously
attended by people from this and neighboring towns.   The Declaration
of Independence was read by Hon. John Wilson, and an oration delivered
by Hon. Alfred Johnson, Jr.   There was a public dinner and "after the
cloth was removed" the usual exercises followed.   There was a celebration
also at Brooks, in which many of our townsmen participated.   The Declaration
was read by Phineas Ashmun, Esq., oration by Rev. Jesse Briggs.   There
was a dinner, followed by the "regular 13," the only sentiment volunteered
possessed the rare merit of originality and savored strongly of the
shop: "Enemies to Liberty, may they be lathered with aqua fortis and
shaved with a handsaw."   Palermo and Montville celebrated the afternoon
with a hail storm, which swept over territory about two miles in length
and one in width, scattering hailstones the size of bullets, and demolishing
most of the window glass within its path.   Taking the exercises of the
day in this section as a whole, there certainly was no lack of variety.
       Immediately following the Fourth came "Cook Kimball from Hallowell"
and established the first book-bindery we ever had here.   He was a good
workman, but there was little work for him to do; specimens of his workman-
ship may be met with occasionally in some of our old libraries; half
bound in sheep with leather corners was the prevailing style.
       During a portion of this year the Steamer Patent, Captain Cram,
was plying between Bath and Eastport, touching at this place; her first
trip to the east was made early in June, her last to the West about
the middle of November.   She came very near making her last trip for
all time on the 23d of August.   She arrived here on that day from Eastport
and left for the west about eight o'clock in the evening with fifty

passengers. She had reached a point near the Bluff when she came in collision with the steam-brig New York, Capt. Harrod, bound hither. One of her wheels was smashed, her mainmast broken into three pieces, two of which fell on deck, and she was in other points severely injured. A number of the passengers were on deck at the time of the collision, but no one seriously injured; some of them were knocked overboard, but were rescued without suffering any great detriment from their involuntary salt-water bath. She was towed back to her wharf by the New York, which left the next morning for Eastport. A more serious calamity was in store for her. Early in the evening of the same day when about four miles from Petit Menan Island, she was found to be on fire. All efforts to extinguish the fire for two hours were unavailing. It continued to make rapid headway, and at the expiration of that time the passengers and crew, between thirty and forty in all, took to the boats and made for the island, abandoning her to her fate. She burned to the waters edge and sank in forty fathoms of water. She was a staunch boat, had been recently repaired and refitted, and was on her first trip for the season.

Funeral obsequies in honor of Ex-President John Adams and Thomas Jefferson, who died on the fourth of July preceding, took place here on the 10th of August. A procession formed in the vicinity of the Conference-room was escorted by the Belfast Light Infantry to the Unitarian Meeting-house; during its progress minute guns were fired and the bell was tolled. The stores and all places of business were closed and the flags on the shipping in the harbor were at halfmast; the interior of the church was draped with black. The exercises consisted of a dirge, prayer by Rev. Mr. Frothingham, an original Ode written for the occasion, and a Eulogy pronounced by Hon. Alfred Johnson, Jr.

The brig Monticello of about 200 tons burthen, owned by Joel Hills and Co., was launched on the 8th of October; her first voyage was to the Sabine river. The schooner Experiment, owned by John H. Connor and Annis Campbell, both residing here, went ashore at Monhegan on the 28th of November. She was stripped and abandoned by the crew, but after they left she was got off and towed into port by the islanders.

At the annual Spring meeting Bohan P. Field, Robert Patterson 2d and John Palmer were chosen Selectmen, Nathaniel H. Bradbury, Clerk, and Thomas Marshall, Treasurer. At a meeting held the week following for the election of a Register of Deeds for Hancock county the whole number of votes thrown was 253; no choice was effected. At the annual Fall meeting another trial was had and the number of votes thrown was 230; on the Congressional ticket 289 were thrown. Ralph C. Johnson, Esq. was elected Representative to the Legislature.

A school census taken this year shows that there were 1183 in town between the ages of four and twenty-one. The disease which had prevailed and had been so fatal during the preceding summers had not entirely disappeared; the number of deaths during the year was about fifty.

The year 1827 opened with a war of the elements and a declaration of war by the staid pedestrians on our streets against the boys and their hand-sleds. A violent snow-storm followed by rain, a high gale, an unusually high tide and severely cold weather, covered our wharves, from which large quantities of lumber had been swept, and our streets, with a coating of ice, affording the boys the best "coasting" they had enjoyed for several years. It was high tide with them in that branch of business when "the Selectmen and 160 others" declared war against them through the Gazette and handbills, announcing that they had associated themselves for mutual protection and pledging themselves to indemnify and hold harmless any person who should "demolish the sled or other vehicle" belonging to or in possession of "any boy found coasting in the streets or highways." There are no statistics showing the number of "sleds or other vheicles" destroyed, but the fact is well authenticated that the boys abandoned coasting when the ground was dry enough for them to play ball.

With the commencement of the year Arnold and Whittier began running a tri-weekly mail stage between Augusta and this place "on the new road called the Eastman road;" so named in honor of Thomas Eastman, Esq., who was one of its originators, who was quite a prominent man in the county, one of the Associate Justices of the Court of Sessions, and who kept a tavern for many years in Palermo in the vicinity of Eastman's corner. That corner will be remembered by some of our elderly people, probably, as being in the vicinity of the field where the ancient "Perlarmo Musters" were held.

On the 7th of February the act incorporating the County of Waldo, constituting Belfast its shire town, was approved by the Governor--Enoch Lincoln. At a town meeting held on the 19th a commitee consisting of William Crosby, William Avery, Alfred Johnson, Jr., Thomas Bartlett and George W. Webster was unanimously chosen "to carry into effect a vote passed at a meeting held September 11, 1826 relative to finishing the Town House for the reception of the Courts for the County of Waldo;" a vote was also passed "to raise the sum of six hundred dollars to defray the expenses of finishing said House."

The vote of September 11th referred to was, in substance, that if the Legislature should establish the county the town would, at its own expense, and without charge to the county, suitably finish and prepared the Town House for the use and occupation of the Courts--and that the same might be used gratuitously so long as the Courts should be held there. The second story was accordingly finished for court and jury rooms. The first term of the Court of Common Pleas was held there on the fourth Tuesday of July then next, Judges Perham and Smith presiding; the last term of the court held there was on the first Tuesday of October 1853; Judge Appleton presiding; the next term, in January 1854, Judge Rice presiding, was held in the new Court House; the old one was converted into a school-room.

By the act of incorporation the new county did not become organized as such until "from and after July 3d then next," but provision was made for the appointment of county officers in advance; the lion's share fell to Belfast. The following named persons residing here received appointments, as follows: Alfred Johnson, Jr., Judge of Probate, Joseph Williamson, County Attorney, Hugh J. Anderson, Clerk of Courts, Bohan P. Field, Chief Justice of the Court of Sessions. Joseph Hall of Camden was appointed Sheriff and Nathaniel M. Lowney of Frankfort, Register of Probate. The Associate Justices of the Sessions were Joseph Shaw of Thorndike and Thomas Eastman of Palermo. Mr. Anderson, afterwards Representative in Congress and Governor of the State, is the only one of the number now living.

The steamboat Patent, Captain Cram, commenced her trips early in May between Portland and Eastport touching at this and other ports; her last trip for the season was made in October. The steamboat Waterville, Capt. Porter, was here September 28th and left the next day for Bangor. It is not remembered that she was here at any other time during the season.

About the middle of May another Caravan, styled magniloquently the "Elephant Caravan," made its appearance and exhibited in the back-yard of the Eagle Hotel. It consisted of the "Great India Elephant," a camel, leopard, lama and "other minor animals," music on the "ancient Jewish Cymbal." This Caravan, like the one which preceded it, was accompanied by "a new and elegant collection of Wax Statues." Our people and those in the back towns had not forgotten the lesson they learned two years before, and let the "India Elephant, minor animals, Jewish Cymbal and wax statues" severly alone.

On the 23d of May Robert Miller died aged sixty-six. He was one of three Brothers, James, Robert and David, sons of James Miller who came here to reside in 1769 and died in 1794 aged eighty-two. James was for many years the owner and occupant of the house and land best known now as the old Frothingham place; before its sale to Rev. Frothingham

known as the Jimmy Miller place.   He removed from this place to Pine
Township, now Perrysville, Pa., in 1824 and died there in 1840.   David
resided the greater portion of his life in Northport.   Robert always
resided here until a short time before his last sickness.   He was the
owner of Lot 37, the next Lot southerly from Main street, on which now
stands some of the finest dwellings in the city, the Unitarian, Universalist,
Methodist and Baptist Churches, the Custom House and Postoffice, Hayford
Block, the old Town Hall and the brick schoolhouse.   He was a man of
quiet, reserved habits, regarded by many as unsocial, that trait in
his character may be attributed, perhaps, to the fact that he was never
married; that he was a rigidly honest man no one ever questioned.   The
following incident in his early life is narrated in White's History
and in Rev. J. L. Locke's Sketches of the early History of Belfast, published
in the Progressive Age in 1856.

During the Revolutionary War, in 1781, General Wadsworth and Major
Burton were taken prisoners by the British and confined in the fort
at Castine.   They succeeded in making their escape and after wandering
through the forest reached this place.   They made themselves and their
condition known to the elder Miller, but declined to accept the hospitality
proffered by him at his own house, through fear that they might be discovered by their pursuers and that he might suffer in consequence.   His son,
James and Robert, went with them about a mile into the forest where
they built a rude camp of evergreens to which they carried food for
the fugitives until the search for them being abandoned they left, and
by the aid of a pocket compass, furnished to them by Mr. Miller, found
their way through the forest to Thomaston, and from thence went to Portland.

CHAPTER XXI. (1827.)

The Fourth of July this year was a gala day for Belfast. It was not only the fifty-first anniversary of American Independence but the birthday of the county of Waldo also. A national salute was fired at sunrise. At 11 A. M. a procession was formed at the Conference-room which proceeded under a volunteer military escort, commanded by Col. Phillip Morrill, to the Unitarian meeting-house, the interior of which was very tastefully decorated with flowers and evergreens. The services there were introduced by appropriate music and prayer by Rev. Mr. Frothingham. The Declaration of Independence was read by William White, Esq., then resident in the place, now deceased, prefaced by remarks on the origin and history of that celebrated State paper. The oration was delivered by William Stevens, Esq., then resident here, now in Lawrence, Mass. At the conclusion of the services in the Church the procession was reformed and proceeded to a booth erected on the Common where a dinner was provided by Col. Nathan Stanley. Hon. William Crosby presided at the table, assisted by several Vice-presidents. After the cloth was removed the regular "13" and numerous volunteer toasts were drank. Among the volunteers was the following by our now venerable fellow-citizen, Hon. Albert G. Jewett, then a young man on the brink of entering the professional career in which he has since become eminently distinguished: "Citizens of Waldo--generous and patriotic; may you continue to be fired with the same holy ardor in the support of your liberties that your ancestors were in achieving them."

There was a Ball in the evening numerously attended, at Phoenix Hall, which was very beautifully decorated with flowers, evergreens and transparencies. Take it all in all it was the happiest day and evening ever known in Belfast; filled to overflowing with light, life and buoyancy. The effort of years had been crowned with success; hope had ended in fruition; the county of Waldo was a fixed fact, and Belfast was a shire town!

Looking back to that day what a cloud of sadness steals over the memory of the few remaining who participated in its festivities! Of the crowd who sat down at that table in the booth how few now walk our streets! Of the twenty-six who gave utterance to sentiments on that occasion, twenty-one have travelled "the way to dusty death!" Of the five Managers of that Ball, one only, an old man now of three score years and ten, is the sole survivor! "O Death in Life, the days that are no more!"

There were on that day ten county officers; there were resident here eight Justices of the Peace and Quorum, nineteen Justices of the Peace, two Notaries Public, ten lawyers, three clergymen, six physicians, two Coroners.--fifty-six in all; of that number there are now living Hon. Ralph C. Johnson, Hon. Hugh J. Anderson, Hon. William Stevens and Hiram O. Alden, Esq.; they, and no more. Bohan P. Field, Robert Patterson, 2d, John Palmer were Selectmen. Nathaniel H. Bradbury, Town Clerk, Thomas Marshall, Treasurer, there were three Auditors of Accounts, five police officers, thirteen surveyors of Highways, two Constables, ten Firewards, three Tythingmen, twenty-one Surveyors of lumber, five School-committee-men, fourteen School Agents, eighty in all; nine of that number are still living.

About this time one Joseph J. Sager, from Hallowell, came here to reside; his wife, Phoebe, a milliner and dressmaker, had been residing here for some time. He was a saddle and harness maker by trade and worked for awhile in a shop in a wooden building which stood on the site of the saloon now occupied by Mr. Richard Carter. They both removed from this place to Gardiner. While residing there Mrs. Sager died suddenly, October 5, 1834; the circumstances attending her sickness and death aroused suspicion that she died of poison. Her husband was arrested, indicted for her murder, and at a term of the Court, held the same month was convicted. He was hung January 2, 1835, at Augusta, in compliance with the sentence of the Court. Those were the days when justice was administered speedily and without delay.

On the third of September a meeting of the Belfast Light Infantry was held for the choice of officers. Henry Colburn was elected Captain in place of Joel Hill, resigned, Samuel B. Hanson, Lieutenant, and Charles Palmer, Ensign. Mention has heretofore been made of Capt. Hills; Mess. Hanson and Palmer are still living here. Mr. Colburn was a native of this place, son of Ebenezer Colburn who came here early in the century. He was for eleven years the faithful clerk of the late John Angier, Esq., in his store. He afterwards engaged in trade and still later kept a tavern at the Head of the Tide at a time when that locality was quite a place of business. On the election of President Harrison, he was appointed Postmaster, having been recommended at a citizen's meeting and held the office until the election of President Polk. During his term the office was kept in the westerly end of the old Telegraph building. He represented the town in the Legislature of 1847. He removed to Boston about 1849 where he died in the winter of 1874; his remains were brought here for interment. A few words will serve for his obituary; he was one of the "noblest works of God," an honest man; such was the eulogy pronounced upon him by all who knew him.

September 18th was a famous "Muster Day" here. Governor Lincoln and General Hodgdon, Major General of the Division, were present. Our militia organization was at the time in a very dilapidated condition. According to the annual return made to the Adjutant General there were fifteen companies belonging and attached to the Regiment; the number of effective privates in the Roll, not including warrant officers, was 219. Whether the "blood thirtsy" Major General was mortified at the beggarly account of rank and file which he had to offer for the inspection of the "Commander in Chief of the Army and Navy of the State," or whether the fit came upon him to magnify his office by finding fault with his inferiors, is a question on which there was a diversity of opinion at the time and was regarded by the community at large as of about as much consequence as the other question, "Who struck Billy Patterson?" Out of it, however, grew a war of words; a very bloodless battle. A Court Martial was held, on charges filed by the Major General against the Colonel of the Regiment and some of his subordinates. The result was that the subordinates were acquitted and the Colonel found guilty of the smallest specification filed against him; in other words, the roar of the lion amounted to nothing more than the squeak of a mouse.

On the 26th of September the Rev. Nathaniel Wales was ordained Pastor of the Congregational Society connected with the first Church in the place. The services, held at the Unitarian meeting-house, were as follows: Introductory Prayer by Rev. John Sawyer, Sermon by Rev. John Smith of Bangor, Consecrating Prayer by Rev. Mighil Blood of Bucksport, Charge to the Pastor by Rev. Benjamin Tappan of Augusta, Right hand of Fellowship by Rev. Stephen Thurston of Prospect, Address to the Church and people by Rev. Mr. Pomeroy of Bangor, Concluding Prayer by Rev. Mr. Loper. Mr. Wales continued to be the Pastor of the Society until he died, January 20, 1829, aged 36.

The notorious Mrs. Anne Royal, authoress of the Black Book and other works, made us a visit in October, tarrying about a week. She was one of the characters of the day; a traveling sponge; holding the pen of a ready writer, and wagging the tongue of a blackguard. Her tongue and pen were the implements employed to blackmail every prominent member of the community; it cost only a dollar to silence both. There were few who did not cheerfully pay the price of exemption from being hung up, in dark colors, in her protrait gallery.

On the night of Oct. 26th, the store of Mr. Liberty B. Wetherbee, now deceased, was broken open by two young men who were captured by Mr. Wetherbee and a friend who was watching with him in the store. At the next term of the Court of Common Pleas they were convicted of the crime and sentenced to two years' hard labor in the State Prison. One of them was John Palmer, Jr., a resident of this place, who figured somewhat conspicuously in the Salem murder a few years afterwards, of

which mention may be made hereafter, the other was James Preble, with
a large number of aliases. There are some elderly ladies still residing
here who are not particularly pleased, even now, at being reminded that
they once had the honor of an introduction to Mr. James Preble, alias
Mr. George Needham, alias Lieut. Pleasants of the Mexican Navy. It
happened in this wise: for several days before the store-breaking he
had been stopping at the Spa, then kept by Mr. Ladd, who had been a
trader in the village, and was the father of several fine daughters.
They made a party for their very handsome and gentlemanly guest and
invited their young friends from the village, male and female, who were
quite happy to accept the invitation. They were, of course, introduced
to "Lieut. Pleasants of the Mexican Navy," and were, of course, captivated
with his personal appearance and exceedingly courteous manners. Within
twenty hours afterwards the finely moulded wrists of the gallant lieutenant
were ornamented with steel bracelets, and he was on his way to jail.
It is not known that any of his numerous female admirers attended his
trial and sat by his side during its progress.

A monument built of wood was erected this year on Steele's ledge,
an appropriation having been made by Congress for that purpose. It
remained there until October 13, 1833, when it went adrift in a violent
storm, came sailing up the river and floated into the dock. It was
subsequently sold at auction for five dollars, that being the highest
bid, and taken across the river to the flats opposite Lewis' wharf,
where it remained for several years. During those years it was used
as a pier to which vessels made fast when occasion required.

Among the business men who came here and the changes in business
during the year were the following: Nathan Heywood came here from Albion,
and was for several years deputy sheriff and jailor. Mayo Hazeltine
purchased the stock in trade of his brother Benjamin and opened a store
at No. 5 Phoenix Row; he was afterwards in trade here for many years
in connection with Hon. R. C. Johnson, under the style of M. Hazeltine
& Co.; he afterwards removed to Boston and did a large and successful
business until his death, in Boston, Dec. 5, 1843, at the age of thirty-eight.
Maj. Chase came to the village and commenced business as watch-repairer,
jeweler, gun and locksmith in the wooden building which stood opposite
the Eagle Hotel. Mr. Wm. O. Poor, having purchased the stock of W.
& J. T. Poor, apothecaries and druggists, opened a store opposite the
same hotel, at the sign of the mortar; the same mortar, now more than
half a century old, wonderfully improved by age, hangs over his store
door on High street. Nathaniel M. Lowney, Esq., having been appointed
Register of Probate of the new county removed to this place from Frankfort
and opened an office at No. 6 Phoenix Row. Thomas H. Carr came here
from Lubec and on the 27th of November became landlord of the Maine Hotel,
succeeding Col. Stanley. He continued to be its landlord until 1829,
when it ceased to be a public house.

During the larger portion of the year there was a society styled
the Belfast Debating Society. Its meetings were well attended and the
discussions of the questions before it were almost uniformly very creditable
to the parties participating in them.

At the annual spring meeting the Selectmen, Clerk and Treasurer
of the last year were re-elected. The sum of $1,500 was raised for
the support of schools; $400 for support of paupers; $60 for ringing
the bell; $500 for the payment of debt; $300 for incidental expenses,
and $3,000 in labor on the highways. The duties paid by retailers of
liquors for licenses, amounting to about $300, was appropriated for
the support of paupers, a very significant appropriation.

At the annual fall meeting Ralph C. Johnson, Esq., was elected
Representative. The Gubernatorial vote was nearly unanimous for the
incumbent, Gov. Lincoln. The great struggle was on the election of
Register of Deeds and Treasurer for the new county. The whole number
of votes thrown was 256. The candidates were George Watson, Manasseh
Sleeper, Wm. Barns, Henry Cargill, and Nathaniel Patterson of this place,
Frye Hall of Hope and Isaac Adams of Unity; no choice was effected.

At the next trial the candidates were Messrs. Watson, Sleeper, Barns, Hall and Patterson; number of votes thrown, 272; no choice. Under the provisions of law, Ralph C. Johnson, Esq., was appointed County Treasurer by the Court of Sessions.

The whole number of houses and stores in the town at this date, according to White's History, was four hundred and fifty. The number of deaths during the year was twenty-nine--a fraction less than one in a hundred of the estimated population. Three of the deceased had reached a very advanced age, viz: John Burgess, 93; Wm. Cunningham 92; Jane Covil about 90.

CHAPTER XXII. (1828.)

This year, 1828, was an uneventful one to the people of our town generally, but not to the compiler of these annals, who on the 15th of October announced to the public that he had commenced the practice of his profession at No. 13 Main street in a room over the store occupied by F. A. Lewis; the fate of that building has heretofore been told.

There was a custom in those days called "wetting the sign." Perhaps no explanation of the term is necessary now; in a few words it was this; any person commencing business, without regard to profession or occupation, was expected to invite the community, especially his acquaintances, to partake of some refreshments when his sign was raised; the omission so to do was regarded as evidence of extreme penuriousness. On the afternoon when the compiler's sign was raised and while the painter was making it fast to the building, his friends, not few in number, gathered in a shop in the vicinity of his office and partook of the refreshments usually provided on such occasions. On going out to look at the sign it was discovered that the painter inadvertently--perhaps intentionally--had omitted a very important letter; as a consequence the sign was taken down, the missing letter supplied, and upon being put in place the next day it was "wet" again in the presence of a still larger assemblege.

On the 8th of January, Thomas Pickard, proprietor of the Eagle Hotel, announced to the public that he was in occupation of the premises as landlord, Mr. Appleton having left in December previous, and that he should "keep his larder well supplied with the best provisions the market afforded and his bar with all kinds of choice liquors." As an antidote for the bane referred to in the latter part of the foregoing announcement, Doctor Chamber's remedy for drunkenness, which was seized on with avidity by many who lacked the moral strength to resist the tempter, was rapidly growing in public favor. It was a powerful medicine but failed to prove a remedy for the disease for which it was prescribed. The dealer in medicine made his profit from the sale of it but it did not materially diminish the profits of the rumseller. Mr. Pickard continued to keep the hotel until April, 1829.

On the 12th of March the last number of the Belfast Gazette was issued, and on the 19th the Waldo Democrat appeared to fill the vacancy; it was the first newspaper here to raise the Democratic standard. It advocated the election of John Quincy Adams and, so far as type and ink could avail, consigned Andrew Jackson to perdition.

There was a daily mail stage this year between this place and Augusta, leaving Augusta every day, Sunday excepted, at noon and arriving here at 8 p. m.; leaving here at 9 a. m. and arriving at Augusta at 5 p. m. There was also a daily mail between here and Thomaston and a tri-weekly to and from Bucksport. The fares were from here to Augusta $2.50, to Thomaston $2.00, to Bucksport $1.50.

Two buildings were destroyed by fire this year. On the 16th of October a building owned by Hon. Thomas Marshall which stood on the site of the building now occupied by Clark and Fernald, marble-workers, was burned. It was a building about which clustered many pleasant associations, it having once been the publishing office of the Hancock Gazette and the book and stationary store of Mess. Fellows and Simpson, its publishers. The school-girls of those days remember it as the place where they were wont to go to purchase their pens, ink and paper, and the boys of those days equally well remember it as the place where they were wont to go to meet the girls. It is the place now where grave-stones are made; but not to mark the graves where the hopes and loves of half a century ago have long lain buried.

On the night of November 28th a saw-mill on Wilson's stream, as it was then called, owned by Hon. John Wilson, was burned. There was no more angling for trout at the tail of that mill; prior to that time it had been one of the favorite localities on the stream. Many a "fry" have the boys had in its immediate vicinity who were themselves long

since "food for worms," or who now walk with canes and have learned
not to be indignant when they are called "old men."

The schooner Mechanic, Isaac Clark, master, which ran for many
years as a packet between this place and Boston was launched on the
11th day of December from the yard of Messrs. Haraden & French near
the late Foundry and Sash Factory.   The schooner Albert, John Shute,
master, was launched in the year previous.   They were both as much in
advance of the coasters which had been plying between the same ports,
in style of finish and accommodations, as the steamer Cambridge is in
advance of an ordinary steam-tug.

A sad casualty occurred on the Albert on the night of February
11, 1829.   She was lying at Bishop's wharf, now Lewis', loaded and ready
to sail for Boston, when she was discovered to be on fire.   All efforts
to extinguish the fire was unavailing until she was scuttled by boring
holes in the run when she soon filled.   Two young men, part of the crew,
both residing here, Thomas Reed, Jr., and George W. Merriam were suffocated
and burned to death in her forecastle; their bodies were found lying
at the foot of the stairs.

The Belfast Debating Society and the Waldo Club, an association
of a similar character and object, were both in flourishing condition
this year.   The discussions in both took a wide range; from the question
"whether the substituting of bank paper for specie had been productive
of more good than evil" to the question "ought old bachelors to be taxed
for the benefit of old maids."   It was the custom to take the sense
of the meeting, at the close of the discussion, by ayes and noes.   At
the meeting at which the question last named was discussed a majority
of those whose names were called were bachelors, old or young; but the vote
was almost unanimous in favor of taxation.   One of the members who was
suspected of being on the brink of matrimony caused no little merriment
by replying, when called on to vote aye or no, that he was "on the fence";
a position occupied about that time by a large portion of our local
politicians.

December 25th was a great day for "sportsmen."   A lot of turkeys
were "distributed" at the Spa and a still larger lot of turkeys, chickens
and geese were "exposed to marksmen in the rear of Mr. Frothingham's
meeting-house," according to the advertisement; "refreshments" also
were provided.   Rum, gunpowder and the Gospel were slightly mixed on
the occasion.

This year, after a long and virulent contest which embittered the
personal relations of many respectable members of the community, Waldo
Avenue was located from the McKeen school house, or the McMillan house,
terms used indiscriminately at the time, to Bridge street.   The opponents
of the road favored a location from the point above named to a point
near the house of George W. Bruce; the house now occupied by Messrs.
Walton and Harriman on High street beyond Field's hill.   The Avenue
was not continued from Bridge to Main street, its present terminus,
until 1830.

At a meeting held November 3d for choice of Presidential Electors
the vote was for Adams 195, for Jackson 79.   The result was a surprise
to the Waldo Democrat, for in the month of June preceding the "Jackson
party" in this place, so far as was known, consisted of--ONE!   He was not a
man possessed of the mesmeric power of which some men have of rallying
hosts around the banner they fling to the breeze;--on the contrary he
was a man of repulsive manner and with few personal friends; but he
was honest, doubtless, in his conviction, for he was in the war of 1812
and personally acquainted with Gen. Jackson.   Some of the mad wags of
the village, who cared as little about who should be the next President
as they did about the mystery of the Aurora Borealis resolved to have
some sport out of his idiosyncrasy, as it was regarded.   They accordingly
notified a meeting of the "friends of Andrew Jackson" to be held at
the Court house, at which several vigorous Resolutions were passed and
a contribution was taken to defray the expenses of the campaign.   On

looking into the hat it was found to contain one-half pistareen, equal
in value to a dime of our present currency, a four pence half-penny,
one cent, and a handful of pieces of tin about the size of a dime; the
half pistareen was the contribution of the "Jackson party"!

On the next morning an old horse belonging to the individual referred
to was found, moored head and tail, in front of No. 3 Phoenix Row, painted
with stripes like a zebra and the words "A. Jackson." Whereupon the
Committee elected at the meeting held at the Court-house published an
advertisement in the Democrat, illustrated with the picture of a jackass,
the substance of which was as follows: "The Jackson Committee of Belfast,
feeling themselves highly insulted by the coalition, in painting and
otherwise disfiguring the noble animal rode by the "Hero" at the battle
of the Horse-shoe, offer the funds raised for other purposes, for the
detection of the perpetrators of the daring outrage committed on Monday
night last. The Committee entertain no doubt but Clay is at the bottom
of this! It is indeed a full and decided proof of the corrupt bargain
and sale!" The only signature attached was "Jackson Committee." The
"bargain and sale" referred to was the alleged coalition between Clay
and the friends of Mr. Adams which resulted in the election of the latter;
one of the battle-axes used in the Presidential war then raging.

It was not then dreamed by those who laughed at the boys' frolic,
that the Jackson party of one would grow to be seventy-nine by November
then next; still less that they themselves would be roaring, ramping
Jackson-men within the next twelve-month; yet such proved to be the
fact; one of the illustrations of the truth that "we know what we are,
but know not what we may be."

Among the business men who came here this year, not now living,
or residing here, was Charles Goodwin, who opened a dry goods store
in No. 1 Pickard's building, next door to the Eagle Hotel; when he left
here he went to Portland. William Center, "from Boston," opened a store
of the same kind at No. 3 Phoenix Row; he afterwards removed to a wooden
building which stood on the site of Dr. Moody's store; when he left
this place he went to Brunswick to reside. John S. Ayer, now resident
in Bangor, opened a store for the sale of English, W. I. and Domestic
Goods, at No. 11 Phoenix Row. A new firm under the name of P. & E.
T. Morrill, consisting of Philip and Ephraim T. Morrill, was formed;
both of them are dead.

Nathaniel C. Bishop, better known as Cony Bishop, was keeping a
lottery office here this year. He was a simple, inoffensive man, with
a heart free from guile; as a natural consequence in a community constituted
as ours then was, he was made the subject of many a rough practical
joke, which amused the community but reflected no credit on the perpetrators
of them. Although a vender of lottery tickets he did not lack "the
vision and the faculty divine;" witness the following from one of his
advertisements:

"Did you ever drop in to see Bishop
 The man who sells fortunes so many?
He'll show you the way you can fish up
 A purse full of gold for a penny."

He subsequently removed to New York where he acquired a reputation
by no means enviable and died since this year began. An account of
the tragic-comical scene at his burial, in which his widow was the principal
actor, and the post-mortem examination of his body has recently been
the rounds of the newspapers.

In the fall of the year, the Village School District purchased
the lot of land next southerly from the Town Hall, or the old Court
House, and voted to erect thereon a brick school-house of sufficient
dimensions to accommodate four hundred children, that being about the
number then attending school.

At the annual spring meeting Bohan P. Field, James McCrillis and Samuel Gordon were elected Selectmen; Nathaniel H. Bradbury, Clerk; Thomas Marshall, Treasurer. At the annual fall election there was a very spirited contest in the matter of election of County Senators and Member of Congress; the highest number of votes thrown on any ticket was 348. William Stevens, Esq., was elected Representative to the Legislature.

CHAPTER XXIII. (1829.)

This year opened with extremely cold weather; the mercury standing at 13 degrees below zero at 8 o'clock in the morning, at zero at noon, and 12 degrees below at nine in the evening. Mrs. Phoebe Sager issued here "Last Call" to her customers, as she was "to leave Belfast in ten days positively;" it would have been better for her, if there is profit in length of days, had her ten days notice been ten years.

On the 21st of January the Waldo Democrat, after a lingering sickness of forty-five numbers, died and "gave no sign." On the sixth day of February the Republican Journal, White and Rowe, Publishers rose from its ashes. The publishers announced in their prospectus that the political character of the paper was to be decidedly democratic and that it would never hesitate to propagate republican sentiment. What would the Republican Journal of this day and the Progressive Age say, in view of the modern definitions of the terms democrat and republican, to sailing under such a flag!

On the morning of February 29th two wooden buildings on Main street, on the site of the brick stores now occupied by E. and L. Robbins and Robert F. Clark, were burned; they were occupied on the first floor as stores, on the second as lawyers' offices. A small building just southerly of them, occupied as a shoe-maker's shop, was torn down to stop the progress of the fire in that direction. A brick store occupied by Peter Osgood and Company standing on the site of the store occupied by Albert C. Burgess, was the barrier in the other direction. The "town pump" was out of order at the time; had it not been the fire would have been confined, probably, to the store where it originated. The only other building in town burned this year was the house of Shepherd B. Blanchard, near the easterly line of the town; the fire occurred in the morning of December 30th.

The inauguration of President Jackson, which occurred on the fourth of March, was celebrated here by the firing of cannon, ringing the bell, patronizing the bar of the Eagle Hotel, and other testimonials of rejoicing. Although there were but seventy-nine who voted for him in November previous, when the dark cloud of "coffin handbills" lowered in the east, there were hosts of devotees to "hail the rising sun."

The corporators named in the Act incorporating the "Waldo Agricultural Society" met at the Court House March 27th and organized by the election of Ebenezer Everett, Esq., of Montville as President, and the late James White, Esq., of this place as Secretary. Hon. Ralph C. Johnson is the only one of the corporators who is now living.

On the 8th of April a newspaper called the Maine Farmer and Political Register made its appearance. In dimensions and typographical execution it was about the same as the Journal then was. Benjamin F. Bond and Edward Palmer were its publishers. Mr. Bond was of Hallowell and by trade a printer. He came here from Castine, where he had been the publisher of the Eastern American, which died on his hands. He sold his interest in the Farmer to Mr. Palmer August 12th and went to Bluehill, where he commenced the publication of a newspaper called the Bluehill Beacon and Hancock County Journal, which lived nearly two years. He then removed to Boston and died many years ago. Mr. Palmer continued to publish the Farmer until October 1830 when its publication was suspended. He is a brother of our fellow citizen Charles Palmer, Esq. After retiring from the business of publishing, he was for awhile a clergyman; since then he has devoted most of his time to various reformatory movements and published several essays treating of the same and kindred subjects, which have been widely circulated. The views advanced in them have not always been in unison with popular sentiment; but the lucid argument and earnest sincerity with which he has endeavored to enforce them reflect credit alike on his head and heart. He is now residing in New York.

On the same day that the Maine Farmer appeared, David and Asa Eastman, sons of Hon. Thomas Eastman of Palermo, announced to the public that they had taken the Eagle Hotel, succeeding Thomas Pickard, its late

landlord. Under their administration the hotel was kept to the satisfaction
of the public, but as an almost necessary consequence without any great
profit to themselves; the custom of the place at that time was not sufficiently large to create a demand for the rooms of "circumambient construction" from which their predessor anticipated, but failed, probably,
to realize a handsome revenue.

The market price at this time of some of our products was as follows:
butter 12 to 14 cents per pound; cheese, new-milk, 6 to 8; beef 4 to
5; veal 5 and 6; eggs 10 and 12 cents per dozen; potatoes per bushel
33 cents; wheat, good-seed, 1.75; rye 1.00; corn 75 cents; oats 25;
barley 67: boards, merchantable, per M. feet 7.50 and 8.00; shingles,
No. 1., pine and cedar, 2.50 per M.   The ears of potato raisers were
cheered by the announcement that potatoes were selling in Boston for
fifty cents and that freight on them from this port was six cents per
bushel.

On the 5th of May the good people of our village experienced quite
a scare.   The schooner Lucerne, launched about a month previously from
the shipyard of Bishop and Wright, made an excursion in the Bay with
about sixty of our town's people, old and young, on board.   When about
a mile from the Monument, with all sails set, she was struck by a flaw
of wind and upset.   Many on shore were watching her at the time and
three vessels lying at the wharves were immediately manned and started
to her assistance.   The Castine Packet, Captain Skinner, who is well
remembered by many still living, was within a short distance of her
when she capsized and went promptly to her relief; fortunately no lives
were lost.   A short time before the Lucerne went over she swept along
like a bird past the Packet jogging leisurely along under main sail
and jib, and some wag on board of her calling to the bluff old captain
inquired if he was at anchor.   What the reply was is not recorded; probably
a growl.   When he laid his sloop along side the capsized Lucerne a few
minutes later, and discovered that all on board were safe, he exclaimed
in his usual gruff but good natured manner, "By the god's, sir, who's
at anchor now!"

About this time a Club was formed under the name of the Round Robin
Club.   Its object was a mystery to the uninitiated for a long time;
in fact as long as it existed.   The gossips and Paul Prys of the day
were sorely puzzled.   Its meetings, or "convocations" as they were styled,
were regularly notified by the Scribe in the newspapers; sometimes they
were held in the "Outer," at other times in the "Inner Temple."   The
Club continued until its members became exhausted by the pertinacity
of those who were diligently seeking to ascertain its object and the
character of its proceedings and then died.   One old lady asserted unhesitat-
ingly that "no good would come of it," another that "all the young men
who belong to it ought to be oystersized by all the girls," and the
editor of the Farmer perpetrated the conundrum, "Why is a certain Club
in this village like a highwayman?" and answered it by adding, "Because
it is Round Robin."   The compiler of these Annals is the only surviving
member of the Club.

There was no public celebration of Fourth of July in this place
this year, but a large number of the townsmen participated in a Celebration
at Montville, where an Oration was delivered by William Stevens, Esq.,
then a resident here.   In lieu of "the Fourth" we had a "Theatrical
Company," the first which ever came so far east; the Company lingered
and loafed in and about this locality for some two months.   Their performances were in Academy Hall, where Shakespeare and other more modern
dramatists were mercilessly slaughtered.   Richard 3d, George Barnwell,
Pizarro, the Stranger, were among the victims, and "to the great and
enthusiastic admiration of large audiences," as the local journal of
the day said.   Such theatrical performances in these days would be hissed
out of Hayford Hall.   The professional education of the principal tragedian
consisted in playing the "Ghost" in Hamlet; the leading comedian was
the son of a Boston policeman whose acquaintance with theatricals was
limited to turning the foot-lights up and down and aiding the scene-shifters
occasionally.

The "New York Caravan" followed, comprising the African Lion with "full flowing mane and superior carriage," the Royal Tiger "imported in the ship Columbia" the Polar Bear" inhabiting the frozen regions of the North," the Hyena "one of the most blood-thirsty animals that inhabits the forest, "Dandy Jack and pony, the Dog-faced Baboon and a collection of monkies; admittance 12 1-2 cents. The general impression in the community was that it was the cheapest concern of the kind, in every sense, that had ever visited us.

Several buildings were erected and vessels built this year. Among the buildings were the county jail and jailer's house, the brick school house on the common, the brick block at the corner of Main and Church streets, built by Hon. Joseph Williamson, now occupied by A. D. Chase, Augustus Perry and others, the fire-proof brick block on High street, also built by Mr. Williamson, now occupied by H. L. Lord, the Eastern Express Company, Geo. R. Sleeper, and others, the brick store on Main street now occupied by E. & L. Robbins, built by Hon. William Crosby, on the site of one of the wooden buildings burned in February of this year. The schooner Samuel was built at the shipyard of Haraden & French, and the schooner President Jackson in a shipyard at the Head of the Tide.

The corner stone of the jail was laid on the 26th of June by the contractors for its erection, Messrs. Jeremiah and Joseph Berry. Under it were deposited copies of the local papers, the Journal and Farmer, and a bottle of "Old Jamaica," prepared for the purpose, would have been, but from some hitch in the machinery the laying of the corner-stone was delayed so long that the contents of the bottle evaporated. It was shrewdly suspected that some young attorneys at law, who were inspecting the premises at the time with a view simply of ascertaining what the accommodations were to be provided for the unfortunate criminals who might be sent there, knew more about that bottle and its contents, than they were disposed to tell. The building was of stone, thirty by twenty and a half feet in dimensions, and two stories high; the walls of the lower story were two feet thick, of the upper eighteen inches. At the November Term of the Court of Sessions the building was accepted and notice given that on and after the 23d day of the same month it would be used and occupied as the common jail in and for the County of Waldo. Nathan Heywood was the first jailer. It continued to be used as the county jail until 1851, when it was demolished and a new one erected.

The first occupants of the brick block at the corner of Main and Church streets, were James W. Webster, who occupied the store on the corner, Dr. Moody, who occupied the room over it, and Messrs. Chase & Sibley, who occupied the store next beyond it. The first occupants of the fire-proof block were Mr. Williamson, its owner, Judge Johnson, R. B. Allyn, Esq., H. O. Alden, Esq., the Clerk of the Courts, Register of Deeds, Register of Probate, and the Post Office. The first occupants of the store on Main street, were P. R. Hazeltine on the first floor, and William G. Crosby in the room over it.

Several important business changes occurred this year. John S. Kimball and H. G. K. Calef, formed a co-partnership under the name of Kimball & Calef, and commenced business on the wharf now known as Lewis'-- the firm was dissolved in November, 1831. Mention has heretofore been made of Mr. Kimball; Mr. Calef is now and has been for many years residing in Boston. The law firm of Wilson & Stevens was dissolved; both of them have been already mentioned; a more extended notice of Mr. Wilson will hereafter appear. Noyes P. Hawes came, bought out the old book store of W. R. Simpson, and offered for sale at No. 17 Main street, the store now occupied by Woods, Matthews & Baker, a large assortment of books and stationary; the supply was entirely beyond the demand. He also established a "circulating library," far beyond anything that has since existed here in pecuniary and literary value. It contained between six and seven hundred volumes, and was in receipt of twenty reviews and other periodicals. Additions were made to it as valuable

and popular works issued from the press.   Dr. Richard Moody came here
to reside; his office was in the room now occupied by Cox & Field.
The firm of Whittier (David) & Patterson (Edward) was dissolved; the
former died here in 1849; the latter at sea, in 1833.   The firm of Chase
& Sibley--Nathan W. Chase and Reuben Sibley--was formed and commenced
business in store No. 9 Main street.   On the dissolution of the firm
Mr. Chase removed to Bangor, where he died many years ago.

At the annual spring meeting, Bohan P. Field, James McCrillis and
Samuel W. Miller were chosen Selectmen; N. H. Bradbury, Clerk; Thomas
Marshall, Treasurer.   The following sums were raised: for support of
school $1200, of paupers $400, for fencing burying-ground $100, ringing
the bell $50, incidental expenses $550, to be expended on roads $300
in money and $3000 in labor.   A third trial for election of Representative
to Congress took place; the whole number of votes thrown was 323; the
candidates were Joshua W. Hathaway, Leonard Jarvis, Samuel Upton, Philip
Morrill, Jere. O'Brien and John G. Deane--no choice was effected.

At the annual fall meeting the number of votes thrown on the gubernatorial ticket was 519; the candidates were Jonathan G. Hunton and Samuel
E. Smith.   The contest was a hard and very bitter one; the plurality
for Smith in this place was 139.   Peter Rowe, Esq., was chosen Representative to the Legislature.   Another trial, being the fourth, to elect
a Representative to Congress resulted in no choice; an equally unsuccessful
trial took place on the 30th of November.   The candidates were Joseph
Williamson, Esq., of this place, Jarvis, Upton and Deane; Messrs. Hathaway,
Morrill and O'Brien having left the field.   At the sixth trial, in the
spring of the next year, Leonard Jarvis, Esq., of Ellsworth was elected.

There were forty deaths in town during the year; eight were drowned
and three burned to death.   Three had lived more than four score years.
Among the deceased were Capt. Robert Emery, Dr. William Poor and John
Angier, Esq.; brief biographical sketches of them will be found in the
succeeding chapter.

CHAPTER XXIV. (1829.)

On the morning of February 21st, Capt. Robert Emery, one of our worthiest and most respected townsmen, was drowned in Portland harbor, aged thirty-five. He left here for Boston as passenger on the schr. Washington, which was compelled by a heavy storm to run into Portland. While lying at anchor she was run into by a large brig, and her crew and passengers supposing she was about to sink left her and went on board the brig. Capt. Emery returned to the schooner for the purpose of saving his papers, which were in a portable desk in the cabin. He succeeded in finding the desk and threw it onto the deck of the brig, but in the attempt to get on board himself he slipped, the deck being covered with snow and sleet, and fell overboard. It was supposed at the time that he was killed by being crushed between the two vessels. On the 27th of May following his body was found near Fort Preble, was carried to Portland and buried with the usual solemnities.

Capt. Emery was a native of Boothbay and came here to reside about 1808. He was a half brother of Mr. Eben Pierce and of the late Capt. David Pierce, both of this place, and the father of Messrs. James and Rufus H. Emery now residing in Bucksport, of our fellow citizen Mr. Robert Emery and of the late Thomas B. Emery, of the Custom House, who died in October, 1871, in the forty-fifth year of his age. His wife was a daughter of George Hopkins, who came here in the early part of this century and built the house at the intersection of Main and High streets, well known for a long time as the Huse Tavern or Maine Hotel.

At the time of his decease Capt. Emery had been engaged for several years in the business of furnishing outfits for vessels employed in the fisheries. He occupied a store, store-houses and cooper's shop in which he manufactured barrels, located on Puddle Dock. He was an honest man, a useful member of society, a prominent member of the Masonic Fraternity, and his loss was deeply deplored in a wide circle of friends.

Doctor William Poor, father of our fellow citizen Mr. William O. Poor, died on the 17th of September, aged fifty-three. He was born in Andover, Mass., from which place he removed to Andover in this State and thence to this place in the autumn of 1815. His first place of residence here was a building which stood at the junction of Main and Washington streets, burned in the great fire of 1865, on a portion of the site of which the store now occupied by Mr. F. M. Lancaster stands. In that portion of the building standing on Main street he kept for sale an assortment of drugs and medicines; the portion standing on Washington street he occupied as a dwelling. The compiler of these annals was then a boy just commencing the study of the Latin language, and like many other boys deeply conscious that he knew a great deal more than many men did who were old enough to be his grandfather; and he vividly remembers now the quiet humor with which the doctor asked him one day to translate the Latin inscriptions on the drawers containing his drugs and medicines, and kindly smiled at the blunders he made in his translations. The last residence of the doctor was the house near the intersection of High and Miller streets, now occupied by Mr. Martin P. White. For many years after his decease it was known as the "Poor house."

Doctor Poor was a quiet, unassuming man, fond of his profession and of scientific pursuits. There was a certain quaintness in his character and conversation which strongly reminded those who knew him of the physician of the then olden time. He was eminently a humane man; a warm sympathizer with all who were sick or suffering;

"He had a tear for pity, and a hand
Open as day for melting charity."

He was compelled by failing health to abandon to some extent the practice of his profession, but retained in a remarkable degree the respect and confidence of his patients to the close of his life.

In this connection an anecdote of the late Isaac Allard Esq., father of our fellow citizen of the same name, a man of "infinite jest, of most excellent fancy," most kindly remembered by all who knew him, occurs to the compiler. Mr. Allard was occupying the house formerly occupied by Doctor Poor; just south of it laid the old graveyard, on a portion of which now stands the Baptist meeting house, "Where are you living now, Allard?" said a friend from the country, meeting him one day on the streets; "in the Poor house--next door to the graveyard," was the reply.

On the 18th of November died John Angier, Esq., father of our fellow citizen Mr. Oakes Angier, aged fifty-one; his widow died the last winter, 1874, in the ninetieth year of her age. Mr. Angier was born in Bridgewater, Mass., and came here in 1803; in 1804 he married and purchased of Paul Giles the house on High street opposite the westerly end of Phoenix Row, which he occupied during his life and which his widow occupied after his decease. In the same year he built a wooden store, which was burned in 1823, on the site of the brick store now occupied by his son, and which he occupied to the date of his decease. He was one among the many originals we had among us in the early part of the century; such as are always to be met with in a newly settled country. He was an impulsive man, thoroughly independent in word and action, no time-server, no hypocrite, not always as particular in his choice of language as comports with a refined taste, but with a heart as full of kindness as ever throbbed. Ardent in his attachments, he was, as is usual with men of his temperament, equally ardent in his aversions.

No man ever lived here who thought less of what is usually denominated "position" or shrunk more sensitively from official responsibility. He had been here but a few years when a meeting of the west-side militia, in whose ranks he was enrolled, was held for the election of officers. On counting the votes it was ascertained that he was elected Captain. "What?" he exclaimed when the announcement was made, "What? me captain! Who in ---- ever heard of a Captain Angier! I won't be!"

He was a man of rather impetuous temperament and when excited was prone to indulge in language more forcible than he ordinarily used; more so sometimes than was actually necessary to give force and energy to his utterances. It might have grated harshly on the ears of some; not so with those who knew him well, and knew that, to use the homely adage, "his bark was worse than his bite." While on a journey to the eastward his attention was attracted to a cow feeding by the roadside to which he took a sudden fancy; he bought her and sent her home by packet. A few days after her arrival she strayed from the pasture in which she was kept. After an ineffectual search for her through the village he despatched one Hamilton the next morning to hunt for her. H. was not distinguished for power of intellect or celerity of movement. As the day wore on and he did not make his appearance Mr. Angier grew exceedingly nervous pacing the platform in front of his store, back and forth, until he was almost of fever heat. Endurance had almost ceased to be a virtue when just before sunset H. made his appearance slowly descending Field's Hill, his usual companions, three dogs, at his heels. As soon as he came within hailing distance Mr. Angier screamed to him at the top of his voice, "Where's the cow?" H. stopped in his tracks and screamed back, "Squire, what color is your cow?" "Blue, by ----!" was the reply yelled back. "Blue, like Angier's cow" became a by-word which even to this day is heard in our streets.

It is not to be inferred from the foreoing that Mr. Angier was at all times impetuous; numerous instances are remembered when all around him were in a high state of excitement and he was cool and self-possessed. He had at one time a favorite horse which he purchased down east. He was driving down Main street, crowded with ox-teams, when the horse became frightened, wheeled suddenly, dashed wildly through and among the teams and concluded the performance by overturning the sleigh and scattering its fragments in every direction. Mr. A. fortunately retained possession of the reins; an excited crowd gathered about the wreck;

he was the only one who was cool and collected. "Well," said he, addressing the horse, "you've done it now, haven't you? Do you know what I'll do with you? I'll send you back to Miramichi!"

Although not a man of quiet temperament he possessed a large fund of quiet humor; many amusing anecdotes are remembered of him in this connection; one must suffice. A dancing school was an unknown institution here until several years after the commencement of this century. The first one was kept by a teacher who came here from Peterboro, N. H.; the second and third teachers came from the same place; it seemed as if Peterboro was destined to be the source from which all our dancing-masters for successive generations were to be derived. When the first elephant ever here was exhibited her keeper was accustomed to put her through a clumsy perforance which he called dancing. He was engaged in that performance when Mr. A. went in to look at her. "What is she doing?" he asked a by-stander. "Dancing," was the reply. "Dancing, is it!" said he. "O! I see; come from Peterboro', didn't she!"

It was not unusual with him to assume an air of harshness which was altogether alien to his nature. He contracted one fall with a man to manufacture for him a lot of shingles of certain quality and dimensions for a special purpose and paid for them in advance. The day came and passed when by the terms of the contract the shingles were to be delivered at his store. Several weeks afterwards the man made his appearance but without the shinbles. Mr. A. began to upbraid him in the severest language for dishonesty in not fulfilling his contract. "Squire," said the man as soon as he found a chance to put in a word, "I didn't mean to cheat you; I'll show you why I havn't made your shingles"--and began taking off bandage after bandage from his right hand until it was fully exposed, fearfully swollen, the flesh nearly gone from the thumb--the bare bone sticking out--a most pitiable sight. "-- --!" exclaimed Mr. A.; "d--n the shingles! Harry," calling to his clerk, "put up twenty pounds of pork for this man." "But, Squire, I can't pay you"--"Put him up twenty pounds of flour, Harry." "But, Squire I--" Mr. A. took another look at the swollen hand, the fleshless thumb--"Fifty pounds, Harry, and two gallons of molasses, pound of tea,--" "But Squire, I'll never be able--" and the poor unfortunate fairly broke down, tears streaming from his eyes, while Mr. A., his own eyes fast filling, rushed for the door screaming, "Harry! fill his pung up with anything he wants;" pausing a moment at the threshold, "go over to the house and tell 'em to give you some dinner while Harry's putting up your things. D--n the shingles! Don't say shingle to me till your thumb gets well."

Is not the heart of the reader of the foregoing narrative, briefly and imperfectly told, prompted to adopt the language of Sterne in his Tristram Shandy? "The accusing spirit, which flew up to heaven's chancery with the oath, blushed as he gave it in; and the recording angel, as he wrote it down, dropped a tear upon the word and blotted it out for ever."

Hamilton, the man who hunted all day for the blue cow, was himself somewhat of an original, but is particularly remembered for the involuntary ride he took one evening. He had contracted the very bad habit of adjusting all domestic difficulties by beating his wife. Some of our villagers who were unwilling to bide the law's delay constituted themselves court and jury and brought in a verdict that the next time Hamilton gave his wife a beating he should have a rough ride. They had not long to wait; the shrieks of the poor woman gave notice a few evenings afterwards that he was at his devils work. He was thereupon seized, placed astride a split cedar rail taken from a fence near by, and treated with a free but rather rough ride through the principal streets in the village and back to the starting point. The rail was found the next morning in a conspicuous place near his house with a card nailed to it bearing the following inscription:

"Hamilton's horse is long and thin--
When he beats his wife he'll ride him agin."
It proved to be his last experience in "riding on the rail."

CHAPTER XXV. (1830.)

With this year commenced another decade in this century. According to the national census, then just completed, the population of Belfast was 3077; an increase of 1051 since 1820. That population consisted of 1585 males, 1492 females. There were 68 persons between the ages of 60 and 70; 24 between 70 and 80; 12 between 80 and 90, and one over 90. The population of the county was 29,784; the population of the towns composing it was 22,002 in 1820; showing an increase in ten years of 7928.

The cauldron of reform, social, moral and political was bubbling violently here and hereabouts this year. Anti-gambling, anti-liquor-drinking, anti-running-in-debt, anti-litigation, anti-extravagance-in-living and various associations of similar character were organized. Alas for poor, weak human nature!--it was but a brief time before the witches who mixed the broth were detected in appropriating it to their own private use. A natural feeling of disgust followed the detection; reaction followed, and as a usual consequence the good cause suffered. Scheming, selfish men, and honest but deluded fanatics, strove to seduce the honest and credulous into the worship of strangeGods; but the result was then--as it always will be until human nature is sanctified--the deceived and led astray soon became iconoclasts, the strange Gods were cast down and broken to fragments and the priests officiating at their altars were tramped in the dust.

Early in the year the "Belfast Lyceum" was organized and a Constitution adopted. The first officers elected were William Stevens, Esq., President, Oliver A. Washburn, Vice-Pres., Justus Hurd, Sec. The first article in the Constitution declared that its object was "the diffusion of Useful Knowledge;" it contemplated the purchase of "a library and apparatus to illustrate the sciences." Its meetings were held semi-monthly through the year. Among the Lecturers residing here were Rev. William Frothingham, Hon. Alfred Johnson, Jr., Doctors Monroe, Alden, Moody and Barker, William Stevens, William G. Crosby and Albert Bingham, Esquires, Mess. Samuel Upton, H. G. K. Calef, Edward Palmer and Francis H. Upton.

There were two fires this year, neither of them in the village. The dwelling house of Nicholas Jefferds at the Head of the Tide was burned, with the greater portion of its contents, in the afternoon of the 28th of January; the dwelling house of Nathaniel Patterson on the east side of the river was burned in the evening of Sunday the 19th of July. There is a tradition that the fire was discovered by a young man and woman who were hanging on a front gate on the west side of the river about 10 o'clock of the evening above referred to.

The noon mail of the 8th of February brought the intelligence that Jonathan G. Hunton had been declared by the Legislature to be the Governor elect. There had been a long and bitter contest in the organization of the Legislature which occasioned the delay. The friends of the successful party were of course jubilant; the afternoon was devoted to ringing the bell, firing cannon, et cetera, and in the evening the Eagle Hotel, then kept by the Mess. Eastman, was illuminated. The 22d Washington's Birthday, was commemorated by a military ball.

Hiram O. Alden, Esq., was appointed Post Master on the 18th of January, to succeed Hon. Joseph Williamson, and on the first day of February he removed the Post Office from the building on Main street nearly opposite the Eagle Hotel, where it had been kept for many years, to a room in Williamson's fire-proof block, erected the year before; the westerly portion of the store now occupied by Mr. George R. Sleeper. It continued to be kept there until the latter part of April, 1833, when it was removed to rooms in the westerly end of the old Telegraph building, next to the Eagle Hotel.

Early in the year the county offices were removed from chambers in Phoenix Row, where they had been from the organization of the county, to Williamson's fire-proof-block, where they remained until the present Court House was completed. The Probate Office was in that part of the

block now occupied by Mr. Henry L. Lord as a store, the Clerk's Office
in the room over it, the Registry of Deeds in the room opposite now
occupied by Judge Williamson. In the rear part of each room there was
a fire-proof vault in which the records and all valuable papers connected
with the office were kept.

The Fourth of July was celebrated by the Belfast Light Infantry
with an address by Albert Bingham, Esq., and a dinner at the Eagle Hotel,
at which a number of guests were present. The Hotel was kept at that
time by one of the brothers Eastman, and Mr. Chas. Rogers. After leaving
here Mr. Rogers was interested in several public houses in different
sections of the country and finally became a prominent employee at the
St. Nicholas in the city of New York. On the morning of December 31,
1866, he was murdered while removing some snow from the yard of the
house he was then occupying in New York. No satisfactory reason for
the commission of the crime has ever been assigned and the murderer
has never been detected.

On the 7th of August, for the first time, a Democratic Convention,
pure and undefiled, was held at the Court House. But a small portion
of the "bone and muscle" composing it is now extant. Of those deceased
all save a few were comforted in their last days by the reflection that
they had "always voted the Democratic ticket." Enough, however, fell
from the faith to verify the old adage that "times change and we change
with them."

The old meeting-house on the east side of the river, built in 1792,
which had not been occupied for some years as a place of stated public
worship, was sold this year at public auction by vote of its proprietors.
It was sold for fifty dollars, and soon afterwards was demolished.
Benjamin Kelley was the purchaser.

On the 20th of October the Rev. Ferris Fitch was ordained Pastor
of the First Congregational Church and Society connected therewith;
the exercises were as follows.

Introductory Prayer by Rev. Mr. Loper of Hampden. Sermon by Rev.
Mr. Shepard of Hallowell. Charge to Pastor by Rev. Mr.Blood of Bucksport.
Right hand of Fellowship by Rev. Mr. Thurston of Prospect. Address
to the people by Rev. Mr. Adams of Camden. Concluding Prayer by Rev.
Mr. Duncan of Jackson. The ordination services were at the Unitarian
meeting-house. Mr. Fitch continued to be Pastor until May 15, 1832,
when the connection between him and the church was dissolved by mutual
consent. His successor was Rev. Silas McKeen, who was installed February
28, 1833.

On the 3d of November the first number of the Maine Workingmen's
Advocate made its appearance. It was of the same dimensions and typographical appearance as the Maine Farmer, the last number of which issued
in the previous month. John Dorr, Esq., who was for several years a
book-seller here, and whose store was in the wooden building at Nesmith's
Corner on the site of the one now occupied by Mr. David Lancaster, was
its proprietor. Mr. Dorr is still living in Augusta. Its political
character was anti-Democratic. At the close of its fifth volume its
name was changed to the American Advocate, the publication of which
ceased in April, 1836. During the greater portion if not the entire
period of the publication of the first named paper it was under the
editorial management of Samuel Upton, Esq., a prominent politician of
the day. He resided a while in Bangor after leaving this place, and
removed thence to Washington, where he died in 1842, aged fifty-seven.

During a heavy gale in the evening of December 15th, about twenty
rods in length of the east bridge, built in 1806, was swept away; no
attempt was made to repair it but a new bridge was built on the site
of the present free bridge as narrated in a previous chapter.

At the annual spring meeting Peter Rowe, James McCrillis and Samuel
W. Miller were elected Selectmen, Joel Hills, Clerk, succeeding Mr.
Bradbury who declined a re-election having held the office nearly five
years, and Frye Hall, Treasurer. There were sixty-six officers elected

at that meeting; of that number there are but five now living. At the fall meeting Governor Hunton and Hon. Samuel E. Smith were the candidates for gubernatorial honors; the vote here was 236 for Hunton, 287 for Smith.   There was a ballot also for member of Congress; 222 votes were cast for Leonard Jarvis, 179 for John S. Kimball and 55 for Samuel Upton. Peter Rowe, Esq. was re-elected Representative to the legislature.

On the morning of April 6th Mr. Joseph White of Salem, Mass., was found in his bed murdered by a blow on the head and several stabs in the body.   It was not known or suspected that he had an enemy, and there were no indications that any property had been stolen from the premises. The commission of such a crime in one of the most moral and quiet towns in New England, without any apparent motive of revenge or plunder, produced a sensation of astonishment and horror which spread far and wide.   A committee of Vigilance was appointed and upon information communicated to them several suspected individuals were arrested; among them Richard Crowninshield, Jr., and his brother George; Richard was eventually found to be one who committed the murder; he did not wait for trial by a jury but committed suicide on the 15th of June by hanging himself in his cell.

Before the occurrence of this event, however, and while the Committee were pursuing their investigations, Mr. Joseph J. Knapp, a respectable merchant residing in Salem, received a letter mailed at the post-office in Belfast, May 12th, signed Charles Grant, Jr., asking for a loan of $350,--alluding to many circumstances connected with the murder--and concluding with the threat that if the money was not sent before the 22d, he (Grant) "would wait upon him with an assistant."   The answer to the letter was to be addressed to the writer at "Prospect, Me."

Mr. Knapp was the father of Joseph J. Knapp, Jr., for whom as subsequently appeared the letter was intended.   He was of course unable to comprehend its import, and immediately placed it in the hands of the Committee of Vigilance, who promptly adopted measures for the arrest of its writer.   Joseph G. Waters, Esq., of Salem and George Jones, a Police officer of Boston, were sent here, arriving just before the 22d, the time limited for the reply to it.

There were then two Post-offices in Prospect; the one in that part of the town which is now Searsport village was called the West Prospect office.   An officer was stationed at this and the other office and also at the office in this place and letters were sent to each of the offices addressed to Charles Grant, Jr.   On the 24th a young man called at the West Prospect office and inquired if there was a letter for him, giving the name of Charles Grant, Jr.; he was immediately arrested by the officer stationed there and brought here; on this arrival it was at once discovered that the self-styled Charles Grant, Jr., was John C. R. Palmer, Jr., whose parents were residing here, and who was convicted some two years before of breaking into Mr. Wetherbee's store and sent to the State's Prison; from which he had been discharged some five months.

He admitted that he wrote the Grant letter and stated that he was in Salem on the third of April, three days before, and again on the ninth, three days after the murder, that on the second of April a proposition was made to him by one of the Crowninshields to assist in the murder and to receive therefor a third part of $1000, which Joseph J. Knapp, Jr. had offered to pay to the person who should commit the act; that he declined the proposition and left Salem the next evening; that when he returned, on the 9th, one of the Crowninshields told him that the dagger used in committing the murder had been melted.

Upon the strength of this information Joseph J. Knapp, Jr. and his brother John Francis were arrested; both of them were afterwards convicted and hung; George Crowninshield was acquitted.

From the confession made by Joseph J. it appeared that through the agency of his brother John Francis he procured the murder to be committed by Richard Crowninshield.   His wife was a relative of the murdered man, and the expectation that she would inherit a portion of his estate, should he die intestate, was the motive which prompted the murder. He had himself stolen from the iron chest of Mr. White a few days before the murder a paper purporting to be his Will; it proved to be an old Will which had been revoked by one of later date which was found in the chest after the murder.

CHAPTER XXVI. (1831.)

Doctor John Scollay Osborn died on the thirteenth of February of this year, aged sixty. He was married in 1791, being then but little more than twenty-one years old, and very soon afterward came here from Epsom, N. H. He was the first one of his profession to make this place his home. Soon after coming here he built a house in 1795, on the site of the present American House, which remained there until the Eagle Hotel was built; it was the first framed house erected on Main street; particular mention was made of it in an earlier chapter. Some years after it was erected he built another house on the site now occupied by the Court House, to which he removed and in which he resided until his decease.

In the early part of his professional life Dr. Osborn was quite too much attracted by gay and jovial associations, and the good cheer usually accompanying them, to be a close student of books; but he was a careful observer of cause and effect, and from his largely varied experience in practice became a skillful physician. About 1815 a marked change took place in his modes of thought and conduct. To the great surprise of his townsmen he made his appearance in our streets one day, for the first time, arrayed in Quaker garb, using the language peculiar to that sect, and announcing that he had joined the Society of Friends; to their faith he held fast to the close of his life. He was ever after spoken of as the "Quaker Doctor" or, being a man of small size, as the "Little Quaker." There was no other one of that sect residing here.

He was a man of irascible temperament, but with the change of religious faith came a wonderful self-control and power to resist and overcome that natural infirmity. It was not in his nature to form warm personal attachments, but once formed they were constant; his friendship never grew cold whatever might be said or done to chill it. He continued in the practice of his profession until near the close of his life, and for many years after his death it was not unusual to hear, in seasons of sickness, from the lips of those whose family physician he had been for years, the language of regret that the "Little Quaker" had left them.

On the evening of the Annual Fast the members of the Belfast Lyceum commemorated their anniversary at the Unitarian meeting-house, with music by the Belfast Musical Society, an address by William Stevens, and a poem by Wm. G. Crosby, Esquires. Among the lecturers of this year, residing here, were Doctor J. P. Alden, Richard Moody and Thomas C. Barker, William H. Burrill and Otis Patterson, Esquires, Messrs. James W. Webster, Francis H. Upton, Charles H. Upton and Nathaniel C. Bishop.

In the latter part of March there was a very severe rain storm and freshet which was more destructive of property than any which had occurred for many years. The highways in this vicinity were rendered almost impassable, except on foot or horseback, for several days. Nearly all the bridges on the road to Camden, the bridge at North Searsmont and several others on the Augusta road, and every bridge of magnitude between this place and Bangor, were destroyed in whole or part. The bridge at the Head of the Tide was entirely destroyed. The highways in every direction were seriously impaired, and for several days the mails were transported, principally, on horseback.

The old east bridge having become impassable, as described in a previous chapter, a ferry was established just easterly from it by the Court of Sessions in the month of May, and James Langworthy was appointed Superintendent. The ferryman's office was "the old centre store on Bishop's (now Lewis') wharf." The ferry was discontinued when the present bridge was completed. To what extent it was patronized is among the things unknown. It is certain, however, that the income derived from it was not sufficiently large to induce the worthy deacon to retire from active business.

On the seventeenth of June died William White, Esq., aged forty-eight. He was born in Chester, N. H., graduated at Dartmouth, and completed his legal education in the office of Hon. John Wilson in this place. He commenced the practice of his profession in Union in 1809. He removed thence to Thomaston and to this place in 1813. He was twice married. His first wife was the daughter of the late Phineas Ashmun, Esq., of Brooks, his second of Samuel Gordon, Esq., who once resided in this place at the Head of the Tide. He was a brother of the late Hon. James White; no descendant of his is now residing here. At the time of his decease he was the owner and occupant, and had been for several years, of the house on Main street now occupied by Mr. Alden D. Chase.

Mr. White was a sound lawyer and skillful debater. A venerable member of the Bar of this county who was present at the last argument he ever addressed to a jury speaks of it as one of the most brilliant and logical to which he ever listened. He retired from practice several years before his decease and devoted much of his remaining years to literary pursuits. One of the fruits of his literary labor was the History of Belfast of which mention was made in the first chapter of these annals. His last days were saddened by disease, mental and physical, and his sun went down in clouds; but he is remembered as a nobly, generous-hearted man, as the possessor of talents of the highest order, and as one who under a different combination of circumstances might have maintained a position in the front rank of his profession.

The Journal of June 29th announced that a balloon was "about being constructed in this place, if a sufficient sum should be raised by subscription to meet the expenses; that it would ascend on or about the Fourth of July, and that it was thought that a dog or cat would be sent up with it." The money was raised, the balloon constructed, and the day, July 13th at 7 p. m., fixed for its ascension. The people assembled at the time announced on the common in front of the Unitarian meeting house to witness the performance; but the balloon caught fire before it was fully inflated and neither dog, cat, or balloon ever ascended.

On the 29th of June the frame of the North Church was raised. It was noticed in the newspapers of the day as an indication of an improved public sentiment, that no ardent spirits were used at the raising." The building was not completed until in the early part of the next year. Col. Benjamin S. Dean of Thomaston was the architect, Joel Hill, Benjamin Houston, Samuel Upton, Luther Gannett, Martin Gilmore and Frye Hall were the building committee. The proprietors of the building transferred to the church Jan. 25, 1836, the control of it and of the site on which it stands, in accordance with the original design of the builders, and the church accepted the trust. A sale of the pews was commenced on the 9th day of February 1832, and on the 14th the house was dedicated. The Dedicatory Prayer was offered by Rev. Dr. Gillett of Hallowell and the sermon was preached, from 1 Tim. 3.15, by the Rev. Ferris Fitch, Pastor of the society. The dedication was followed by a "three days meeting." The bell was rung for the first time for religious services on Sunday the 22d day of January. The vestry in the basement was finished and first opened for devotional meetings on the evening of July 20, 1836. Up to the time of the erection of the house the society had occupied as a place of worship the conference room, mentioned in a previous chapter, which was erected about 1823.

The Belfast Light Infantry under command of Captain Mixer celebrated the Fourth of July by an excursion to Castine in the schooner Mechanic, Capt. Isaac Clark, leaving here at 7 a. m. and arriving back at 9 p. m. They were accompanied by a large number of their townsmen and were very pleasantly and generously entertained by the Castine Artillery, Captain Rogers.

During the month Carl Blisse, the Tyrolese Vocalist, gave a series of entertainments at Phoenix Hall. It was our first practical acquaintance with the style of melody which was at that time, perhaps still is, peculiar to the Swiss. He was followed in due time by other musical artists claiming to be natives of that country--the Swiss Bell-ringers included.

About 2 o'clock in the morning of August 9th an alarm of fire called out the firemen and people generally. An out-building of the Academy was found to be in flames; the work doubtless, of some sportive incendiary.

The Waldo Agricultural Society held a "Farmer's Festival" on the 26th of October. The exercises at the Unitarian meeting house consisted of music, prayer by Rev. Mr. Frothingham and an address by Hon. William Crosby. The places of exhibition were the court-house and the common west of it. The largest premium awarded was three dollars: the smallest seventy-five cents.

Among the business changes during the year were the dissolution of the old firm of Haraden and French, and the formation of the new firm of Ayer and Whiting; consisting of John S. Ayer, who is now living in Bangor, and Barzilla G. Whiting, who left here many years ago; he ultimately went to California. They occupied store No. 11 Phoenix Row, the same now occupied by Charles D. Field. Mr. Haraden continued at the old stand on the Ladd and Morrill wharf, now owned by W. B. Swan & Co. and Mr. French opened a store on French's wharf, now Frederick's; both stores were burned in the fire of 1873. Noyes P. Hawes purchased the book-bindery of Cook Kimball, and Mr. Edwin Fenno came here from Augusta to take charge of it; in March following he became the proprietor of it; he married a daughter of Rev. Mr. Frothingham and is now residing in Washington, D. C. John W. Wales, druggist and apothecary, who had for several years occupied a store which stood on the site of the one now occupied by Albert C. Burgess, sold out his stock in trade to Mr. Samuel Locke; in March following Mr. Locke sold out to Dr. Hollis Monroe; all of them are dead. The dry-goods firm of Center (William) and Howard (Daniel) was dissolved; they were occupying at the time a wooden building at the intersection of Main and High streets where McClintock's block stands; Mr. Center continued the business at the same place and Mr. Howard resumed his former business of cabinet-making. Solyman Heath, Esq., now residing in Waterville, afterward Reporter of the Decisions of the Supreme Court, came here and opened his office at the corner of Main and High streets, and Nathaniel Patterson, Jr., Esq., late Judge of the police court, removed from this place and opened a law office in Prospect, now Searsport. Nathaniel Woodman, hatter, commenced business in the building on High street now occupied by the Belfast Livery Company; he subsequently removed to Searsport; he died many years ago.

At the annual spring meeting Peter Rowe, Hugh Ross and Samuel Otis were chosen selectmen, James W. Webster, Clerk, Frye Hall, Treasurer, Messrs. Ross and Otis declined the office, and at a subsequent meeting Nathaniel M. Lowney and Henry Goddard were elected in their stead. At the same meeting an amended code of by laws as adopted. It provided among other things for the election of a Board of Police officers, to consist of five, and made it part of their duty "to take up and imprison for the term of twenty-four hours any and all persons who shall at any time be found drunken and disorderly about the streets of the village disturbing the peace and good order thereof."

At the annual fall meeting the whole number of votes thrown on the gubernatorial ticket was 386, being 137 less than the number thrown the year preceding. The candidates were Hon. Samuel E. Smith and Hon. Daniel Goodenow. Hon. Thomas Eastman of Palermo and Hon. Jonathan Thayer of Camden were elected county Senators, the first elected after Waldo became a Senatorial District. James W. Webster, Esq., was elected Representative to the Legislature.

CHAPTER XXVII. (1832.)

The Waldo Bank, the first one established here, was chartered February
11th, this year, with a capital of fifty thousand dollars. Of the eighteen
corporators named in the charter, three only are now living; Hon. Ralph
C. Johnson, Hon. Hugh J. Anderson, and Hiram O. Alden, Esq. The meeting
of the stockholders for organization was held on the 24th of March.
Ralph C. Johnson, Joseph Williamson, Rufus B. Allyne, Thomas Marshall
and Hugh J. Anderson were chosen directors; Mr. Johnson was elected
President and Mr. Alden, Cashier. The Banking-room' was in Williamson's
Fire-proof-block in the easterly half of the store now occupied by George
R. Sleeper. Early in the next year Mr. Alden resigned the office of
Cashier; James White, Esq., was appointed to succeed him and the office
was removed to Number 6 Phoenix Row, at which place it was kept, Mr.
White continuing to be Cashier, until March 20th, 1838, when the charter
was surrendered and the Bank ceased to exist, save for the purpose of
closing its affairs. The investment did not prove a profitable one
for the stockholders; not, however, by reason of any lack of fidelity
or integrity on the part of the directors. The Bank was on the high
tide of prosperity when the wildland-speculation fever attacked the
community. Money was flowing freely; almost every other man whose notes
were in the market held a bond or a deed of one or more townships of
wild land, and was regarded as not only solvent, but rich; his paper
of the deepest rose-colored tint. When the fever subsided, and the
bubble burst, the Waldo Bank, like a great many other banks and individuals,
found that there was a much larger quantity of suds than soap in its
safe.

At the annual spring meeting held on the 8th of April, Nathaniel
M. Lowny, Henry Goddard and James Gammons were elected Selectmen, James
W. Webster, Clerk, Frye Hall, Treasurer, and Arvida Hayford, Jr. Collector
of Taxes. For the first time Road Commissioners were elected in lieu
of Highway Surveyors; the Commissioners elected were William Salmond,
Hugh Ross, Nicholas Jefferds, Nahum Hunt, and Joshua Adams. Several
young men, very old ones now, who during the last year had been caught
in the trap matrimonial, were elected hog-reeves. One of them distinguished
himself during his official term by arresting a swine of portentous
magnitude one evening and finding himself with a litter of pigs on his
hands before reaching the town-pound.

The monies raised at this meeting were as follows; for support
of schools $1500; of paupers, $500; incidental expenses, $500; ringing
the bell, $50; payment of debts, $700; repairs of highways, $300; in
labor and materials for same purpose $5,000. At the same meeting a
vote was passed authorizing the town treasurer to purchase a sufficient
number of Greenleaf's Map of Maine to furnish one to each school-district
in the town.

On Sunday the 20th day of May the Rev. Ferris Fitch pastor of the
North Church, preached his farewell discourse to his parishioners, the
connection existing between them having been dissolved on the 15th.

This year had its freshet as well as the year proceeding; it occurred
in the month of May. The streams in this place and vicinity rose very
suddenly and a large number of bridges, mills, dams, were swept away.
Among them, in this town, the bridge across little River near the grist-mill
then known as Eastman's, the bridge with stone abutments on the main
road at the Head of the Tide, together, with a sawmill and several dams
on the same river, and in Searsmont three bridges on the northerly route
to Augusta, and the bridge near Hazeltine's mills on the southerly route.
The mail from the west due here on the 20th did not arrive until the
23d, and then on horseback. The rain storm was a very severe one, lasting
eight days. The fall of rain through the summer of this year was unusually
large.

The Fourth of July was observed in the due form and with public
services at the Unitarian Meeting-house. The declaration of Independence
was read by Rev. Alfred Johnson and an oration delivered by Solyman
Heath, Esq.

There was no snow on the ground on the 16th of June, but that did not prevent a gentleman then residing here from taking a sleigh-ride driving his "gray mare Kate," from Rowe's corner, where Hayford Black now stands, to Brown's corner in Northport and back again, on a wager of one hundred and fifty dollars that he could not perform the feat in one hour; he won the wager by doing it in fifty minutes. The event is doubtless remembered by some still living as "Tom Pickard's sleigh ride."

On the evening of August 6th and 7th a concert was given at the Court House by Miss C. J. Clark, a minute specimen of female humanity, twenty-nine years old, three feet and three inches tall and "well-proportioned;" at least, so the village newspapers said. She hailed from Virginia; probably came from some distance from there; but her singing was, to say the least, of a very respectable order.

A democratic Convention was held at the Court-house on the 18th of August at which Joseph Williamson, Esq. of this place and Ebenezer Knowlton, Esq. of Montville were nominated for County Senators, Frye Hall of this place for County Treasurer, and Ephraim Fletcher, Esq. of Lincolnville for Presidential Elector, General Thomas Sawyer, Jr. of Brooks, was Chairman of the Convention, and Albert Bingham, Esq. of Unity and Henry W. Cunningham, Esq. of Swanville were the Secretaries. The nominations were made, of course, "with great unanimity;" but what a terrible rattling of political dry-bones there would be should a majority of the delegates present at that Convention meet in a democratic convention held in these days! There was an anti-Masonic Convention held here on the same day.

On the first day of September the copper-fastened schooner Comet, 128 tons burthen, was launched. She was a famous packet in her day and for many years plied between this port and Boston under command of Captain James Young. She was in existence and still running a few years ago. Captain James Young resided on the east side of the river. He was a faithful, worthy, honest man. He died at Calcutta Oct. 23, 1858, aged 58. At the time of his death he was master of the ship Lady Blessington.

At the annual fall meeting, held Sept. 10th, the whole number of votes thrown on the gubernatorial ticket was 450; of this number 261 were for Smith, Jackson candidate, 148 for Goodenow, Clay candidate, 42 for Carlton, Anti-masonic candidate. Messrs. Williamson and Knowlton, nominated at the Democratic Convention, were elected Senators, and James W. Webster, Representative to the Legislature. Frye Hall was elected County Treasurer. At the Presidential Election, November 8th, the vote was for Jackson 311, Clay 182, Wirt (anti-masonic) 22.

On the 11th of September the announcement was made to the public that the new East bridge, the present one, was passable for travellers; a few carriages had passed it in the month preceding.

The 18th of the same month was a pleasant June-like day, and Muster day! The most conspicuous objects were a few men on horse-back, bedizened with gold and silver lace and feathers, and a large number of men on foot who looked as if they wished the d----l had the men on horseback. There was the usual amount of drinking, swearing, rows and dances; a beautiful page in the history of morality, it was not thought to be at time, for the perusal of the then rising generation.

The Waldo County Agricultural Society held its annual Cattle-show and Exhibition on the 24th of October. The exhibition of manufactured articles, vegetables &c. was in the town hall; the cattle-show was in the rear of it. The largest premium awarded was ten dollars; the smallest fifty cents. An address was delivered at the Unitarian Meeting-house by Hon. Alfred Johnson, Jr. The number attending the Show was unusually large, and the animal and vegetable productions exhibited were in every particular very creditable to the farming community.

There was quite an excitement and no little alarm here during the summer occasioned by the appearance of the Asiatic Cholera in some of

in some of our large cities and the apprehension that it might visit
this section of the country.   There was a general "house-cleaning" of
streets, gutters, cellars and cess-pools under the supervision of the
Board of Health.   Quarantine regulations were established under which
all vessels arriving from any port where the disease was supposed to
exist were prohibited from coming to the wharves, or anchoring within
six hundred yards of low water mark; vessels having on board emigrants
from any European port were subjected to a quarantine of thirty days
before landing their passengers.   A vessel commanded by Capt. Josiah
Simpson, Jr. arriving from New York about the 17th of July was put in
quarantine for twenty-hours.   It is believed that she was the first
vessel ever quarantined in this port.   Various articles recommended
by physicians as a preventive or remedy, such as laudanum, camphor,
chloride of lime &c. rose suddenly in their market value.   The pestilence
prevailed to some considerable extent in New York, there were a very
few cases in Boston, or questionable character, but none in this place
or vicinity.

The Lyceum still kept up, but the public mind was so engrossed
with the pending Presidential canvass that it lingered rather than lived.
Few lectures were given; the exercises before it were principally of
the nature of discussions; the literary powers of the village were beligerent.

Among the buildings erected this year were the brick stores on
Main street now occupied by F. A. Follett and Robert F. Clark.   The
first occupant of the one first named was James B. Norris, who after
leaving this place resided in Augusta where he was for several years
a deputy sheriff.   From there he went to Boston where he held an office
for several years in the Custom House and died not many years ago.
The first occupant of the other store was Charles F. Angier, who died
in this place April 12, 1859, aged forty-nine; he was a brother of Mr.
Oakes Angier.

The following is a list of the vessels built and registered or
enrolled here during the year; schooners Scioto, 140 tons, Two Sons,
65 tons, Nantucket, 125 tons, Commerce, 136 tons, Wm. and Harris, 65
tons, Comet, 128 tons, Alhambra, 126 tons, Margaret, 125 tons, Capital,
124 tons.

Among the business changes of this year were the following.   The
firm of John Haraden and Son, composed of the late John Haraden and
his son Daniel was formed and commenced business in a wooden building
which stood at the intersection of Main and Church street, on the site
of the Savings Bank.   It was removed in 1850, when the brick building
now standing there was erected, and is now the dwelling of Mr. E. C.
Hilton on Church street nearly opposite the Court House; the firm was
dissolved the same year.   Mr. Haraden, Senior, died March 15, 1867 in
his eighty-eighth year.   F. N. Holway, who had previously been in trade
in Montville with Samuel Atkins, Esq., under the style of F. N. Holway
and Co., came here in October and commenced trade in the northerly half
of the Nesmith store on the site now occupied by J. C. Thompson.   After
leaving this place he went into trade in Syracuse, N. Y., where it is
supposed he is still living.   Liberty B. and John E. Wetherbee, brothers
and natives of Brookfield, Mass., commenced business here, under the
style of L. B. and J. E. Wetherbee in the store then No. 17 Main street,
now occupied by Woods, Matthews and Baker, in the month of December.
When the copartnership terminated, John E. left and was for some years
resident in Cleveland, Ohio, where he died about 1847.   The senior partner,
Mr. L. B. Wetherbee, remained here in trade until his decease in October
1860 aged sixty-three.   He was a quiet, unobstrusive, worthy member
of society.   The firm of Jackson (Samuel, Jr.) and Quimby (William)
which was formed in November 1830 was dissolved in April.   During that
time they occupied a wooden building erected in 1830 by James and Samuel
B. Miller which stood on the site of the easterly portion of the Custom
House.   At the time of the erection of the Custom House it was occupied

by the late Samuel S. Hersey; it was removed to a site on Church street about where the store now occupied by Pote and Quimby stands. Soon after the great fire of 1865 it was again removed to the corner of Main and Washington streets and now constitutes a portion of the building occupied by F. M. Lancaster. After the dissolution of the firm Mr. Quimby continued to occupy it until 1838. Mr. Jackson died at Portsmouth, N. H., October 9, 1838 aged thirty-eight.

The number of deaths in the town this year was forty-seven.

CHAPTER XXVIII. (1833.)

The winter of this year was a very severe one. No rain fell until the twelfth of March, but in its stead came a series of snow storms. The extreme cold weather and deep snow operated almost an embargo on all teaming. Cordwood reached the unusually high price of $3.50 per cord; there was much suffering among the poor in our village for lack of an adequate supply of fuel. The market value of some of the produce of the country was as follows: corn per bushel $1.12, rye, $1.25, butter per pound, one shilling, pork, round hog, per pound 5 to 7 cents; beef, on the hoof, 5 cents, hay per ton, $8 to $10, potatoes per bushel 25 cents. Early in May abundant supplies came in the form of salmon, shad and alewives; the price of salmon was at first as high as 15 to 17 cents per pound, but soon fell to ten cents.

On the 23d of January the schooner Bellino, Joseph Simpson, Master, Edward Patterson, Supercargo, sailed for Gibralter and ports on the Mediterranean. On her return passage she touched at Havana; on her eighth day from that port, the 19th of July, Mr. Patterson died after a few days sickness and his body was committed to the ocean sepulchre in which his father, Capt. Robert Patterson, was entombed less than three years before. The Bellino arrived here on the 27th bringing the sad intelligence of his death; sad not only to his kindred but to the community at large, of which he was a general favorite and very promising member. His age was twenty-eight.

Rev. Silas McKeen was installed Pastor of the First Congregational Church and Society on the 27th of February. The services were as follows: Sermon by Rev. Mr. Root of Dover, N. H., Installing Prayer, Blood of Bucksport, Charge, Pomeroy of Bangor, Right-hand of Fellowship, Thurston of Searsport, Address to Church and Society, Tappan of Augusta. The pastoral relation between Mr. McKeen and the church and society was dissolved November 16, 1851. He removed from this place to Bradford, Vt., where he was installed as Pastor of a church in that place and where he still resides. His successor was Rev. E. G. Cutler who was installed in 1842.

On the evening of April 19th a fire broke out in the third story of a large wooden building called the Babel, on the westerly side of Main street about where the stores now occupied by Mess. Manly E. Dodge, William C. Marshall and B. C. Dinsmore and Son stand. The fire had considerable progress when it was discovered. There was a prevailing sentiment that if "the town pump had been out of order," and the fire-engine absent on an excursion, and the building as a consequence, burned to its foundation, there would have been no cause for regret except so far as its owners sustained a loss by its destruction. In October following there was a change of ownership and it was razed by cutting out the lowest story thereby reducing it from three stories to two. It was finally destroyed by fire in 1846.

In the night of the 16th the sawmill at the Head of the Tide known as Cochrans Mill was burned; the fire was occasioned, it was said, by friction of the machinery.

On the 12th of June the old Merriam house so called which stood on the easterly side of Main street, as then located, at its junction with Front street, was removed to the site on Front street, as now located, which is now occupied by the stores of Newell Mansfield and F. A. Knowlton. After its removal it was occupied for several years as a store by P. and E. T. Morrill. It was built, prior to 1805, by Wiggin Merrill; it was burned in the fire of 1865. The removal was regarded as a great improvement as it almost entirely obstructed all view of the water from Nesmith's Corner. It was owned previous to its removal by John Merriam, Esq., once a member of the Court of Sessions of the county and a prominent magistrate of the place. He subsequently, about 1822, built a large wooden house on Main street on the westerly portion of land now owned by the United States; it was known in later days as the Carney house. About the time the United States made its purchase this house was purchased by Hon. James White and removed to the premises on Waldo Avenue then

occupied by him, now occupied by Mr. Alden D. Chase. Mr. Merriam died
in this place in April 1832, aged fifty-five.

On the 20th of June the steamer Connecticut bound to Portland touched
here, bearing back from Bangor a host of land-speculators who had been
there to attend a large sale of public lands. Those were the days when
a large portion of the population in our large towns were all agog on
speculation; when men ordered "pumpkin pine" for breakfast, "granite
quarry" for dinner and supped on "water-privileges." The steamer stopped
several hours to afford opportunity for passengers to take a look over
our insignificant little village. We had but one livery stable then
and its proprietor put money in his purse by letting his horses to the
strangers to ride round the place; "one dollar an hour for a horse"
was his price, "provided you don't sweat him." There was no great danger
of any such result, except as the consequence of very immoderate driving,
for the weather for the entire month was unusually cold. The prevailing
winds were from the northeast, there were quite heavy frosts several
nights, we had one terrific thunder storm and two hail storms. Among
the passengers on the Connecticut was William P. Fessenden, Esq. then
a young man, since then one of Maine's ablest representatives in the
Senate of the United States: the compiler well remembers how much his
old college classmate enjoyed his ride through our streets and his frequent
injunction to the driver of the horse, "don't sweat him!"

The Cholera excitement of the last year prevailed during the summer
portion of this, but in a modified form. There was excitement, of course,
because the pestilence was in closer proximity to us--several cases
being reported at Bangor--but it was shorn of its worst element of terror.
The Board of Health resumed its duties and gave public notice that on
the 15th of July the dwelling houses and premises in the village would
be visited by them "in order to ascertain their situation as it respects
cleanliness." The "dwelling houses and premises in the village" were
never in more cleanly condition, probably, than they were found to be
on the day announced for the visitation of the Board; it is quite questionable whether they have ever been in so good condition since that day.
The pestilence passed by us and with the first fall frosts all was quite
on the Passagassawaukeag.

The only public celebration of the Fourth of July in town was at
the Head of the Tide. The exercises of the day were the reading of
the Declaration of Independence by Mr. Lewis F. Shepard, an oration
by Mr. Henry W. Piper, and "a sumptuous dinner prepared in Colburn's
best style" at the Maine Hotel, kept by Captain Henry Colburn. At the
close of the dinner a large number of toasts were given, which were
"received with loud cheering, and rounds of applause, accompanied by
the discharge of artillery; no ardent spirits were used at the table."
The officers of the day were Capt. David Otis, President, Major John
Russ and John McClure, Esq., Vice-presidents, Col. Moses Woods and Mr.
George U. Russ Marshals.

During a portion of this month there was an exhibition at Phoenix
Hall of "16 was figures as large as life!" Among them were the pirates
Gibbs and Wansley, "with the ropes about their necks by means of which
they were launched into eternity," the Deputy Marshall who greased the
ways, the Siamese Twins, and Joseph J. and John F. Knapp the conspirators
in the Salem murder. The proprietors assured the public in their handbills
that there was "nothing in the exhibition to create undue excitement
in the most timorous minded person." Admittance 25 cents; after a week's
trial reduced to 12 1-2.

In October Bailey Pierce, Esq. from Frankfort, became landlord
of the Eagle Hotel, succeeding Thomas Pickard. He was afterwards Clerk
of the Courts for the County of Waldo, during the first administration
of Governor Kent. He died in 1844 aged fifty-seven.

At the annual spring meeting James W. Webster, James McCrillis
and Peter H. Smith were elected Selectmen, James W. Webster, Clerk,
Frye Hall, Treasurer. At the annual fall meeting the whole number of

votes thrown on the gubernatorial ticket was 391; for Dunlap, regular Democratic candidate, 217; for Smith, irregular, 51; for Goodenow, Clay candidate, 69; for Hill, antimasonic, 54. There was no choice of Representative until the fifth trial was had. Charles Gordon, who afterwards resided in Searsport, who was for many years Cashier of the Searsport Bank, a worthy, excellent man, was the regular candidate of the Democratic party; James W. Webster was the candidate supported by the disaffected Democrats and the largest portion of the "Opposition." Salathiel Nickerson was the candidate of the anti-masonic party. At the last trial there were 470 ballots thrown; Mr. Webster received 236 and was elected. It was regarded at the time as a triumph over the "Office-holding Junto," so styled.

In the night of Saturday the 12th of Oct. a southeasterly gale commenced and increased in violence until nearly noon of the next day. The tide was higher than had been known here since the September gale of 1815; great destruction was caused among our wharves; several of them were washed almost entirely away. Large quantities of lumber, cord-wood and bark were swept away from them and lost. Acres of the shores on both sides of the river when the tide went out were strewed with lumber of various kinds and the debris of the destroyed wharves. The Monument on Steel's Ledge was swept off; the wooden portion of it with the Spindle on it came sailing up the river and grounded: its future history has been heretofore told. There was a large number of vessels in the river and harbor, but they all rode out the gale without sustaining any serious injury.

Among the vessels built, registered or enrolled at this port during the year, were the schooners Temperance, 137 tons, Isabella, 129, Oneco 128, Moro 124, Cassius, 120, Catherine, 107, Marengo, 99, and the Bahama, 83 tons.

The Lyceum still maintained a lingering existence until near the close of the year, when an attempt was made to infuse vitality into its meetings, the attendance on which had been growing small by degrees and beautifully less, by holding them on Sunday evening, when it was supposed they would be more fully attended; the experiment was tried but did not succeed. The Lecturers during the year residing here were Rev. Silas McKeen, Doctor Richard Moody, William Stevens, Solyman Heath and Samuel Upton, Esq., and Mr. George Childs. In December a Mr. Harrington delivered one or more Lectures on the Steam-engine and Astronomy, illustrating his lectures with models of a steam carriage and railway, and a transparent Orrery.

Some time during the summer a large collection of wild animals was exhibited here under the name of the National Menagerie. Among them were four tigers; two of which were said to be domesticated. In confirmation of the fact the keeper was accustomed to enter their cage and play with them. He presumed once too often on their good nature. He went into their cage one day, just before the close of the annual tour, a whole man, and was taken out, as soon as it could be done with safety, in pieces; the result, doubtless, of the "exuberant playfulness of the domesticated tigers" on that occasion.

There are few, probably, of those who read this chapter who have not seen the poor old shattered fragment of humanity who recently "shuffled off this mortal coil," after vibrating between the public poor-house and the sources of private charity for more than half a century--Asa Day. There are comparatively few, however, who know how or when he acquired his military title of Lieutenant. He was indebted for it to the strong feeling which had for some time existed against the system of militia trainings and which may be regarded as having culminated this year: in this locality at least. He was elected Lieutenant of the Militia Company, as the speediest method of rendering the organization so ridiculous that no man of military propensities would accept the position of an officer: the method adopted answered the purpose and the Company soon afterwards lost its organization.

The Lieutenant was not disposed, however, to wield a barren sceptre. Being in command he ordered his company out on two occasions for election of officers. His order was obeyed with more than usual alacrity and with full ranks; but Bedlam let loose could not have played wilder pranks than were played on those occasions. In the estimation of those who participated in them the end, probably, justified the means; and this was one of the means adopted to render ridiculous a system which had become almost unendurably odious. Looking back, however, through the sober-hued glasses of more than forty years it cannot but be seen that the motive power was the mental imbecility of an inoffensive old man; too much so to be used for any purpose, least of all for sport. Poor old Day! It cannot be said of him, as has been often said of others as little worthy of the eulogy as he, "he lived beloved and died lamented," but it can be said of him truthfully that all who took note of him in his long, wearisome struggle with old age and penury were glad for his sake when the struggle was over and life's journey ended, although its end was in only a pauper's grave.

Among the business movements of the year were the following: Col. Moses Woods, father of our fellow citizen, Mr. William M. Woods, commenced trade in the store at the Head of the Tide previously occupied by Messrs. S. and W. B. Otis. Col. W. died in May, 1840, aged about forty-one. Nathaniel Wiggin commenced the business of manufacturing boots and shoes in the room over the store now occupied by Augustus Perry; he died in Sept., 1862, aged forty-nine. The firm of Furber, (James P.) and Bean (Joseph) was formed and opened a hat store in a wooden building which stood at the intersection of Main and High streets on the site of the store now occupied by Richard H. Moody. The firm continued during the life of Mr. Furber; he died in 1865, aged fifty-four. A new Iron Foundry was established at Gannett's Mills, on the east side of the river. Luther Gannett, Samuel A. Moulton, both of this place, and Daniel Bates of Boston were its proprietors. Mr. Gannett died at Bridgewater, Mass. about 1865. Mr. Moulton's death has been before noticed. The copartnership existing between the proprietors was terminated in 1835; their successors were Eastes and Kimball. The firm of Kimball (John S.) and Gordon (Samuel A.) was formed and commenced business on Kimball's wharf, now Lewis'. Mr. Gordon continued in trade here for awhile after the dissolution of the firm and then removed to Hallowell, where he died soon afterwards. Mr. Kimball's death has been already noticed.

On the 13th of April Col. Jonathan Wilson of this place was drowned while attempting to pass with his son-in-law, Capt. David Green, from Eastport to Carlow's Island bridge, which he had been building under a contract with its proprietors. The boat in which they were was swamped, their perilous situation attracted the attention of persons on shore who hastened with all possible despatch to their rescue. Capt. Green was taken from the boat to which he was clinging almost exhausted and Col. Wilson was found floating on the surface, buoyed up by a heavy cloak he had on, but life was extinct.

Col. W. was born in Chester, N. H., in 1762. The exact time when he came here is not known, but he was one of the selectmen in 1790. He was elected Town Clerk in 1800 and held that office for thirteen years under successive re-elections. He was the first Representative of the town in the General Court of Mass., having been elected in 1802, and was re-elected for six terms between that date and the year 1813. He was one of the most enterprising among our early townsmen, and to his energy more than any other source probably, was the town indebted for the East Bridge erected in 1805. It was through his instrumentality mainly that the charter was procured and his name stands first on the list of the corporators. He was chairman of the board of managers under whose supervision the bridge was built and was its first toll-gatherer. He was a man highly respected for his integrity, and his death was deeply regretted by the large circle of friends and acquaintances in which he moved.

CHAPTER XXIX. (1834-5)

There were two fires this year.   Just before day-break of January
12th, the toll-house on the easterly end of the east bridge was burned.
About ten o'clock in the morning of the 22d a fire broke out in the
second story of a wooden building nearly opposite the Eagle Hotel, occupied
by John Dorr, Esq., publisher of the Working Men's Advocate.   The fire
was communicated to an adjoining building occupied by Mess. White and
Rowe, publishers of the Republican Journal, in the chambers, and by
Nathaniel Frost on the first floor. Both buildings were entirely consumed,
and the contents of the two printing offices sadly mixed but partially
saved.   The office of the Advocate was removed to a chamber in the old
Babel, and the Belfast Bookstore to a room under it.   The Journal Office
was removed to a chamber in the building on High street now owned by
the Belfast Livery Company.   Mr. Frost re-opened in the store now occupied
by Robert F. Clark, then known as Number 4, Crosby's Building.   Both
the buildings burned were owned by Hon. Joseph Williamson, father of
Judge W.   Before the close of the year he erected on their site the
brick stores now occupied by Mess. John S. Caldwell and Henry H. Forbes.
The first occupants of the one first named were John M. Gould on the
first floor and The Republican Journal in the room over it; of the other,
Daniel Lane, Jr., on the first floor and the Custom House in the room
over it. Col. Lane was Collector at the time.
     Mention has been made of the Belfast Bookstore. In the month following
its removal Mr. Dorr connected a book-bindery with it under the charge
of Mr. H. G. O. Washburn, who came here from Hallowell. He subsequently
became a co-partner with Mr. Dorr and still later the proprietor of
both bookstore and bindery and kept them for some time in the old Nesmith
store at the corner where Mr. David Lancaster's store stands.   From
thence he removed to the brick store now occupied by Mr. M. P. Woodcock,
which he continued to occupy until his decease in 1866, in the 55th
year of his age, leaving a reputation for integrity without spot or
blemish.
     The Belfast Screw Dock was completed and in working order on the
first day of May.   It was located on the easterly side of Holt's wharf
near the westerly end of the East bridge.   Abraham Libby was its first
agent.   It was maintained for several years but was not in the end a
successful enterprise; its last annual dividend of profits was thirty-seven
and a half cents on a share.
     At the annual spring meeting Nathaniel M. Lowney, Isaac Allard
and Joseph Eayres were elected Selectmen, David W. Lothrop, Clerk, for
the first time, Samuel French, Treasurer, and James Y. McClintock, for
the first time, Collector of taxes.   The monies raised were, for support
of schools $1350, of paupers $500, for repairing and building highways
$1400 in cash, and $5000 in labor at $1 per day, for payment of debts
$1300, incidental expenses $500, ringing the bell $50.
     The 2d day of July witnessed the largest concourse of people in
our village which had ever been seen here; attracted by the Menagerie
of Waring, Tufts and Co. which was on exhibition for that day only on
the Common near the old Court-house, and a collection of Wax Figures
on exhibition at Phoenix Hall.
     The 3d brought to our wharves the steamer McDonough from Portland
bound to Bangor with the Portland Rifle Company on board.
     The 4th was celebrated as the anniversary of our National Independence
and of the Belfast Light Infantry by ringing the bells, firing cannon,
an oration at the Unitarian Meeting-house by Col. James W. Webster,
and a public dinner.
     We were permitted to look at the new steamer Bangor on the afternoon
of the 14th as she lay off the mouth of our river for half an hour on
her first passage between Bangor and Boston.   On the 26th, and again
on her return on the 29th, she actually touched our wharf to land and
receive passengers.   She was under the command of Capt. George Barker.
She did not favor us in the same way during the summer; our river was
quite too narrow for the steamer, her captain and his speaking-trumpet
to turn round; it increased in width as passengers from this port increased
in numbers.

Mr. Lewis Bean, father of our fellow-citizens Joseph and Lewis Bean, died on the first day of August, aged fifty-five. He was a native of old York, and came here to reside, with his brother Josiah, father of Captain Andrew D. Bean, about the year 1809. They commenced the business of manufacturing hats in the Babel under the style of L. and J. Bean. A year or two afterwards he erected a wooden building on Main street about on the site of the stores now occupied by E. C. Hilton and Carle and Morrison which he occupied in part as a dwelling; contiguous to it was his hatter's shop. The buildings were burned in the fire of 1865. His brother Josiah built the house on High street now occupied by Martin P. White and another building just westerly from it which he occupied as a shop. It is now occupied as a dwelling. He removed from this place to Brooks about the year 1825 and died there in 1853 aged about sixty-four. Lewis remained here and continued in active business at his original stand until near the close of his life, sustaining to the end an unblemished character for integrity, fair dealing and industry in his vocation.

Captain Hutson Bishop, mention of whom has been heretofore made, died on the sixth of the same month at his house on Church street, the brick house now owned by Governor Anderson, aged forty-two.

A Democratic County Convention was held here on the 9th, and a Whig County Convention at Brooks on the 16th; it was the first Whig Convention held in the county. It was in this year in fact that the Whig Party was born; it died in its twenty-first year.

At the annual fall meeting, September 8th, the whole number of votes thrown was 627; for Dunlap, Demo., 346, for Sprague, Whig, 263, for Hill, anti-masonic, 18. Charles Gordon, Esq., was elected town representative.

Hon. Abial Wood of Wiscasset died at the Eagle Hotel on the 26th of October aged sixty-two. He was one of the Bank Commissioners of the State and was here on an official visit to the Waldo Bank. He completed his examination on Monday, was attacked the same night by bilious fever and died on Sunday morning following. His wife, who survived him, was the widow of Francis Anderson, one of the earliest merchants in the place, uncle of Governor Anderson.

The first noticeable event in the year 1835 was the death of Major Samuel Houston at the age of eighty-two. He was the son of Samuel Houston, one of the original proprietors of the town, who was the successor of John Mitchell as town clerk and captain of the Belfast militia; Samuel Jr. succeeded his father in the office last named. He served in the army during the war of the Revolution and was for a portion of the time a member of Washington's Body-guard. He will be remembered by some still living as the veteran soldier who for many years was wont to contribute to the festivities of Fourth of July by singing the old and favorite song of the soldiers of the Revolution, Washington and Liberty.

During a portion of the months of February and March our harbor was blockaded by ice extending as far across the Bay as Turtle Head. Sleighs passed from the main to the islands. James Y. McClintock, Esq., had the credit of being the first one to venture across from this place; he drove from our wharves to the island and thence to West Prospect, now Searsport. The great body of ice left about the middle of March; there remained a bridge across the river about half a mile in width below the wharves. Some of our enterprising townsmen soon cut a canal through it enabling vessels lying at its outer edge to come up to town. We glorified ourselves greatly over our ship canal of half a mile in length; it continued to be the theme of occasional boasting until February, 1844, when it was utterly dwarfed by the canal seven miles long cut through the ice in Boston harbor to enable the British steamer to go to sea.

At the annual spring meeting Nathaniel M. Lowney, Isaac Allard and Dennis Emery were chosen Selectmen, David W. Lothrop, Clerk, Rufus B. Allyne, Treasurer.

On the 8th of April the steamer Bangor came in, it being her first appearance for the season. She continued her trips regularly through the season between Bangor and Boston, touching at Saturday Cove for passengers bound to and from Belfast. We did not consider ourselves fairly treated, taking into consideration the probable patronage from this place, which according to estimate would average ten passengers for each trip! During August and September the Bangor, Capt. Samuel H. Howes, and the Independence, Capt. Thomas Howes, ran in connection. Each of them made one through trip per week; leaving Boston at 3 p. m. for Portland and Portland for Bangor at 7 a. m. the next day. The fare from Boston to Portland was $3.00; from Portland to Bangor, "and found," four dollars.

The steamer Sandusky, Capt. Seward Porter, stopped here early in July on a trip to Bangor. A hope was entertained that she or some other boat would be put on the route, touching at Belfast; hope was doomed to wait some time before it ended in fruition.

On the 5th of June a Menagerie of beasts and birds from the New York Zoological Institute was here. With it came an omnibus containing paintings of the Conflagration of Moscow, &c., a collection of wax statues and busts, "androides, or animated automatons," &c.; the proprietor was a blind man and had but one arm.

On Sunday, July 12th, for the first time in this place, our ears were regaled with the music of a Church Organ; one having been purchased by subscription and set up in the Unitarian Meeting-house. It was from the manufactory of Mr. Henry Erben, of New York, and cost eleven hundred dollars.   The organist on this occasion was Mr. Frederic N. Palmer, brother of Charles Palmer, Esq., now a practising physician residing in Mass.; Miss Aurelia A. Quimby afterwards wife of Albert Merrill, Esq., of Portland, daughter of Mr. William Quimby, was the first organist permanently employed.   This was the second Organ for which the Society had contracted.   The first one was shipped on the Schooner New Packet at Newburyport, which left for this place in the afternoon of the fourth of June and was wrecked on the breakers off Franklin Island on the morning of the fifth, the light on that island having been mistaken for the light on Monhegan.   In a very few minutes after the schooner struck she was an utter wreck; she and her cargo a total loss.   Her crew and passengers, among whom was Col. James W. Webster who had been to Newburyport to purchase the organ, barely escaped with their lives by climbing up a precipitous rock against which the stern of the vessel was driven; they were hospitably entertained by the keeper of the Light, Mr. Thomas Hanna.   By the terms of the contract with the owner of the Organ it was not to be paid for until it was set up in the Church; the loss, consequently, fell on him. A liberal present was made to him in considera- tion of his misfortune.   The contract price for the organ was six hundred dollars.

Captain Nathan Swan, father of Mr. William B. Swan, died on the 30th of June, aged fifty-two.   Capt. Swan came to the village to reside about 1819; prior to that time he had resided at Poor's Mills.   He was a Deputy under Sheriff Adams, and several of his successors, held various municipal offices, and was captain of the Militia company at the time this place was occupied by the British; he was the first captain of infantry who appeared on parade armed and equipped with a spontoon. Our venerable fellow citizen, Ralph C. Johnson, was ensign of the company at the time.   He established a Bakery in a building which stood on the site of the Sanborn House, and from 1828 until near the time of his decease he kept a restaurant in the building at the junction of Main and Washington streets now occupied by Anson E.Durham.

The celebration of Fourth of July was under the exclusive auspices of the Democratic Party, which held a County Convention here on the same day. The Declaration was read by Albert Pilsbury, Esq., and an oration was delivered by John W. Frost, Esq.; both young men just admitted to the Bar.   Mr. Pilsbury studied law in the office of H. O. Alden,

Esq., Mr. Frost in the office of Judge Johnson. Mr. Pilsbury soon afterwards opened an office in Calais, and Mr. Frost in Bangor. In 1853
Mr. P. was a member of the Executive Council and in the year following
was the Democratic candidate for Governor of the State. He was subsequently
for eight years U. S. Consul at Halifax where he died in June, 1872,
in his fifty-seventh year.   Mr. Frost after leaving Bangor, where he
edited a newspaper for awhile, established his residence in Brunswick,
Georgia.   From thence he removed to New Orleans in 1847, where he was
the editor of the New Orleans Crescent.   In 1851 he became involved
in some political difficulty to which a Dr. Thomas G. Hunt was a party.
It resulted in a duel between him and the doctor; the duel was fought
near New Orleans, and Mr. Frost was killed.   Escort duty was performed
on the occasion of the celebration by the Belfast Light Infantry under
command of Capt. Alexis Morrill, a brother of Philip Morrill, who after
leaving here resided for many years at Norwalk, Ohio, near which place
he was killed by a railroad accident in October, 1872.   There was a
public dinner at the Town Hall prepared by Mr. Herbert R. Sargent, who
died in March, 1848.

On the evening of Sept. 4th the "Wandering Piper," as he was styled,
piped at the Court House; he was apparently about forty years of age,
tall, athletic and a Scot. There was an air of mystery about his movements;
he piped for money but bestowed in charity the greater portion of his
receipts.   One theory was that he was an eccentric nobleman travelling
in disguise; another that he was testing on a wager the hospitality
and liberality of the American people as compared with the people of
some other country. He traveled on his mission, whatever it was, throughout
the Union.   The amount which he had received and expended for charitable
purposes up to the time of his arrival here was said to have exceeded
thirty-five hundred dollars.   Two Female Benevolent Societies were the
recipients of his bounty in this place, to each of which he gave five
dollars.   It is not known that the secret of his pilgrimage was ever
discovered.

During the summer our poeple were all agog on the subject of a
railroad to Quebec. A reconnoisance and partial survey of the route
was made under the supervision of Col. S. H. Long of the U. S. Army
corps of topographical Engineers.   Numerous meetings were held, speeches
still more numberous were made, resolutions adopted and even the prophetic
authority of Scripture invoked to prove that a railroad from Belfast
to Quebec was one of the hidden things to be revealed; the revelation
has been for a long time delayed. It may come at last--"line upon line--
here a little and there a little."

The steamboat Patent arrived here on the morning of September 10th,
having been purchased by a company of our townsmen to ply between this
place and Bangor.   She made her first trip to Bangor on the 21st in
four hours and a half; she was six hours making her return trip.   Her
engine had contracted a very bad habit of "fainting away," as the stage
driver said who ran in opposition to her.   The truth was that she was
an old, worn out, broken down affair, and the whole enterprise resulted
disastrously to all concerned.

Coupled with the foregoing movement was a project to build a steamboat
wharf 500 feet long commencing at the end of Durham's wharf; a little
south from the present upper steamboat wharf.   A company was formed
and money to come extent expended but the project was never carried
out.

On the 29th of September Daniel Webster passed through our village
on his way from Bangor to Wiscasset, tarrying only about one hour; long
enough, however, to have an interview with his old friend and brother
Member of Congress, Hon. John Wilson.   Some of his political friends
learning that he was here set themselves at work making preparations
to give him a salvo of artillery; but he was "o'er the hills and far
away" on the road to Belmont before the "barzen war-dogs" uttered their
first "howl."

    At the annual fall meeting General Apathy achieved a brilliant victory.   The whole number of votes thrown on the gubernatorial ticket was 217; for Dunlap 211, for King 1, Scattering, 5.
    The burying ground, afterwards styled Grove Cemetery, were purchased of Wm. Avery, Esq., this year and a contract made for fencing it.   The number of deaths in town during the years was thirty-eight.

CHAPTER XXX. (1836.)

The conflagrations in this year were as follows. On Sunday evening, January 10th, a fire broke out in a blacksmith's shop in the rear of the Eagle Hotel, occupied by R. M. Monroe and Robert W. Quimby; the building was consumed with all its contents, which were combustible. Between seven and eight o'clock in the evening of October 15th an extensive conflagration occurred in the banking-room of the Waldo Bank; thirteen thousand dollars of its bills were utterly consumed. There were strong suspicions that the directors and cashier were accessory to the act. The bills were all of the denomination of one, two and three dollars, the re-issue of which was prohibited by law as it then was, and hence no serious loss was sustained by the stockholders. In the afternoon of the 25th a one story double dwelling-house situated on the Judge Read farm, on the Northport road, was burned; it was one of the oldest framed houses in town.

Mr. Jonathan White, who came here to reside in 1795, died on the 11th of January, aged sixty-nine; his brother Robert, who came here in 1795, died July 30th, 1840, aged seventy. The lives of these two brothers were so intimately blended that notice of the two in connection seems to be peculilarly appropriate. They were born in Chester, N. H. After coming here to reside they became the owners of lots of land in close proximity to each other, on the Northport road, and continued to occupy them during their lives. They married sister, daughters of the venerable James Patterson, one of the earliest settlers in the town. Jonathan's farm was the one now known as the Pickard place; the one which was purchased at the time of the Quebec Railroad excitement with the expectation on the part of the purchasers that the depot would be located on it; the price paid for it was five thousand dollars. Robert's farm was the one which is now, and has been since his decease, in occupation of his son William B. At the time he purchased there was a log house upon it in which he commenced housekeeping and in which his son, Hon. James P. White, was born. In 1803 he erected the framed dwelling-house recently removed from the site on which his son William B. is now erecting a house. All his children now living reside in this city; at one time they all resided with their several families, seven in number, on the same street. Jonathan erected his house, still standing where it was erected, at a little earlier date. All his surviving children reside here, except his son Jonathan, who resides in Rockland. Their descendants constitute the most numerous family, probably, in town. They were both worthy men and good citizens; faithful in the discharge of their obligations and exemplary in the performance of all the duties devolved upon them.

The "Belfast and Quebec Railroad Corporation" was incorporated March the ninth. There were sixteen corporators named in the charter; the only survivors are Ralph C. Johnson, Hiram O. Alden, Hugh J. Anderson and William G. Crosby. Intelligence of the passing of the act was received nere with most emphatic demonstrations of joy. On the evening of the 11th the Eagle Hotel was illuminated, there was a grand entertainment at which the "solid men" of the town as well as the "young and vigorous" were present, there was a perfect avalanche of toasts and speeches, and steam enough let off, could it have been utilized, to propel a locomotive to the Canada line: or to adopt the phraseology of the day, "from the storm-tossed Atlantic to the placid bosom of the Saint Lawrence!" An instrumental survey of the route was commenced on the sixth of June, under the directions and superintence of Colonel Long, and was completed to the Canada Line in the latter part of September. There were various reasons why the road was not built; one was the parties could not be found to take the stock; the others need not be recapitulated.

The Belfast Bank was incorporated April 1st, with a capital of fifty thousand dollars. There were twenty-six corporators named in the charter, eleven of whom are still living. The meeting for organization was held June 3d; Joseph Williamson, Daniel Lane, Paul R. Hazeltine, Thomas Pickard, James P. White, Salathiel Nickerson and John Haraden

were chosen directors.   At a subsequent meeting of the directors Mr.
Williamson was elected President and Albert Bingham was appointed cashier.
The office of the bank was in the second story of Williamson's fire-proof
block, that portion now occupied by Mr. George R. Sleeper, until 1857,
when it was removed to the room now occupied by the Belfast National
Bank, in which bank the original one was merged in March 1865. The succession of presidents of the old bank and new, after Mr. Williamson, has
been John S. Kimball, James White, Thomas Marshall, James P. White.
Nathaniel B. Bradbury succeeded Mr. Bingham as cashier and held the
office nineteen years, at the expiration of which time his son, Mr.
A. H. Bradbury, the present cashier, was appointed.
      The steamer Bangor made her first trip from the west for the season
on the ninth of April; the ice in the river prevented her from going
beyond Frankfort.   She ran through the summer as a day-boat between
Portland and Bangor, connecting with the Portland and Independence,
which ran as night-boats between Portland and Boston.   She made two
trips per week, and for the accommodation of Belfast passengers Mr.
H. N. Lancaster ran a stage on boat-days between this place and Saturday
Cove, which still continued to be the landing place for "passengers
for Belfast."   The Independence took the place of the Bangor occasionally.
On her last trip from Portland to Bangor, in the latter part of September,
she struck on a rock in the river near the latter place and sank in
about an hour in twenty fathoms water.
      Captain William Avery died May 13th aged fifty-two.   He was born
at Preston, Conn., and came here to reside permanently about 1813.
He had been here occasionally for several years previously buying and
shipping lumber.   He was originally a ship-master.   After establishing
his residence here he engaged in trade in one of the stores opposite
the Eagle Hotel which was burned in 1834, which he continued to occupy
until he retired from active business about 1832.   He and Mr. James
P. White, under the name of Avery & White, were in copartnership from
1823 to 1828.   He was married in 1820, and in 1821 built the house at
the corner of Church and Miller streets now occupied by his son-in-law,
Mr. Daniel Lane; from thence he removed in 1833 to the Durham house
on Wilson's Hill, where he died.   The prominent characteristic of Capt.
Avery was good nature.   He was always pleasant, patient, forbearing;
never excited by passion, however sorely tempted.   "How shall I know
him if I meet him on the street?" inquired one who had never seen him.
"Know him?" was the reply.   "You can't help knowing him; he's a stout
man and always has a smile on his face.
      A Menagerie and Circus combined exhibited here on the sixth of
June.   From this place it moved eastward and ultimately to the British
Provinces.   It was on its return to the States on board the Royal Tar
at the time of her destruction by fire, October 25th, near Fox Islands,
not far from the place where the steam-brig New York was lost a few
years before.   More than thirty human beings perished and all, or nearly
all, the beasts, birds and reptiles belonging to the Menagerie.
      The Fourth of July was celebrated by the Belfast Light Infantry
under command of Capt. Benjamin P. Swan and the Belfast Artillery under
command of Capt. Mayo Hazeltine.   There was a military procession, an
address by Col. James W. Webster at the Unitarian meeting-house, and
a public dinner at the Town Hall.   Capt. Swan was the son of the late
Capt. Nathan Swan and is now residing, where he has been for many years,
at Natchez, Miss.   Capt. Hazeltine, a brother of Paul R. Hazeltine,
Esq., at that time a member of the firm of M. Hazeltine and Company,
has been before noticed.   There was a public celebration also at Sandypoint
at which an oration was delivered by our fellow-citizen William H. Burrill,
Esq., then residing in Prospect.
      This was the year of the celebrated Knox Convention, held June
30th, at which Alfred Marshall of China was nominated for Congress;
out of which grew a bitter political contest which at one time put in
jeopardy the integrity of the democratic party in this District; but

out of which grew also the Belfast Intelligencer a weekly newspaper printed in this place, the first number of which issued the 17th of November. Like the Journal, whose rival it was, it was democratic in politics. Frederic P. Ingalls was its publisher, Hon. Joseph Williamson its editor and principal proprietor. Its office of publication was removed to Frankfort, now Winterport, in November 1837, where it continued to be published until January 1839.

James F. O'Connell, the "tatooed man," exhibited himself and told his story at Phoenix Hall on the evening of the 23d of August. His story was, in brief, that he lived for several years on an island in the Pacific, was adopted by the natives, found favor and acquired distinction among them, and in conformity to their custom was tattooed. The fancy-work on his body sufficiently indicated that he had been subjected to the process, but whether under the circumstances represented by him was regarded as somewhat questionable. There was nothing incredible, however, in his narrative and nothing tending in any great degree to impeach his veracity.

The Light Infantry made trial of their marching capacity in the month of September by a visit to Bucksport, leaving here at 1 p. m. of the 12th and arriving home on the 14th at 5 p. m. The day intervening was passed in military evolutions at Bucksport in company with the Bucksport Light Infantry and the Bangor Independent Volunteers, and in "having a good time generally."

On the 3d of October the Town Clock on the Unitarian Meeting-house began to tell us how the hours rolled on. It was the joint handiwork of Major Timothy Chase and the late Phineas P. Quimby. It was built at a machine shop at the Head of the Tide where the Foundry now is, there being at that time no machine shop in the village. Three of the dials, the one in front having been made and put in a place at the time the Meeting-house was finished, were manufactured by our venerable and highly esteemed fellow-citizen, Mr. Wm. Frederick, whose place of business was at that time on Spring street.

Mr. Quimby died at his residence in this place January 16, 1869, in his sixty-fourth year. He was a native of Lebanon, N. H., a younger brother of Mr. William Quimby, father of Mr. John H. and George A. Quimby. He was educated to the trade of watch and clock making; but being naturally of an inventive and investigating mind he found his principal employment outside the routine of professional occupation. Having become deeply interested in the art, science, of Mesmerism, then in its comparative infancy in this country, he devoted the last twenty years of his life to the development of its principles, especially with reference to the healing art; reducing those principles to practice he wrought out wonderful results. The theory he propounded did not always meet with acceptance, but its practical results commanded respect. No man ever did more than he to promote the growth of the science to its present vigorous manhood. Its workings are still among the mysteries; but when the veil is lifted, as soon or late it will be, in the catalogue of those who were the earliest and ablest priests officiating at the altar of the Unknown Power, will be found the name of Phineas Quimby.

Deacon Tolford Durham died November 13th, aged ninety-two. The exact time when he came here to reside is not known, but he was one of our earliest settlers. He was a subaltern in the Belfast Militia when Samuel Houston, senior, was Captain, and had charge of the company at Castine under General Lovell in 1779. Early in this century he held various municipal offices; he was one of the managers, under whose supervision the east bridge was built and was its second toll-gatherer. He was the first Postmaster in town; during his official term the office was kept on the eastern side of the river. James Nesmith was appointed to succeed him and since that time it has always been kept on the west side. Deacon Durham became a member of the First Church in 1799, was chosen deacon the year following and continued to hold this position during his life.

At the annual spring meeting, April 11th, Ralph C. Johnson, Isaac Allard and Arvida Hayford, Jr., were chosen Selectmen, David W. Lothrop, Clerk, and James White, Treasurer.

At the annual fall meeting the whole number of votes thrown on the gubernatorial ticket was 410; for Dunlap, Dem. 277; for Kent, Whig, 133. There was no choice of Representative to the legislature. At the second trial, on the 19th, there were 534 votes thrown and Ralph C. Johnson elected; he was the candidate of the Whig party and a portion of the Democrats.

At the Presidential election in November there were only 288 votes thrown; 202 of which were for Van Buren, 86 for Harrison.

There were thirty-seven deaths in town during the year.

CHAPTER XXXI. (1837.)

The winter of this year is memorable for its snow storms. Snow fell, the wind blowing a gale all the while, during five days of the first week in January. At noon of the 8th the mail arrived six days over-due. As late as the 25th of February the snow in the woods lay four feet deep on a level; there were drifts in the roads six and seven feet deep, through which avenues and canals were cut very much after the fashion of 1873.

A "Citizen Watch" was organized early in the year and was maintained through the winter. It was a purely voluntary association. The watch for each night consisted of six, one of whom was constituted Captain of the Watch, who earned his laurels by providing suitable entertainment for his subordinates.

The Rev. Alfred Johnson, father of the Hon. R. C. Johnson and the late Judge Johnson, died January 12th, aged seventy. He was born at Plainfield, Conn., graduated at Dartmouth, with the highest honors of his class in 1785, was ordained to the ministry at Freeport, in this State, in December 1789, and continued to reside there until he came to this place and was installed Pastor of the First Congregational Church in September 1805. His pastoral relation terminated in 1813. He was no ordinary man; under other circumstances, in some broader field, he would have been recognized as a power. Had he been born in a country where Roman Catholicism was the prevailing religious creed, and educated to the priesthood, a mitre would not have been beyond his grasp. Had he been born in Scotland, and in the days of the Cameronians, he would not have been a whit behind the noblest and most fearless of their devoted leaders; no voice would have rung from hill-top and valley louder and clearer than his; there would have been no hand readier than his, if need called, to wield "the sword of the Lord and of Gideon." He was a bold, strong thinker, a thoroughly fearless and independent man. He was a man of commanding presence, of great physical power, and endowed with a voice that, when occasion called, rang like a trumpet. For many years he was called to exerise the office of Chaplain at our military musters. No one who ever saw him on those occasions, as the compiler of these annals often did when he was a boy, can forget him as he stood there, his broad massive brow uncovered, his herculean form looming up above all around him, his voice ringing out far above and beyond the crowed awed to silence as he poured forth his prayer for the soldiers that they might put on the whole armor of God--that they might stand having their loins girt about with truth--having on the breast-plate of righteousness--taking the shield of faith, the helmet of salvation, the sword of the Spirti--and having done all--to stand! It was a scene worthy the pencil of the artist.

Mr. Johnson was a learned man in his profession; too learned, probably, for the congregation to which he ministered. He could not have been, could he have made the effort, a sensational preacher; he could not have toyed with tropes and figures. He was a man of stubborn facts; and in his dealings with them he was a Boanerges. He had not the art to make his hearers weep; but he had the power to make them tremble. Perhaps in these our days the art is preferable to the power. If so it need only be added that it is well that his labors ceased when they did.

The steamer Bangor made her first appearance for the season in our waters on the second of April, going up the river no farther than Frankfort on account of the ice. She continued her trips regularly through the summer.

At the annual spring meeting, April 17th, Nathaniel M. Lowney, Isaac Allard, and Arvida Hayford, Jr., were chosen Selectmen, David W. Lothrop, Clerk, James White, Treasurer. The meeting was very fully attended, the exciting cause being the disposal of the town's proportion of the "Surplus Revenue" which under an Act of Congress had been apportioned among the States. A vote passed by a large majority to distribute the

portion coming to this town among its inhabitants, per-capita, and it
was "divid" accordingly.   William Salmond was appointed to make the
distribution and it was commenced on the 19th of June.

On the 26th of April Mr. Isaac C. Brown, of the firm of Brown and
Nickerson, a man highly esteemed for integrity of character, respected
and beloved in his social and domestic relations, committed suicide;
he was about thirty years of age. He had been for some months suffering
from partial aberration of mind, superinduced by bodily disease; the
burden had become heavier than he could bear and he sank under it.

At an election held May 8th, Hon. Hugh J. Anderson was elected
Representative in Congress from this district over Alfred Marshall,
nominated at the famous Knox Convention, and all others.   The whole
number of votes in this place was 602; 430 of which were for Mr. Anderson.
Immediately after his election he resigned his office of Clerk of the
Courts and Nathaniel M. Lowney, Esq., was appointed his successor.
Mr. Lowney's appointment vacated the office of Register of Probate and
William H. Burrill, Esq., was appointed Register.

In the afternoon of the 11th of May James Enright, a shoemaker
by trade, who resided in this place for about fifteen years, committed
suicide by hanging himself on the limb of a tree on the eastern side
of the river. He was about forty-five years old.

On the 25th of May the office of The Republican Journal was removed
from Williamson's Block on Main street to rooms in the second story
of the wooden building at the south end of Phoenix Row now occupied
by N. G. Prescott and Co.   On the 8th of June The Journal made broad
its phylactery by adding one column to each page in width and two inches
to each column in length; the addition being equal to six columns of
the former size.

The old firm of P. and E. T. Morrill suspended payment, in other
words failed, on the 19th of June. The event was not altogether unanticipated, although upon a large number in this town and vicinity the blow
fell heavily and unexpectedly.   Col. Morrill, the senior partner, a
native of Methuen, Mass., had been in business here for many years and
had been the means of furnishing employment for a large number of operatives
and promoting many public enterprises.   He was an active, enterprising,
public-spirited, business man; visionary perhaps in many of his schemes
and too prone to venture beyond his financial depth; notwithstanding
the losses which his failure entailed on many of his townsmen, it is
not known that the imputation of dishonesty was ever attached to him.
It was through his agency, and in no small measure at his cost, that
the lower portion of Main street at its junction with Front street was
widened and many of the streets southerly of Main street and westerly
of Church street were located.   He always took an active part in all
movements having for their object social or moral reform and a deep
interest in the development of the agricultural resources of our county.
After removing from this place he resided at Glenburn in the county
of Penobscot where he devoted his time and energies to agriculture,
and where he died February 16, 1862, aged seventy.

There was a "Democratic Celebration" here on the Fourth of July.
The Declaration of Independence was read by Hon. Alfred Johnson and
an Oration delivered by Ephraim K. Smart, Esq., of Camden.   Mr. Smart
had just then acquired quite a reputation and high position for a young
man in his party by his contributions to The Journal over the signature
of "Bibulus."   The procession was escorted by the Light Infantry under
command of Capt. Benjamin P. Swan.   There was a public dinner at the
Town Hall, at which the toast was given which perplexed the brains of
all who heard it, the deep significance of which has not to this day
been fathomed: "Daniel Webster electioneering on the Ohio--Grouping
for trout in a peculiar river." The political character of the celebration
was not universally acceptable;   The Belfast Volunteers and the Belfast
Artillery observed the day by performing field-duty on the eastern side
of the river, near the mouth of Goose river, and partaking of a collation

in camp.   The Belfast Volunteers was the name of an independent company
composed principally, if not entirely, of residents on the east side
of the river, of which Moses H. Young was then captain.
     There was a public celebration also in a neighboring town, attended
by a number of our townsmen, and a public dinner, at which among the
sentiments given "after the cloth was removed" the "Memory of General
G. Washington" was not forgotten, and the "American Fair" were remembered
as "the recruiting officers for our Army and Navy;" a townsman who had
recently sustained a heavy loss by fire was kindly remembered in the
sentiment " ---- ----.   Suffering the flames of elements and consuming
fire, may he rise to a Phoenix who will cheerfully entertain and receive
the applause and favor of the Public."
     The lots in the new burying yard, Grove Cemetery, were offered
for sale at auction on the 7th; the bids were for choice of lots at
a minimum price of one dollar; but few of the lots were sold.   It was
contemplated that the proceeds of the sales should be expended in laying
out and adorning the grounds.   The committee of the town having the
matter in charge were Timothy Chase, Hiram O. Alden, Philip Morrill,
Nathaniel M. Lowney, James White, Thomas Bartlett and Frye Hall.   Messrs.
Chase and Alden are the only surviving members; with the exception of
Col. Morrill all the others occupy chambers in the Cemetery.
     On the 17th of the same month the frame of the Baptist Meeting-house
on High street was raised; on the 17th of November the bell purchased
for it arrived, and on the 20th of December the house was dedicated.
The dedicatory services were as follows: Invocation by Rev. Mr. Thurston
of Prospect, Dedicatory Prayer and Sermon by Rev. Mr. Smith of Waterville;
Reading of the Scriptures by Rev. Mr. Frothingham, Concluding Prayer
by Rev. Mr. McKeen, Benediction by Rev. Mr. Aspenwall, all of this place.
On the Saturday following, the pews were offered for sale at public
auction; they had been appraised and marked according to their estimated
value; the first choice sold for about forty dollars.
     On the 22d of July the public house now kept by Josiah N. White,
at that time a wooden building without an outside lining of brick, was
opened as the Phoenix House by Eben W. Hilton, landlord.   It had been
formerly occupied for stores and offices, but was fitted in the fall
of 1835 for a hotel.   At the time of its completion it was called the
Belfast Hotel.
     An event occurred on the 21st of August of a novel character for
this place, which brought together a crowd of some two thousand spectators;
a race between two horses--Sleepy David" and the "Elliot Mare."   The
race-course was on the Northport road.   "Sleepy David" was the victor.
     Captain Isaiah Skinner, who had for thirty-three years ran a Packet
between this place and Castine, died this month at the latter place
aged seventy-two.   During that long series of years, covering the third
part of a century, no accident of a serious nature befell him, his passengers
or any property entrusted to his charge.   He was a careful, faithful,
uniformly temperate man.   There was occasionally a roughness in his
demeanor which to those who did not know him well savored of rudeness;
but the rough shell covered a precious kernel--an honest heart.   He
was buried at Castine.   The people of the town erected a marble tablet
to his memory.
     At the annual fall meeting there was some rather hard work done.
The whole number of votes thrown on the gubernatorial ticket was 539;
for Parks, Dem., 296, for Kent, Whig, 241, for Scattering, 2.   James
McCrillis, Esq., was elected Representative.   The result of the balloting
was for some time doubtful.   It will be remembered that Kent was elected
by a little less than two hundred majority.   The Whigs of Belfast "held
on" until the 22d of November, when they gave vent to their pent-up
joy by firing seventy-five guns at noon and a supper at Phoenix Hall
in the evening, of which about one hundred and fifty partook.   A great
quantity of patriotism found utterance in song, speech and sentiment.
Of the orators of that evening there is but one now living; and he is
only an "Old Settler."

There was an addition this year to our local newspaper literature. On the 30th day of December appeared the first number of the Waldo Patriot. It was of the same dimensions as The Journal, but unlike that in politics was thoroughly Whig.   It was published by John Dorr, Esq., and edited by Solyman Heath, Esq.   At the close of its first volume it was united with the Kennebec Journal, published at Augusta by Luther Severance, Esq., of which Mr. Dorr became part proprietor.

The number of deaths in town during this year was thirty-seven.

CHAPTER XXXII. (1838.)

The year 1838 was exceedingly lean in local events. The people were too busily engaged in political manipulations to take a hand in anything else; there was hardly room for anything to happen save "Election." The contest between the two great parties, Whig and Democratic, was bitterly personal, especially in this locality. The Whigs were the victors at the spring election; the tables were turned at the fall election with a terrible whirl. The Democrats carried everything before them. They were the "outs" and fought with desperation; the "ins" were equally desparate in their efforts to retain possession of the loaves and fishes. It was a regular "bread and butter" campaign.

The political power of the State was in the hands of the Whig party, Edward Kent having been elected Governor. The doctrine that "to the victors belong the spoils," although up to that period regarded by the party as heretical, became practically an article in its creed. Col. Geo. Thatcher of Monroe was appointed Sheriff of the County in place of Jacob Trafton removed; Bailey Pierce, Clerk of the Courts, in place of N. M. Lowney removed; Solyman Heath, Register of Probate, in place of Wm. H. Burrill, removed; and Webster Kelly, County Attorney, in place of Charles R. Porter removed. All the appointees, except Col. Thatcher, resided in this place; Belfast was "provided for."

Col. Thatcher was a son of Judge Thatcher of the Supreme Court of Massachusetts, once Member of Congress. He was born in Biddeford in 1790, graduated at Harvard in 1812, studied law with Hon. Cyrus King of Saco, where he commenced practice in 1815. He removed from Saco to Monroe in 1835 and resided there until 1841, when he was appointed Collector of Customs for this port, and came here to reside. In January, 1845, he resigned his office of Collector and returned to Monroe, where he resumed business and resided until 1853, when he removed to Westford, Mass., where he died suddenly June 12, 1857, aged sixty-six. He was a high-minded, kind-hearted, honorable gentleman.

Mr. Kelly was a lawyer by profession. He was born in Salisbury, N. H., and graduated at Dartmouth in 1825. He commenced the practice of his profession at Frankfort from which place he removed to Belfast. He held the office of Deputy Collector under Col. Thatcher, Collector of Customs for this port, appointed in 1841, and during that term resided in Frankfort. While residing in this county he continued in the practice of the law and stood confessedly at the head of the Waldo County Bar. He removed to Bangor in 1846, and from thence to Boston in 1850. He was rapidly acquiring rank at the Suffolk Bar, when on a visit to his friends in New Hampshire he was taken suddenly ill and died at Henniker, July 4, 1855, aged forty-nine.

Two Mormon preachers visited our village on the 23d of February and held forth in the evening to a large assemblage, attracted by curiosity to learn somewhat of the faith of the "Latter-day Saints." The men were both illiterate; they may, perhaps, have had the gift of the Spirit; one of them certainly had the gift of gab to a very extraordinary degree. He took his text from one of the Epistles of St. Paul, and evoked a malediction on all who should preach other doctrine than "Christ and Him crucified." No converts to the faith were made here. They were more successful on some of the islands at the eastward to us, on which they had been laboring.

In the month of April following a series of "protracted meetings," as they were styled, were held by the various religious denominations in our place; not, probably, to neutralize the effect produced by the Mormon preacher, but from an honest conviction that something should be done to check the rising tide of immorality and irreligion. There were those who doubted the expediency of the movement, questioning the permancy of its apparently good results, but all were agreed that the morals of our village needed reform sadly.

One of the results of the Knox Convention and the dissensions in the Democratic party growing out of it, of which mention was made in

a preceding chapter, was the removal of Col. Daniel Lane from the Collector-
ship of this Port and the appointment of Nathaniel M. Lowney, Esq.;
this event occurred early in the spring. David W. Lothrop of this place
was appointed Deputy Collector and Inspector in place of Nathaniel H.
Bradbury and Isaac Allard of this place was appointed Deputy Collector
at Frankfort in place of Benjamin Shaw.

At the annual spring meeting, April 16th, Nathaniel H. Bradbury,
Thomas Marshall and James Gammons were chosen Selectmen, Henry Colburn,
Clerk, and John Haraden, Treasurer. They were all Whigs with the exception
of Mr. Bradbury, who was a member of that branch of the Democratic Party
which assumed the name of Conservative. The largest number of votes
thrown was 478.

On the third day of May died Asa Edmunds, Esq., aged eighty-one.
He came to this place from Connecticut; the year of his coming is not
known to the compiler. He was by profession a school-teacher and continued
to practise his vocation until far advanced in years. He was a Sergeant
in the army of the Revolution and was one of the picked men who under
Major William Barton crossed over to Rhode Island in the night of July
9, 1777, and captured and brought off Major General Richard Prescott
of the British army. He was Chairman of our Board of Selectmen at the
time the British took possession of our town in 1814; the same who replied
to the bearer of the flag of truce, as narrated in a previous chapter,
that had we received earlier notice of the coming of his Majesty's troops
we should have been prepared to give them a different reception. Master
Edmunds was a large, portly gentleman--such a one as Shakespeare had
in his mind's eye, probably, when he described the Justice--"of fair,
round belly, with good capon lined," and from the peculiarity of his
personal appearance was sometimes called by the bad boys of the day,
"Toad Edmunds." He was the father of Alvan Edmunds, a highly respected
and worthy townsman, grandfather of the late Charles C. Edmunds, and
great-grandfather of the late Norman N. Edmunds. Father, son, grandson,
and great-grandson all rest in the same plot in Grove Cemetery; the
family is extinct.

Master Edmunds was a prominent member of the Masonic Fraternity.
The first code of by-laws of Belfast Lodge was framed by him, it is
said, in 1817; although the first printed code, drafted by Samuel Gordon,
James Poor and Timothy Chase, was not adopted until 1822. Master Edmunds
was the first Treasurer of the Lodge. A truthful portrait of him, not
an elaborate work of art, hangs in Masonic Hall.

The Menagerie of June, Titus, Angevine and Co. was exhibited on
grounds near the Academy on the 19th of June from 1 to 4 o'clock p.
m. The proprietors claimed in their advertisements that "in the collection
would be found a greater variety than any heretofore offered." The
public were willing to take their word for it; very few came to see
for themselves how the fact was.

In the afternoon of the ninth of July a party of five gentlemen
left this place on a hunting and fishing excursion among the islands
in Penobscot Bay. They arrived at Owls Head in the evening and passed
the night there. Leaving there in the morning of the next day, with
a light wind and under a bright summer sky, when about two miles out
from the Head one of their number, Eben W. Hilton, was killed by the
accidental discharge of his rifle, the ball entering on the right side
of his chin and lodging in his head. He lived about two hours but in
an insensible state. His remains were brought here and interred on
the 12th in Grove Cemetery. Mr. Hilton was the only son of Col. Eben
Hilton of Wiscasset, and at the time of his untimely death was only
twenty-six years of age. He came here to reside in 1834. At the time
of his decease he was, and had been for nearly a year, the landlord
of the Phoenix House. His brother-in-law, Mr. Thomas W. Lothrop, succeeded
him in the month following.

The Siamese Twins, alias "The United Brothers Chang-Eng," received
visitors at the Eagle Hotel on the 13th and 14th of July, and on the

16th and 17th the "American Arena," or Circus Company, A. Turner and Sons, Proprietors, exhibited their "beautiful steed of horses and first-rate Equestrian Performers," for twenty-five cents, children under ten years of age half price.

The annual fall meeting was held on the 13th of September. The whole number of votes thrown on the gubernatorial ticket was 751; for Fairfield 447, for Kent 299, Scattering 5. Fairfield was the successful candidate. James McCrillis was elected Representative.

On the 17th of the same month the Eagle Hotel, which had been vacated by Mr. Bailey Pierce, was re-opened by Messrs. Pickard and Sawyer, under the name of the "American House and Belfast Stage and Steamboat office." The change of name wrought no change in the management of the house; the new landlords followed in the footsteps of their illustrious predecessors and announced in their advertisement that their larder would be kept supplied with the best the market afforded and their bar well furnished with the Choicest Liquors; "bar" in italics, "choicest liquors" in capitals. Mr. Sawyer died at the American House on the seventh of December, 1839, aged thirty-two. He was the son of Capt. John Sawyer of Portland. He had resided in this place at the time of his decease but little more than a year; long enough to secure the esteem and confidence of the community.

On the 30th of this month the Brig Carroll of this place, commanded by Capt. Josiah Simpson, arrived at New York, bringing two giraffes, male and female; it was the first male of the species ever brought to this country. Two females, the first ever imported, arrived a few months earlier, and were the great attraction of the day among quadruped-fanciers. With the giraffes Capt. Simpson brought two Arabs as their keepers and attendants. N. B. They did not belong to the corps of "Arabs" who made their first appearance at the polls in this place at the Election held this month.

We had unusually cold weather through the month of November; for many days the mercury was below zero, and for a good portion of the month we had good sleighing. The newspapers throughout New England pronounced it the coldest November we had experienced since 1815, and predicted that it would be remembered as "the cold November."

The science of Phrenology was introduced to us in December by Doctor Bartlett in a course of four Lectures at the brick schoolhouse.

The steamer Bangor, Capt. Howes, made her two trips per week, during the usual season this year. The discovery had been made that there was sufficient depth of water to admit of her coming within half a mile of our wharves, and passengers we received and landed at a landing-place where McGilvery's shipyard now is, at the foot of Allyne street.

The last number of the Waldo Patriot issued on the 21st of December. The prediction made at its birth that it would "die a yearling" was fulfilled.

For the first time in the annals of Belfast, Christmas was recognized as one of the noticeable days in the calendar. There were religious services in the evening at the North Church, Unitarian, Baptist and Methodist houses. The services at the Unitarian house were after the manner of the Episcopal Church.

The number of deaths in town during the year was thirty-four.

CHAPTER XXXIII. (1839.)

The Democrats having regained possession of the public crib, John Fairfield being Governor, a new distribution of the corn followed as a matter of course. The poor Whigs who had held possession of it for a year only and who had barely begun to learn how to nibble the kernel from the cob, were loath to give it up; but there was no escape from the clutches of party destiny. George Thatcher was removed from the office of Sheriff and James Y. McClintock was appointed in his place; Bailey Pierce from the office of Clerk of Courts and William H. Burrill appointed; Webster Kelley from the office of County Attorney, and Charles R. Porter of Camden appointed; Solyman Heath from the office of Register of Probate and William H. Codman of Camden appointed; Belfast's share of the corn was smaller than it was the year preceding; but her teeth were longer and sharper and could gnaw deeper into the cob.

There were several fires in our town this year, but no one of magnitude. In the night of January 19th the shoemaker's shop of Mr. George Durham, on the east side of the river, was entirely consumed by fire. On the night of September 30th the barn of Jona. Durham, with all its contents, hay and grain, was burned; it was without doubt the work of an incendiary. On the fourth of November an old building known as the "Quaker House," standing on premises now owned by Hon. W. H. McLellan, was burned; it was of trifling value, but the burning of it afforded sport for the boys and stimulated the men to look into the condition of our "Fire Apparatus;" which was found to be in a very unfit condition for a contest with the "consuming element."

Early in this year measures were adopted by the Universalist Society preliminary to erecting their meeting-house on Court street. The work progressed so rapidly that on the fifth day of September the vane was placed in position on the spire, and on the 30th of October the house was dedicated. The Dedication Sermon was preached by Rev. Frederic A. Hodsdon, then of Levant in the county of Penobscot. He was subsequently settled as Pastor of the Society; more particular mention will be made of him hereafter.

There were two very heavy and destructive gales this year; one in the month of January, the other in December. The January gale was said by our oldest inhabitants at the time to be the heaviest ever experienced here. There was a large number of vessels at our wharves and in our harbor, some of which were seriously injured and barely escaped shipwreck. The new ship Lausanne, on whose account there was considerable anxiety, rode out the gale nobly in the middle of the Bay. More damage was sustained in neighboring ports than in this.

The December gale was almost unparalleled for violence and the amount of damage done to shipping on the coast. Among the vessels totally lost was the schooner Deposite of this place, Simon G. Cottrell, Master. She was driven ashore on Lakeman's Beach in Ipswich Bay at midnight. Of the seven on board of her, four perished, viz: Capt. Cottrell, aged about twenty-eight, Albert, son of Mr. William Durham of this place, aged about nineteen, a man by the name of Doyle, of Bucksport, and a negro, name unknown. The three saved were Mrs. Cottrell, wife of the captain, George Emery, son of the late Jonas Emery, Esq., and Chandler Mahoney, all residents here. The schooner Boston of this place, Charles Thomas, Master, laden with wood and timber, bound to Salem, was totally lost. A letter from the master to the owners, received soon afterwards, informed them that "all on board were saved except one, and he was lost."

The schooner Mary Frances, of and from this port, Frederic Worden, Master, bound to Boston, was driven on to a ledge in Gloucester harbor where she laid nearly all day showing signals of distress. Towards evening, while the gale was at its height, she was boarded by the Custom House Boat and her crew and passengers taken off. In a few minutes afterwards she parted her cable and drove to sea; she brought up on a beach in Marshfield then owned by Daniel Webster. Her cargo was landed in good order and in the Spring following she was got off and brought to this place. Captain Worden, whose pleasant face is still seen daily

in our streets, informs the compiler that while the schooner laid there
and he and others from this place were engaged in getting her off, they
were often visited by the great statesman, who jocosely remarked to
them that he should "have to charge pasturage for the schooner."   He
adds that one of the party employed, whose political notions did not
coincide with those of Mr. Webster, was wont to discuss with him the
great questions of the day; but that in all their discussions he invariably
came off "second best."   Among the passengers on the Mary Frances was
our fellow citizen B. F. Blackstone, Esq., now residing at City Point.

The "frugal swains" who fed their flocks on the eastern side of
the river derived great satisfaction from the capture of two loup-cerviers,
or "lucervees," in the month of February.   They were caught in traps
and were believed to be the individuals who had committed havoc among
the sheep in that locality during a portion of the year preceding; they
made no admission of guilt, but after their decease there was no mortality,
except from causes called natural, among the sheep who grazed on the
banks of the Passagassawaukeag.

The steamer Bangor commenced her trips early in the season, about
March 20th, making but one trip per week until the ice left Penobscot
river; after that she made two trips per week through the season, connecting
at Portland with the steamer Portland, J. B. Coyle, master, for Boston.
Capt. Howes was still master of the Bangor.

The last term of the old Court of Common Pleas was held here; it
terminated on the first day of April; it was held by Judge Perham.
With it terminated his tenure of judicial office; he was not appointed
to a place on the Bench of the Court substituted for the Common Pleas,
the District Court, which became a Court of law on the second day of
April.   The Bar of the County passed a series of resolutions on the
occasion complimentary to the Judge, to which he made a very feeling
and truly eloquent reply.   Judge Perham had held his office from 1822,
a term of seventeen years.   He was not a man of brilliant talents--he
was not an eminent jurist; but he was an honest man   and discharged
the duties of his judicial station with fidelity, courage and impartiality.
No Judge of any Court of whom the same can be truthfully said can ask
for a higher eulogium.

The 18th day of April was Fast Day; our eyes opened in the morning
to see the ground well covered with snow which fell in the night preceding
and was still falling briskly.   The "fast nags," with sleighs, boys
and girls attached, did a fast business through the day.   Report said
that the snow fell, fifteen miles back of us, to the depth of a foot.
There was a great Temperance Rally in the evening at the North Church.

The last week in April was peculiarly a week of excitement in the
village.   A fine looking, portly   gentleman, of noble and resolute
mien, arrived in the noon stage at the American House.   The driver of
the stage lost no time in whispering to the hostler and bar-room loafers
that he was the notorious Bill Johnson--the "Hero of the Thousand Islands"
--the "Buccaneer of the Lakes"--the "Canadian Patriot."   During the
hour which elapsed before the stage left hosts of our curious villagers
thronged the entrance to the house and the bar-room to gaze at the distinguished stranger.   No one ventured to address him as he stalked through
the hall and various apartments wrapt, as he seemed to be, in the mantle
of thought--dreaming, perchance of plans for the deliverance of Canada
from the york of oppression, of victories to be achieved over her oppressors.
Just as the stage was leaving the driver whispered in the ear of some
confidant that the stranger was not Bill Johnson but a flour-merchant
residing in Salem, Mass.   The fact was, as afterwards developed, that
the stage-driver, who was a bit of a wag, had adopted that method of
humbugging the gossiping loafers who hung round the hotel and that the
flour-merchant, who was himself a wag, had combined with the driver
to carry out the joke.   The only man who could be found the next day
who was willing to admit that he went to the hotel to see "Bill Johnson"
was the Editor of The Journal, Mr. Cyrus Rowe, who frankly admitted

in his next paper that he did go, not only once but twice, to gaze at the "Canadian Patriot;" and asserted that the sight of a man so good looking as he was in Belfast, although he was only a flour-merchant, was "good for sore eyes."

During the same week arrived the man who acted as pilot of the British fleet when it came into our harbor in 1814--Wiggin Merrill. He was the son of Mr. Wiggin Merrill of whom mention was made in one of our earliest chapters. Mr. Merrill had not been here for twenty-five years. He was warmly welcomed by his old friends and intensely stared at by the generation which had grown up during his absence. It is due to him if living, if not to his memory, to add that on the occasion referred to he acted as pilot not voluntarily but by compulsion.

In the month of June Dunlap's celebrated paintings of "Christ Rejected" and "the Crucifixion" were exhibited here at the Unitarian Meeting-house and were very generally visited.

There was a Democratic Convention held here on the Fourth of July, but there was no public commemoration of the day as our National Anniversary. In the evening there was a display of "fire-works;" the first exhibition of the kind ever witnessed here.

At the annual spring meeting Nathaniel H. Bradbury, Thomas Marshall and James Gammons were re-elected Selectmen, Henry Colburn, Clerk, John Haraden, Treasurer. They were all nominess of the Whigs. The party was of course in high glee; but at the annual fall meeting, September 15th, the Democrats swept the board, carrying all before them and electing their candidate for Governor, Fairchild, by a majority of more than six thousand. The whole number of votes thrown in this place was 670; 390 for Fairfield, 280 for Kent. Benjamin F. Blackstone, Demo., was elected Representative.

On the 24th of September the district Court held its first session here, Anson G. Chandler, Judge, presiding.

On the morning of the 28th died William Moody, Esq., of apoplexy, aged sixty-four; he was in the Court room the evening preceding in apparently perfect health. He was born in Byfield, Mass., in 1775, was married in York, Me., in 1802, and came here to reside in January 1803. He was educated a merchant and for a while after he came here was in trade; but in 1813 he became the Agent of Thorndike, Sears and Prescott, of Boston, proprietors of large tracts of land in this vicinity, succeeding in office the late Phineas Ashmun, Esq., of Brooks. He continued to be the agent of the Proprietors until the close of his life. He occupied at one time the dwelling house which stood on Front street opposite the site of the Belfast Foundry, which was burned in the fire of 1815; at the time he occupied it the garden in front of the house extended to the shore. He afterwards occupied the Lymburner, or Locke house, at the junction of Beaver, then Range, and High streets for many years and until he became the owner and occupant, in 1825, of the house on Church street now occupied by his son-in-law, General Webster. His widow survived him, dying in 1856, aged eighty-two.

Mr. Moody was passionately fond of music. His name is found at a very early date prominent in the musical annals of the town. For a long series of years he was the leading spirit of the choir in the Unitarian society. He was a man of rather indolent habit of body, President of the "Lazy-Club" which existed here in the early part of the century--but possessing a large amount of mental activity. He was an honest man, social and kindly in his intercourse with friends and neighbors, liberal in his religious views, but exceedingly tenacious of his own opinions. No better testimonial to his integrity and fidelity in the discharge of duty can be found than the inscription on the monument erected to his memory in Grove Cemetery: "William Moody, For 26 years the confidential agent of the Proprietors of the adjoining country. This monument is erected by David Sears, of Boston, 1840, in honor of his virtue and services."

Mr. John Cochran, father of our fellow-citizen of the same name, died on the 30th of October, aged ninety. He was born at East Boston, then known as Noddle's Island. He was one of the six original Proprietors of the town who came here to reside in 1770, and at the time of his decease was the only survivor of the original thirty-two. After him came another John Cochran from Wenham. To distinguish them one was called Wenham Johnny the other Boston Johnny. Mr. Cochran first settled on one of the lots purchased by Judge Read in 1806. Before removing to the place on which he died he lived on the lot known as the Salmond Lot; the one just southerly of the Academy lot. He was a very worthy man and highly respected. The monument erected to his memory in Grove Cemetery bears the following inscription: "He was one of the memorable Tea Party at Boston, Dec. 16, 1773."

Among the vessels launched this year were the schooners Rocket and Albert Vinal from the yard of Master Lemuel R. Palmer, the bark Don Juan from the yard of Master Joseph Rolerson, and the bark Hualco from the yard of Master James L. Burgin.

The number of deaths in town during the war* was thirty-seven. There was more than the usual mortality among them "who do down to the sea in ships." Among them were Capt. Joseph Houston who died at St. Augustine, Florida, Captain James Cunningham and Ambrose Farrow who died in the West Indies, Capt. Philip Eastman who died at Hampton Roads, Capt. Simon Cottrell of the schooner Deposite, and Capt. William Oliver Greely, the place of whose death is unknown, but whose vessel was seen for the last time in Mobile Bay in February of this year.

*"year" See note p. 122

CHAPTER XXXIV. (1840.)

With the year commenced another decade in the century. According to the National Census then just completed, our population was 4194; an increase of 1117 from 1830. Belfast was then one of the nine cities and towns in the State containing over four thousand inhabitants. The increase in the population of the county during the same term was 11,745; but within that time Vinalhaven and been annexed to the county, which accounts for a portion of the apparent increase.

There were several fires this year, but none of magnitude. The house of Mr. Simon Knowles, on the outskirts of the town, was destroyed by fire about the 25th of February, with its contents. In the morning of June 18th, the barn and porch attached to the dwelling of Capt. Benjamin Linekin were burned; the fire commenced in the barn and it was only by the greatest exertion that the house was saved. On the night of June 27th the house of Capt. John Doyle, on Main street, was burned. He and his family were absent from town at the time and the house was unoccupied. No doubt was entertained that it was the work of an incendiary. The house stood on the site of the one now occupied by Mr. Cyrus Patterson. In the evening of October 8th, "Muster Day," a large barn on the Col. Morrill lot, so called, located half a mile from any building or road, was burned. The general impression was that it was the accidental work of some one who, excited by the evolutions of the muster field, had sought the seclusion of a hay mow to cool off his military ardor; it was thought also that a pipe had something to do with it. Another barn in the neighborhood belonging to Mr. Jonathan Durham was burned in the evening of the 12th; it was the second barn which Mr. Durham had lost by fire within about a year.

Hon. Alfred Johnson's term of office as Judge of Probate for this county expired on the first day of March by Constitutional limitation, and Hon. Jonathan Thayer of Camden was appointed his successor. William H. Codman, Esq., of Camden, resigned his office as Register of Probate and Charles Palmer, Esq., of this place was appointed.

The steamer Bangor made her first appearance for the season on the 11th of April but was not yet able to come nearer our wharves than the landing referred to in a previous chapter. On the 25th she passed by on her way up the river with three hundred troops destined for Houlton. On the 16th of June she touched here at 4 A. M., to take delegates to the Whig State Convention to be held at Augusta on the day following; there was no Maine Central Railroad with a branch to Belfast in those days. She made her last trip for the season in the latter part of November.

On the 19th of May Mr. Edward Wight committed suicide by cutting his throat with a draw-shave. He was an honest, upright man. For some time before he committed the act he had been laboring under mental aberration. He was about sixty-eight years of age.

The Fourth of July was celebrated by the Democrats at Black's Corner in Prospect, now in Searsport, where an Oration was delivered by Hon. J. G. Dickerson of this city, then residing at West Prospect. There was a public dinner in a bower provided for the occasion. The day was commemorated here by the Whigs with an Oration by Lucius H. Chandler, Esq., then of Thomaston, and a public dinner in the McFarland Grove; no longer a Grove but the site of numerous handsome edifices. It was the first public demostration made in this place by the supporters of General Harrison for the Presidency. There was a long procession which marched through our streets to the Grove, preceded by the party emblems, the "log cabin" and "hard-cider barrel" mounted on wheels--the "political Jaggerell" as the editor of the Journal styled them--there were banners floating in the air, ensigns borne by horsemen, mottoes displayed in every direction, and a crowd as confident of success and as happy in the anticipation of it as Fourth of July ever gazed on. The celebration was no more palatable to the Democrats than their party celebrations of previous years had been to the Whigs; but with comparatively few exceptions they submitted to it with a very good grace. How could they

help it?   The "log cabin," with the smoke curling from its chinmey,
was a facsimile of the genuine article, the faces peering from its door
and windows were most mirth-provoking, the mottoes on the banners were
hard hits; but good-natured ones, there was not the slightest odor of
vinegar about the hard cider, every heart was full to overflowing and
every face radiant with joy.   Under such a combination of circumstances
men who could not conscientiously "Hurrah for Tippecanoe and Tyler,
too" could not find it in their hearts to grumble at those who did.

A Whig Convention was held here on the 15th of August, at which
Sanford A. Kingsbury of China was nominated for Congress, and Doctor
John Huse, of Camden for Presidential Elector.   A Democratic Convention
had been held previously at which Alfred Marshall of China was nominated
for Congress and John B. Nealey of Monroe for Elector.   Mr. Nealey died
on the 5th of October, and Thomas Bartlett of Hope was substituted.
It is a matter of history that Messrs. Marshall and Huse were the successful
nominees.

At the annual spring meeting the municipal officers of the year
preceding were re-elected by increased majorities.   The contest was
on strictly party grounds and the Whig ticket prevailed.   At the annual
fall meeting, September 14th, the number of votes thrown for the gubernatorial ticket was 784; for Fairfield 431, for Kent 353, Benjamin F.
Blackstone was elected Representative.

The first number of the Waldo Signal, Whig in politics, appeared
on the 17th of October, Mr. Charles Giles, a practical printer, son
of Paul Giles, of whom mention has heretofore been made, was its publisher.
It was enlarged in dimensions in 1846 and assumed the name of the State
Signal.   Isaac N. Felch, Esq., was its editor until October 1847 when
a sale of the paper and office was made to William L. Avery of this
place and Horace K. Kimball of New York.   Mr. Giles subsequently engaged
in mercantile pursuits.   He was postmaster in this place from 1849 to
1853.   At an early period in the War of the Rebellion he enlisted in
the Fourteenth Maine Regiment and fell in the battle of Baton Rouge,
August 5th, 1862, aged about 45.   Mr. Felch was a native of Parsonsfield,
a graduate at Bowdoin of the class of 1838 and by profession a lawyer.
He was Deputy Collector under M. C. Blake, Esq., in 1849.   After leaving
this place he was for a short time editor of the Portland Evening Courier.
He was a member of the Legislature for several sessions.   He died at
Hollis, April 21st, 1870, aged fifty-four.

At the Presidential election, November 2d, the whole number of
votes thrown was 791; for Van Buren 423, for Harrison 368.   It will
be remembered that the State went for Harrison.   On the 6th the Whigs
of Belfast were so assured of the fact that they ran up the "Tippecanoe
flag."

On the 5th the schooner Rodney of this place, Elias Libby, Master,
bound to Boston with a cargo of leather, potatoes and spars, was lost
in Barnstable Bay, Mass., with all hands, four in number; Capt. Libby,
aged about twenty-nine, John O'Neal, about thirty-four, Grancelo Thurston,
about thirty, all of this place; the fourth one, name unknown, came
from Belmont.

The dormant energies of the shooting men in our village were awakened
this month by the temporary resuscitation of the old-time shooting-match.
Matches were announced to be held at Searsmont, North Searsmont, and
Belmont Corner.   The party announcing the match at the last named place
being of strong democratic proclivities, and of sportive temperament
withal, advertised that "it would afford an excellent opportunity for
his political friends to furnish themselves with a good supply of poultry
for their expedition up Salt River."   The match was largely attended
by sportsmen from this place "without distinction of party."

Among the vessels launched here this year were the brig Metamora
and bark Wyandot from the yard of Master Rolerson, the brig Gallio from
the yard of Gilmore, Sweetser & Co.; the brig New Orleans from the yard
of Master Palmer, and the brig Columbia from the yard of Master Burgin.

The Wyandot, Capt. Mann of Bluehill, from Honduras bound to Bremen, with a cargo of logwood, was last seen on the 20th of September, 1842, in the Gulf of Mexico; a heavy gale came on the next day since which time she has never been heard from. Her first mate was Otis Skinner, son of the late Capt. Isaiah Skinner; her second mate was a son of the late Jonathan Durham.

The portion of the year which elapsed between the commencement and close of the Presidential Campaign was replete with incidents. A summary of them would occupy more space than the scope of these annals will admit; no selection from them would be satisfactory to the compiler on those who remember them as he does, or convey to the mind of those who do not any adequate idea of the reality. It was a "real jolly campaign," with none of the little feeling which has attended any previous one or any one which has succeeded it for many years.

The head quarters of the Whigs--the Tippecanoe Club--was Phoenix Hall; that of the Democrats the chambers in a building opposite on the site of which Mr. Arnold Harris's store now stands. For some time before election meetings were held in both places nearly every evening in the week, at which addresses were made. As much sound, solid argument might have been heard at one place as the other; but the Whigs quite early in the campaign invoked the aid of music. Their songs were of a popular character and attracted an audience often when the eloquent tongue failed so to do. Many of them were of purely local character and were for that reason more attractive and popular. "If you would only stop singing," said a prominent member of the democratic party one day to the compiler, "we could do something; but as soon as you strike up a song at your Hall our men rush off to hear it, no matter who is speaking."

It was pretty much so; and those who came to listen to the song were very apt to linger long enough to listen to the speech that followed. "If a man were permitted," said Andrew Fletcher of Saltoun, "to make all the ballads, he need not care who should make the laws of a nation." It was true when he uttered it--nearly two centuries ago--and what was true then is true now. "I never heard the old song of Percy and Douglas that I found not my heart moved more than with a trumpet," said Sir Philip Sidney. Song is mightier than logic in its effect on the popular mind.

It can hardly be expected of the compiler to concede that such was a fact in the "Log Cabin and Hard cider" campaign of 1840; but that logic and song worked very well together was rendered very apparent by the result of the contest. "Hard times," "corruption in high places," "wasteful extravagance at the White House," may have been true and good causes for a change of Administration. It was so contended at the time: but

"Old Tip's the boy to swing the flail,
    Hurrah, hurrah, hurrah!
He makes the Locos all turn pale,
    Hurrah, hurrah, hurrah!
He'll give them all a tarnal switchin'
When he comes in to clear the kitchen,
    Hurrah, hurrah, hurrah,
        Hurrah, hurrah, hurrah!"

and other melodies of similar character added potency to the truth.

Since the occurrence of the events to which this brief allusion has been made more than the third part of a century has elapsed. How many of those who then joined in the chorus, "Hurrah, hurrah! For Tippecanoe and Tyler too," are now voiceless! How many of the lips then eloquent are silent! Harrison, Van Buren, Tyler, Johnson, those rival candidates for the highest offices within the gift of the people, for whom as representative men all that music and eloquence were poured forth--all gone! "What shadows we are--what shadows we pursue."

The number of deaths in town this year was forty-five.

—————

Last week the compiler of the annals was made to say that "the number of deaths in town during the war was thirty-seven". It should have been "during the year." The proof-reader makes suitable apology to the "Old Settler", and proposes at an early day to present to him as a peace offering, a ----better pen.

CHAPTER XXXV. (1841)

With this year came about another revolution of the political wheel,
the Whig spoke, which had been "down" for the two years preceeding,
came "up again." Edward Kent was once more Governor; as a natural consequence, such had become the law of party, the official guillotine was
again put in operation.   James Y. McClintock was removed from the office
of Sheriff and Joseph Muzzy, of Searsmont, was appointed in his place;
William H. Burrill from the office of Clerk of Courts and Solyman Heath
appointed;   Charles Palmer from the office of Register of Probate and
Bohan P. Field, Jr., appointed; Charles R. Porter from the office of
County Attorney and Joseph Williamson appointed.   Hon. Ralph C. Johnson
was elected a Member of the Executive Council from this District, but
declined to accept the office and Hon. Thomas Marshall was elected in
his place.

The 12th volume of The Republican Journal closed with its issue
of January 28th.   The next volume began under the proprietorship of
Rowe and Griffin (Benjamin).   Mr. Griffin, under whose editorial charge
it had been in part for the four months next preceeding, became sole
editor.   His connection with the paper continued until he left for California
in 1849 in the barque Suliote from this place.   He was at one time,
while connected with The Journal, a Member of the Board of Education
of this State.   After his return from California he was for awhile editor
of the Providence Daily Post; afterwards of the Syracuse Democrat.
He died at Fayetteville, N. Y., March 14, 1874.   He was a man of high
intellect; his editorials were always characterized by vigorous thought,
simplicity of style, and a fairness which did honor to him as a man
and a politician.

On the third day of March Rev. Darius Forbes was installed Pastor
of the Universalist Society.

The inauguration of President Harrison, March 4th, was observed
by a Ball at Phoenix Hall--the old battle-ground of the Tippecanoe Club--and
a supper at the American House.   Ralph C. Johnson, Paul R. Hazeltine,
James W. Webster, Albert Bingham, Henry Colburn, William H. Connor and
Jacob Johnson were the managers.   Dancing commenced at 6 p. m.--Supper
at 11; the good, old-fashioned hours were observed, it will be noticed.
Four of the seven managers are still living.

With the inauguration of President Harrison the sceptre departed
from the Democratic Judah of the Nation, as it had already from that
of the State.   Col. George Thatcher of Monroe was appointed Collector
of Customs for this Port in place of Nathaniel M. Lowney, removed, Norman
E. Roberts, Deputy Collector, in place of David W. Lothrop, and Webster
Kelly, Deputy Collector and Inspector at Frankfort in place of Isaac
Allard.   In the foregoing official changes Belfast was kindly remembered;
two of the three appointees being residents here.

It seemed good to the Whigs that there should be a change in the
Post Office also.   A meeting was notified and held at the Court House
for the purpose of nominating a suitable person to be recommended for
the office of Postmaster in place of the incumbent, Hiram O. Alden,
Esq.   The whole number of votes thrown at the meeting was seventy-five;
fifty-nine were for Henry Colburn, and he was accordingly recommended
and appointed, but did not take possession of the office until July
1st.   He held the office until the change in the National Administration
in 1845.   During his term the office was kept in the building since
known as the Telegraph Building, in that part of it nearest the American
House.   A brief biography of Mr. Colburn has been given heretofore.

President Harrison died on the fourth day of April.   The announcement
of the event was received here with becoming demonstrations of sorrow.
The bells were tolled, the newspapers, The Journal and the Signal, were
dressed in mourning, and on the Sunday following a funeral sermon was
preached by Rev. Mr. Forbes at the Universalist Church.   The Day of
National Fasting and Prayer, appointed by President Tyler, May 14th,
was observed by appropriate religious services at the Unitarian Church,
in which the people united without distinction of political party or

religious denomination. The house was draped with the emblems of mourning and a discourse peculiarly appropriate to the occasion was preached by Rev. Mr. McKeen of the North Church.

According to the valuation taken for the purpose of assessing the State Tax for this year the number of Polls in town was 802, and the value of estates was $658,523. There were owned in the county 3,851 horses, 5,168 oxen, 9,606 cows, 47,518 sheep and 4,930 swine. The tons of shipping owned by parties residing here was 16,441.

The steamer Bangor made her first appearance here this year on the third of April and her last on the third of December. She ran regularly through the season.

"A splendid and combined Attraction of Equestrian and Gymnastic Performances, with a beautiful collection of Living wild Animals, comprising the Stupendous Giraffe, Elephant, and every variety of Beasts, Birds and Reptiles"--so read the hand-bills--was exhibited here on the 30th of June. The manager "pledged" himself that the exhibition should be "of a strictly moral character." When the account was made up the balance in favor of the morals of our village was not alarmingly large.

The public celebrations of Fourth of July throughout the county were "Temperance Celebrations." In this place the day was celebrated under the auspices of the Belfast Independent Temperance Society. A long procession marched through the principal streets to the Unitarian Church, where an Address was delivered by Andrew T. Palmer, Esq. At the close of the services at the Church there was a dinner at Phoenix Hall. "The 13 regular toasts" were drank in the best of "Adams' Ale;" the last one in order is worthy of preservation: "The Ladies! how can we be temperate in our love for them!--and who would sign the pledge if it applied to them the rule, touch not, taste not, handle not!" In the evening there was a ball at Phoenix Hotel. The day was a happy one to those who participated in its festivities, and to the community in general.

A course of Lectures on Phrenology, illustrated by "suitable apparatus and public examinations," was delivered at the Court House this month by Mr. Vining. A seceding Shaker--Carter by name--lectured on Shakerism; giving a description of the ceremonies, songs, modes of worship, &c., of the disciples of Mother Ann Lee; one of the last subjects which might have been expected to be seen on the dissecting table of the lecture-room. Three Lectures on the condition and prospects of Poland were delivered in August by Major Tochman, a Polish exile. Poor Poland! The patriotic and sympathetic resolutions passed by the good people of the village at the close of the Lectures, although gratifying doubtless to the Lecturer, rendered but little substantial aid or comfort to her oppressed people.

During the month of August extreme drought prevailed in this vicinity. The fields became so parched and dry that many were compelled to feed out hay to their cattle. There was so great lack of water on some of the islands in the Bay that the cattle on them were brought off to the main. On the 11th of September came rain; the first that had fallen, with the exception of two slight showers, since the 26th of July.

Phoenix Hall was converted into a "Dramatic Saloon" for a portion of the month of September and occupied by a company of strolling play-actors, the most prominent of whom was a Mr. Forbes. They were supplemented by a "home production" composed of several of the young men of our village under the title of the Thespian Society, who occupied the same Hall and gave several historic exhibitions; among them the tragedies of "Douglas" and "Revenge."

In the month of September and October Dr. Collyer lectured here on Animal Magnetism, or Mesmerism, with practical illustrations of the theory then new, and in its infancy, but since that time wonderfully developed. To a large majority of audiences he was a "setter forth of strange gods." "What will this babbler say?" asked the "Epicureans and the Stoics" of our village. They were not the first, nor the last, who have seen works wrought approximating to the miraculous and still doubted or hesitated to credit the evidence of their own senses. It is too late now for observing and reflecting minds to deny the existence of the power, or faculty--by whatever name it may be called--which the Lecturer advocated and illustrated.

In November, for the first time, a Daguerreotype Artist, Charles W. Perkins, made his appearance in our village. His rooms were in the second story of the building on High street on the site now occupied by Clark and Fernald, Marble workers.

A new "Coach Line" from this place to Augusta, on the New County Road, as it was then called, passing through Belmont, Searsmont, Liberty and Windsor, was established this month by Thomas W. Lothrop. The coach left this place three days in the week at 8 a. m. and returned on the days next following.

Christmas was celebrated at the Universalist Church by appropriate religious services in the evening. The house was very tastefully decorated and a Discourse delivered by the Pastor, Rev. Mr. Forbes.

Among the vessels built and launched this year were the brig Tonquin from the yard of Master Carter, the brig Ohio from the yard of Master Burgin, the ship Octavius from the yard of Master Rolerson, and the ship Dumbarton from the yard of Master Palmer, each of about 600 tons burthen; the barque Ovando from the yard of Master Perkins, the brig Lisbon at Russ' Point, and the brig Arixene built by James Y. McClintock.

At the annual spring meeting Nathaniel M. Lowney, Benjamin F. Blackstone and Samuel Haynes were chosen Selectmen, David W. Lothrop, Clerk, and Timothy Chase, Treasurer. The only contest was on the election of Clerk, in which 538 votes were thrown. At the annual fall meeting the whole number of votes thrown on the gubernatorial ticket was 734; for Fairfield, Dem., 432; for Kent, Whig, 299; for Curtis, Abolitionist, 3. Fairfield was the successful candidate. Nehemiah Abbott, Esq., was elected Representative; Ephraim K. Smart of Camden and Joshua F. Elliot of Knox were elected Senators.

The memorable event of this year was the movement here and throughout the country in behalf of temperance; a movement which originated in Baltimore the preceding year, known as the Washingtonian; the history of it is familiar to all. It was, briefly, a movement initiated by inebriates; the only weapon with which it contended, and the banner over it was--Love. Love for the intemperate, hate for that which made him so rather than for those who placed temptation in his path. The results of the efforts made were almost miraculous. Tens of thousands were snatched, or rather snatched themselves, as brands from the burning. Love proved mightier than legislation, as God's law is mightier than man's.

An association was formed here early in the month of May styled the Independent Temperance Society of Belfast. It was composed of those who "had been in the habit of using intoxicating liquor as a beverage." Prominent among its members were many who had been equally prominent in the large company of recognized inebriates; still more of those who had been known as moderate drinkers. No one was admitted as a member who belonged to any temperance society whose platform contained the plank of legal force. Meetings were held regularly in this and neighboring towns, and similar associations were formed throughout this county. Why did not the movement continue until this day, and why, like many other movements inaugurated to promote the cause of temperance, did the interest in it die out, are interesting questions; to furnish an answer to them does not come within the scope of these annals. God's law wrought better results through the instrumentality of the Washingtonian reform movement than man's law has ever wrought since. God's law has never been repealed; and the human heart, for the government of which it was enacted, is the same now, subject to the same influences, that it ever was.

A Temperance Convention, largely attended, was held here on the 18th of December. An Association styled the Waldo County Washingtonian Total Abstinence Society was organized and a Constitution adopted. Among the Resolutions passed at the meeting was the following: "Resolved, that the laws granting licenses to a certain portion of the community to sell intoxicating drinks are not founded upon moral and Republican principles; because, if the business be inconsistent with the public good, no law can make it right; and if it tends to promote the public good the monopoly thus established by law, as well as the excise required, is entirely at variance with true Republicanism; and, therefore, all such laws ought to be repealed." Such was the solemn protest, the earnest appeal of the inebriates of 1841--the poor, tempted slaves of appetite struggling for freedom. What answer do we, the men of this generation, make to them and those following in their footsteps? "Ho, every man that thirsteth!--Come up to our city rum-shop, sanctioned by public opinion and the law of the land, and drink your fill of liquid damnation; and to encourage you in so doing, we promise as a municipality that when all manhood shall be burned out of you, when your eyes have become bleared, your hands palsied, your wives and children are naked and starving, we will clothe and feed you and them, free of charge at the city Poor-farm!"

A Ladies Temperance Fair was held at Phoenix Hall on the evenings of the sixteenth and seventeenth. The Hall was beautifully decorated and the merchandise offered for sale was of a very attractive character. The amount realized from the sales made was about three hundred and fifty dollars. A few statistics connected with this Fair may not be uninteresting to the fair--if any such waste time in reading these annals. The tables at the Hall were in charge of thirty-four ladies, twelve of whom were married, twenty-two unmarried. This was thirty-three years ago; ten of the twelve married ladies and fifteen of the twenty-two unmarried are now living; a wonderful tenacity of life. Of the twenty-two then unmarried, eighteen have since married; four only have escaped. A strong encouragement or warning, to all young unmarried ladies interesting themselves in Temperance Reformation.

CHAPTER XXXVI. (1842.)

"Turn about is fair play" is an old adage, but was rather an unpalatable one to the office-holding Whigs about this time. The Democratic party was again in the ascendancy, John Fairfield having been elected Governor. The political guillotine was again in motion. Israel Cox of Searsmont, now of this city, was appointed Sheriff in place of Joseph Muzzy, removed; William H. Burrill, Clerk of the Courts, in place of Solyman Heath; Chas. Palmer, Register of Probate in place of Bohan P. Field, Jr., and Jonathan G. Dickerson, County Attorney in place of Joseph Williamson. Hon. James White was elected Treasurer of the State.

In the month of February Messrs. Townly and Burnham gave two concerts of vocal and instrumental music at Phoenix Hall. Townly had before that time resided here for awhile, and during that time officiated as organist at the Unitarian Church.

Prior to this year our connection with the outside world through the medium of steam had been limited to one steamboat, making at the most two trips per week between this place and Boston. This year, during a large portion of the summer season, we had a steamboat at our wharves every day in the week save Sunday. Since that time we have been, like Oliver Twist in Dickens' story of that name, constantly "asking for more." The old Bangor led off in the early spring, but soon retired from the field. She made her last call and fired her parting gun on the 25th of April. A change took place in her ownership and in the month of August following she left Boston for the Mediterranean where she was to be employed, as contemplated by her owners, as a towboat. She plied for awhile as a freight and passenger boat between Smyrna and Constantinople under the name of Yeni Demia, sailing under the Turkish flag. She was first put on this route in 1834 and had continued to make her trips to this time between Bangor and Boston with remarkable regularity, never having met with any serious accident.

She was followed, April 27th, by the Express, Captain J. B. Coyle, and by the Telegraph, Capt. S. H. Howes, on the 18th of May. These boats ran in opposition for awhile. The fare to Boston was reduced to one dollar. On the third of June eighty-seven from this place took passage on both boats for Boston, on the sixth, seventy, and on the twenty-eighth between eighty and ninety. A large number of our good people availed themselves of the low fare to visit the metropolis of New England who had seldom, if ever before, visited the shire town of the county. Marvelous were the tales told by them on their return; among them, that there were "taverns enough in Boston to accommodate thirty-five hundred people."

The steamer Huntress ran for awhile between Portsmouth and St. John's, touching at this place on her return trips, and connecting at Portsmouth with the railroad to Boston.

Among the beneficial results of the steamboat opposition of this year were the discovery of the wonderful fact that steamboats could come to our wharves, and the construction by Mr. Daniel Merrill of the wharf now known as the Upper Steamboat Wharf. Mr. Merrill fitted up rooms for bathing at the end of his wharf on a scale altogether beyond any thing ever attempted here. The men of those days, however, had not learned that there was any affinity between cleanliness and godliness, and for lack of patronage the enterprise was soon abandoned.

The Rev. Elbridge G. Cutler was ordained Pastor of the First Congregational Church and Society on the fifteenth of June. The exercises on the occasion were as follows: Invocation, reading of Scripture and prayer by Rev. James P. Stone of Prospect; Sermon by Rev. Dr. Tappin of Augusta; Ordaining prayer by Rev. N. Chapman of Camden; Charge by Rev. Isaac Rogers of Farmington; Right hand of Fellowship by Rev. Uriah Balkam of Union: Address to the people by Rev. L. Wiswell of Jackson; Concluding prayer by Rev. R. Page of Levant.

Mr. Cutler was born at Farmington and died at Reading, Pa., whither he had gone for the benefit of his health, April 28th, 1846, aged thirty-four.

He was eminently successful in his labors in the ministry while residing here and left behind him a name which is still kept as a precious treasure in many yearts.   On the receipt of the sad intelligence of his decease a funeral discourse was preached at the North Church by Rev. Stephen Thurston of Prospect.

Mr. Charles Spear, well remembered by the business men of that day, commenced running an express between Bangor and Boston on the steamer Telegraph this year.   The business was conducted, and never more promptly and faithfully, under the name of Spear & Co.; the company being Mr. David Bugbee of Bangor.

The evening of June 23d was eminently a Lecture evening. Mr. Abbott, the "Sailor Preacher," lectured at the Academy on temperance, a Mormon at the Court House on the doctrine and creed of the "Latter-day Saints," and a Millerite at the Methodist Meeting-house on the millennium.

The Fourth of July was ushered in by the ringing of bells and a rain-storm of short duration.   The day passed off very quietly with only one "row" and a very marked decrease in the consumption of rum. There was no public celebration here, but there were several--all on temperance principles--in different parts of the county, some of which were attended by large delegations from this place.

On the eighth of July the office of the Republican Journal was removed to chambers in the northerly end of the old Telegraph Building.

The United States steam frigate Missouri, under command of Captain John T. Newton, arrived here from Castine on the 24th of August.   She remained until after noon of the 26th, when she left for Camden.   While here she was visited by crowds--five thousand people according to the estimate of one of her officers--from this and towns adjacent.   She was the first war-steamer that had visited any American port on this coast east of Boston and was said to be at the time the largest steamship in the world.   She was subsequently destroyed by fire, originated by the breaking of a glass vessel containing spirits of turpentine, while lying in the harbor at Gibraltar.   Among the young lieutenants on board her while here were Simon B. Bissell, now a Commodore on the retired list, and John A. Winslow who was in command of the Kearsage when she captured and destroyed the Alabama, and who died within the last year.

A Farmers and Mechanics Convention, so called, assembled here on the 27th of August; its principal professed object being to devise measures for the suppression of litigation. The projectors of the movement overlook-ed the fact that human nature must be marvellously purified before man will conform his life to the precepts of the Gospel his tongue is so fond of preaching.   We should indeed have a Heaven on earth if men would cease from contention and do unto others as they would that others should do unto them; but it is idle to look for that day until the prayer is answered, "The kingdom come!"--Litigation was neither suppressed or checked by the convention.

One Harmon Quiggle relieved himself of the burthen of a very un-musical name and a charge of larceny by committing suicide in the jail on the 27th of September.   It was somewhat questionable, however, whether the poor unfortunate, who was of intemperate habits, intended suicide, or whether his death was the consequence of taking laudanum left in his cell by a former occupant as a means of exhilaration.   However that may have been, there was no more Quiggle.

The house and barn of Mr. George Durham on the Stanley road, the road leading from Belmont Avenue by the premises now occupied by Hon. Albert G. Jewett, were burned in the night of October twenty-sixth. On the 17th of December at about ten o'clock in the evening the Academy was discovered to be on fire and was entirely consumed.   It had been removed and repaired about two years before at a cost of about two thousand dollars.   These were the only destructive fires during the year within the memory of the compiler.

In the month of November, about the 19th, the schooner Enterprise of Salem, Captain John Shute of this place Master, was lost at sea with

all on board.   Two of the crew, Silas Reed and John McDonald, belonged
here.   The wreck was seen by two vessels and one man was discovered
on it lashed apparently between the pump and the stump of the mainmast.
The attempt was made to take him off, but as the sea was running very
high and the wind blowing a hurricane the attempt was unsuccessful;
such was the report at the time.   The wreck was afterwards boarded,
Nov. 22d, by the keeper of the Mt. Desert Light who found no person
on board.   Captain Shute had previously been master of the President
Jackson and the Albert of this port.   Many still living cannot fail
to remember him.

In the month of May Mr. John Lord delivered a course of lectures
on the Middle Ages.   They were of high literary order and exceedingly
interesting, but did not attract a large audience.   In October Doctor
G. W. Ellis delivered a course of lectures on Phrenology.   In December
Mr. Springer, known previously to that time as Editor of the Maine Farmers
Almanac, delivered a course on Astronomy, which was very well attended.

The interest in the temperance movement referred to in our last
chapter kept up and numerous lectures were given during the year.   The
annual meeting of the Waldo County Washingtonian Total Abstinence Society
was held on the 15th of December at the Unitarian Meeting-house.   In
the evening there was a presentation of a prize banner, a gift from
the Ladies' Temperance Society.   It was presented by Miss Caroline M.
Kimball, daughter of Hon. John S. Kimball, now the wife of Charles P.
Brown, Esq., of Bangor, and received by Mr. Samuel Thompson in behalf
of the East Belmont Society, to which it had been awarded as the society
which had made the greatest and most efficient progress during the year.
The presentation and reception of the banner were accompanied by very
appropriate addresses.   The Convention was then addressed by Hon. Ether
Shepley, Judge of the Supreme Court then in session here, and by other
gentlemen.

Among the vessels built and launched this year were the brig Topliff
of about 175 tons burthen from the yard of Master Rolerson, the brig
Venezuela of about 200 tons from the yard of Master Carter, and the
barque Rio of about 250 tons from the yard of Master Palmer.

At the annual spring meeting Nathaniel M. Lowney, Benjamin F. Blackstone
and Samuel Haynes were re-elected Selectmen, David W. Lothrop, Clerk,
and Timothy Chase, Treasurer.

At the annual fall meeting the whole number of votes thrown on
the gubernatorial ticket was 646; for Fairfield, Demo., 405; for Robinson,
Whig, 241.   Nehemiah Abbott, Esq., was re-elected Representative.   This
was the first election at which the people voted for Clerk of the Courts
and County Attorney; William H. Burrill, Esq., was elected Clerk, and
Jonathan G. Dickerson, Esq., County Attorney.

The volume of our local literature was enlarged by the publication
in December of a phamphlet of forty-seven pages, from the press of Rowe
and Griffin, entitled, "New Views upon the Bible and its Abuses by the
Priests," by Jonas S. Barrett.   The "views" of the author were quite
beyond the comprehension of his fellow townsmen; they were a sort of
cross between the doctrines of Emanuel Swedenborg and the mysticism
of the Transcendentalists.   Mr. Barrett was a very honest man in his
business transactions, and was very sincere, doubtless, in the opinions
he entertained and expressed in his pamphlet; but it is very questionable
if he made any converts to his peculiar faith.   He resided here for
many years and was a useful member of society in his vocation.   He removed
from this place to California, where he died on the twelfth day of September
1864, at Auburn, aged sixty-five.

In the same month of this year died Mr. Samuel French, who came
here to reside in the early part of this century, about 1811, aged fifty-nine.
The mention of his name will recall to the minds of all who knew him
the life-long companion and friend, and for many years copartner in
trade, John Haraden, who died March 15, 1867, in his eighty-eighth year.
"Haraden and French" is one of the names engraved on the memory of all

who lived here when that firm was one of the prominent business houses
in the place; a firm whose reputation for integrity and fair dealing
was without spot or blemish. They were both born in Gloucester, Massachusetts, and were both house-wrights by trade. Mr. French was the master-
builder of the Unitarian Meeting-house. They both wrought at their
trades until 1823, when they formed a copartnership as commission merchants
and dealers in general merchandise and commenced business at a store
standing at the end of Morrill's wharf, then so-called. They subsequently
occupied a store on the site of the one now occupied by Messrs. W. B.
Swan & Co. The house on High street now occupied by Mr. Lemuel R. Palmer
was built by Mr. French; he was occupying it at the time of his death.
The brick block at the intersection of Main and Church streets, now
occupied in part by the Belfast Savings Bank, was built by Mr. Haraden.
    There was a striking resemblance in the character of these two
men. They were both quiet and unassuming, with no ambition to be known
save as industrious members of the community and good citizens, attending
to their own business and not intermeddling with the business of others.
Neither of them had any aspiration for official position, but both of
them were repeatedly elected by their fellow-townsmen to occupy and
perform the duties of important municipal offices.
    There was a quaint and quiet humor about Mr. Haraden not possessed
by Mr. French. At the time the Whittier building, now occupied by Woods,
Mathews and Baker and others, was erected, Mr. Haraden was at work at
his trade and employed on it. He accidentally fell from the staging;
one of his arms was broken and the other dislocated at the shoulder.
A neighbor who called to condole with him remarked that he was very
unfortunate in meeting with such an accident. "Unfortunate!" replied
he, "I think I was very fortunate. I only put one arm out of joint
and broke the other; I might have broke my neck." He was part owner
of schooner *Bellino* at the time she made a very unsuccessful trip to
the Mediterranean, bringing back a cargo of beans, for which there was
no market here. The owners met for the purpose of settling up the voyage
and deciding what should be done with the almost valueless return cargo.
Loud and long were the lamentations of the other part-owners over their
bad luck, in which Mr. Haraden did not participate. "What's the use
of crying over spilled milk?" said he; "we've saved our beans and all
we want now is pork; if we can only get that we shall have pork and
beans to live on."
    Mr. French died in the maturity of manhood, leaving no child.
Mr. Haraden lived until the grasshopper became a burthen and died leaving
several daughters but only one son, our fellow citizen Mr. Daniel Haraden.
    The average retail price during the year of some of the leading
commodities in our market was as follows: Beans per bushel, $1.25 to
$1.50; wheat, $1.25 to $1.50; oats, 40 to 42 cents; corn, 80 to 90 cents;
potatoes 25 to 33 cents; flour per barrel, 7.00 to 7.25; hay, per ton,
10.00; butter, per pound, 14 to 16 cents; cheese, 7 to 10; mutton, 2
to 3; chickens 4 to 5; turkey 6 to 7; clear salt pork 8 to 10; beef,
on foot, 3 to 3 1-2; geese 20 to 25 cents apiece; they were not sold
by weight then; eggs 14 cents per doz. Molasses, per gallon, 25 to 30;
tea per pound, Souchong, 54 to 62; old Hyson 75 to 100.
    Among the prominent business men who died this year were Peter
H. Smith, for many years a trader here, who died in April, aged fifty-five;
Capt. Samuel B. Miller, brother of the late Capt. James Miller, joint
owner with him of the Robert Miller lot, who died in May, aged fifty-one,
and Capt. William Grinnell who died in December aged seventy-nine.

CHAPTER XXXVII. (1843.)

The winter of this year is memorable for its extreme cold weather and the quantity of snow which fell. The "oldest inhabitant" spoke of it as the coldest winter we had experienced and the one in which more snow had fallen than for thirty years previous. According to a memorandum kept by a gentleman in this vicinity there were forty snow-falls between the 24th of November and the 7th of April; the depth of the snow which fell being twelve feet and seven inches. The snow in the woods was three feet deep on a level on the first day of April. Quite a number of deer were seen in the immediate vicinity of our village, driven from the forests in search of food by the depth of snow or by the wolves, who were reported as being plenty in the forests of Penobscot and Washington counties. One of them--a deer, not a wolf--was captured in March while swimming from the eastern side of the river in the direction of the steamboat wharf.

There was quite an excitement in our village early in January occasioned by the arrest of one of our business men on a charge of passing counterfeit bank-bills and the sudden departure between two days of two others who were suspected of being his accomplices, or, rather, of being wholesale dealers in the commodity which he disposed of only at retail. He was taken to Boston, tried, convicted and sent to the House of Correction. The parties in whose hands he was a mere tool escaped well merited punishment; but both found before they passed beyond the reach of earthly tribunals that the way of the transgressor is hard. The business had been carried on in this county to considerable extent, and very successfully, as the counterfeits were so well executed as not to be distinguishable from the genuine, except by the practised and skillful eye. The crime was regarded, and very properly, as one of the deepest dye, the counterfeits being of the smallest denominations, such as were most in circulation among the poorer classes, who were the least qualified to distinguish between the genuine and the counterfeit.

In the same month and the month following there was an extensive religious revival prevailing here. It commenced in the Methodist Society, then under the charge of Rev. Theodore Hill, a very earnest and effective preacher, and extended to all the religious societies in the place. Prayer and Conference meetings were held in all of them, and a universal solemnity pervaded all classes in the community. No one, not even the most faithless or obdurate, manifested the slightest disposition to ridicule or cast any obstruction in the path of the movement. The boisterous and ribald songs with which our streets had resounded nightly gave place to the equally enlivening but more spiritual ones of "We shall see a light appear" and "When the Lord of Glory cometh." Large additions of membership to the several churches were made as the fruit of the seed sown during the revival. On the first Sunday in May, fifty-one united with the North church, then under the pastoral care of Rev. Mr. Cutler; more in number than during the whole six years next preceding.

In the afternoon of February 12th occurred the first fire of the season. A house owned by Mr. Benjamin Brown, at the corner of Market and Pleasant street occupied by three families, was discovered to be on fire. The fire was extinguished but not until after considerable damage had been done to the building and its contents. A one story house on Miller street, beyond what was then called "Jail Hill," occupied by Abiathar Smith, was burned in the night of the twelfth of July. On the night of July 28th an extensive tannery at the Head of the Tide, conducted by Mr. Amos Peaslee, owned by Mr. Southwick of Danvers, Mass., was entirely destroyed by fire with a large quantity of hides and leather; the estimated loss was about eight thousand dollars. The fire was supposed to have originated from friction of the machinery in grinding bark. A barn owned by Col. Watson Berry, father of our fellow-citizen Mr. Franklin W. Berry, at the Upper Bridge settlement, with its contents, about sixteen tons of hay, was burned on the evening of the second of December. His dwelling-house was barely saved by tearing away a shed

which nearly connected it with the barn.   The zeal of our people so
far outstripped their discretion in saving the furniture in the house
that it might have been about as well for the Colonel had the whole
been left to the tender mercies of the flames.

While on the subject of fires it will not be amiss to mention that
a town meeting held on the eleventh of December a vote was passed to
raise two thousand dollars for the purchase of an engine, fire apparatus,
&c., and our now venerable fellow-citizen, Major Chase, was appointed
sole agent to make the purchase.

Washington's birthday, the 22d day of February, was celebrated
throughout the country by the Washingtonian Temperance Associations.
The celebration in this place was at the Unitarian Church; the ground
floor and galleries were crowded.   The house was beautifully decorated
with flags and floral ornaments.   The exercises of the evening were
introduced with prayer by Rev. Mr. Hill of the Methodist Church, followed
by music from a selected choir, and an address by Hon. Alfred Johnson
worthy the occasion.   It was listened to with the most intense interest
and was replete with classic wit and sound argument.   It was subsequently
published in pamphlet form and had a very wide circulation in this and
other States.   A republication of it at this time, although its doctrines
might not be in accordance with the popular sentiment of the day, would
be productive of benefit to the cause of temperance.

The afternoon of the 28th was devoted by a large portion of our
population to gazing at a luminous body in the sky, apparently in close
proximity to the sun, which was subsequently ascertained to be a comet.
It was visible to the naked eye until about sunset; and for some minutes
after the sun sank below the horizon a luminous strip was visible, apparently in its track.   The advent of this wanderer of the sky had not been
predicted by the astronomers and its unexpected and unannounced appearance
furnished occasion for many fearful forebodings.

In the month of March, Bradford S. Foster became landlord of the
public house at the foot of Main street on the site of the store now
occupied by L. A. Knowlton and Co.   It had been occupied previously
by Hiram Littlefield, professedly as a Temperance House.   It was afterwards
occupied by John Hussey and by Josiah N. White, now of the Phoenix House,
and was long known as the Farmers Inn.

A new and in this locality unheard of method of contributing to
the support of ministers of the gospel was inaugurated this spring under
the name of Donation Parties.   Since that time they have become of frequent
occurrence; but the question then raised, whether the money paid for
the purchase of a ham is not of more value to the pastor than the ham
is after being eaten by his parishioners, all but the bone, still remains
an open question.

There was another important question on which the public mind in
this locality was much exercised about this time; and that was whether
the article of female dress denominated a bustle was or not conducive
to the health, or beauty of the sex.   Male physiologists were down on
it in severest manner, the medical faculty unanimously denounced it;
artists failed to discover in it the "line of beauty."   No one came
to its rescue save the "artless bard," who in a "paroxysmal" parody
of Moore's, "This world is all a fleeting show" broke forth in the columns
of the Journal with

"Bustles are not an empty show
  For man's illusion given;
They're filled with bran, or stuffed with tow,
They stick out 'bout a feet or so,
  And look first rate, by heaven!"

The poet came off victor in the conflict.   Physiologist, medicine-man,
artist to the contrary notwithstanding, the article of dress still has
a name and a place.   All efforts to curtail it will be unavailing so
long as women sternly and steadfastly asserts her inalienable right

to imitate in her person the pattern of the symmetrical bumble-bee.

At the annual spring meeting the monies raised for expenses for the municipal year were as follows: for the support of schools 1800,00, for support of paupers 600,00, for construction and repair of highways 700,00 in money and 5000,00 in labor, for payment of debts and expenses 1500,00. An effort was made to pass a vote instructing the selectmen not to license retailers of ardent spirits; it failed because those engaged in the business, and their friends, and those who disapproved of the arbitrary measures adopted by some of the indiscrete advocates of temperance opposed it.

The following town officers were re-elected: Nathaniel M. Lowney, Benjamin F. Blackstone, Samuel Haynes, Selectmen, David W. Lothrop, Clerk, Timothy Chase, Treasurer.   Messrs. Chase and Blackstone are the only members of the municipal government for the year who are now living.

Mr. Lowney was the son of William Lowney, a graduate of Dublin College, Ireland, originally a school teacher by vocation, who came to this place from Monmouth, Maine, and died here in 1815, aged seventy-six. Mr. Lowney, who was never of vigrous health, commenced the study of medicine with the late Doctor Hollis Monroe but after a while abandoned it and studied law in the office of the late Judge Johnson.   After being admitted to the Bar he opened an office at Frankfort where he remained a few years and then returned to this place. He occupied, successively, the office of Register of Probate and Clerk of the Courts for the county of Waldo, and afterwards the office of Collector of Customs for this port.   For many years he was a member of our Board of Selectmen.   He was never fond of the practice of his profession, and is best remembered as an active, earnest, influential politician of the Democratic school. The role he played was not an assumed one; he was by nature antagonistic to any and every thing that was tinctured with aristocracy; it may be said of him truthfully, that he was born a Democrat, and that he never sold his birthright for a mess of aristocratic pottage.   There has never been in this county a political partisan who exercised a more controlling and extensive influence than he did. He died at his residence on Church street, purchased by him of Fellowes and Simpson, the first publishers of The Republican Journal, now occupied by his widow, on the tenth day of May 1855, aged fifty-seven.

Mr. Haynes was born in Durham in this State and came here to reside in 1825.   He was by trade a shoemaker, but abandoned that vocation after residing here several years and engaged in business as a druggist and apothecary; he occupied the northerly store in the old Nesmith Building, on the site of the store now occupied by J. C. Thompson.   He was for several years in succession a member of our Board of Selectmen, was at one time Master of Phoenix Lodge of F. and A. Masons, and at all times one of our worthiest, most highly respected and esteemed fellow townsmen.   He died at his residence on Church street, built by him, now occupied by his widow, on the sixth of January 1861, aged fifty-nine.

Mr. Ansel Lothrop was the son of Ansel Lothrop, Esq., who resided in this place in the early part of this century and removed to Searsmont, when it was part of Greene Plantation, where he died in 1834.   Mr. L. was for some years engaged in trade in this place alone and as a member of the firm of Lothrop & Woodman. For many years he was our town clerk, deputy collector of Customs for this Port and Register of Deeds.   He was a member of the Executive Council for the year 1837 when Robert P. Dunlap was Governor. He died on the 29th of May, 1849, aged forty-one, and was buried with the honors of the Odd Fellows, of which Fraternity he was a prominent member.

During the month of March the throat distemper and scarlet fever prevailed here and proved fatal in many cases, especially among the young, although those of mature age did not in all cases escape.   On the thirteenth of the month the Hon. Bohan Prentiss Field, father of our fellow citizens Charles D., Bohan P. and B. F. Field, died in his sixty-ninth year.   He was born in Northfield, Mass., graduated at Dartmouth in 1795, and pursued his legal studies in the office of Hon. Samuel Dana at Amherst, N. H.   Soon after his admission to the Bar, in 1799, he came to Maine and opened an office at North Yarmouth.   He came here to reside in the year following; he was the first lawyer who established his residence within the territory now constituting the County of Waldo. The office he occupied, built by him in the year he came here, stood on the site of the store now occupied by S. Sleeper and Son; it remained there until it was burned in the fire of 1865.   He was married in 1807, and built the house on the hill, long known as Field's Hill, now occupied by his son B. F. Field.

When the county of Waldo was organized, in 1827, he was appointed Chief Justice of the Court of Sessions and held the office for ten years, when the Court was abolished, performing the duties of the office during that time faithfully and impartially and to the entire satisfaction of the people of the county.   His associates on the bench were Joseph Shaw of Thorndike and Thomas Eastman of Palermo.   He was a well read lawyer, a safe and sound counsellor; he was never an enthusiastic practitioner of his profession, finding, like many of his professional brethren of that day, occupation more congenial to his taste in agricultural pursuits.   He was often selected by his fellow townsmen as arbitrator between them in their matters of difference, and speaking of him in that capacity Mr. Willis, in his "History of the Law, Courts and Lawyers of Maine," very truthfully remarks, that "no man entered on the investigation of the rights of parties freer from passion or prejudice, and no one exercised a sounder judgment.   Such was his known integrity of character and singleness of purpose that he received a thousand unsought tokens of public favor and confidence.   Few men ever died more highly esteemed and respected by all who knew him."

Mr. Field retired from the practice of his profession some years before his decease, but the high position he held to the last in the estimation of his professional brethren appears in the resolutions adopted by them at a Bar meeting held immediately after his decease; they constitute a most truthful eulogy of the man and the lawyer.   "Resolved, that we cherish the highest respect for his memory, for his talents, industry, moral worth, and gentlemanly deportment; that we hold him up to all as a worthy example of disinterestedness and faithfulness in the discharge of the duties of his profession; that we honor him as the one who first came to practice law within the limits of the county, and as the father of the Bar; and that we will attend his funeral as mourners."

The remaining annals of this year will be found in our next chapter.

CHAPTER XXXVIII. (1843.)

The sixth day of April, 1843, was Fast Day. Snow began to fall
in the evening of the 5th and continued through the night and until
afternoon of this day. It was estimated that the fall was twelve inches
at least in depth. At four P. M. there was not a sleigh-track visible
on Church street. The natural inference was that the good people in
that locality were complying with the request of the Governor by devoting
the day to "humiliation, fasting and prayer, and abstaining from all
labor and recreation inconsistent with the usual solemnities of the
occasion."

The Telegraph, Captain J. B. Coyle, was the first steamer to put
in an appearance at our wharves this spring; she arrived on the first
day of April. She was advertised to ply between this place and St.
John, N. B., but did not long continue on the route. She was soon followed
by the Charter Oak, Captain S. H. Howes, and the Huntress, Captain Thomas
C. Jewett. The first sailed under the advertised flag of the "Peoples
Anti-monopoly, Anti-corporation line!!!" and plied between Bangor and
Boston, touching for awhile at Portland; the latter under the flag of
the "Steamboat and Railroad Line," plying between Bangor and Portland
and connecting at the latter place with the Eastern Railroad to Boston.
Competition led to a reduction of rates for freight and passage until
the fare from this place to Boston was only one dollar and fifty cents.
It continued until September when the Huntress was taken off the route
and the "Anti-monoply" was swallowed by the "Steamboat and Railroad."
After that our only steam connection with Boston was per Charter Oak,
via Portland, and Eastern Railroad. There was no small amount of growling
here on the occasion and the proprietor of the Stage Line between this
and Augusta advertised that he would carry passengers for one dollar
and arrive in Augusta in season to take the steamer from that place
to Boston on Monday and Thursday. The Charter Oak was here on her last
trip for the season on the seventh of December. The new steamer Penobscot
touched here on the 26th of June on her way from Portland with passengers
to attend the Maine Conference of Churches at Bangor. On the 29th she
came down the river on a pleasure excursion, called here for passengers,
thence to Castine where she remained a few hours and thence back to
this place and Bangor. She was intended to ply between Boston and St.
John, but was soon taken off and put on the Kennebec route.

Many of our good people went to Boston on the steamers to unite
in the commenoration of the battle of Bunker Hill, June 17th, and to
celebrate the completion of the monument. Daniel Webster was the orator
on the occasion and among those assembled were President Tyler and many
other distinguished national and State officials. It seemed to be a
day when the nation went up to the earliest altar of our national liberty
to lay upon it a nation's offering of gratitude to the Ruler of Nations
for unnumbered mercies and blessings, and prayer that so long as that
granite monument pointed toward Heaven there might be "Peace on Earth."
Our gratitude was sincere; so was our prayer; but, as the honest old
clergyman of the olden time said, "What's the use of praying for rain
until the wind changes!" The various experiences of some of our unsophisticated townsmen on that occasion have a place in the memory of their
surviving contemporaries; the record of them in these annals might afford
amusement to the generation which has succeeded, but--"Let the dead
Past bury its dead!"

The Fourth of July was celebrated under the auspices of the Washingtonian Temperance Associations. Fifteen societies were in attendance from
different towns in the county. Two military companies, the Hancock
Guards, from Castine, and the Frankfort Artillery helped to swell the
large concourse of people. The literary exercises of the day, at the
Unitarian Church, were the reading of the Declaration of Independence
by Hon. Alfred Johnson and an oration by Col. Charles W. Cutter of Portsmouth,
N. H. A public dinner was served in the large chamber of Mr. Daniel
Merrill's store-house on the steamboat wharf, at which there were about

six hundred guests.   The Prize County Banner was awarded to the Frankfort Washingtonian Society and was presented by Miss Caroline F. Alden, daughter of Doctor J. P. Alden, and received by the late Benjamin Shaw, Esq., of Frankfort, now Winterport.   A banner was also presented to the Belfast Washingtonian Society, the gift of the "Martha Washingtonians" of this place, by Miss Abigail Marshall, daughter of Hon. Thomas Marshall, afterwards Mrs. F. W. Berry, now deceased, and received by James H. Smith, Esq.   A banner was presented to the Juvenile Cold Water Army of Belfast, the gift of the Misses Temperance Society, by Miss Frances Towne, daughter of the late Thomas Towne, now Mrs. Richard Briggs of Boston, and received by Master Samuel F. Burd, now deceased.   The presentation and receipt of the banner in each instance were accompanied by appropriate remarks. The day passed off very joyously and was crowned at evening with a "Ladies' Temperance Picnic Party" held at the house of Mr. Benjamin Hazeltine, father of C. B. Hazeltine, Esq.

The 15th of July was celebrated by Mr. Jonas S. Barrett, of whom mention was made in a former chapter, and his disciples, as the anniversary of the day when he commenced writing his "New views of the Bible." He resided at the time on Peach street, near High street.   A grove of evergreens was extemporised in front of his house and a flag-staff raised from which floated a white banner bearing the inscription "Opening of the Seven Seals" and the representation of a Bible with seven clasps, three of them broken.   At nine o'clock in the morning seven cannon were fired, emblematic of the seven thunders that announced the opening of the seven seals.   A bugle, drum and fife furnished music for this occasion, and a plain, substantial dinner was provided for all who were disposed to partake of it.   Sixteen sat down at the table; four more than sat at the table with Him whose second advent the new Evangelist asserted had already occurred.   Mr. Barrett received his numerous visitors very courteously and conversed freely with all disposed so to do on the peculiar religious views entertained and promulgated by him in his pamphlet.

During the month of July there was a very prevalent influenza, attributable doubtless to very sudden and extreme changes in the weather, but after the fashion of all time attributed to the National Administration. It was denominated the "Tyler Grippe"; a grip which was effectually unloosed at the Presidential election of the year following.

A course of Lectures on Phrenology was delivered this month by Doctor A. Bartlett.   The lectures was illustrated by skulls, plaster casts and drawings of heads, and public examinations.   In November Mr. C. P. Castanis, by birth a Greek, gave two lectures descriptive of the manners and customs of his native country, the massacre at Scio, the place of his nativity, &c.   They were exceedingly interesting.   During the same month and the month following a course of lectures on Anatomy and Physiology was delivered by Doctor Calvin Cutter, author of several popular works on anatomy and Physiology and anatomical outline plates designed for use in schools, and families.   One or more lectures on Mesmerism, a subject then attracting much attention, were given by Mr. Phineas P. Quimby, illustrated by experiments with a subject when under the influence of mesmeric sleep, as it was they styled.   Lectures were given at several of the Churches by a Mr. Bowen, a blind man, on the education of the blind.   On the 25th of October Elihu Burritt, the "Learned Blacksmith," gave a lecture at the Baptist meeting house on the Policy of Peace.

In the month of August the office of the Republican Journal was removed to chambers in the brick building on Main street, then newly erected, now occupied on the ground floor by M. F. Carter & Co.   On the 7th of October Mr. Rowe, one of its proprietors, sold his interest in the paper and office to George C., brother of his copartner Benjamin Griffin, and the paper was thereafter conducted under the name of G. C. & B. Griffin.   In bidding farewell to his patrons and the public, Mr. Rowe remarked that "if in his connection with the Journal he had unjustly offended any one, he asked that forgiveness which he most freely accorded to those who had injured him." He devoted his time to collecting his bills, forgiving and being forgiven, until 1846, when he re-purchased the interest of George C. and the old name of Rowe and Griffin was resumed.

Our village was enlivened on the morning of the 13th of September by the advent of a caravan of wild beasts, birds and reptiles, preceded by a car drawn by four elephants in harness. A large concourse of people witnessed the exhibition. The proprietors announced in their hand-bills that their collection embraced "all the animals in the United States!"

For several days this month there was an exhibition at the Town Hall of wax statuary, of life size, representative of the Last Supper.

At the annual fall meeting, held on the 11th, the whole number of votes on the gubernatorial ticket was 658; for Hugh J. Anderson, regularly nominated democratic candidate, 398, for Edward Kavanagh, irregular, 102, for Edward Robinson, Whig, 185, for Appleton, Abol., 24. Mr. Anderson was the successful candidate; it was his first election to the office. Our fellow citizen Joseph Bean, of the firm of Furber and Bean, was elected Representative to the Legislature; he was then known as Joseph Bean, 2d, there being another townsman older than he of the same name.

In October the erection of a one story building in the rear of the Unitarian church was completed; it was known as the Unitarian Vestry. Religious services were held in it for the first time on the evening of the fifteenth of the same month. It was removed some fifteen years ago to Bridge street, near Waldo Avenue, and is now a school-house.

The business of ship-building was not so brisk this year as in the year preceding. The only vessels built and launched so far as the compiler remembers, were the ship Lady Arbella of about 400 tons burthen, the brig Mazeppa, of about 200, and the barque Ralph Cross of about 300; they were all launched from the yard of Master Rolerson.

The Mails arriving and leaving during this year were as follows: to and from Thomaston and Bangor daily; our "Western Mail" then went by the way of Thomaston; to and from Augusta and Ellsworth tri-weekly; to and from Albion and Dixmont semi-weekly; to and from Gardiner weekly; our Western Mail left at four o'clock in the morning and arrived at from 8 to 11 in the evening. Post office open every day except Sunday, from 7 a. m. to 9.30 p. m. Sunday was a day when, it was presumed, no one cared to receive or mail a letter. How is it now? Have we become less scrupulous in our observance of the Sabbath than we were then? or, have we become more thoroughly appreciative of the truth that "the Sabbath was made for man," and that man therefore may make such use of it as his taste or inclinations suggest? or--perhaps for our own credit it is better that we should not pursue the inquiry.

The annual meeting of the Waldo County Washingtonian Total Abstinence Society was held on the 11th of December. Prior to this date harmony had pervaded all the councils of the Society and great and good results had followed its labors. The time had come at last when the apple of discord was to be thrown into its feast by the introduction of a resolution that "all who retail ardent spirits as a beverage in the county of Waldo are a nuisance." After a long and earnest discussion the resolution was adopted; it was the death-blow to the original Washingtonian movement in this locality. The status of the business of retailing ardent spirits at that time may be gathered from the report made to the County Society by the secretary of the Belfast Washingtonian Society, from which report it appears that "we have sixteen licensed retailers, two taverns, fourteen stores and dens underground." The report proceeds, "that we are happy to add that Belfast village is blessed with an American House kept by the present landlord, Mr. Lancaster, on total abstinence principles." It is gratifying to know that the House, although its proprietorship has been frequently changed, still maintains its well deserved and established reputation.

Among the noticeable deaths of this year in addition to such as have been already named, were those of Captain John Doyle, who for many years ran a packet between this place and Eastport, who built the house on Main street now occupied by Cyrus Patterson, and died at Eastport in August aged thirty-five; Mayo Hazeltine, brother of our fellow citizen Paul R. Hazeltine, for many years a merchant in this place and of whom mention has heretofore been made, who died in Boston, December 5th, aged thirty-eight, and whose remains were brought here for interment; Alvan Edmunds, son of Asa Edmunds, father of Charles C. Edmunds, who died June 6th, aged sixty-three, and Ebenezer Colburn, one of the earliest settlers here in this century, grandfather of our fellow citizen William T. Colburn, who died January 15th, aged eighty-five.

CHAPTER XXXIX. (1844.)

This year opened with three feet of snow on the ground, the travelling so heavy that our mails were two and three days behind time, and the mercury twelve degrees below zero. On the principle that "misery loves company" we found great comfort in the fact that the inclement weather extended over all the northern States. The harbor of New York City was frozen over for a distance of twelve or fifteen miles from the city; Boston harbor was frozen up as far down as the Light, and a canal was cut through the ice seven miles in length to enable steamers to go to sea. Our own harbor was so frozen that sleighs passed between Islesborough and the main. The ice extended as far as Owl's Head. There was good skating from East Thomaston to the Fox Islands; an event which had not occurred for fifty years; at which time, it was said, foxes, which were very numerous on the islands, came off to the main. We were brought in contact with open water on the 27th of March by cutting a canal through the ice as far out as the Monument.

For the first time in this locality the amusement of riding on "ice-boats," up and down our river, was introduced. The ice-embargo on this Port was so effectual and of such duration that, according to an estimate made on the 5th of April, there were then at least ten thousand cords of wood and bark piled on the wharves at the village and at the Point, then called Russ's, now City Point, awaiting shipment. The river above the upper Bridge was, even on that day, blockaded by ice. It was predicted at the time that "the young men of our village would have gray hair on their heads before this harbor would be so thoroughly closed by ice again." The prediction has been fulfilled; for the heads of many of those young men have been for many years whitened with the "blossoms of the grave" and a similar state of facts has never since occurred.

The Fire Engine, for the purchase of which an appropriation was made as stated in a previous chapter, arrived here early in January. It was built by W. C. Hunneman and Co., of Boston, and cost, including hose, hose-carriage and appendages, $1017.50. It was named the Hydrant. A new fire company was forthwith organized under the name of Hydrant Engine Company, No. 2, and the following officers were chosen: Stephen B. Day, Foreman, Curtis B. Merrill, assistant, John W. White, Joseph Bean, 2d, Benjamin Griffin, Directors, Matthew C. Hazeltine, Clerk, Nathaniel Merrill, Foreman of Leading hose, Joseph Dennett, Assistant, Joseph Ames, Jr., Foreman Suction Hose, Charles Giles, Assistant, Josiah Hall, Jr., and John S. Caldwell, Hoseman, William Beckett and Daniel Murch, Polemen, Alden D. Chase, Torchman. The old engine, Vigilance, was thoroughly repaired and James P. Furber was chosen Foreman and Amos R. Boynton, Assistant.

There was a strong feeling of hostility to the purchase of the new engine prevailing in the eastern part of the town, and at a public, or "Anti-engine" meeting held by the residents in that section, a resolution was adopted to resist the payment of any tax assessed for the payment of its cost. Wiser counsels prevailed, however, and the feeling of hostility gradually died out.

On the first day of March the first number of a newspaper called the Peoples Advocate and Independent Democrat made its appearance. As its title indicated, it was of Democratic proclivities; it was printed and published by Lewis Richardson. It professed to be the organ of the true Democracy, supported the regularly nominated Democratic candidates, State and national, but opposed the local nominations of its party. The publication of it was suspended before it reached the close of its second year.

Mr. Richardson was a practical printer but had been engaged in trade for some years in this place. He was of nervous temperament, honest in his convictions, by nature antagonistic to all chicanery and demagogism, and not the man for the place which by the force of circumstances he was called for a while to fill. After he left this place he was joint publisher, 1846-7, with Mr. John Porter of the Limerock Gazette,

now the Rockland Gazette, at East Thomaston, now Rockland. He afterwards
went to California, but returned to Rockland, where he died in 1867.

On the morning of Sunday, the 10th of March, the first fire of
the season occurred. It broke out in the second story of a brick block
on Main street, owned by the late Rufus B. Allyne, Esq., which covered
the site of the stores now occupied by Albert C. Burgess, A. B. Matthews
and John B. Wadlin. On the ground floor were three stores; one occupied
by the late Benjamin Hazeltine, another by our fellow citizen A. N.
Noyes; the other was unoccupied. One of the rooms on the second floor
was occupied by Mr. Allyne as a law-office; the others as workshops
and storerooms. The roof of nearly the whole building was burned, but
the fire was extinguished before it reached the ground floor. Suspicion
pointed out a young man, John Greene, as the incendiary; he was arrested
and subsequently convicted and sentenced to the State Prison for five
years. He admitted his guilt and stated that his object in entering
the building was to rob Mr. Allyne's safe; that failing to obtain an
entrance to it he took from his office such articles as he thought might
be of value to him and then set the building on fire. He had formerly
been employed by Mr. A. as man-of-all-work about his house and premises.
He asserted that he had an accomplice who came with him from Boston
but who decamped immediately after the failure of their attempt to break
into the safe. The value of taxable property saved through the instrumentality of our new engine furnished a very convincing argument in answer
to the reasons assigned by our people in the eastern section of the
town why they should not contribute their portion of the money paid
for it.

About midnight of the eighth of July an old tenement, then recently
occupied by Asa Day, was burned; the handiwork of some sportive incendiary;
it stood on the street leading to the bridge. An unoccupied house and
barn at Mason's Mills were destroyed by fire in the night of the nineteenth,
and on the night of the twenty-sixth an old barn, the property of widow
Alden, was burned; it was an ancient local landmark, being the same
temporarily occupied by the British troops when they were here in 1814;
this fire, doubtless, was the work of some of the "gay and festive cusks"
of our village, quite a number of whom were running at large between
July and December of this year.

At the annual spring meeting, March 18th, Thomas Marshall, Benjamin
F. Blackstone, and Samuel Haynes were chosen Selectmen, David W. Lothrop,
Clerk, and Timothy Chase, Treasurer. The only representative of the
Whig party on the Board was the chairman of the Selectmen. The largest
number of votes thrown was 580. The monies raised were as follows:
for the support of schools $1800, for support of paupers $800, for
incidental expenses $500, for repairs of bridges, &c., $700, for payment
of debts $1500, for highways, in labor, $4000. A vote was passed by
a very large majority to instruct the Selectmen not to grant licenses
for the sale of spirituous liquors.

The first steamer of the season was the Portland, who made her
appearance at Saturday Cove on the 19th of March; it was as near as
she could come on account of the ice; she reached our wharves, for the
first time, on the second of April. The Charter Oak followed her before
the close of the month and continued to run through the season, connected
with the Eastern Railroad at Portland; the fare from this place to Boston
was $3.50. She was taken off the route for one trip, in June, to convey
delegates to the Whig State Convention in Augusta, and the steamer Frank
took her place; very much to the annoyance of certain people then styled
Loco Focos, who were saved from bursting only by giving vent to their
indignation in the columns of The Journal. The Portland was again on
the route in the fall of the year but suspended her trips on the 18th
of December.

A schooner of about 90 tons burthen, named the Squirrel, built
by Mr. William Tilden, was launched on the 11th of April, and a brig
of about 200 tons, named the Maria Spear, from the yard of Master Rolerson,
on the 28th of September.

Mr. A. H. Park, a nephew of the late Capt. Andrew W. Park of this town, who died in September 1867, aged eighty-one, a man blind from his birth, delivered a course of lectures at the Court House in the month of May on Astronomy!   It was one of the last topics on which it would be supposed that a blind man could discourse intelligently; yet his lectures were very interesting and evinced that he was master of his subject.   He is now living in Massachusetts engaged in the business of milk-farming.

In the same month Mr. B. S. Foster, firm in that faith which is "the substance of things hoped for," re-opened the bath-rooms on Merrill's wharf.   There is no evidence on the Valuation-book that he derived any income from the enterprise.

Mr. Daniel Ring became landlord of the Phoenix House the same month, and in December following Mr. John Hussey became landlord of the public house at the foot of Main street, then called the Farmers House, afterwards the Farmers Inn.

On the 29th of the month one John S. Trafton, about twenty-five years of age, was found by some boys who were playing in the woods about half a mile from the village suspended from the branch of a tree with a rope around his neck.   From the appearance of the body, and various circumstances, it was inferred that he had been hanging there for several days.   A Lodge of "Odd Fellows," called the Passagassawaukeag Lodge, was instituted here on the 29th of June, and the following officers were elected: David W. Lothrop, N. G., Samuel G. Thurlow, V. G., Ansel Lothrop, S., and George R. Lancaster, T.   The meetings of the Lodge were held in Phoenix Hall which was thereafter known for many years as Odd Fellow's Hall.   The old Anti-masonic feeling against "secret societies" had not become entirely extinct, and on the 27th of December the Rev. Richard Woodhull, of Thomaston, delivered a lecture at the Baptist Meeting-house in defence of the Order and explanatory of the object and design of the institution.   The claims for charity upon this Lodge became heavier than it could bear, and in 1857 its Charter was surrendered to the Grand Lodge.   The Messrs. Lothrop, two of the original officers, are dead.   Mr. Lancaster, "our George," now resides in Bangor. Mr. Thurlow is now and for many years has been our worthy Postmaster.

There was no formal celebration of the Fourth of July in this place beyond ringing the bells and firing India crackers.   There was a large gathering of the Democracy at Bangor; Hon. Levi Woodbury of New Hampshire was the orator of the day.   There was also a Democratic Celebration at Black's Corner, in Prospect, and a Temperance Celebration at Frankfort. At the former place the oration was delivered by J. G. Dickerson, Esq., at the latter by Rev. S. H. Hayes.   All of the above celebrations were attended by large delegations from this place.

The "American Olympiad, instituted for the advancement of refined equestrian and gymnastic exercises, with a most splendid Bugle Band in a magnificent Chariot drawn by six beautiful Arabian horses," which being translated means a circus, exhibited here, for one day only, in the afternoon and evening of the 12th of July.

At the annual fall meeting there were 861 votes thrown on the guberna-torial ticket; for Anderson, Dem., 478, for Robinson, Whig, 366, for Appleton, Abol., 17.   Joseph Bean was re-elected Representative to the legislature.   An Act in relation to "Town Courts," and the question of summer instead of winter sessions of the legislature, were submitted to the people at this election.   The Act referred to became a law so far as Waldo was concerned and in January following Manasseh Sleeper, Esq., was appointed Justice of the Town Court of Belfast.   The movement in favor of summer sessions was successful.

A granite cistern was placed near the junction of Main and Franklin streets, on the locality now known as Custom-house squre, in the month of September.   It was supplied with water through pipes connecting with several reservoirs and was intended especially for the benefit of horses and cattle coming into our village from the country; the surplus water escaped into a reservoir under the cistern. The expense of its construction was defrayed by private subscription. After the Custom-House was erected it came to be considered rather an obstruction in the way of business and was removed not many years since to the place it now occupies near the corner of Pierce's Block.

Notwithstanding the political turmoil of this year there came a time when music, other than campaign songs, found an audience. Early in the season the Bath Quartette Club gave a concert at the Court House; still later the "Congo Melodists," who in these days would be styled Negro Minstrels, gave two concerts at Washington Hall; and later still the Baker Family, consisting of three brothers and their sister, gave two at the same place.

The schooner Borneo of Beverly, George S. Durham of this place, Master, bound hence to Bermuda with a hold full of lumber and provisions and a deck load of cattle and hay, was capsized at sea about the 13th of September. The wreck was fallen in with about the 20th, and her supercargo and crew were taken off. They had been on the wreck seven days without water or provisions, with the exception of a few raw potatoes. The next day after the schooner was capsized, Capt. Durham, who with all on board were lashed to the foremast, unlashed himself and in the attempt to go aft was swept from the deck and lost. The late Edmond Wilson of this place was supercargo. Messrs. Lucius Stephenson and Chandler Mahoney, two of the crew, are still living here. Stephen Murch, who was cook, died here a few years since. The only other one of the crew was Mr. Anson E. Durham, whose brother was Master of the schooner. Any one desirous of interviewing Mr. D. can do so by calling at the City Fish Market, corner of Main and Washington streets, where the angler with a silver hook, or one baited with scrip, can catch as nice a fish as ever swam in the sea.

Among our townsmen, prominent in our business circles, who died this year were Bailey Pierce, Esq., who came here from Frankfort, was for a while landlord of the Eagle Hotel, afterwards Clerk of the Courts of this county during the first administration of Governor Kent, and afterwards engaged in trade, who died April 3d aged fifty-six; Captain William Barnes, for many years a ship-master afterwards in trade here, who died April 23d aged forty-nine; Norman E. Roberts, Deputy Collector of this Port at the time of his death, which office he had held from 1841, who died December 7th aged thirty-six, and Samuel Jackson, one of the earliest inn-holders in the village, who died December 20th aged sixty-six.

The annals of this year will be continued in our next chapter.

CHAPTER XL. (1844-5)

The principal occupation of our voting population from early spring until the middle of November of this year, 1844, was the discussion of the political questions of the day, the tariff and the annexation of Texas, the merits of the candidates for the Presidency of the two great parties, Whig and Democratic, making or listening to public speeches, and attending political meetings and conventions. The Presidential candidates were Clay and Frelinghuysen, Polk and Dallas.

The former were nominated at a Whig Convention held at Baltimore on the first day of May. About five days afterwards the news reached here and the Whigs were excessively jubilant. The latter were nominated at a Democratic Convention held at the same place on the 27th. Intelligence of the event reached here about the first of June, and was welcomed by the Democracy with a salute of twenty-six guns and a banquet at the Phoenix House.

The campaign was inaugurated in this place on the 9th of March by the formation of the Belfast Democratic Association, of which Josiah Farrow was President, Benjamin F. Blackstone, Timothy Chase and Richard Moody, Vice-presidents, William T. Colburn, Secretary, James P. Furber, George Patterson, Alfred J. Libby, George Hemenway and Abraham N. Noyes, Directors; all of them are still living, and residing here with the exception of Messrs. Farrow, Furber and Libby.

The meetings of the Association were held in a room over the store on High street then occupied by Mr. William S. Brannigan, then styled No. 12 Phoenix Row, now occupied by N. G. Prescott & Company, until June following, when they began to be held in a hall over the store of Furber and Bean on Main street. The hall was fitted up as a reading-room, well furnished with seats, and its walls decorated with numerous portraits of distinguished democratic statesmen; it was kept open to visitors at all times except Sundays. A flag staff was erected in front of it from which floated the "star spangled banner". Two large signs were affixed to the front of the building, one bearing the words Democratic Hall, the other, "Polk and Dallas"; the latter was so constructed that it could be illuminated. It was dedicated on the 24th of June, on which occasion addresses were made by J. G. Dickerson, Esq., of Prospect, John K. True, Esq., of Montville, Andrew T. Palmer and Nathaniel Patterson, Esqs., and Hon. Alfred Johnson of this place. Judge Dickerson is the only one of the orators on the occasion now living.

The young Democracy of the town following the example of their elders, formed an association called the Young Hickory Club. The Club was organized July 9th, and the following officers were elected: David Haynes, President, Henry E. Burkmar and Alden D. Chase, Vice-presidents, Hiram Chase, Corr. Sec., Joseph S. Noyes, Recording Sec., James H. Spring, Alfred J. Libby and Cornelius L. Wilder, Directors. The meetings of the Club were held in Democratic Hall.

In imitation of the Democrats the Whigs formed a "Clay Club" on the first of June and for a while held their meetings in the old Masonic Hall, in the Babel. They afterwards erected a building on High street, opposite Phoenix Row, to which they gave the name of "Washington Hall". The building still stands there, remodeled by building a basement story and in other particulars; the basement is now an engine-house and the rooms over it are occupied by Mess. Hersey and Woodward. A Liberty Pole was erected, surmounted by a ship, below which floated the American flag with the names of Clay and Frelinghuysen. The design over the door in front was an eagle perched on a globe bearing in his talons the word "Protection". The hall was dedicated on the evening of the 31st of July with songs and speeches. The dedicatory address was by William G. Crosby, Esq. Addresses were also made by Solyman Heath, Esq. and Franklin Muzzy, Esq., of Searsmont.

A mass convention of the Whigs of the county was held on the Square in front of the Unitarian church on the 26th of August. The speakers on the occasion were Richard F. Perkins, Esq., of Augusta,

Hon. John C. Park of Boston and Ex-Gov. Kent; and in the evening Lucius
H. Chandler, Esq., of Thomaston, at Washington Hall.

Two days afterwards a Democratic mass convention was held on the
Common.   The convention was addressed by Albert G. Jewett, Esq., then
of Bangor, Col. Cullen Sawtelle of Norridgwock, Hon. Nathan Clifford,
now Judge Clifford, and Robert Rantoul, Jr., Esq., of Boston; and in
the evening by Wyman B. S. Moore, Esq., of Waterville.   At noon a free
collation was provided on the Common.

At the Presidential election the whole number of votes thrown was
741. Of these 443 were for Polk, 291 for Clay, and seven for Birney.

The first noticeable local event of the year 1845 was a Concert
at the Unitarian Church for the benefit of the poor in our village;
the amount realized from it was about eighty dollars.

On the fourth of February Benjamin Wiggin, Esq., of Bangor, now
residing in Boston, took possession of our Custom House, having been
appointed Collector of this Port in place of Col. George Thatcher, resigned.
The following subordinate officers were appointed for this place; Ansel
Lennan, now residing in Bangor, Deputy Collector, Capt. D. D. Pinkham,
Deputy Collector and Inspector, Bradford S. Foster, Weigher, Gauger
and Measurer.   The officers appointed by President Tyler did not find
much favor with the new Administration; Mr. Wiggin shared the same fate
with others occupying the same status, and in the month of April he
was removed and Nathaniel M. Lowney, Esq., was appointed in his stead.
No changes were made in the subordinate officers.

Early in the year a portion of our territory was taken from us
by act of the legislature and made a component part of the town of Searsport,
which was incorporated February 13th and held its first town-meeting
on the third of March.

On the 4th of March our Democratic townsmen fired twenty-seven
guns in honor of the inauguration of President Polk.

The matter of the Belfast and Quebec Railroad was again called
up, and the time allowed by the original charter for its construction
having expired an Act was procured from the legislature extending the
time for building and completing it to December 31, 1860.

We were not deficient in the matter of amusements such as singing,
&c., during the year.   In the month of February came the Augusta Glee
Club and gave two Concerts at Washington Hall, and the Harmoneon Family,
who gave us the same quantity, although not of the same quality, as
a portion of their minstrelsy was of the negro type.   The same family,
or another under the same name, was here in September.   In the month
of March we had a series of "Moral and Dramatic Entertainments" at Washington Hall; in other words a theatrical company was there "doing" Richard
III., Damon and Pythias, and other feats of the same character.   The
"American Olympiad" again made its appearance, on the 17th of June;
but this time with its "refined Grecian athletic and equestrian exhibitions"
and the "sublime Spanish spectacle, with splendid steeds gorgeously
caparisoned, called the Andalusian Entry."

Neither were we, without instruction and amusement in the lecture-room.
Albert Merrill, Esq., delivered a very interesting lecture on Phonography
on the 18th of February.   John Coffin Nazro, "Professor of the Divine
Art of Oratory," lectured on the evening of Fast-day, April 7th, on
Temperance, taking the scriptural standpoint, as he styled it.   He concluded
his lecture by advising his audience to "drink good liquor only and
put their trust in the Lord!"   In the same month Dr. George W. Ellis
gave a course of lectures, with practical illustrations, on Phrenology.

The steamers on the eastern route this year were the Portland,
Capt. Thomas Rogers, the Charter Oak, Capt. S. H. Howes, and the Penobscot,
Capt. T. G. Jewett.   The Portland made her first appearance for the
season on the 12th of March.   The Charter Oak soon followed and made
her last trip on the 8th of December.   The Penobscot came for the first
time June 25th and left on her last trip to the west on the 28th of
November.   The new steamer Bangor, propeller, touched at our wharf on

the 14th of August with a party of excursionists from Bangor. On the
31st, while on her passage from Boston to Bangor, she took fire when
a few miles from Castine and was entirely destroyed, with the exception
of her hull, which was iron, and a portion of her machinery. She was
run into a harbor in Islesborough and her hull was afterwards towed
to Bangor. There were about thirty-five passengers on board all of
whom were fortunately saved, a large quantity of freight, most of it
for parties in Bangor, valued at thirty thousand dollars, was totally
lost.

At the annual spring meeting Thomas Marshall, Benjamin F. Blackstone
and Daniel Putnam were chosen Selectmen, Henry Colburn, Clerk, Timothy
Chase, Treasurer. Mr. Colburn resigned his office in December and Joseph
Wheeler was chosen to fill the vacancy. Of the 98 officers chosen at
the above meeting forty are dead.

The first fire of the season occurred in the morning of the 23d
of April; a building on the premises of Mr. Eben Pierce, not far from
his house and barn, was partially destroyed by fire. It was occupied
by Henry Carlton as a joiner's shop. In the night of the 26th a barn
on the eastern side of the river was burned. In the evening of May
26th the old Foundry building, so called, situated near Rolerson's ship-yard,
previously occupied as an iron foundry and with much of the old machinery
still in it, was entirely destroyed. It was afterwards ascertained
that it was set on fire by some boys for the purpose of pilfering old
iron, brass and copper from the wreck. There were numerous fire alarms
during the year but the foregoing are the only ones remembered where
there was any considerable loss of property.

On the 27th of June The Republican Journal made its appearance
enlarged by the addition of a column of reading matter and otherwise
improved. On the 26th the Waldo Signal appeared under the name of the
State Signal, with an additional column; its publishers were Charles
Giles and Company. It was under the editorial care of Isaac N. Felch,
Esq., who edited it until its name and ownership were changed in 1847.

Mr. James M. Torry became landlord of the Phoenix House in the
month of June, and Mr. H. N. Lancaster, proprietor of the American House,
built the piazza in front of it and enlarged and improved it in other
particulars.

The same month brought about a change in our Post office. It had
been so well conducted for the four years preceding that it was not
deemed advisable to take it "out of the family", and thereupon Mr. William
T. Colburn was appointed to succeed his uncle, Mr. Henry Colburn. While
Mr. Colburn, the newly appointed postmaster held the place, which was
until there was a change in the national administration, the office
was kept, with the exception of a few months, in the store occupied
by him on Main street, now occupied by Mr. H. H. Forbes.

There was no organized celebration of the Fourth of July, yet it
did not pass uncelebrated. Numerous fishing parties passed the day
on the Bay and ponds, the boys were unusually industrious in the work
of firing crackers, and one of our "brazen war-dogs howled" at intervals
through the day, and into the evening. The last "howl", uttered in
Main street, brought down a shower of window-glass. There was a dance
in the evening at Democratic Hall.

On the evening of the 10th the young ladies of the Unitarian Society
held a Levee for the purpose of raising funds to remodel the pulpit
in the Unitarian Meeting-house. On the 13th, Sabbath religious services
were inaugurated at Washington Hall, which received the appellation,
for the time being, of the Seamen's Bethel.

A Division of the Sons of Temperance, styled Belfast Division,
No. 9, was opened and its officers installed on the 16th of July. The
officers were Edward Baker, W. P., Charles Giles, W. A., Lewis Richardson,
R. S., Charles W. Milliken, T., Calvin Hervey, C., J. W. Sherwood, A.
C., James H. Smith, I. S., I. C. Abbott, O. S.

The first day of August, the anniversary of the emancipation of the British West-India slaves, was commemorated at the Unitarian Church. An address was delivered by Rev. Frederic H. Hedge, then residing in Bangor.   It was a brilliant performance.   He gave a history of African slavery on this side of the Atlantic, tracing it back to the age of Columbus--of the efforts of Clarkson and others for its abolition and their ultimate success--portrayed in glowing colors the incongruity of slavery with a Republican form of government and contended for vigorous action for its abolition.   As the last resort for us of the North he squinted hard at dismemberment of the Union;--the last but effectual mode for ridding our skirts of the sin and its curse.

At the annual fall meeting there was but little excitement.   The whole number of votes thrown on the gubernatorial ticket was 640; 338 for Anderson, Dem., 290 for Morse, Whig, 12 for Fessenden, Liberty, or Abol.   There was no choice of Representative to the Legislature. At a meeting held on the Monday following, Henry Colburn, Whig, was elected.   Hon. David W. Lothrop was elected County Treasurer, William H. Burrill, Esq., Clerk of the Courts and William H. Weeks, Esq., of Unity, County Attorney.

The brig Arixene of this place, Capt. William McClintock, sailed for Philadelphia on the 11th of November laden with ice and was lost about 100 miles from Nantucket on the 16th; her officers and crew were rescued from the wreck by the schooner Montreal of Portland.

On the 27th of November the "Sturgess property," so called, at the junction of Main and High streets, was sold at public auction for $5330.00; the late Rufus B. Allyne, Esq., was the purchaser.   The same premises are now covered by the store occupied by Calvin Hervey, Johnson Block and McClintock's Block.

The work of launching vessels commenced this year in January and terminated in December.   The following were launched from the yard of Master Rolerson: Jan. 25th, barque Prospect of about 235 tons, May 31st, schooner Helen McLeod, 100, December 31st, barque Santee, 202, and brig Marshal, 220; the Santee was launched at 10.30 a. m., by sunlight, the Marshal at 11 p. m., by moonlight.   The following were launched from the yard of Master Carter: April 14th schooner Mary Farrow of about 140 tons, July 20th, schooner Malabar, 125, and October 8th, schooner Governor Anderson, 125.   The schooner Otter, of about 130 tons, built by Mr. William Tilden, was launched the 22nd of February; the schooner Peytona 96, built by Master Burgin, on Lane's Wharf, June 18th; the schooner Samuel Lewis, 100, from the yard of George U. Russ, at Russ' Point, June 24th; the brig Charles Edward, 150, from the yard of Master Palmer, October 1st, and the brig Samuel Potter, 150, built by Mr. William Tilden, October 30th.

Christmas was celebrated at the Universalist Church, which was decorated for the occasion, with religious services on Christmas Eve, and an Exhibition given by the Sunday-school teachers and scholars on the evening following.

CHAPTER XLI. (1846.)

Early in January of this year the offices of Sheriff of the county and Register of Probate were vacated by the expiration of the official terms of the incumbents, and James Y. McClintock was appointed Sheriff and Charles Palmer Register of Probate. Mr. McClintock appointed Axel Hayford his deputy in this town.

The first public lecture of the year was on the 14th by William L. Avery, Esq. afterwards editor of the Signal and Planet, before the Sons of Temperance. On the 29th Rev. F. A. Hodsdon gave a lecture on Odd Fellowship at the Universalist Church, and on the 12th of March Rev. Cyril Pearl lectured on the same subject at the Baptist Church. Doctor Darling gave a course of lectures on Physiology in the month of May at the Court House. In November there was a lecture by a Mr. Norton on Astronomy and one on the Magnetic Telegraph. Numerous lectures were given during the year on the subject of temperance.

Washington's Birthday--February 22d--was commemorated here, as it was throughout the Union, by the Washingtonian Temperance Associations. A very admirable address was delivered at the Unitarian Church, in the evening, by John K. True, Esq. of Montville. Mr. True removed to Mt. Vernon, O. in November following and died there in August of the next year aged thirty-two.

The first musical entertainment of the year was a "Charity Concert" at the Unitarian Church, on the evening of February 26th, for the purpose of raising funds for the purchasing of fuel for the poor in our village; the net amount realized was $78.72. The compiler was one of the committee selected to distribute the fund and painfully remembers to this day the reluctance with which he left his bed soon after daylight on the morning following, to answer the call of an antique specimen of the feminine gender who came to demand her portion of the fund and threatened a law-suit if it was not paid over forthwith!--The Misses Macomber, whose various excellences of character were duly certified by "Our George," gave a series of vocal and instrumental concerts in April. The Peak Family was here in August and gave two concerts at the Baptist Church.

This year was prolific in fires. How far the rivalry between the two engine companies or the curiosity to see them "break her down" contributed to the result is problematical. The first occurred soon after noon of the 6th of March, when a fire broke out in that portion of a building belonging to the Holt estate which was used for storing oakum, &c.; the other portion was occupied by a family. This portion, with its furniture in it, was saved although in a damaged condition; the other portion was destroyed. The fire was attributed to the attraction of cohesion between the spark from a pipe and the oakum. In the night of the 5th a small house on Bridge street, previously occupied by William Murch, but at that time unoccupied, was burned. Between 2 and 3 o'clock of the morning of the 20th fire was discovered bursting through the side of a new wooden building on Church street, owned by Hon. Joseph Williamson, occupied on the ground floor by J. C. Morse and Co., dealers in dry goods, and Alfred Richards, grocer, and in the second story by the Sons of Temperance. The engines were immediately on the spot and by great exertions prevented a wide spread conflagration. The brick block on Main street, then occupied by John Pierce and Beaman and Perry, now by Alden D. Chase and Augustus Perry, was on fire several times. The building in which the fire originated was entirely destroyed, with its contents. It stood on the site of the brick building now occupied in the second story by the Republican Journal, which was erected in 1849. In the night of June 4th a building belonging to John Pierce and Co. near the westerly end of the Bridge was burned, with its contents, the knees and moulds for a contemplated vessel of about 150 tons and a quantity of carpenters tools. At the time the fire was raging a building on the old Distillery wharf was discovered to be on fire; this was soon extinguished. Both were believed to be the work of an incendiary; the one first named certainly was, as one of our worthy citizens, then a young man, can testify, who was crossing the bridge after a somewhat protracted call on the eastern side of the river and saw some one swing a firebrand in the air and then deposit it in a pile of shavings under the building; the flames following instanter. About 10 o'clock in the evening of September 18th a fire broke out in an old store on Puddle Dock, known as the Prince store, owned by Daniel Merrill, Esq. and Captain Wells, then occupied as a work-shop; the fire spread to a dwelling-house known as the Hewes house, owned by Hon. John S. Kimball; both buildings were entirely consumed. The house was occupied by two families who barely escaped, losing most of their household furniture. The wind was very high and apprehensions were expressed that the fire would be communicated to other buildings in the vicinity by the flying sparks. This was the occasion when the young lady remarked, to the great amusement of the by-standers, that she wished "the wind or something else would send some of the sparks to her house it was so long since any of them had been there." On the night of October 16th the house and barn of Col. Watson Berry and a house and barn occupied by Josiah S. Witherell at the Upper Bridge were burned. Nothing was saved except a portion of their furniture and clothing. The fire was first discovered on the roof of Col. Berry's barn; how it came there has never been satisfactorily ascertained. On the morning of the 24th fire broke out on the westerly side of Main street which consumed the following buildings: a store owned by Joshua Pickard, occupied by Luther Coombs, grocer, the old building long known as the Babel, owned by William Tilden and Alonzo Osborn, occupied in a portion of the second story by Mr. T. as a paint-shop, on the lower floor by Hersey and Wilder, tinplate-workers, and William Quimby, provision dealer, and the dwelling house of James Cook, barber. On the site of those buildings, saving that portion of the premises afterwards appropriated to widening the street, about thirty feet in width, now stand the brick stores occupied by Thomas W. Pitcher, Manly E. Dodge, William C. Marshall, B. C. Dinsmore and Son, George G. Pierce and H. E. McDonald. A wooden building owned by the late Benjamin Hazeltine, adjoining Cook's house on the north, was torn down to stop the progress of the fire in that direction; that building is represented by the brick store now occupied by Edward A. Perry. A wooden building which stood at the corner, where McClintock's Block stands, occupied by Ignatius Sargent, grocer, and Hendrie and Bradbury, (A. H.) dealers in hats and furs, was saved only by great exertions.

The Babel was one of the oldest landmarks in our village. It was apparently one building but was in fact two closely united. They were built about 1807; the northerly portion by Deacon Stanley, and Samuel Walton, the southerly by Squire Nesmith, and were three stories high, each story being of the same height; they were reduced to two stories not many years before the fire, as stated in a previous chapter.

We had no reason to complain of the lack of steamboat accommodations this year. On the 8th of March the steamer Portland, Capt. Thomas Rogers, made her appearance on our waters. On the 5th of April came the Penobscot, Capt. T. G. Jewett, on the 8th the Governor, her first appearance here, Capt. S. H. Howes, on the 9th the Huntress, Capt. D. Blanchard, and on the 18th of June the T. F. Secor, her first appearance, Capt. T. B. Sanford. The Penobscot was called the Peoples Line and plied between Bangor and Boston; she was the last to leave the route; making her last trip to the west on the first of December. The Huntress connected with the railroad at Portland but was taken off the route in May and the Governor took her place. The Secor plied between this place and Ellsworth, touching at intermediate points and making two trips weekly; she ran until November. The John W. Marshall, Capt. W. H. Byram, was on the route a few trips in the fall of the year. The Bangor, propeller, Capt. Charles H. Spear, was on the route between Bangor and Boston a portion of the season employed principally as a freight-boat. She was afterwards sold to the Government and her name changed to the "Scourge."

On the 21th of March Phoenix Hall, having been handsomely fitted for the uses of the Odd Fellows, was formally dedicated as Odd Fellows Hall. The dedication address was made by Rev. Richard Woodhull of Thomaston; up to this date a Hall over the store of Mr. Oakes Angier had been used for the meetings of the Lodge.

At the annual Spring meeting, March 23d, Thomas Marshall, Benjamin F. Blackstone and Daniel Putnam were chosen Selectmen, Joseph Wheeler, Clerk, and Timothy Chase, Treasurer.   Mr. Wheeler resigned his office in July following and Henry Colburn, Esq., was elected in his place on the 27th of the same month.

Mr. Colburn was elected Representative at the preceding fall election but having temporarily removed to New York an opinion prevailed that his office was thereby vacated. A town meeting was called to fill the vacancy. It was held on the 6th of April and Samuel S. Hersey was elected. The right to the seat was contested before the legislature and it was awarded to Mr. Hersey.

A theatrical company under the management of Mr. J. C. Myers gave several performances this month at Washington Hall.

The 16th was Fast Day, and the ground was well covered with snow which was falling through the preceding day; it made but a brief sojourn with us.

Samaritan Tent, No. 17, Maine District, of the Independent Order of Rechabites was organized on the evening of the 29th and the following officers were elected, Ephraim Swett, Sh., S. S. Hersey, P. C. R., Benj. Griffin, C. B., Joseph Wheeler, D. R., Isaac Allard, Jr., F. S., W. S. Brannigan, R. S., Ansel Lennan, I., Cyrus Rowe, L., Benj. W. Lothrop, and Joseph Rolerson, C. R. S., S. A. Hammond and Nathaniel Merrill, D. C. R. S., J. G. Sumner, I. G. The meetings of the Tent were held in a hall over the store of Mr. Oakes Angier; it continued in active operation for two or three years.

On the 8th of May, Mr. Cyrus Rowe purchased George C. Griffin's interest in the Journal and the old firm name of Rowe and Griffin was resumed; it continued until January, 1849.

There was no formal celebration of the Fourth of July here but there was the usual amount of bell-ringing and cracker-firing. In the morning there was a parade of the mounted "Fantastics", and in the afternoon several balloons of domestic manufacture were sent up; one of them exploded, the others behaved very properly. In the evening we had quite a handsome display of fire-works.

The firemen of our village were visited on the 9th by the Amory Company from Bangor and the Bagaduce Company from Castine. The visitors were cordially welcomed and entertained at the Phoenix House.   There was a trial of strength between the several companies. Notwithstanding some difference of opinion it was pretty generally conceded that the Amory   threw highest into the air but the Hydrant the longest distance ahead.

On the evening of the 14th some Seceding Shakers gave an entertainment, rather an emaciated one, at Washington Hall.

On the 18th came the "Mammoth Circus," for one day only. This "Mighty equestrian troupe", according to the handbills, was preceded on its entrance to the village by "the New York Brass Band in their costly Chariot, the most superb affair ever beheld, drawn by Ten Splendid Steeds."   The 8th of August was marked by the "Triumphal entrance to the village of the vast and magnificent Van Amburgh's Collection of trained animals, preceded by the colossal Roman Chariot drawn by eight Flemish horses of Prodigious size and weight!" The exhibition was advertised to take place on "High street near Mount Rural." The ruralists were indeed here, and in larger numbers than ever before at a similar exhibition, attracted doubtless by the announcement that Van Amburgh would put his head in the lion's mouth; but it puzzled the topographers of that day, as it would those of the present, to locate Mount Rural. The place of exhibition was in fact a vacant piece of land between High street and Waldo Avenue just northerly from the house then occupied by Hon. Ralph C. Johnson.

In the same month Hon. Alfred Marshall of China was appointed Collector of the Customs for this Port in place of Nathaniel M. Lowney, Esq., whose nomination to the Senate had been rejected. Mr. Marshall removed to this place with his family and held the office until a change of the National Administration in 1849. He resided here for a while after the expiration of his official term, and then returned to China, where he died in October, 1868, aged seventy-one. No changes were made in the subordinate officers during his term except the appointment of his son, Jacob S., to the office of Inspector in place of Capt. Pinkham removed.

At the annual fall meeting, September 14th, the whole number of votes thrown on the gubernatorial ticket was 709; 359 for Dana, Dem., 294 for Bronson, Whig, 56 for Fessenden, Abol. There was no choice by the people; Dana was elected by the legislature at its next session. There was no choice of Representative. At a meeting held on the 21st, at which 769 votes were thrown, Henry Colburn, Whig, was elected.

The building of the brick Academy, the one now standing, on the site of the wooden one which was burned in 1842, was this month completed and opened for the reception of pupils under the tuition of Mr. George W. Field, now Rev. Dr. Field of Bangor, and Miss Elizabeth A. Barnes. It was built by private contributions and cost about $2200.00.

Rev. Edward F. Cutter was installed Pastor of the North Church on the 23d of this month; the installation services were as follows: Invocation and reading the scriptures by Rev. Mr. Bowker of Union, Prayer by Rev. Mr. Freeman of Prospect, Sermon by Prof. Park of Andover, Mass.; Installing prayer by Rev. Mr. Thurston of Searsport, Charge by Rev. Mr. Chapman of Camden, Right-hand of Fellowship by Rev. Mr. Sewal of Castine, Address to church and people, by Rev. Mr. Hayes of Frankfort, Concluding prayer by Rev. Mr. Wiswall of Brooks. Mr. Cutter's pastoral connection with the church and society terminated in September 1855.

On the same day a new Church was organized at the Head of the Tide. The sermon on the occasion was by Rev. Mr. Hayes of Frankfort, Organization of the Church by Rev. Mr. Chapman of Camden, Consecrating prayer by Rev. Mr. Wiswall of Brooks, Fellowship of the Churches, by Rev. Mr. Cutter, Address to the Church, by Rev. Mr. Thurston of Searsport. The ladies of the North Church presented a communion service to the new church as a token of affectionate interest in their enterprise.

On the 13th of October the Sons of Temperance dedicated their new Hall in the attic of the store now occupied by the Messrs. Howes. The address was by Rev. Mr. Kalloch of East Thomaston.

On the 18th the funeral services of Mr. David Robinson, a worthy and much esteemed townsman who died on the 15th aged thirty-five, father of our fellow citizen Mr. Benjamin Robinson, were held at the North Church. His remains were accompanied to the grave by the Odd Fellows, of which order he was a member. The Lodge had been in existence about two years and numbered about two hundred members. Mr. R. was the first one of the brotherhood for whom the funeral rites and ceremonies of the order were required.

The schooner Mariner of this place, owned by our now venerable fellow citizen Robert Patterson, sailed from Tarpaulin Cove for Philadelphia on the 2d of September; she has never been heard from. Two sons of the owner, George W. and David F., Joshua Durham, John B. Haskell, all of this place, and John Tyler of Swanville, were on board of her.

The Superintending School-committees of the county met here in convention on the 3d of November to elect a member for this county of the Board of Education created by the last legislature; Hon. Ebenezer Knowlton of Montville was elected. The Board met at Augusta on the 16th of December and elected William G. Crosby, Esq., of this place

Secretary of the Board.   He held the office until he resigned in July, 1849. Hon. Elisha M. Thurston was elected to succeed him.

The last noticeable events of this year were the Exhibitions of the pupils at the Academy and of the scholars of the Sabbath School at the Universalist Church on Christmas Eve.

CHAPTER XLII. (1847.)

A list of the vessels launched in the year 1846, which should have been embraced in our last chapter, is as follows: Brig, Judge Whitman of about 175 tons burthen, brig Belfast, 191, brig Atlantic, 160, brig Montague, 150, brig Wacamaw, afterwards called the San Jacinto, 185, brig Queen Esther, 188, brig Antoinette, 150, brig General Taylor, 150, brig Leghorn, tonnage not remembered, brig Rolerson, 200, schooner Michigan, 140, schooner Tahmiroo, 127, schooner Comet, 76, schooner Mary Reed, 100, schooner John Farwell, barque Pequot, 200.   Of the foregoing the Michigan and the Judge Whitman, were launched from the yard of Master Carter, the schooner Tahmiroo and John Farwell from the yard of S. C. Nickerson and Co. at the Upper Bridge, the Almatia and schooner Mary Reed at Russ' point, the Wacamaw and Rolerson from the yard of Master Rolerson, the Queen Esther from the yard of Master Palmer and the Antoinette from the yard of John Pierce and Company.   The foregoing are all the vessels launched this year, 1846, within the memory of the compiler.

The vessels launched in the year 1847 were as follows: the brig Nitheroy of about 190 tons from the yard of Master C. P. Carter, the brig President Z. Taylor, 150, from the yard of Mess. White and Connor, V. R. Lancaster master builder, the schooner Melrose, 136, Henry E. Carter master builder, a brig of 168 tons, William Tilden owner, Samuel L. Sweetsir master builder, schooner Major Ringgold, 132, P. J. Carter master builder, brig Judge Mitchell, 146, from yard of Master C. P. Carter, schooner William Stevens, 115, Ezra Holmes master builder, schooner Florian, 133, H. Woodcock master builder, ship Danvers, 413, James S. Burgin master builder, brig Russian, 200, E. Stevenson master builder, brig Orizava, 170, C. P. Carter master builder, bark Grampus, 240, Henry E. Carter master builder, brig Josephine, 200, S. L. Sweetsir master builder, bark Brunette, 250, John G. Hall master builder, and brig Harriet Newell, 194, L. R. Palmer master builder.   The compiler is quite confident but not certain that the brig Saltillo, and the schooners Abby Weld and Sarah A. Smith were launched this year.

The first musical entertainment of the year was furnished by the Union Brass Band at the Court House on the evenings of the 4th and 5th of February.   The Thomaston Brass Band gave a concert at the Unitarian Church in the evening of the third of March for the benefit of the suffering poor in Ireland.   The Hammond Family, seceders from the Society of Shakers at Alfred, gave two Concerts at Washington Hall on the evenings of the 10th and 11th of May.   The Campanologians, or Swiss Bell-ringers, gave an entertainment at the Unitarian Church on the evening of the 15th of July.   The Ethiopian Serenaders followed on the 29th with a burlesque of the Bell-ringers; a very mirth-provoking part of their concert. Mr. and Mrs. Canderbeck, and Mr. Squires gave two concerts on the 22d and 23rd of November.

On the evening of Sunday the 7th of February Major Timothy Chase was assaulted in Church street, while on the way from the post-office to his house, by two ruffians, knocked down and severely injured in his face, arms and otherwise.   The selectmen offered a reward of $300 for the detection and conviction of the guilty parties.   The object of the assault was, it was surmised, to get possession of some warrants which had been issued against parties in the village for violations of the liquor law; the Major's hat, with two warrants in it, was carried off by the parties who assaulted him.

The hall over the store of Mr. Oakes Angier, occupied by the Rechabites was formally dedicated on the evening of the 18th of February.   The address was by Mr. Benjamin Griffin, editor of the Journal.

About nine o'clock in the evening of the 19th we had quite an experience in the way of earthquake; the shock was very sensibly felt here and in the surrounding country.

Washington's birthday was commemorated at the North Church, an address was delivered by Rev. Mr. Cutter.   There was a Ball in the evening at Washington Hall.

Mr. Frederic Sanborn opened the lecture campaign with a course on Galvanism and Electricity at the Academy. A lecture on Common Schools was delivered at the Unitarian Church on the evening of May 22d, by William G. Crosby, Sec. of the board of Education. Professor Beal gave several lectures in July on a new method of reading music called the Numeral Harmony. Lunsford Lane of North Carolina, once a slave, lectured at the Court-house on the evening of August 13th on slavery and its influences at the North, Capt. Andrew T. Palmer, who had just returned from Mexico, gave a very interesting lecture at Washington Hall on the climate, products, and the social and political condition of that country, and the movements of our army in which he had participated, on the evening of the 24th of December; the lecture was repeated the following evening.

The first steamer of the season was the Portland, Capt. Rogers. She arrived March 12th and plied on the route from Boston to Bangor and Eastport, touching at intermediate points, until June when she was placed on the route between Portland and Boston. The Charter Oak, Capt. Byram, came on early in April and ran until her place was taken by the Penobscot, Capt. Asa M. Sanford, in May. The Governor, Capt. Howes, came in May and continued on the route until late in November. Capt. Howes was superseded in the command of her about the first of July by Capt. T. G. Jewett. The Secor, Capt. T. B. Sanford, ran between this place and Ellsworth from early in May until November, and then from Frankfort, after the river closed, to Portland.

Our Collection district was razeed in March by cutting off Bangor and Frankfort and making them part of a new district of which Bangor was the Port of Entry.

Judge Thayer's official term as Judge of Probate having expired by limitation, Joseph Miller, Esq., of Lincolnville, was appointed to succeed him and held his first Court here on the first Tuesday in April.

At the annual spring meeting, March 22d, Nathaniel M. Lowney, James Gammons and Abraham N. Noyes were chosen Selectmen, Nathaniel Patterson, Clerk, and Samuel S. Hersey, Treasurer. The monies raised were $1650.00 for schools, $700.00 for paupers, $1000.00 for incidental expenses, $700.00 for roads and bridges, $5000.00 in labor and materials, and $1000.00 for payment of debts.

Excelsior Encampment of the I. O. of O. F. was instituted on the 15th of April, and the following officers were elected: Ansel Lennan, C. P., David W. Lothrop, H. P., Benjamin Griffin, S., Benjamin F. Barker, I., Darius D. Pinkham, S. W., Benjamin Sargent, T. W., Abram Jordan, S., Martin P. Townsend, G.

On the 15th of May Capt. Palmer with his company of infantry left on the steamer Penobscot for Fort Adams, Newport, R. I., en-route for Mexico.

In the morning of the first of June a young man by the name of Marden committed suicide in his room at the American House. He was found suspended from the bedpost by a silk handerchief round his neck. He had been in the employment of the stage proprietor as hostler.

On the 18th Mr. Bird, the "famed wizard of the East," gave an "exhibition of Mirth, Magic and Ventriloquism" at Washington Hall.

This month, for the first time in our village, ice became a marketable commodity. It was sold at the rate of one cent per pound delivered at the purchaser's house, or half a cent at the ice-house. The ice-house stood in rear of the wooden stores on high street now occupied by Charles H. Mitchell and Andrew D. Bean, and the dealers in the article were Charles U. and Lucius E. Burkmar.

The Fourth of July being Sunday, the day following was celebrated in its stead. In the forenoon there was a parade of the Callathumpian Band and Fantastic Guards, and another of the Firemen, who marched through the streets preceded by our new Brass Band and afterwards practised with their engines. In the evening there was a fine display of fireworks on the Common to the great gratification of hosts of men, women and children and the great grief of one little fellow, a son of Mr. Roger Merrithew of Belmont, who came very near being fatally wounded by the falling shaft of an exploded rocket which struck him on the head. American Hall, the new hall in the American House, H. N. Lancaster landlord, was opened with a public Ball and supper.

About this time there was an exhibition at Washington Hall of "Historical and Scriptural Dioramas and Panoramas on 8000 feet of canvass." One of them was a panorama of Bunyan's Pilgrim's Progress.

The first number of a newspaper, the New Planet, William L. Avery, Esq., and Horace K. Kimball publishers, issued on the 15th of July. It was a folio sheet, with seven wide columns on each page, and was published weekly. After sixteen numbers had been issued its proprietors purchased the Signal and on the 4th of November the State Signal and New Planet, united, made its first appearance. In January, 1849, Mr. Kimball dissolved his connection with the paper, and Mr. Avery continued to publish and edit it until March 3, 1853, when he sold it to Mr. D. P. Prime who changed its name to the Belfast Signal.

Rockwell and Company's New York Circus, "with Fannie Ellsler the most sagacious pony in the world," exhibited here on the 22d and 23d of July, and on the second of August Sands, Lent and Co's "American Circus Company, with the India-rubber man and the English horse May-fly, who dances in an inconceivable graceful style" gave us "an Olympian Festival for one day only."

Rev. M. A. H. Niles was installed pastor of the Unitarian Society on the 11th of August. The services were as follows: Introductory prayer and Charge to the pastor by Rev. Mr. Wheeler of Topsham, Installing prayer by Rev. Mr. Cole of Hallowell, Sermon by Rev. Dr. Gannett, address to the people by Rev. Mr. Miles of Lowell, Right hand of Fellowship and concluding prayer by Rev. Mr. Judd of Augusta. After the Installation the members of the society and clergymen of their own and other denominations dined at American Hall. Mr. Niles was so sick at the time as to be able to be present at a portion only of the installation services. He died on the 17th, aged forty-one. He was born in Deer Isle but early in life removed to Newburyport. Having finished his collegiate and professional course of study he was settled as pastor of a church in Marblehead, and afterwards in Lowell. He first came to this place in the month of May of this year. His funeral solemnities were observed at the Unitarian Church on Sunday the 22d, when a discourse appropriate to the occasion was preached by Rev. Mr. Judd, who died January 26th, 1853.

On the 10th of September a barn on the eastern side of the river was burned; it was supposed that it was set on fire by a poor, unfortunate, half-crazed person by the name of Wilson. This was the only fire during the year, so far as the compiler remembers, by which any building was destroyed. On the morning of December 7th a wooden building at the foot of Main street, owned by Josiah Farrow, Esq., and occupied by Mr. N. Chapman as a block-maker's shop, was found to be on fire. The loss on the building and contents was estimated at $400.00; the building however was not so much injured but that it was repairable.

The dedication of the new Meeting-house at the Head of the Tide took place on the 22d of September and Rev. Samuel Souther was installed Pastor of the church on the same day.

At the annual fall meeting the whole number of votes on the ballot for Governor was 766; 444 for Dana, Demo., 304 for Bronson, Whig, 17 for Fessenden, Abol. and 1 "scattering." There was no choice of representative to the legislature. The candidates were Nathaniel M. Lowney, Demo., William Pitcher, Whig, and numerous others of divers party stripes. At a meeting held on the Monday following Mr. Lowney was elected.

The Waldo County Agricultural Society, which was organized under a new Act of Incorporation at the Court-house on the 15th of July, held its first Cattle Show and Fair at Belmont Corner on the 20th and 21st of November. The amount distributed in premiums was about one hundred and seventy-five dollars.

The Teachers Institute for this county, the first one held under the Act of the last legislature which created the institute, commenced on the 15th and closed its session on the 24th; its catalogue contained the names of 77 male and 68 female pupils. The session was held in the brick schoolhouse. Evening lectures were delivered by Mr. W. B. Fowle of Boston, Rev. S. H. Hayes of Frankfort, Rev. E. F. Cutter, S. Souther and S. Heath, Esq., of this place, Rev. S. Thurston of Searsport and the Sec. of the Board of Education. At the annual convention of the School Committees Benjamin Griffin, Editor of the Journal, was elected member of the Board for this county in place of Hon. Ebenezer Knowlton who declined re-election.

The Waldo Mutual Insurance Company, (Marine), was duly organized and commenced business on the 24th of November. Josiah Farrow, Esq., was elected President and Nathaniel H. Bradbury, Esq., Secretary. There were eighteen corporators named in the Charter twelve of whom are still living. The first Policy issued by the company was on the brig Antoinette, Dec. 2d, 1847; the last was on the Ship C. W. White, Dec. 8th, 1858; at which date the Company ceased doing business. Both the above vessels were built here; the Antoinette was afterwards lost at sea with all hands; the C. W. White is still in full life.

Among the brick buildings erected this year was "Johnson's Block" on High street. Its first occupants on the ground floor were Mr. Horatio H. Johnson, owner of the block and Mr. William O. Poor; on the second floor Mr. Samuel Locke, brother of our fellow citizens John L. and Horatio J. Locke and Mrs. M. B. Towne wife of the late Thomas Towne. The third story was first occupied by the Sons of Temperance. In the construction of the block, Eben. Edwards was master-mason, William Winslow master carpenter, and the stone-work was by N. and E. Hawkes. One of the wooden buildings removed from the premises to make room for the new brick block is now part of the dwelling-house of John Cunningham on Miller street, beyond jail-hill. It was originally the work-shop of the late Job White, axe-maker, and while occupied by him stood in the vicinity of the Universalist Church on what is now called Court street. The brick block at the corner of Main and Beaver streets, formerly occupied by Daniel Faunce and Company, now by Charles H. Sargent and Daniel Sylvester, was built this year. A wooden building which stood on the premises, occupied by Faunce and White, was removed on the 31st of March and now constitutes part of the wooden block on Church street owned by Josiah Mitchell. The construction of the brick block commenced on the first day of April and was completed on the 17th of June; when "Daniel" was again at the "old stand" and offered goods for sale "as cheap as at any store in town for the same kind of pay". The first occupant of the westerly end of the block, now occupied by Dr. Sylvester, was Mr. S. G. Thurlow, our present post-master, who took possession of it on the 27th of July. On the "burned district" of the Babel fire of the year preceding, two brick stores were built by the late Alonzo Osborn, two by the late James Cook, and one by the late Benjamin Hazeltine. The brick addition to the American House, larger in capacity than the original house, was built this year by the proprietor, Mr. H. N. Lancaster, and the "rooms of circumambient construction" were remodeled!

Mention should have been made in our last chapter of the erection in 1846 of the brick block on Main street now occupied on the ground floor by Col. Hiram Chase and Mr. M. P. Woodcock. The store now occupied by Mr. W. has always been a book-store; its first occupants were Mess. Washburn and Jordan. The first occupant of the office above it was Hon. Nehemiah Abbott. The first occupant of the store now occupied by Col. Chase was his father Major Timothy Chase. The room above it was first occupied by the Collector of Customs for this District, Gen. Marshall. It continued to be occupied by the Collector for the time being until the Custom House at the head of Main street was built; the office was removed to that building Jan. 1, 1857.

CHAPTER XLIII. (1848.)

This year opened with a gloomy sky and a general feeling of gloom pervading our community. On the second day of January the funeral obsequies of our worthy and enterprising townsman, Capt. Joseph Rolerson, his wife and son Charles, were observed at the Universalist Church. They perished in the wreck of the brig Falconer, which was lost in Ipswich Bay on the 18th of December, on her passage from St. Johns, N. B., to Boston, laden with passengers and coal from Sidney. Fourteen of the passengers also perished. The remains of the Captain, his wife and son, were brought to this place for interment. He was a member of the Lodge of Odd Fellows and was buried with the usual rites and ceremonies of the Order.

A Lyceum was maintained during a large part of the year, excluding the summer months. The exercises consisted of lecturers and discussions. Among the lectures were Rev. Messrs. Edward F. Cutter, Joseph Ricker, Nathan C. Fletcher, Hon. Joseph Williamson and James W. Webster of this place, Rev. Stephen Thurston of Searsport and William H. Codman, Esq., of Camden.

The musical entertainments of the year commenced on the 21st of January with a concert at the Unitarian Church by the Belfast Brass Band; they gave another in May--Mr. Wyeete and his "wonderful family, from Glasgow, Scotland," gave a "Grand Olio, or musical entertainment," at Washington Hall on the 14th of June.--The "Kilmiste Family from Europe" gave two or three "Grand Vocal, Instrumental, and Terpsichorean Entertainments" at the same place in July and August. --Barnekoy and Company gave a concert on the 8th of August. --A "Grand, Vocal, Sentimental, Instrumental, Ethiopian and Operatic Soiree" was held at Washington Hall on the 11th of October by the Harmoneons, and on the 24th, Mr. Dempster, a somewhat celebrated vocalist, gave a concert at Osborn's Hall. This hall was in the brick building on Main street erected the year preceding by Mr. Alonzo Osborn.

At the annual spring meeting, March 6th, Nathaniel M. Lowney, James Gammons and Abram N. Noyes were elected Selectmen, Nathaniel Patterson, Clerk, Daniel Haraden, Treasurer. The monies raised were for support of schools $2,500.00--being about $900.00 more than ever before raised--for support of paupers and insane $900.00, for incidental expenses $700.00, for payment of debts $1,000.00, for repairs of roads and bridges $1,000.00 and $5,000.00 in labor and materials. A vote was passed to allow for labor of men and oxen on the highways 12 1-2 cents per hour.

The new Hall of the Sons of Temperance in Johnson Block was formally dedicated on the evening of the tenth; the address was by Rev. N. C. Fletcher.

On the 28th Mr. Martin Cross announced to the public that he had become landlord of the Phoenix House.

The first steamer to make her appearance was the Admiral, Capt. Thomas Rogers, March 7th. Beside her there were on the route between this place and Portland and Boston, the Senator, Capt. Samuel Seymour, who made her first appearance on the 6th of June and her last on the 20th of July, when her place was taken by the Governor, Capt. T. G. Jewett. The new steamer State of Maine, Capt. S. H. Howes, touched here for the first time on the 6th of July, and made an excursion down the Bay the day following. She left this route on the 13th of November. The W. J. Pease, a new boat, made her first appearance here on the 10th of April; she was commanded by Capt. T. B. Sanford until early in July when Capt. William Flowers took command of her. The Penobscot and the Charter Oak were also on the route a portion of the season. The Secor resumed her trips between this place and Ellsworth on the 13th of May. At one time in the summer the fare from this place to Boston was reduced by competition to one dollar.

The pulpit in the Unitarian Church which had bravely maintained its position for thirty years yielded at last to the demand of fashionable Christianity and was converted into a desk, from which Rev. Cazneau Palfrey preached for the first time on Sunday the 16th of April. While

the change was being made the religious services of the society were
held in the Vestry.   Doctor Palfrey was installed Pastor on the 19th.
The religious services on the occasion were as follows: Sermon by Rev.
Dr. Thompson of Salem, Mass., Installing prayer and Charge to the Pastor
by Rev. Dr. Parkman of Boston, Fellowship of the churches by Rev. Mr.
Cole of Hallowell.   Address to the people by Rev. Mr. Cutler of Portland.
In the evening there was a parish "Pic-nic" at Osborn's Hall.   Dr. Palfrey's
pastoral connection with the society was terminated by his resignation
in April 1871.   His farewell discourse was preached on the 16th of that
month.   He still resides here, esteemed and beloved by the members of
the society to whom for nearly a quarter of a century he broke the bread
of life, and respected by the community at large.

There were but few lectures this year, aside from those before
the Lyceum and Temperance Associations.   Mr. Wakefield delivered one
on the Magnetic Telegraph on the evening of the 21st of April, Dr. N.
Wheeler delivered three on Phrenology in the month of May, and Dr. Gregory
three or more in August on the professional education of females as
physicians.

The first number of the Maine Common School Advocate was issued
on the first day of May.   It was published by Rowe & Griffin and edited
by the Secretary of the Board of Education.   It was published semi-monthly
until August 1, 1849, when it was discontinued for lack of patronage
sufficient to pay the cost of publication.

About 10 o'clock in the evening of the first of May the first fire
of the season occurred.   A small wooden building on the Lincolnville
road, a short distance beyond jail hill, was burned with all its contents.
It was occupied by a widow and her two small children, who were in bed
and asleep when the fire broke out and barely escaped with their lives.
The general opinion was that the fire was kindled by a mean, cowardly
scamp who lacked the moral courage to resort to the law of the land
for redress of a real or fancied injury.   In the morning of November
21st a barn belonging to Capt. Isaac Smalley, on the road to the Head
of the Tide, about a mile from the village, was wholly consumed with
the ell connecting it with the house in which he lived.   How the fire
originated was never known.   The policy of insurance on the buildings
had expired but a few days before the fire.   There were frequent fire
alarms during the year, but the foregoing are the only instances within the memory of the compiler when there was a serious loss of property.

The following is a list of the vessels launched this year, so far
as remembered; the ship Bothnia of about 460 tons, brigs Rockingham,
148, Georgiana, 172, Lady of the Lake, 148, Carlann, 191, Marine, 215,
Martha Rogers, 198, Xenophon, 245, Roscoe, 199, Huron, 206, General
Marshall, 200; barks Ortona, 276, Martha Anna, 272, Suliote, 263, E.
Wilson, 248, Oakes Angier, 193; schooners Lamartine, 142, Henry Dunster,
145, Cameo, 70, Sea Bee, 80, Rebecca Fogg, 135.   The work of launching
commenced in April and terminated in December; eight of the above vessels
were launched in October.

The "Circus and Menagerie" of June, Titus, and Co., was here for
one day only on the 30th of June, with "the Lion Queen, Miss M. A. Randolph,
who entered the wild beasts' lair and exhibited her astonishing command
over the wild natives of the Desert."

The Fourth of July was celebrated by the Odd Fellows, who were
out in full force and regalia.   Preceded by the Brass Band they marched
from their Hall to the Unitarian Church, where, after prayer by Rev.
N. C. Fletcher and the reading of the Declaration by L. W. Howes, Esq.,
an oration was delivered by Rev. Albert Case of Worcester, Mass.   At
the close of the exercises they proceeded to Merrill and Pitcher's store-
house, near the steamboat wharf, where a dinner was provided by Mr.
Benjamin Sargent.   The only startling event of the day was the death
of a little boy, son of Mr. Jacob Ames, who was killed by being thrown
from a wagon.

A "Rough and Ready Club" was organized on the 5th at Washington Hall. Samuel G. Thurlow was elected President, Joseph Dennett and Horatio N. Palmer, Vice-Presidents, and Charles Giles, Secretary. Daniel Putnam, Edwin C. Kimball, Prescott Hazeltine, Daniel Faunce, Ephraim K. Maddocks, Samuel Edwards, Edmund P. Brown, Daniel Lane, Jr., and Samuel A. Blodgett were chosen a "Committee of Ways and Means." What the duties of this committee were is somewhat uncertain; but it is very certain that they found "ways and means" to rally at the polls a larger number of voters for "Old Rough and Ready" than ever before came up in this town to the support of the Whig candidate for the Presidency.

On the 7th Robert W. Quimby re-opened the Bathing-house on the steamboat wharf in connection with a refreshment room, and Luther Coombs opened the New England House, which he pledged himself to "conduct on strict Temperance principles." Since that time the house has been much enlarged and improved in its exterior and interior arrangements. The oldest portion of it was originally the dwelling-house of Benjamin Eells, erected about 1807. Some of the patrons of the house while Mr. Coombs was landlord cannot fail to remember the plaintive music of his voice when humming the stanza commencing with, "How long, dear Savior, O how long."

One of the engrossing tonics of public interest this year was a contemplated railroad from this place to Waterville. An act incorporating the Belfast and Waterville Railroad Company passed the legislature on the 29th of July. Prior to that time a route had been surveyed under the direction of Mr. Butterfield of Lowell, Mass., chief engineer, the expense of which was defrayed by the contributions of our townsmen. The route was found to be feasible and every thing seemed to presage the construction of the road; but the death-dew thrown on the enterprise by some of the wealthiest in our community proved fatal to it, as it had previously to every enterprise of a public nature. Time, which "cuts down all both great and small," according to the Primer, has gradually relieved us from the incubus; the people have cause for gratitude that they have taken the business into their own hands, although at this late hour, and that our town is no longer the "Sleepy Hollow" which sordid avarice once made it.

Lieut. Amos H. Billings, who left this place as sergeant in Capt. A. T. Palmer's company, died at the Bite Tavern in Boston, on his way home from Mexico, on the first day of September. His body was brought here and buried on the third, on which occasion a very impressive funeral discourse was preached by Rev. N. C. Fletcher.

At the annual fall meeting, September 11th, the whole number of votes thrown for Governor was 762; 419 for Dana, Demo., 306 for Hamlin, Whig, 37 for Fessenden, Abol. Daniel Putnam, Whit, was elected Representative to the legislature.

West's celebrated painting, "Christ healing the sick," was on exhibition this month at the Unitarian Church.

The second annual session of the Teachers Institute for this county was held at the North Church, commencing on the 24th of this month and closing on the third of November. The members of the Board of Instruction were Rev. William Warren of Windham, Hon. E. M. Thurston of Charleston, Mr. J. E. Littlefield of Bangor, and Dr. George S. Rawson of Feltonville, Mass. The lecturers were Rev. Messrs. Palfrey, Cutter and Fletcher of this place, Rev. Stephen Thurston of Searsport, and Messrs. Warren and Littlefield of the Board of Instruction. The School Committees held their annual Convention on the 30th of October and elected Hon. Hugh J. Anderson member of the Board of Education for this county. The second annual Fair and Cattle show of the Waldo County Agricultural Society was held in this place, commencing on the 26th of October.

On the second of November the "State Signal and New Planet" obliterated the last part of its title from the planetary system, and was thenceforward known as the State Signal. On the 26th of the month previous its office was removed to the building now occupied by M. E. Dodge.

At the Presidential election, November 7th, the votes thrown were for Cass, Demo., 366, for Taylor, Whig, 360, for Van Buren, Freesoil, 72. The Whigs were very naturally elated by the success of their candidate and held a jubilee at Washington Hall on the evening of the sixteenth, which was to them in a twofold sense "Thanksgiving Day". The Hall and several buildings in its vicinity were brilliantly illuminated; also the street in front by burning tar-barrels; lanterns were suspended around the ship on the top of the flag-staff. The Hall was filled to repletion with happy as well as thankful hearts. Addresses were made by several gentlemen and the tables spread under the supervision of Mr. Robert W. Quimby were bountifully laden with viands of the "rough and ready" order. During the afternoon and evening a salute of a hundred guns was fired. One solitary incident occurred to mar the festivities of the evening. Some evil-disposed and reckless person fired at the lanterns on the flag-staff with a rifle and succeeded in breaking one or two of them. As an indication of party hostilities it was contemptible; as an act putting in jeopardy life or limb it was, at the best, inexcusable.

During the month a theatrical corps under the management of Mr. George Goodnow gave several exhibitions at Washington Hall.

Among the buildings erected this year were the following. The brick store on Main street now occupied by Thomas W. Pitcher, built by James Y. McClintock; its first occupant was Sherburne Sleeper. The building next northerly from it, now occupied by M. E. Dodge, built by Hiram E. Pierce; its first occupants were Thurlow (S. G.) and Pierce (H. E.) and the Signal and Planet. The brick block on Church street built by Hon. Joseph Williamson, now owned by W. H. Simpson and occupied in the second story as the office of the Journal. Its first occupants were Frye Hall and Son, (Elisha H.), grocers, and John Haraden and Son, (Daniel), dealers in general merchandise; the latter occupied only while they were erecting their brick building on the corner opposite. The second story was occupied as a dwelling by different tenants.

Among the noticeable local events of this year were the opening of the magnetic telegraph office, the deaths of Manassah Sleeper, Esq., and Hon. John Wilson, two of our oldest inhabitants, all which are entitled to fuller notice than the limits of this chapter will admit and must be deferred until our next.

--NOTE. In our last chapter the "Old Settler" is made to say that his old friend Samuel Locke was "Horatio's" brother, instead of father. The only apology the type-setter has to make is that the word father was written so legibly that he thought it must be a mistake!

CHAPTER XLIV. (1848.)

The important local event of this year, last in date, was the opening of telegraphic communication between this place, Bangor and Thomaston. The first printed despatch which came over the line from Bangor read as follows: "Nov. 23, 11 1-2 A. M. The Kenduskeag stream has some ice in it but the river is free yet." 12 m. Deers plenty. Poultry abundant since Thanksgiving Day. Mutton chops hot and above par. Shooks well shaken up by the late gale. Boards boarding out for the winter along shore. Fish froze up. Daguerreotypes taken by lightning at half price. Sugar's riz." The first printed despatch which passed over the line from Thomaston was on the 30th; it announced the accidental and instantaneous death of Edward Merrill, brother of Nathaniel and Curtis B. Merrill, then residing here. News by the British steamer arrived at Halifax, forwarded by express to St. Johns, passed over the line thence to Boston and the south on the 16th of February following for the first time. The Maine Telegraph Company organized under its charter on the 4th day of January 1849. The office of the Company in this place was opened in the second story of the building since known as the Telegraph Building; it remained there until it was removed to the room in McClintock's Block where it now is. William H. Simpson, now proprietor of the Journal, was the first operator here.

Manasseh Sleeper, Esq., familiarly known as Judge Sleeper, father of our fellow citizens Sherburn and George R., died this year on the 28th of June in his sixty-ninth year. He was born in Poplin, N. H., and came to this State in 1802, residing for a while in Bath, where he taught school for two or more years. In 1814 he came here to reside, having married a daughter of one of our earliest settlers, Thomas Whittier, Esq., the first landlord of the Whittier Tavern. He opened a store in the building on Main street then called the Edmunds shop, since that time converted to a dwelling house and now occupied by Messrs. Howard and Kittridge. He removed from that to the building which stood at the intersection of Market and High streets, on ground now belonging to the North Church, of which mention has frequently been made in previous chapters. It was while he was occupying this store that it was broken into one night by one Morang, who had been in his employment as hostler, and a quantity of merchandise stolen. The thief was arrested, convicted and sent to the States prison. The stolen goods were accidentally found some time afterwards partially buried in the forest in the town of Hope, but so much decayed as to be valueless. In connection with this larceny there is an anecdote which Mr. Sleeper was accustomed to tell with much gusto, although it told rather hard on himself. "Morang," said he to the criminal, after he was convicted "while you was about it why didn't you steal more goods?" "Well, Squire," was the reply, "I would have taken more dry goods but they were marked so d--d high that I could not afford to; there wasn't any chance for a profit." After the robbery, on the principle of "locking the barn-door after the horse is stolen," Mr. Sleeper put a lock of extra dimensions on the store door; anyone desirous of seeing the key to it can do so by calling on Mr. Daniel Haraden, at his store, at any time in the day except during the "ten minutes" when he is "at the wharf."

Mr. Sleeper was for some time landlord of the old Whittier Tavern and afterwards of the Huse Tavern. He opened the last named to the public on the fourth of July, 1820, raised a sign bearing the Coat of Arms of the new State, and gave to the house the name of the Maine Hotel; a name by which it was ever afterwards known. When he left the Hotel he removed to the house which he built in 1818, at the junction of Church and Spring streets, now occupied by Dr. Flanders. It was the second house built on Church street, the first being the one now occupied by Edwin Salmond. He continued to reside there until his decease. He was often elected to important municipal offices. In the memorable "Small Pox year" he was chairman of the board of selectmen; the onerous and delicate duties devolving on him in the season of excited public feeling were performed independently and fearlessly but to the acceptance of the community at large. He was one of the founders of Belfast Lodge of F. and A. Masons, which was chartered in 1816, was its first Master, and delivered the first public address before it on the anniversary of St. John the Baptist, 1823.

After leaving the Hotel he devoted the larger portion of his time to surveying land, the duties of Notary Public, and Justice of the Peace, until the almost exclusive jurisdiction of criminal offences committed within the town was conceded to him; he became in fact the Police Court of the village. When the law creating Town Courts was enacted he was appointed by the Governor to the office of Judge of the Town Court of Belfast; an office which he held until compelled by failing health to abandon the discharge of its duties. In the exercise of his judicial duties no man ever had reason to complain that in judgment he failed to remember mercy. It is told of him that not infrequently when compelled by the evidence before him to impose a fine for violation of the law on a party who was so unfortunate as to be destitute of the means to pay it, he would set him at work in his garden and assume the payment himself. Out of this habit grew the jocose remark, that "the Judge has sentenced the party to two days hard labor in his garden." His manner of administering an oath was peculiarly impressive; the following is illustrative of the fact. He was trying a case in which an elderly female of not very refined character or impressible temperament was a witness, to whom he administered the oath in his usual manner and resumed his seat. There was deep silence pervading the Court-room, broken only by the exclamation of the witness, "My God! how solum!"

Although not ordinarily sportive in his demeanor he possessed a large fund of quite humor on which he often drew, sometimes even in the Court-room, as the following anecdote will show. Some boys were brought before him charged with the heinous offence of appropriating to their own use certain tar-barrels for the purpose of a bonfire on the evening of the Fourth of July. The little fellows were in a terrible state of trepidation, anticipating nothing less than confinement in the county jail as the sentence of the court. Their surprise may be imagined when the judge with great solemnity, but with a merry twinkle of the eye, ordered them to be discharged on giving bonds to "keep the peace against all tar-barrels for the term of one year!" As a truthful annalist it becomes the duty of the compiler to add, that one of the young culprits was the present editor of The Republican Journal. To this event in early life may be attributed his passion for the rooster, rather than the tar-barrel, as the symbol of patriotic joy.

Although not possessing any legal education beyond that acquired in the discharge of his duties as a magistrate, his decisions in cases pending before him were almost uniformly in unison with the law involved; appeals from his decisions were not infrequent, but the instances were rare in which those decisions were not sustained in the higher court. He was called in his declining years to bear a heavy burthen of physical and mental infirmity, but bore it patiently and resignedly to the end. He left four sons and two daughters, all of whom save one, the wife of the late Hon. James White, are still living.

Hon. John Wilson, who died on the 9th of July, aged seventy-one, was a native of Peterborough, N. H. He graduated at Harvard in 1799, in the same class with the late Rev. William Frothingham, pursued his legal studies in the office of his elder brother, James, and in 1803 came here and commenced the practice of his profession. In 1807-8 he erected the house formerly occupied by his son-in-law, Hon. Albert G. Jewett, destroyed by fire in April 1867, on the hill ever since known as Wilson's Hill. About a year previously he married a daughter of Andrew Leach, Esq., of whom particular mention was made in an early chapter, whom he survived; he afterwards married Miss ---Tinkham of Wiscasset, who survived him. He had a large practice in the counties of Hancock and Washington, as well as at home, until 1824, when in consequence of exposure to a severe storm he was attacked with a fever, from the effects of which he never wholly recovered. He was a member of the 13th and the 15th Congress; and that, it is believed, was the only public office he ever held; his inclinations did not naturally tend in that direction. He was an able lawyer, occupying a position in the front rank of his profession, an ingenious, not an eloquent advocate, an inflexibly, upright man. No shadow of dishonesty or chicanery rests on his memory. He was a man of popular manners and a universal favorite. He was one of Nature's noblemen and in whatever situation he might be placed he was ever the courteous gentleman. He had a natural fondness for agriculture and always took a deep interest in the agricultural welfare of the surrounding country. His personal efforts in that direction, although they failed to add to his material wealth, had the effect to stimulate others to good works whose reverence for "the Almighty Dollar' was greater than his. He was one of the earliest and most persistent advocates for the erection of our county, and was the first one, so far as known, to suggest the name it bears. Wilson's Hill and Wilson's Stream, two of the ancient landmarks in our city, are indebted to him for their appellations.

A minute biographical notice of Mr. Wilson, one that would do ample justice to him, would require more space than can be spared from these brief annals. A few anecdotes, selected at random, may suffice to illustrate the character and peculiarities of the man more vividly, perhaps, than can be done in any other mode within the power of the compiler.

He was a man of fine physical organization, of great physical strength when a young man, cool and deliberate in all his actions, and of unflinching courage. Soon after he commenced practice he had occasion in the argument of a case to comment with more than ordinary severity on the conduct and character of a prominent witness. The witness very indiscretely, as the result proved, determined to have redress by inflicting personal chastisement, and watching an opportunity when Mr. Wilson was alone in his office went in and commenced an attack on him. It was but the work of a moment for Mr. W. to seize him by the collar and place him, not very gently, in a horizontal position on the floor; he then very deliberately sat down on him. A brother lawyer who happened to come in at the moment and saw the condition of the prostrate man, without any apparent sign of life about him, exclaimed, "Why, Wilson, the man's dead!" "Yes," replied Wilson, "yes, I am aware of that, and I am the Coronor's Inquest sitting on the body!"

He was naturally of rather indolent habit and was of course a member of a Club existing here in the early part of the century called the Lazy Club. One of its unwritten by-laws provided that no member, under any circumstances, should run when he might just as well walk. He was discovered one day running leisurely down the steepest part of the hill on which he lived, and the fact was reported to the Club. Being put upon trial he set up in defense that he had not violated the law, the intention of which was to punish unnecessary labor; for the reason of his running was that it was less labor to run than it was to hold back! It does not appear of record what the adjudication of the Club was; the presumption is, from the well recognized precedents of the day, that the ingenuity of the defence was admitted, but that the "pound of flesh" was exacted.

Neither fear, favor, affection or the hope of reward ever influenced him to abandon a position which he held to be tenable consistently with truth and justice, nor to withhold an opinion which he felt duty required him to express. He was once a witness in a cause when it became important to prove by his testimony, and that of others, that the reputation for truth of a material witness was not good. In reply to the usual question, Mr. Wilson testified that the general reputation of the witness for truth was bad. The emphatic manner in which the word was spoken so irritated the witness that he broke in upon the proceedings by saying: "I suppose, Mr. Wilson, you'd swear that I am the worst man that ever was!" "No, doctor," replied Mr. W., deliberately folding his arms across his breast as was his habit, "I would not swear to that; but I am ready to swear that you are the worst man I ever knew or read of."

He had a remarkable memory. No testimony in any case he tried escaped his notice when he came to the argument; hence his arguments were always exhaustive, but necessarily prolix and sometimes tedius to those not personally interested. A friend once asked him if it might not be that his arguments were too long. "Did you ever hear any of my clients complain of their length?" was his reply.

He possessed a wonderful degree of self-possession and forbearance. No instance is remembered in which he exhibited any anger, however much annoyed. About the last time he appeared in the Court-house he was arguing to the Judge presiding a question of law, and having stated a legal proposition the counsel on the other side, a young member of the profession, in a rather contemptuous tone of voice remarked "Who ever heard of such a principle of law as that!" Mr. Wilson, without moving a muscle, or exhibiting the slightest resentment at the rude interruption, or taking his eye from the Judge, proceeded to say, "My brother inquires who ever heard of such a principle of law as that which I have just stated. The obvious inference from the remark is that he never did; but your Honor and I heard of it thirty years ago." It is needless to add that the interruption was not repeated.

Daniel Webster was a member of Congress at the same time with Mr. Wilson and stood deservedly high in his estimation as a lawyer and advocate. "What did you think of Mr. Webster?" said he one day to a townsman who had just returned from Court at Wiscasset where Mr. Webster had argued an important case. "Well," was the reply, "I liked him very well; but he didn't say any thing more than any lawyer in this place could have said," "Very likely" said Mr. Wilson; "if he had only thought of it?"

This imperfect sketch of the life and character of a man who was one of the ablest intellectually who ever resided here cannot have a more fitting conclusion than the resolution adopted at a meeting of his professional brethren on the day before his funeral: Resolved, that in the death of Hon. John Wilson, one of the earliest members of the legal profession in this county, we deplore the loss of an able counsellor, a faithful friend, a courteous gentleman and an honest man.

CHAPTER XLV. (1849.)

The California typhoon, which had been gradually drawing nearer and nearer to us, reached this latitude with the opening of this year. The new bark Suliote, Josiah Simpson, Master, was advertised to sail for San Francisco with passengers and merchandise. The first invoice was a company of about twenty-five, the largest portion being young men, who arrived here from Bangor in the afternoon of the 25th of January. They were met at the bridge by a delegation of their co-adventurers from this and other places, and the Brass Band, and escorted to the hotel, where they were received with three times three cheers from the large concourse of people assembled in front of it.

As a token of respect and an expression of interest in the enterprise, a collation was tendered to the adventurers by our citizens at Washington Hall on the evening of the twenty-seventh. Tables were spread on each side of the hall, extending its whole length, under the supervision of Mr. Benj. Sargent. At the close of the repast eloquent addresses were made by Rev. Messrs. Palfrey, Cutter, Ricker, Ex-Gov. Anderson and Mr. William O. Poor, all of this place, to which responses were made by William H. Weeks, Esq., of Unity, Mr. A. H. Johnson of Stillwater, Benj. Griffin, Esq., then late editor of The Journal and Captain Simpson. At the conclusion of the entertainment the company dispersed with three cheers for the captain, crew and passengers of the Suliote, and three in response for the citizens of Belfast. It was a season of great excitemen in our ordinarily quiet village.

The Suliote sailed about two o'clock p. m. of the 30th. A salute was fired and cheers was exchanged as she left the wharf. She carried with her, in addition to her officers and crew, fifty passengers. Some idea of the miscellaneous character of her cargo may be formed from the fact that her manifest was over nine feet in length. The occupations of her passengers were equally miscellaneous; fifteen of them were mechanics, eleven lumber or millmen, five merchants, four farmers, three surveyors, two mariners, one chemist, one artist, one printer, one dentist, one apothecary, one hatter, one lawyer, and three who having no stated occupation designated themselves gentlemen. Only five of the passengers were residents of this place. One of them, Mr. William L. Torrey, the Artist of the expedition, is still residing in California; the other four returned one after another; the only one of them now living is Mr. Curtis B. Merrill, who resides in Standish in this State.

Two days after she sailed it was discovered that there were but two casks full of water on board that were fit for use, owing to the fact that all the casks, with the exception of those two, were not properly cleansed before being filled. She was compelled to put into Port Prayer, Cape de Verd Islands, for a supply, where she arrived on the 22d of February. She arrived at Rio Janeiro on the 20th of March. On her passage round Cape Horn in the night of the 16th of April in a very severe gale Edwin Paul Simpson, son of the captain, was washed overboard and lost. He was about eighteen years old, a worthy, intelligent youth, of frank and generous disposition, and the favorite of all who knew him. It was a dark, tempestuous night--the sea running so high that no ship's boat could live in it. Captain Simpson returned home by the way of the Isthmus; although from boyhood his life had been passed on the ocean he never went to sea again. The Suliote arrived at San Francisco about the 18th of July without farther loss or accident. She is still afloat, changed in rig to a schooner, and is now a coal-carrier.

After Capt. Simpson returned from California he engaged in merchantile pursuits. In 1852 he built the wharf still known as Simpson's Wharf. He was the owner of the house on Church street now occupied by his son, the editor of the Journal. While employed in making some improvements about the premises he took a severe cold the effect of which was fatal; he died September 23, 1860, aged sixty-two. He was regarded one of our worthiest and most enterprising townsmen; his hand and voice were ever in favor of public enterprises, and his loss was a loss not merely

to his family and friends but to the town. This is but an expression
of public sentiment; the compiler, whose personal and business relations
with him were of the most intimate character, cannot do justice to his
own feelings without adding that the green blanket which Nature kindly
spreads over her sleeping children never covered a truer, warmer, more
genial heart than his.

On the 9th of January Dr. Palfrey delivered the last lecture before
the Lyceum. --Doctor Young commenced a course on Chemistry on the tenth;
his second was delivered on the evening following, but for lack of patronage
sufficient to pay expenses the course was abandoned. --Mr. Holt of Bloomfield
gave a highly interesting and beautifully illustrated lecture on Palestine
at the North Church on the sixth of February. --Dr. Josiah Prescott,
who had previously resided in this place, lectured on Hydropathy, or
the cold water cure, in the month of March; but the mercury was quite
too low for success in the way of conversions to the faith he held.
--On the 15th of July a colored man, John Randolph, who claimed to be
a nephew of the celebrated John Randolph of Roanoke, lectured at the
Unitarian Church to a crowded house. He commenced by tracing his "geology"
as he termed it, back to Pocahontas--dwelt at great length on the achieve-
ments of his own "industrious"--and concluded by satisfying his audience
that he was an arrant imposter, humbug and ass. He was followed in
August by Henry Bibb, another individual of the colored persuasion,
who gave two lectures at the Baptist Church, embracing a narration of
his escape from bondage. He was far superior to his predecessor in
brains and honesty and his narrative was quite interesting. All the
lectures with which we were favored this year, so far as remembered,
are embraced in the foregoing.

On the 12th of January Messrs. Josiah N. White and Jesse Black
announced to the public that they had become landlords of the Farmers
House, succeeding Mr. John Hussey.

On the same day the firm of Rowe and Griffin, publishers of the
Journal, was dissolved. Mr. Griffin being about to sail in the Suliote
sold his interest in the paper to Mr. George B. Moore, who became joint
proprietor with Mr. Rowe. On the 6th of April following, Mr. R. sold
out his interest to Mr. Levi R. Wing and soon after left for California
by the overland route.

Mr. Moore continued to be connected with the paper as editor or
proprietor until he removed to Camden, having received the appointment
of Inspector of Customs at that place. After the expiration of his
official term he was for a while a contributor to the columns of the
Eastern Argus, and still later editor of the Portland Advertiser. While
occupying that position he died on the fifteenth day of March, 1864,
aged thirty-eight. Mr. Moore was a native of Searsmont, and by trade
a printer. He served his apprenticeship in the Journal office. He
was a man of a high order of talent, wielded the pen of a ready writer,
and had he not been deficient in what is termed worldly wisdom might
have reaped the pecuniary reward to which his labors richly entitled
him; but he was wedded to his profession and no alien love was permitted
to steal between it and him. He left many warm friends by whom his
early departure was sincerely deplored.

In the evening of February 10th a shop in Mr. S. C. Nickerson's
shipyard at the Upper Bridge was destroyed by fire with its contents,
tools, moulds, etc. About midnight of the 12th a small house near Front
street, owned by Dr. Cass, was burned. In the evening of August 13th
a work-shop in Carter's ship-yard was burned; supposed to be the work
of an incendiary. A house on the eastern side of the river occupied
by Bancroft Wyman was burned in the night of the 15th of June. In the
evening of October 27th a small house on Bridge street, then recently
vacated by a tenant of dubious character, was pried from its foundation
tumbled down the bank and then burned by a company of "Regulators" who
constituted themselves the guardians of the morals of the village for
the time being. No criminal prosecution followed although the act was
regarded by all reflecting men as an outrage on property.

Washington's birthday was celebrated under the auspices of the
Temperance Society at the Unitarian Church. An address was delivered
by Rev. Mr. Cutter. The patriotic boys of the village closed the evening
with a tar-barrel illumination.

For two or three weeks before this date we had very severely cold
weather. On the morning of the 16th the mercury stood at twenty-two
degrees below zero. The bay was so frozen over on the 20th that a party
from Castine came across on skates and an iceboat.

At the annual spring meeting, March 12th, Prescott Hazeltine, James
Gammons and Abram N. Noyes were chosen Selectmen, Nathaniel Patterson,
Clerk, and Daniel Haraden, Treasurer. The monies raised were $2,500.00
for schools, $1,000.00 for paupers and insane, $1,000.00 for incidental
expenses and $1,000.00 for payment of debts. At an adjourned meeting
held April 2d the sum of $4,500.00 in cash was raised for making and
repairing highways and bridges, and for the first time Road Commissioners
were chosen in lieu of surveyors. The commissioners chosen were Hiram
O. Alden, James White and Thomas Marshall. They made a contract with
the late Isaac Allard to keep all the highways in town, with the exception
of those in the village district, in repair for the term of five years
for the sum of $2,250.00 per year. According to the Report submitted
to the Meeting, there were then fifty-six miles of highways in the town.

The steamers began to make their appearance this month. They were
the W. J. Pease, Capt. William Flowers, the Admiral, Capt. William Hutchins,
the Governor, Capt. Thomas Rogers, and the Penobscot, Capt. Samuel Seymour,
which ran until July when she was sold to run on the route between New
York and Philadelphia. She was succeeded by the Kennebec, Capt. Asa
M. Sanford. The Secor, Capt. Thomas B. Sanford, plied between this
place and Sedgewick. We missed the State of Maine, and the pleasant
face of her gentlemanly commander, Capt. Samuel H. Howes. He had been
on our waters about fifteen years, commanding successively the Bangor,
Telegraph, Charter Oak, Governor and State of Maine steamers. He died
at Cambridge, Mass., on the 23d of March.

The first gun from Washington under the new administration heard
in this locality was before the close of the first month of its existence.
Our postmaster, Mr. William T. Colburn, was the victim; his brother-in-law,
Mr. Charles Giles, came manfully forward and occupied the post of danger.
He removed the post-office to the room now occupied by Doctor Sylvester,
at the junction of Main and Beaver streets, early in May; it continued
there during his official term. Mr. Giles, it will be remembered, fell
at the battle of Baton Rouge, August 5th, 1862. The earth that covers
him in his last sleep once belonged to President Taylor; the same from
whose hand he received his appointment as postmaster.

About noon of April 5th George A. Durham, son of the late Jonathan
Durham, was found dead in his barn suspended by a rope from one of the
big beams. It was supposed from the fact that his neck was dislocated,
that after adjusting the rope he leaped from the beam. He was about
28 years of age, unmarried, in easy circumstances pecuniarily, intelligent,
exemplary in conduct and highly esteemed among his acquaintances. No
cause for the act could be surmised save sudden mental derangement.

The musical season was opened by Thayer's Minstrels, who gave several
concerts at Washington Hall early in April. --Mr. Howard, the "American
Ole Bull," talked with his violin at the Court House on the 29th of
May to a small audience; he deserved a larger one but --he was only
a fiddler!" --The Saxonian Orchestra performed at the same place on
the 18th of June. --The celebrated Hutchinson Family sang at the North
Church in the evening of 4th of July. --In the evening of the 9th Mr.
Mooney, the "Irish vocalist," gave a musical entertainment consisting
of Irish songs and ballads at the Court House. --The Elenas, two Italian
boys, Annibale aged fourteen and Lucini eight, gave two concerts this
month; the eldest played on the piano, the youngest on the violin. --Charles
Currier and Company gave several musical entertainments, connected with
the drama, at Washington Hall. The dramatic preponderated over the

musical--the spirit over the understanding. --The Riley Family, consisting
of three sisters, aged respectively eight, twelve and sixteen, and one
brother, gave a vocal and instrumental concert at the Court House on
the first of November. --"Dr. Ness's Oratorio and Concert Company" gave
"one of their inimitable and unique entertainments" at Washington Hall
on the evening of the 4th of October.   There are some living, probably,
who remember the attitude struck by the principal female artiste preparatory
to commencing her "Fancy Hornpipe," and the "uncertain sound" given
forth by the well-greased Fiddle-strings on the occasion.   The man who
furnished evidence of his identity by the transfer of the black wig
is not forgotten, probably; nor the rise in the market value of hen-fruit
which succeeded the "entertainment."   It was "unique," certainly, before
and behind the curtain, and would be "inimitable," it is to be hoped,
in these days.
    There was an exhibition of statuary at the same hall for several
days in April; it consisted of twenty-three figures and was said to
be representative of the trial of Our Saviour before Pilate.   The figures
were described in the hand-bills as "exceedingly life-like".   The likeness
to Pilate was recognized at once by one of our "oldest inhabitants",
who still lives waiting patiently for the day when "he shall go up in
a fiery chariot."
    Early in June Maurice C. Blake, Esq., of Camden, was appointed
Collector of the Customs for this District in place of Hon. Alfred Marshall,
removed; he entered on the duties of his office on the 2d of July.
His subordinate officers were Isaac N. Felch, Dep. Collector and Inspector,
and Horatio N. Palmer, Inspector.   Soon after the expiration of his
official term Mr. Blake went to California and established his residence
in San Francisco, where he still resides, occupying a judicial station
the duties of which he is performing with credit to himself and to the
acceptance of the community.
    Fourth of July passed off very quietly.   There was less display
of patriotism than usual in the way of punch, guns, crackers and bells;
an indication that the "pride, pomp and circumstance" of rum and gunpowder
had in a measure departed.   A large number of our people passed the
day out of town; many went on an excursion trip made by the steamer
Governor.   The only public parade of the day was that of the engine
companies, who turned out in the morning for a trial of strength.
    On the 30th an "indignation meeting" was held by the original subscrib-
ers for the construction of the cistern in Fountain Square, as it was
then called, now Customhouse Square.   Certain nefarious bipeds, ignoring
the fact that the cistern was constructed for the purpose of quenching
the thirst of quadrupeds, had been in the habit of using the water it
afforded for the base purpose of washing carriages and harnesses.   Whereupon
the meeting referred to was held and sundry indignant and heart-stirring
resolutions were adopted; one of them was as follows: "Resolved, that
the uses to which the water has thus been appropriated are destructive
to boot leather, inductive of consumption, and ruinous to the long dresses
of the ladies, and for these reasons should be discontinued";--and they
were.   The meeting was reported to have been "harmonious from fountain
head to outlet."
    The bill of mortality for this year was larger than ordinary.
It contained the names of Judge Read, Capt. Ephraim McFarland, Hon.
David W. Lothrop, Mr. Thomas Bartlett, Frye Hall, Esq., Capt. David
Whittier, Nathaniel Wilson, Purser in the Navy, Major John Russ, and
Capt. Annis Campbell--most of whom are identified more or less with
the early history of our town.   Particular mention of many of them has
already been made in these annals; brief biographical notices of the
others will be found in our next chapter.

CHAPTER XLVI. (1849.)

The first week in August was signalized by the exhibition at Washington Hall of a grand Panorama of the Mississippi and Ohio rivers.   On the 6th came the "Hippoferaean Arena!"   It made its entrance to the village preceded by the "Sacred Egyptian Dragon Chariot of Isis and Osiris, drawn by ten Egyptian Camels."   The "beautiful Fairy carriage drawn by twenty Liliputian Ponies bringing up the rear of the procession, the toute ensemble of which surpasses anything which language can express!" --at least, so the handbills read.

During a heavy thunder-shower on the 7th the office of the Telegraph Company was entered in the absence of the operator and the relay magnet demolished.   The burglar was well known here by the name of Chain Lightning; the general opinion was that he made his way into the office on the wire.   What the consequence would have been to Lightning, or the operator had he been at his post, was problematical.

At the annual fall meeting, September 10th, the votes for Governor were as follows: Hubbard, Demo., 321, Hamlin, Whig, 260, Talbot, Freesoil, 29.   Daniel Putnam, Whig, was re-elected Representative to the legislature by 331 votes against 268 for all others.

During Election week the "Fakir of Ava," and his Fakiress, gave three exhibitions of their skill as magicians at Washington Hall.

The Waldo Argricultural Society held its third annual Fair and Show here on the second and third of October.   Rev. Mr. Fletcher delivered an address at the Unitarian Church on the evening of the first day, and in the evening of the second there was a large gathering at the Town Hall, with music, feasting and dancing.

A session of the Teachers Institute commenced on the 23d and closed on the 2d of November.   The Board of Instruction consisted of Hon. E. M. Thurston, Sec. of the Board of Education, Dexter A. Hawkins, now a prominent citizen of New York, and Dr. George S. Rawson of Feltonville, Mass.   During the session public lectures were delivered by Rev. Messrs. Palfrey, Cutter and Ricker and W. G. Crosby, Esq., of this place, Rev. Mr. Wiswall of Brooks, and Messrs. Thurston and Rawson of the Board of Instruction.

The construction of a marine railway on the flats near Miller's wharf was commenced this fall.   It was not completed until March following. On the 26th of that month the first vessel, a schooner of 75 tons, was taken onto it.   The premises are now occupied by David W. Dyer and Son.

The California fever which was raging at the opening of the year had not entirely subsided at its close.   A company of about forty adventurers for the golden land purchased a bark of 274 tons, built by Oakes Angier and others, launched from the ship-yard of Master Carter, October 20th, and named the William O. Alden in honor of our fellow citizen who was to take the command of her.   She sailed for San Francisco, under command of Capt. Alden, on the morning of the 8th of December; she arrived there on the 6th day of May following.   The Argonauts of her predecessor, the Suliote, were bid God-speed when they left us with speech and prayer; those of the W. O. Alden with a complimentary ball at the new Foundry and a supper at the New England House on the evening of Thanksgiving Day, the 29th of November.   A list of the managers at that Ball will not be without interest to those who remember it; they were Samuel G. Thurlow, CHARLES GILES, William B. Swan, John B. Wadlin, Lewis W. Howes, HARVEY P. HUTCHINSON, GEORGE B. MOORE and NOAH G. CLARK.   Those in small caps have gone to "walk the golden street;" the others, with the exception of Mr. Howes, are still living here.   Nineteen of the thirty-eight passengers on the bark were residents in this place; six of them are dead; three of them are resident in California; four only of them are now resident here.

Among the vessels launched here this year were the following: Brigs, L. R. Palmer of about 200 tons, China, 176, R. Patterson, 227, I. B. Lunt, 180, Reindeer 160; barques, Alexina, 245, Rhone, 349, Wm. O. Alden, 274, A. R. Taft, 318, Lillias, 398; schooners, D. P., 120, City Point, 100, Abby Gale, 105.

The Belfast Foundry Manufacturing Company was organized on the 18th of August. During the summer a building was erected by the company on the site occupied by the one burned in the fire of 1873. That building was burned in the night of June 24, 1851; the building erected in its stead was completed early in the year following.

Our last chapter closed with an enumeration of those once prominent in our business community who died this year. The list embraced, with others, the names of Hon. Nathan Read, Capt. Ephraim McFarland, and Hon. David W. Lothrop, all of whom have been noted biographically in previous chapters.

Thomas Bartlett, the contemporary of John Haraden and Samuel French, and like them a housewright by trade, came here from New Hampton, N. H., about 1804. He commenced house-keeping in the house on Puddle dock now occupied by Mrs. Isaac Clark and resided there until he built the house on Market street about 1825, now occupied by the widow of the late Judge Patterson. He was on his return from Canada, where he had been to visit some relatives, when he was attacked by cholera at Manchester, N. H., and died after a few hours illness, on the 15th of June, aged sixty-nine. He was a thoroughly honest man, possessed the entire confidence of the community and was universally respected.

Frye Hall, Esq., who died suddenly in the evening of August third, the day of the National Fast, was the father of the late Joseph F. Hall and father-in-law of our worthy fellow-citizen, Dr. Richard Moody. He was a native of Methuen, Mass. In 1806 he left his native town and came to Camden; he went thence to Hope, where he was residing when he was elected Register of Deeds for the new county of Waldo, in 1828. He then came to Belfast, and for most if not all of the remainder of his life occupied the house on Church street, corner Park street, now owned by Manley E. Dodge. He held the office of Register, and that of County Treasurer with slight interruptions, for about twenty years. Soon after coming here he became a member of the First Congregational Church and always took a deep interest in the welfare of that Society. He was a prominent member of the Masonic Fraternity and at the time of his decease was D. D. G. Master of the 9th District. He was buried with the rites and ceremonies of the Order; no man, probably, ever led a life more in conformity to its precepts than he did. In the performance of his duties as a public officer he was eminently faithful; he was an upright man, an exemplary and useful member of society.

Capt. David Whittier, who died October 15th, aged sixty-one, was the son of Thomas Whittier, Esq., whose name has frequently appeared in these annals. He commenced "following the sea," as a profession, in early life and was for many years a successful and skilful shipmaster. He abandoned that vocation about 1821 and ever after made this his place of permanent residence. The only voyage he made after that time was to Jacksonville, Fla., then an almost unknown region. In 1822 he built the brick block on Main street, known as Whittier's Block; a large and notable enterprise for that day. He engaged in mercantile business soon afterwards with his brother-in-law, Captain, now Rear Admiral Joseph Smith of the U. S. Navy; the name of the firm was Whittier and Smith. In connection with their mercantile business they established a livery stable and were the first to bring to this place a "nine passenger coach". Capt. Smith having been called to active service retired from the firm, and a new firm was formed under the name of Whittier and Patterson, consisting of Capt. W. and Edward Patterson, which was dissolved about 1831. With that terminated Capt. Whittier's active connection with trade, although he still continued to occupy as an office and counting room the store now occupied by A. J. Harriman and Company.

He was a kind-hearted, benevolent man. He was the organizer of an association formed here in 1826, called the Infant School Society, the object of which was to maintain a school for children between the ages of three and seven, and to furnish tuition gratuitously to all whose parents were unable to pay for it. The school continued to flourish for many years under his fostering care.

He was an ardent politician, and never flinched from the expression of an opinion or the performance of an act which in his judgment duty demanded. Naturally of ardent temperament, and fearless in giving utterance to his sentiments, it was not strange that he should incur the hostility of those who were equally ardent and of different political proclivities; but to his credit be it said, he never forgot his friends in futile attempts to conciliate his foes. It was sometimes said of him that he was arbitrary and over-bearing; but it was never said of him that he failed in the performance of any Christian duty to the poor and afflicted or was faithless to his friends. Captain Dave, as he was familiarly called, left many such by whom he is still kindly remembered.

Nathaniel Wilson, a native of this town, son of Col. Jonathan Wilson of whom frequent mention was made in our earliest chapters, died at the Tremont House in Boston on the 27th of October in his fifty-ninth year; his remains were brought here for interment. At the time of his decease he was a purser in the navy; an office he had held for more than twenty years. He was a lieutenant in the army in the war of 1812, was in several engagements with the enemy, particularly at the battles of Stone Mill and Plattsburg, where he won the reputation of an intrepid and gallant soldier. At the close of the war the regiment to which he belonged was disbanded, and he was appointed to a place in the Custom-house at New Orleans. He remained there until he was appointed Purser, in 1829. He was on the East India station in the Constellation, and returned a short time before the commencement of the war with Mexico, when he was ordered to the Gulf on the flag-ship Cumberland. At the close of the war he was stationed at Portsmouth, N. H., from which post he had been recently relieved at the time of his death.

Although but a brief portion of his life after attaining to manhood had been passed here, he was strongly attached to the place of his nativity. He provided by his last will and testamnt that all his estate, after payment of certain legacies and annuities for life to his three sisters, two of whom are still living, should constitute a fund the annual income of which should be appropriated to the promotion of a general education in his native town; the method of appropriation to be determined from time to time by its inhabitants. The amount of the bequest when realized will probably amount to nearly thirty thousand dollars. It was a munificent gift; one for which he will ever be respectfully and gratefully remembered by us and those who are hereafter to occupy our places.

Captain Annas Campbell was born at Hawke, now Danville, N. H., in 1776. He came here to reside in 1800, purchased the farm on the Belmont road now owned by Mr. Franklin Banks, built a log house on it near the location of the present buildings, into which he moved with his family the year following. He continued to occupy it until he built the one story framed house which he occupied at the time of his death; it is now a part of the house occupied by Mr. Banks. The only one of his children now living is the wife of our fellow citizen Mr. Sullivan Hicks. Captain C. derived his title, by which he was always known, from having held the office of Captain of a company of cavalry which was organized in this town in 1803. He was by occupation a farmer. None of the various enterprises which were started in the early days of our village diverted his attention from his chosen vocation. He commenced life here on his farm, and there he finished it on the 12th day of December in the seventy-fourth year of his age.

Major John Russ who died November 3d aged seventy-five, was one of the many hardy, strong willed, enterprising men who came here to build up a home in this comparative wilderness in the early part of this century. The precise year when he came the compiler has not been able to ascertain; but he was residing here and was a deputy under high-sheriff Phillips in 1804. He was one of the prominent men of the village immortalized in Dolliff's ballad of the Greene Indian War in 1807.

"John Russ then run, without a gun,
  An Indian for to kill;
He took a stake their heads to break,
  Priest Johnson cried, 'Be still!'"

Major Russ was at one time extensively interested in real estate
in the village and in navigation. At the commencement of the war of
1812 he was the sole, or principal owner of a brig just launched; she
lay in the dock westerly of the railroad wharf until the close of the
war; at a heavy loss of course to her owner. The wharf which stood
near the dock belonged to him and was known as long as it remained there
as Russ's wharf. The precise year when he removed his residence and
business to the locality now known as City Point is not remembered.
Prior to his removal it was known as Clay's [Clary's] Point; afterwards,
and for many years as Russ's Point. He was a man of great muscular
power, but never exercised it to the detriment of his fellow-men; like
most of our village originals he was a man of humor but his mirth was
never boisterous. His wife was the daughter of Maj. Gen. George Ulmer,
one of the prominent men in this section of the country in the early
part of the century. Major Russ had a large family of children, one
of whom only, Mr. Francis A. Russ, is now living in this town.

CHAPTER XLVII. (1850.)

The fire-fiend commenced his ravages early this year. In the night of January 25th fire broke out in a wooden building on High street occupied by Edwards and Lennan as a clothing store and tailor's shop and Noah G. Clark as a restaurant. The building, with the entire stock of E. and L., and the building adjoining, occupied by Robert B. Thomas, were entirely consumed. The building first named was owned by J. Y. McClintock and A. N. Noyes; the latter by Mr. McClintock. They booth stood on the present site of McClintock's Block. --On the morning of the 9th the house occupied by Joseph Meek in the rear of the jail was discovered to be on fire. The furniture was removed and the fire extinguished before much damage was done to the building. --Early in the night of March 5th fire broke out in the wooden store at the southerly end of Phoenix Row, now occupied by N. G. Prescott and Co. It was occupied as a dry-goods store by G. W. Moulton, whose stock of goods was almost destroyed by fire and water. The second story was occupied by our fellow-citizen, Mr. E. C. Hilton, as a tailor's shop; his stock was considerably damaged by water. The building, owned by Alden and Crosby, was not seriously injured. --About midnight of March 20th a small house on Cobbett's Lane, owned by Joseph McDonald and occupied by John G. Small, was wholly consumed. --In the evening of April 19th a barn owned by Mrs. Thomas Cunningham in the rear of her dwelling house on High street, which stood on the site of the stores now occupied by Francis Whitmore and F. B. Knowlton, was burned. --About three o'clock in the morning of the 27th the Farmer's House, Josiah N. White, landlord, was discovered to be on fire in the attic and was burned to the ground; the furniture in the house was mostly saved. --In the evening of May 23d a barn about a mile from the village, owned by Dr. Hollis Monroe, was burned with its contents, about twenty-five tons of hay.

Early in January William Rust, Esq., was appointed sheriff of the county, succeeding James Y. McClintock, and Henry W. Cunningham, Register of Probate, succeeding Charles Palmer. Mr. Cunningham accepted the appointment of Deputy and Jailor under Sheriff Rust, and Mr. Palmer was reappointed Register.

Mr.Springer gave several lectures at the Court-house on Astronomy in the winter, and in April Dr. H. G. Darling gave several on Biology and Pschycology; in November Mr. Spencer gave a course on the same topics. Mr. S. F. Green lectured in June on the Cultivation of Memory, and in December Rev. J. W. Hanson, who had just returned from the World's Peace Convention at Frankfort, Germany, which he attended as a delegate from this District, lectured on Peace. The Lyceum was reorganized in November, and the first lecture before it was by Prof. Shepard of Bangor, on the 13th of December, on Reading. It was found difficult to procure lecturers from a distance because, as more than one of those to whom application was made, replied: "I see no railroad to your place." The editor of the Journal at the time hazarded the prediction that "but a few years will elapse before the reply will be: "I see you have a railroad to Belfast and I can reach there in one day from Boston." It required only twenty years to fulfil the prediction!

A company of Ojibway Indians gave two exhibitions illustrative of the manners and customs of their tribe, at Washington Hall in January.

The first steamer of the season was the Admiral, Capt. Hutchins; she came early in March and left the route early in April. She was followed by the Governor, Capt. Rogers, on the 23d of March. The new steamer Boston, Capt. Sanford, made her first appearance here on the 10th of April. The steamer S. B. Wheeler, Capt. A. Michiner, arrived for the first time in April to go on the route between this place and St. Johns; she was sold the next month to go to California. The Lawrence, Capt. Deering, came on in May to ply between this place and Ellsworth in place of the Secor. In the latter part of December the steamer Creole, Capt. Deering, made her first appearance here; she was a celebrity from the fact of her connection with the famous Lopez Expedition, and was intended to run through the winter.

At the annual spring meeting, March 18th, Prescott Hazeltine, James Gammons and Abram N. Noyes were chosen Selectmen, Joseph Wheeler, Clerk, and Daniel Haraden, Treasurer. The monies raised for schools were $2500.00, for support of paupers and insane $1000.00, for incidental expenses $1000.00, for payment of debts $1500.00, for engine purposes $150.00 and $1000.00 for repair of roads and bridges. Ralph C. Johnson, Hugh J. Anderson, Thomas Marshall, James White and William G. Crosby were appointed a committee to draft a City Charter, procure its enactment by the Legislature, and report at the September meeting the comparative expense of a city and town government. A charter was procured at the next session of the legislature; it was approved the 17th of August.

The introduction or a certain Preamble and Resolves and their unanimous adoption at the above annual meeting afforded no little merriment. Prior to this time it had been the custom for many years to select as field-drivers, or hog-reeves, those of our townsmen who during the year preceeding had committed matrimony. The preamble, after referring to the uniform custom, proceeded to set forth "that it had been found to be injudicious and productive of evil; because married men are prone to break out of the pasture, and are bad judges of good fences." The resolves embraced a list of those "who from their strong and unwavering attachment to the state of celibacy--their undeviating walk in the path of virtue and their general affection for the fair sex are justly entitled to the confidence, respect and support of the people for the office of hog-reeve." At the head of the list stood the name of that venerable bachelor, Dr. Hollis Monroe, and at its close that of Dr. E. G. Gould, "Professor of roots and herbs." The list embraced the names of twenty-three of our townsmen. Eight· of them have gone where "they neither marry nor are given in marriage;" fourteen of them, sooner or later, became the prey of the spoiler, Hymen; those who have thus far kept clear of the clutches of death and matrimony, and are still living in our midst, are Benjamin F. Barker, William H. Simpson, William S. Brannigan and Lewis Bean. "The foxes have holes and the birds of the air have nests," but those relics of the noble army of hog-reeves of 1850 are neither foxes nor birds.

The fortunate individuals thus elected to office held a meeting for organization in the week following their election and took oath required in due form. They afterwards held a festival in the hall previously occupied by the Sons of Temperance, in the attic of the store now occupied by the Messrs. Howes. A baked boar's head of the largest dimensions, with an enormous cucumber in his mouth, constituted the center-piece on the table. An address was delivered on the occasion by William H. Simpson, now editor of the Journal, and a poem by his predecessor, the late George B. Moore; a few couplets from the latter may afford some idea of the nature and tenor of both.

"Hogreeves of Belfast!--listen to my lay,
Ye Hogarths and Pugmalions of the day!
No longer wear the bare-legged Muses clog,
Dismount from Pigasus and mount the Hog!
No longer idly seek the Golden Fleece.
    Unsheath your shinging blades and go for Greece!"

A commission was issued to each officer elect of which the following is a facsimile:

IN THE NAME OF THE STATE!
To _____   GRUNTING.
    Reposing special trust in your insticts and animosities, you are empowered to comprehend all vagrant HOGS, great and small, quadruped, biped, and striped, and commit them to durance vile, or like our great prototype, drive the latter down a steep place! Behold at once the object and emblem of your high and august duties. Arm for the conflict, and down with the Bores, be your motto.

Fail not, but accumulate grease, and gather wool, and your children
(!!) shall bristle up and call you great!!!
Given under the broad seal March 19, 1850
                              BENEDICT, the Virtuous!

Among the vessels launched this year were the ship John W. White
of about 550 tons burthen, the Kate Anderson of about 196 tons, the
bark P. R. Hazeltine, 400, the schooners Franklin, 86, Castelene, 76,
F. Patterson, 173, Jane Otis, 82.

There were several concerts, or "musical rehearsals," at the Unitarian
Church in the months of March and April. The Harmoneans were here in
July. In August the "Druid Band" gave several instrumental concerts,
"in the full costume of the Ancient Druids, upon seventy ox-horns as
used by the Priests of Old Britain." The Kilmiste Family was here in
September, the "American Ole Bull" in November, and in the evening of
December 20th Ossian E. Dodge gave one of his "chaste, unique, and fashion-
able musical entertainments" at City Hall.

"Alhambra!--round thee lingers still the radiance
Of jossaunce and loves gentle dilliance."

The Alhambra Saloon was opened to the public on the 30th of April
at 10 o'clock A. M. with a free entertainment at No. 3 Granite Block,
Main street; the premises are now occupied by Wadlin and Merrill. One
of its apartments styled the ladies' saloon was opened with a similar
attraction on the 11th of July. It was a restaurant, fitted up and
conducted on a scale altogether too large for this latitude; far better
adapted in dimensions and surroundings to a city such as Boston then
was. Martin Cross, formerly of the Phoenix House, was its proprietor.
The column of "Fancy Drinks" on its Bill of Fare embraced thirty-three
varieties! The flavor of the largest portion of them is unknown, probably,
to the palates of these days; the method of compounding them numbered
with the lost arts. Here are a few specimen bricks from the edifice:
 Belfast Smasher, Bangor Smasher, Capt. Sutter's Extra, Portland Fancy,
Boston Tod, Thomaston Breakdown, Stonewall, Floater, Conviviality Cocktail,
Bumbo! Some of the oldest of us will doubtless remember the eccentric
individual who, with a friend, undertook to go through the list in regular
order, appropriating one for each day in succession, and who differing
in opinion after several days labor as to the drink at which they had
arrived at the previous day, "to prevent any mistake in the matter went
back and began again."

In the month of May occurred one of the heaviest freshets ever
known here. In the night of the 24th the rain began to fall in torrents
and continued with slight interruptions until the 27th. Market street,
below the Phoenix House, was badly washed and gullied. Four bridges
on the western branch of our river were carried away; that at City Point
was partially destroyed. Two buildings at Gardner's tannery at the
Head of the Tide were swept off; the main works were in imminent danger
and would have shared the same fate, probably, had not the river suddenly
changed its course, completely insulating the tannery and making a chasm
across the road at a point where the water was never known to flow before.
The bridge at Robbins' mill on Little River was carried away. The damage
done in other sections of the county, and State, was far greater.

A new military company, called the Belfast Rifle Company, was organized
on the 24th of June by the choice of Levi R. Wing, Captain; John B.
Wadlin, 1st Lieut. and Noah G. Clark, 2nd Lieut.

Fourth of July was celebrated under the auspices of the Sons of
Temperance. An oration was delivered at the Unitarian Church by Rev.
M. R. Hopkins of Oldtown; Rev. Dr. Palfry officiated as Chaplain, and
the Declaration was read by Mr. William O. Poor. There was a public
dinner in the grove, known formerly as McFarland's Grove, and a display
of fireworks in the evening near the Academy.

President Taylor died on the 9th; intelligence of the event reached
here about eight o'clock in the morning of the next day. At noon thirty

minute guns were fired on the Common, the bells of the several churches
were tolled, and flags were displayed at half-mast on the shipping in
the harbor and at various places in the village. The event was noticed
at several of our churches on the Sabbath following by appropriate discourses
and religious services.

There was a Circus here on the 27th; its only distinguishing feature
was the Appollonicon; a wilderness of pipes which generated various
sounds called music in the bills; it must have been of the kind referred
to as having "charms to soothe the savage breast"; it certainly had
no peculiarly soothing influence on our good people.

At the annual fall meeting, September 9th, the votes for Governor
were for Crosby, Whig, 368, for Hubbard, Demo. 302, for Talbot, Free
Soil, 11.   Joseph S. Noyes, Demo., was elected Representative to the
legislature.

In the evening of the fourth of October, George W. Carey, about
twenty years of age, who was here on business for a mercantile house
in Boston, was found dead in his room at the American House, having
committed suicide by cutting his throat with a razor.

The annual Fair of the agricultural society was held on the ninth
and tenth.   On the evening of the 9th an address was delivered before
the Society at the Unitarian Church by Rev. William A. Drew of Augusta.

The annual meeting of the School Committee was held at the Court-house
on the 23d and Rev. Edward Freeman of Camden was elected member of the
Board of Education for this county.   The Teacher's Institute commenced
its annual session on the 22d and closed on the 2d of November. Messrs.
Dexter A. Hawkins and William H. Seavy composed the board of Instruction.
The session was held in City Hall; it was the first time the hall was
occupied for any public purpose.

A Panorama of the Kennebec river was on exhibition at the same
place in the month of November.

Mr. Martin Cross having relinquished the Phoenix House for a wider
field of operations--the Alhambra--Mr. Josiah N. White became its proprietor
and having thoroughly repaired and refurnished it opened it to the public
under the name of the Belfast Hotel.

The brick block at the intersection of Main and Church streets,
in which the office of the Belfast Savings Bank is now kept, was built
this year by the late John Haraden and Daniel Haraden. The first occupants
of the stores were John Haraden and son and the late Charles D. Field;
the first occupant in the second story was the late Phineas P. Quimby.
Mr. McClintock also built his block at the intersection of Main and
High streets.   The first occupant of the corner store, now occupied
by Richard H. Moody, was the late Samuel Haynes, druggist and apothecary.
The store next below it was occupied as a restaurant by Isaac Clark
Jr. Messrs. William T. Colburn and Isaac Allard were the first occupants
of the premises they still occupy.   It is doubtful whether Mac fully
realizes the blessing they have been to him.   In the second story was
the office of Solyman Heath, Esq., the news-room of The Republican Journal,
and Hoyt's shaving and hairdressing saloon. The whole of the third
story was occupied by The Republican Journal. The fourth story was
finished as a hall, to which the name of City Hall was given; it was
a great advance on any of the public halls we had ever had and the enterprise
of its projector and proprietor was duly appreciated. It was painted
in fresco the next year and a large telescope was placed in the cupola.

The number of deaths in town this year as forty-two.

CHAPTER XLVIII. (1851.)

According to the national census taken last year, just completed, the population of our town was at this time, 5,052; including the territory set off since 1840 it was 5,568; showing an increase of population in the entire territory of 1,374 in the last ten years. The population of the county was 47,229 against 41,535 in 1840; 5,694 gain in ten years. According to the State valuation of last year we had 932 polls and 1,323,979 of estate in town. According to our town tax bills of this year the number of those who paid a tax exceeding one hundred dollars was nineteen; the largest tax, $235.00, was paid by Ralph C. Johnson. The number of those who paid a tax in 1874 exceeding one hundred dollars, was 217! The largest tax, $2,800.00, was paid by the estate of the late Alfred W. Johnson.

The course of lectures before the Lyceum inaugurated the preceding fall was continued this winter. The lecturers were Gen. Sennott, Esq., of Boston, on Popular Delusions concerning the Middle Ages, Rev. Ezra Gannett of Boston on Conversation, Dr. Charles T. Jackson of Boston on A Grain of Corn, Geology and Mining, Rev. A. L. Stone on the True Mission of Woman, Rev. Horatio Southgate on the Domestic life of the Turks, Rev. J. H. Allen of Bangor on American Civilization, Rev. Calvin E. Stowe of Bowdoin College on the origin and history of Alphabetic writing, Rev. Stephen Thurston of Searsport on the relation of the Pulpit to Politics and Government, Rev. Edward F. Cutter on Iceland, Rev. Nathan C. Fletcher on the Natural History of Man, Hon. N. Abbott on the equality of Human Conditions.

The fall course commenced on the 23d of October. The lecturers were H. N. Hudson, Esq., of Boston on Falstaff, Prof. Shepard of Bangor on Charles James Fox, Rev. T. Starr King, of Boston, on Socrates, Charles C. Hazewell, Esq., of Boston, on Roman Slavery, Rev. William Ware, of Cambridge, on the Usefulness of the Fine Arts, Rev. A. L. Stone, of Boston, on Kossuth and Hungary, and Rev. John Pierpoint, of Medford, a poem on Improvement.

There were other lectures and readings during the year. Rev. C. W. Dennison lectured on California, and Prof. Travener gave readings from the Ingoldsby Legends and Hood at City Hall in May. Prof. Grimes gave a course of lectures in July on physiology, phrenology, mesmerism, &c. In August Mr. John M. Spear, the "Prisoner's Friend," lectured on the prevention of crime and the form of youthful offenders, and in September Mrs. Lesdernier gave readings at the Court House. Mr. Charles Whitney gave two entertainments in December, consisting of imitations of distinguished orators, and Rev. Mr. Pierpoint lectured on temperance.

Mr. T. D. Baldwin gave an exhibition of Natural Magic in January, and Mr. Bird, the "Ventriloguist and Magician," gave two exhibitions of his professional skill in June. He was followed the same month by Mr. Harrington, "the greatest ventriloquist in the world," who gave two of his "unique and fashionable entertainments which had been the theme of admiration and delight in all the principal cities and towns in the United States!"

The first steamer to arrive was the Admiral, Capt. Albert Wood. She made her first appearance for the season here on the 7th of March, her last on the 5th of April. The Secor, Capt. C. B. Sanford, followed her and plied between this place and Portland, Sedgwick and Machias until June, when she was sold to go on a route between Newcastle and Portland. The Boston, Capt. Sanford, came on in April. The Lawrence, Capt. Charles Deering, commenced running from this place to Ellsworth and intermediate points in July. The Governor, Capt. Thomas Rogers, ran to Portland in connection with the railroad; her first trip was on the 14th of April.

At the annual spring meeting, March 17th, James P. White, Ansel Lennan and Franklin Brier were chosen Selectmen, Joseph Wheeler, Clerk, and Daniel Haraden, Treasurer. The monies raised were $2,500.00 for schools, $1,000.00 for paupers and insane, $1,000.00 for incidental expenses, $3,000.00 for repair of highways and bridges, $150.00 for

engine expenses.   The amount of the town's indebtedness at this time
was $2,692.75.

The fire record of this year is brief.   The first one occurred
on the night of the 24th of June.   It was the most destructive of property
and the most disastrous to the effective industry of our village that
had ever occurred.   The Belfast Foundry, erected in 1849, and a two
story building near it owned by Mr. Samuel Sweetsir, were totally destroyed.
The actual loss of property uninsured was $21,000.00.   On the morning
of the 29th a blacksmith's shop owned by Mr. William Frederick, which
stood in the rear of the old Farmer's House stable, was consumed with
its contents, a portion of which was property saved from the Foundry
fire.   In the afternoon of October 16th fire broke out in the attic
of the Belfast Hotel.   By the efforts of the fire department the flames
were arrested before any serious damage was done.

Among the vessels launched this year were the following: The Ship
William Frothingham of about 830 tons, bark Ann Johnson, 445, schooners
Judge Tenney, 135, Lone Star, 90, Viola, 86, S. S. Lewis, 71, Magyar,
150, Siam, 149, Arvanda, 83, Blue Belle, 83, Bloomer, 84, Eliza Otis,
110, Clarendon, 115.

There was quite a tempest in our village teapot early in April
occasioned by the announcement that our time honored field-pieces--our
"brazen war-dogs"--were to be transferred to the arsenal at Bangor,
by order of the Governor and Council.   They were removed from the gun-house
to the wharf to be transported on the steamer of the next morning.
During the night they were converted into flying artillery; and when
the sun rose the next morning it shone on the places they occupied when
it went down, but not on them.   The pertinacity with which they clung
to the locality they had known for forty years led to a revocation of
the military order for their removal, and on the 26th they resumed their
old position in the gun-house.

The next local excitement was the examination before Magistrates
of Samuel and John J. Jewell, father and son, on the charge of having
murdered one John N. Cousins, at Monroe on the 26th of April.   They
were bound over and had their trial before the Supreme Court at its
next term in July.   Samuel was acquitted on the ground of insanity;
John J. was convicted on manslaughter and sentenced to seven years hard
labor in the State Prison.   The prosecution was conducted by Attorney
General Tallman and County Attorney Codman; the counsel for the prisoners
were Messrs. Abbot and Howes.

The bell was hung in the belfrey of the Universalist Meeting-house
and rung for the first time on the 13th of May, its weight 1527 pounds.

The first day of July was not quite up to the memorable "Fourth,"
yet was the commencement of an era interesting alike to us, locally,
and the nation at large; the "three cent postage law" went into operation.

Contrary to all precedent, rain began to fall about two hours after
sunrise on the Fourth and continued through the day.   Guns were fired
and bells rung, to the contrary notwithstanding; but the consumption
of India crackers and the expenditure of breath on that musical instrument
the fish-horn were exceedingly limited.   The parade of the Fantastics
was deferred until the next evening, Saturday, and the exhibition of
Fireworks until the next Monday evening.   The old field-pieces and the
Belfast Brass Band furnished the accompaniment on the occasion.

The public musical entertainments of this year, were not numerous.
Thayer's company of Sable Harmonists gave two concerts at City Hall
in July, and the Portland Harmoneans gave one in November.   There may
have been others, but they are not remembered.

Raymond and Company's Menagerie, with Herr Dreisbach and "Hideralgo
the Lion Tamer", were here on exhibition on the 5th of August.   Some
of the proprietors of white skirts who attended the exhibition remember
that it was on Waldo Avenue, on clayey ground, and that there was a
heavy shower in the night preceding.

The old Burying Ground on High street, the first ever occupied on the west side of the river, was abandoned and the removal of its tenants to Grove Cemetery commenced in August. Its site is now occupied by dwelling houses.

In the last week of this month Signor Devoto exhibited his band of trained birds and white mice at City Hall. A Diorama of the funeral of Napoleon was on exhibition at the same place in September.

The annual Show and Fair of the Agricultural Society was held on the 8th and 9th of October. The attendance was unusually large. There was a meeting of the Society at the Unitarian Church in the evening and a ball at City Hall.

The "Maine Law," whose growls had been heard in the distance, began to "show its teeth" in this locality early in August; several of our townsmen were badly bitten. In December came off the affray at Frankfort on board the Steamer Boston, which will be remembered by many still living. It grew out of an attempt to seize certain liquors on board the boat, which attempt was forcibly resisted by the crew. It was a matter of no local importance to us, save that on the arrival of the boat at our wharf the parties charged with violating the laws of the land were arrested and the preliminary hearing was had before magistrates here. Some of the accused parties were discharged by the magistrates and others were bound over to court. At the hearing before the Court some of them were convicted and others acquitted.

The extensive improvements made by Mr. Hiram E. Peirce at the mouth of Goose River, and the erecting of the new bridge across it, just completed, naturally recall to mind the condition of the river and the improvements on its banks a quarter of a century ago. They were, in addition to the saw and grist mills at the outlet of Goose Pond, Mason's saw mill, Kelley's carding machine and axe factory, Whiting's edge-tool factory, White and Kimball's iron foundry, grist mill and turning lathe. Prior to that time there had been on the river near the bridge a grist mill and fulling mill, a trip hammer and a tannery; but they had served out their time and few if any traces of them remain. The facilities for manufacturing furnished by this body of water are so obvious and so great, that it is to be hoped that our enterprising capitalists will at no distant period avail themselves of them, and thereby add to their own and the material wealth of the city as well as to its population.

The condition of the old jail had become such that it became necessary for the security of the public and the comfort of persons committed to it by due process of law that it should be demolished and a new one erected. The granite material in the old one was used in the construction of the new one, which occupied the same site. A temporary cell was built for the reception of criminals then in confinement--the two Jewells-- and parties imprisoned for debt were accommodated with board and lodging in the jailer's house. The stone-work of the new building was done by Edward Hawkes, the brick-work by R. S. Smart, the wood-work and slating by Amos R. Boynton.

Mr. Samuel Locke, father of our fellow-citizens John L. and Horatio J., was a native of Hallowell, and came here to reside in 1825. He was a tailor by trade and confined himself to that vocation the largest portion of his business life; he was for several years engaged in the business of druggist and apothecary, and for a while devoted himself to agricultural pursuits. He was a prominent and active member of the Methodist denomination in this place, and contributed largely by his personal effort and indomitable energy to the promotion of its prosperity and permanence. He was an upright man, a worthy member of society. He sailed in the bark Wm. O. Alden, in December 1849, for San Francisco, in the hope that a sea-voyage and change of climate might be of benefit to his health; that hope did not "end in fruition." He returned in January of this year, and died three weeks after his arrival home, February 19th, aged forty-nine. He was a prominent member of the I. O. O. F., and was buried with the ceremonies of the order; the members of the Masonic fraternity, of which he was also a highly esteemed and worthy brother, attended his funeral as mourners.

CHAPTER XLIX. (1852.)

The first noticeable event of this year was a fire which occurred early in the morning of January first and consumed the workshop of Carter and Co., ship-builders, with its contents consisting of moulds, patterns, lumber and ship-carpenters' tools.   The fire communicated to the house of Aaron Eaton which was also burned.   The circumstances attending the fire were such as to justify the belief that it was kindled intentionally, and at a town meeting held on the 14th the selectmen were authorized to offer a reward, not exceeding one thousand dollars, for the detection of the incendiary.   They accordingly offered a reward of five hundred dollars, but no discovery followed. --In the afternoon of the 11th an alarm of fire from the house now occupied by Mr. B. F. Field called out the engines.   It caught in a closet in one of the chambers and had broken through two places in the roof; but by the energy of the inmates of the house and the aid of a few others it was extinguished before doing farther damage. --In the evening of May 7th an old unoccupied house on the eastern side of the river, known as the Kelsey house, was burned; the work of an incendiary, doubtless. --The buildings occupied by David S. Whittaker on the road leading to the upper bridge took fire about midnight of the 13th of August.   The house was saved, but the barn and ell were destroyed. --Early in the morning of the 30th, during a violent storm, the house of L. J. Cotterell on Cobbett's Lane, now Vine street, took fire from a defective chimney and was consumed. --In the afternoon of September 13th--election day--fire broke out in the furniture manufactory of Daniel Howard, the building now occupied by the Belfast Livery Company.   It caught in the basement and spread with rapidity, but through the vigorous efforts of our fire companies the building was saved although in rather damaged condition.   The firemen were complimented with a supper in the evening at the American House, after which they made an informal call on one of their townsmen whom they had complimented with their votes during the day.

The Lyceum was in a thriving condition this winter; the lectures before it were as follows: Rev. S. L. Caldwell, of Bangor, on Unwritten History; Rev. William A. Drew, of Augusta, on the World's Fair; Rev. George Shepard, of Bangor, on Demosthenes; Rev. Sylvester Judd, of Augusta, on the Uses of the Beautiful; Rev. Theodore Parker, of Boston, on Progress in the Development of Mankind; Rev. E. H. Chapin, of New York, on the Ideal and the Actual; Rev. Dr. Palfrey of this place on the Reading of Fiction, Rev. Joseph Ricker on Earnestness as an Element of Character, and Hon. Albert G. Jewett on Paris and the Parisians.

Bullard's celebrated Panorama of the city of New York was on exhibition at City Hall in the month of January.

The first steamer to arrive was the new steamship Eastern State, Capt. William Flowers, who made her first appearance here on the 14th of January.   The Governor, Capt. Thomas Rogers, made her first appearance for the season on the 12th of April and her last on the 29th of November; she connected with the railroad at Portland.   The Boston, Capt. T. B. Sanford, came on the 12th of April.   She ran on the outside route. The Lawrence, Capt. Charles Deering, came on in May to run between this place and Ellsworth, and Mount Desert, touching at intermediate points.

Early in February three deer, an unusual sight then in this locality, were discovered by some of our "dead shots" on the eastern side of the river.   Had they come to take a last look at the old town soon to be merged in the new city? or a first look at the embryo aldermen already beginning to sharpen their appetites for venison steak and turtle soup? In either case, they paid the penalty of their curiosity.   One of them weighed over one hundred and fifty pounds, and was chased from the woods into the water before he was captured.

We had but few public musical entertainments this year; the public ear was too filled with politics to listen to "the voice of charmers, charm they never so wisely."   The Portland Minstrels were here at City Hall in February, and Mr. Henri M. Jungnickel with Mr. and Miss Wheelock in May; Furber's Minstrels, and the Harmoneans, gave two or more concerts in November.

At the annual spring meeting, 15th of March, Daniel Haraden, William T. Colburn and Franklin Brier were chosen Selectmen, Joseph Wheeler, Clerk, and Augustus Perry, Treasurer. The monies raised were $3,000 for schools, $1,000 for paupers and insane, $1,000 for payment of incidental expenses, $1,000 for payment of debts, $150 for fire engine expense, $3,000 for repairing highways and bridges. The all absorbing question before the meeting was that of establishing a town liquor agency under the provisions of the Maine Law. A motion to instruct the selectmen to purchase liquors and appoint an agent to make sale of them for medicinal and mechanical purposes prevailed by a vote of 206 against 138. Benjamin F. Blackstone, Esq., was appointed agent.

Hon. Alfred Johnson died March 22d, at the residence of his son-in-law, the late Dr. Nahum P. Monroe, in the sixty-third year of his age. He was the eldest son of Rev. Alfred Johnson, who was installed pastor of the first Congregational Church in this place in 1805, brother of the late Ralph C. Johnson and father of the late Col. Alfred W. Johnson. He was born in Newburyport, Mass., Aug. 13, 1789. At the time his father came here to reside he was a student in Bowdoin College, where he graduated in 1808 with the highest honors of his class. He studied law in the office of Hon. William Crosby and on admission to the Bar in 1811 opened an office in the counting-room of the Nesmith Store then kept by his brother Ralph C. In the war of 1812 he was captain of the artillery company in this place, his brother holding at the same time the office of ensign in the infantry. He represented this town and Northport in the General Court when Maine was a part of Massachusetts, and was a member of the Convention which in 1819 framed the Constitution of the new State. He was a member of its first legislature and resigned that position to accept the office of Judge of Probate for the county of Hancock, Sept. 1, 1820. That office he held until March 1, 1827, when he was appointed to the same position in the new county of Waldo. He continued to hold the office until his term expired by constitutional limitation in 1840, when Hon. Jonathan Thayer of Camden was appointed his successor. He was one of the Trustees of Bowdoin College from 1838 until his decease.

He was an able lawyer and a ripe scholar; occupying a place in the front rank of the literati of the State. He possessed a remarkable memory; it may be truthfully said of him, if of any one; that nothing ever escaped him. He was eminent as a conversationalist, and his memory was a perfect treasury of all he had ever read or thought. No more truthful, mental or moral portraiture of the man can be presented than that embraced in the following resolutions adopted at a meeting of the members of the Waldo Bar held on the day preceding his funeral: "Resolved that we lament with profoundest regret the demise of Hon. Alfred Johnson, who for nearly forty years was a member of this Bar, and for a large portion of the time filled an important judicial office. Although during the latter portion of his life he had retired from active practice the profession will long remember him as a sound and correct lawyer, performing the various duties of his official station with signal ability and to the acceptance of the public. Resolved, that in contemplation of the character of Judge Johnson, in all his various situations both public and private, as a lawyer, a legislator and a judge, as a prominent citizen, as a scholar thoroughly versed in classical and general literature, and as a man of social qualities, of genial humor, and of remarkable colloquial powers, we feel that a void has been created in our community which cannot be filled."

Hon. William Crosby died on the 31st of March in his eighty-second year. He was born in Billerica, Mass., June 3, 1770, graduated at Harvard in 1794, studied his profession in the offices of William Gordon, Esq., at Amherst, N. H., and Hon. Samuel Dana at Groton, Mass., was admitted to the Bar of Middlesex county in 1798 and after practising his profession three years in Billerica came here to reside in January, 1802. He erected his office on the site on High street now occupied by the brick store of Mr. Arnold Harris, first removing the fallen trees to make room for it, and in 1804 became the owner, by purchase, of the dwellinghouse on Main street now occupied by his son. He left an interesting auto-biography, covering seventy years of his life, from which it appears that when he first came here in 1801, there were on the site of the present business portion of the city but five framed-houses, a few log houses, one store, one meeting-house, and five Indian wigwams.

Soon after he commenced practice here he was appointed county attorney, and in 1811 chief justice of the Court of Common Pleas for the Third Eastern Circuit, embracing the counties of Hancock, Washington and Penobscot. He held that office until the Court was abolished in 1822. He then resumed practice and continued in it until 1831, when he carried into effect a resolution which he had long before adopted, to retire from active business at the age of sixty. He was a member of the College of Presidential Electors in 1812 and of the Senate of Massachusetts in 1815.

His remaining days after retiring from the practice of his profession were devoted to his books, the study of the natural sciences, the preparation of manuscripts on various subjects, and to agricultural and horticultural pursuits. It would not become the compiler of these annals, sustaining the relation he does to the subject of this brief biographical sketch, to indulge in the language of eulogy; yet it is but simple justice to the man, whose memory is very precious to him, to embody in it a resolution adopted by the members of the Waldo Bar at a meeting held the day after his decease: "Resolved, that the recent demise of the Hon. William Crosby, calls us to mourn the loss of a respected and venerated brother, the oldest member of this Bar, its founder and first President. Although he had retired from active life and for the last twenty years we have not met him in the arena of professional labor, yet he is fresh in our recollection, and will long be remembered as the just lawyer, the able advocate, the impartial judge, and the eminent and beloved citizen." A somewhat extended biography of Judge Crosby may be found in Willis's History of the Law, the Courts, and the Lawyers of Maine.

Early in April Messrs. Holmes and Baker became landlords of the American House, succeeding Mr. H. N. Lancaster. Mr. Holmes is now landlord of the New England House, and Mr. Baker died some years ago.

A town meeting was held on the 30th of April to act on the question of accepting the city charter. The whole number of votes thrown were only 592. The result was the acceptance of the charter by a vote of 314 against 278. The only public demonstration of joy at the result was by the boys, who rang the bells and had a tar-barrel bonfire in the evening. A meeting was held on the 25th of December "to see if the town will vote to surrender their city charter." The vote was so decisively in the negative that there was no further opposition.

A movement was inaugurated this month by School Districts 4 and 5 to purchase the interest of the county and town in the old Court-house and convert it into a school house. It resulted in the purchase of those interests; the interior of the building was re-modeled, and it has to the present day been used for school purposes. In 1862 a contract was made between the School District and the Masonic Fraternity by the terms of which the attic was leased to Phoenix Lodge and the Chapter for the term of ninety-nine years, in consideration of which they constructed the French roof on the building and engaged to keep it in repair during the term of their lease.

Early in May a change was made in the course of the telegraph wire across the river. Up to this date it had crossed at the lower bridge; by the change made it diverged from Bridge to High street, thence on High street and the road to City Point to the red bridge at the Point where it crossed the river and thence to Mason's Mill where it connected with the old line.

Among the vessels launched this year were the ship Northern Chief of about 1136 tons burthen, the barks John Gardner, 487, and Moses Kimball, 499, the brigs Amos M. Roberts, 218, and Mary McCrae, 241, the schooners

Vesta, 99, City Belle, 98, Fred Dyer, 157, J. B., 186, Mazurka, 92, and the Olivia, 97.

The Maine Baptist Convention commenced an annual session of three days at the Baptist Church on the 15th of June. It was largely attended, more than a hundred of the clergy of the denomination being present. A State Convention of the Universalist denomination commenced a three days session on the 22d. This also was numerously attended. Rev. N. C. Fletcher, now residing in Camden, was pastor of the Society in this place at the time.

"And Satan came also among them." Job. 2. 1-2. While these religious denominations were engaged in "presenting themselves before the Lord" those famous Magicians, Professors Baldwin and Wood came "from going to and fro in the earth and from walking up and down in it," and gave two of their "amusing and interesting entertainments" at City Hall. Whether it was through their magical art, or the influence of the Conventions, that the cocks of the casks in the liquor agency were mysteriously turned on the night of the 19th and some two or three hundred dollars worth of liquor "wasted its sweetness on the desert air," is a question to which no satisfactory answer has yet been made.

The remaining local events of this year will be found in our next chapter.

CHAPTER L. (1852.)

There are many still living who will remember with kindness and respect the Rev. Edward D. Very, who but a short time previous to this date was pastor of the Baptist Church in this place. He was drowned near Horton, N. S., on the 8th of June. He was on his return from Cape Blomidon, where he had been with a party consisting of Prof. Chipman and four students of Acadia college, for the purpose of collecting specimens of the minerals found in that locality, when the boat in which they were was upset and they were all, with one of their two boatman, drowned. Mr. Very was a graduate of Dartmouth and studied theology at Bangor. His untimely death was much deplored by his numerous friends here and elsewhere.

Rev. William Frothingham, for twenty-eight years pastor of the Unitarian Society in this place, died on the 24th of June in his seventy-sixth year. He was buried from the Unitarian Church, which was draped with the emblems of mourning, on the Sunday following; the funeral services were conducted by his successor in the pulpit, Rev. Dr. Palfry.

Mr. Frothingham was born in Cambridge, Mass., March 14, 1777, graduated at Harvard in 1799, and was first settled at Saugus, Mass., about 1804. He first came to this place as a teacher and missionary in 1817; at that time the stated religious services of the society to which he minister-ed were held in the academy. In the spring of 1818 he was invited by the Society to become their settled minister. That invitation he accepted in the spring following, and on the 21st of July he was duly installed. He continued to be their pastor until the spring of 1847, when by reason of declining health he was compelled to relinquish the duties of his office. The last sermon he wrote was prepared for Fast Day, April 8th, but was never preached. He was not an eloquent preacher, but there was a simplicity of style and sincerity of purpose in his discourses which were far more effective in producing permanent results than any mere oratorical display ever can be. He was not a controversialist, but sought rather to follow after the things that make for peace and things wherewith one may edify another. No breath of censure ever tarnished his character and his memory is cherished with love and respect by all who knew him.

On the 29th of the same month Henry Clay died in Washington. He also, like the venerable clergyman above noticed, was born in 1777, on the twelfth day of April. On the receipt of the sad intelligence the Whig flag was displayed draped with crape, and the Democratic flag was set at half mast. At sunset minute guns were fired and the bells were tolled.

One more, and the list of those the termination of whose earthly pilgrimage this year we have to chronicle is ended. Daniel Webster died in Marshfield, Mass., on the morning of the 24th of October. On the receipt of this intelligence, in the morning of the day following, a general feeling of sadness seemed to pervade all classes in our community. The flags on the Democratic and Whig flag-staffs floated at half-mast during the day; the flag over the office of the Republican Journal and the revenue ensign on the Custom House were trimmed with crape. At half past twelve o'clock minute guns were fired and the bells on all the churches were tolled. The last words of the dying statesman, "I still live!" acquired a new significance; they became prophetic. The universal expression of sorrow at the announcement of his death demonstrated that he still lived, as he always will live, in the memory of his countrymen.

Fourth of July being Sunday was celebrated on the fifth. A national salute was fired at sunrise, noon and sunset. The national ensign with the names of the Whig candidates for the Presidency and vice Presidency--Scott and Graham-attached, was displayed from the Whig flag-staff erected on the Saturday preceding at the foot of Franklin street. The flagstaff was 120 feet in height and stood, although like the party erecting it sadly shorn in dimensions, until May 5, 1874. Having "outlived its usefulness" and having come to be regarded dangerous in consequence

of its increasing tendency towards the north it was taken down. Hydrant
Company, No. 2, with full ranks, about sixty men, and in full uniform,
red shirts trimmed with blue, glazed hats and belts, marched through
the principal streets in the forenoon, and at the termination of their
parade were entertained at the American House. In the afternoon a company
of mounted Fantastics paraded, and there was a ball at City Hall in
the evening.

The "Consolidated exhibition of Wild Beasts and Equestrian exercises"
was here in the early part of the month. The entertainment "concluded
with the Pageant of St. George and the Dragon." From the spirited demonstrations outside the "pavillion" it was surmised that St. George was the
personage better known here as St. Croix, and that the dragon was none
other than the "Baskahegan Giant" in disguise.

A dramatic company under the management of Mr. John D. McGowen,
who had formerly resided here, gave several performances at City Hall
this month, and in September we were favored with several by the Howard
Dramatic Company under the management of Mr. W. B. English.

On the 12th of August the Neptune Fire Company of Waltham, Mass.,
arrived here from Bangor on the steamer Boston. They were the guests
of Hydrant Company, No. 2, at the American House. The two companies
marched through our streets the next morning prior to the departure
of the Neptunes on the Steamer Governor.

The principal occupation of our people during the summer, not only
here but throughout the State, had been the discussion of the merits
of the Maine Law, analyzing the characters of the several candidates
for the office of governor, and preparing for the political battle to
be fought on the 13th of September. A pleasant episode occurred here
on the 7th which for twenty-four hours smoothed the wrinkled front of
grim visaged war and spread oil on the troubled waters of the political
sea. It was a gala day with Hydrant Engine Company, No. 2. There was
a pleasant, harmonious reunion of men and women of all parties and sects
at City Hall in the evening, on the occasion of the presentation of
a banner by the ladies of Belfast to the company before named. The
presentation speech, beautiful in language and most gracefully delivered,
was by Miss Helen A. Upton; the reply, equally happy and appropriate,
was by Capt. Calvin Hervey. The banner, of beautiful silk, bore on
one side the State coat of arms, and on the other in gilt letters Presented
by the Ladies of Belfast, &c. It was painted by Theodore N. Phillips,
then of this town, and cost about seventy-five dollars. Music by the
Bangor Band and the Belfast Glee Club, appropriate addresses, bouquets,
refreshments, &c., &c., contributed to make the occasion one of much
joy and festivity. The Company paraded the next morning and left on
the steamer for Portland on a visit to brother firemen.

The annual State election came off on the 13th. There was no lack
of candidates or of questions involved in the issue. For the office
of Governor, John Hubbard of Hallowell, the incumbent, was the candidate
of the Democrats, William G. Crosby of this place of the Whigs, Anson
G. Chandler of Calais of the anti-Maine-Law-party, and Ezekiel Holmes
of Winthrop of the Free-soil party. The vote in this place was, 298,
for Hubbard, 505 for Crosby, 4 for Chandler, and 2 for Holmes. There
was no choice by the people; at the next session of the legislature
Crosby was elected. Alfred W. Johnson, Whig, was elected Representative,
Robert White, Democrat, was elected Register of Deeds and County Treasurer,
and Nathaniel Patterson, Democrat, Clerk of the Courts.

It was a hard fought fight, as was also that which followed in
November. Looking over the field of battle at this late date for the
dead and wounded, in a different sense from that in which those terms
are ordinarily used, it is found that the successful candidates for
Register of Deeds, Clerk of the Courts, town Representative, all are
among the dead. Of the four candidates for gubernatorial honors one
only, Ex-Gov. Crosby, is now living. Of the standard-bearers of the
two great national Parties--Pierce and King, Scott and Graham--the last

named is the sole survivor!   "Vain pomp and glory of this world!"

The smoke had hardly cleared away from the State battlefield when the hosts began to rally for another conflict on the National. A Granite Club was organized on the 16th by the Democrats, and a Scot and Graham Club on the 17th by the Whigs. The latter having already raised their flag-staff at the foot of Franklin street, the former raised theirs on the Common in front of the brick schoolhouse. It occupied a very commanding position, and it was very much to the regret of the community, irrespective of party, that it was cut down a few years afterwards.

The sixth annual Agricultural Fair and Cattle Show was held on the 13th and 14th of October. The exhibition was in every respect creditable to the farming community. At the meeting of the Society at the Unitarian Church in the evening of the second day addresses were made by Hon. Albert G. Jewett, Hon. Nehemiah Abbott and Alfred W. Johnson, Esq.

That last name reminds the compiler that he had a duty to perform, pleasant yet mournful, for the discharge of which there will be no more fitting opportunity, probably, than the present; mournful because it is always sad to think or speak of the ties of friendship sundered by the hand of death, pleasant because there is pleasure always in bearing witness to the merits of the departed. Alfred Waldo Johnson, son of the late Hon. Alfred Johnson, was born Dec. 20, 1824, graduated at Bowdoin in the class of 1845, studied law in his father's office, and was admitted to the Bar in 1848. The practice of law had no attractions for him, and after the decease of his father in 1852, he gradually withdrew from it and engaged in business pursuits more congenial to his taste. His business acquaintance with gentlemen interested in the construction of western railroads led him to investigate and finally engage in the business, in which he was eminently successful. In 1852 and 1853 he was elected to represent his native town in the State legislature. He was the candidate for representative in Congress from this district in 1858 and 1860. These are the only offices within the gift of the people for which he ever was a candidate. His military title of Colonel, by which he was familiarly known, was derived from holding the office of aid to the commander in chief of the State. He was one of the four, all young men, appointed in 1853; but one of the four is now living. In July, 1867, he went abroad with the intention of making a tour of the United Kingdom and the Continent. A severe cold which he contracted on the passage, and over exertion immediately after while travelling in Ireland and Scotland, brought upon him or developed the disease, consumption, of which he died. He returned in August of the year following with impaired health, and failed gradually until he died at the St. James, in Boston, on the 14th day of November, 1869, in the forty-fifth year of his age.

He was a man of genial temperament ardent in his attachments, and of unbounded hospitality. He was a well-read lawyer, especially in commercial law; as a financier there were but few superior to him. He believed that wealth was a blessing, but only so far as it was made to contribute to the comfort, welfare and happiness of his fellow-man. Although possessed of large wealth he was not of that class who hug it "to the very verge of the church-yard mould." He was a man of quick sympathies and of many benefactions; but so quietly and unostentatiously were they bestowed that few knew of them save the recipients. In the distribution of his wealth he remembered liberally those connected with him by the ties of kindred and did not forget those to whom he was bound by the ties of friendship. In his will he made a bequest of three thousand dollars to Bowdoin College to found three Scholarships for students in indigent circumstances, and a perpetual bequest of five hundred dollars, annually, to the poor of Belfast, to be distributed among them by his Trustees according to their judgment. There is many a man whose heavy burthen of poverty and infirmity has already been made lighter by his generous bequest, to whom his memory is precious; many a widow and fatherless in our midst who "arise up and call him blessed."

At the Presidential election, November 2d, the votes in this place were 437 for Pierce, demo., 314 for Scott, whig, 17 for Hale, abolition. The result of the contest, the election of Pierce, was welcomed by the democrats with the liveliest demonstrations of joy. Bonfires were kindled, guns fired, bells rung, and democratic banners flung broadcast to the breeze. The machinery of the whig rooster was too terribly shattered to manufacture a single crow.

The County Commissioners advertised this month for proposals to build a new Court House, the interest of the county in the old one having been disposed of. The contemplated Court House was the one now standing at the intersection of Church and Market streets, opposite the North Church. It was erected in the year following. A term of the Supreme Court, Judge Rice presiding, was held in it, for the first time, in January, 1854.

Pierce's Block, at the junction of Church and Franklin streets was erected this year. The ground floor was originally designed for two stores; the largest one was first occupied by the Messrs. Pierce. The hall in the second story was dedicated on Thanksgiving Eve with a ball. The first lecture delivered in it was by Rev. Mr. Brooks of Lynn, Mass., on the evening of December 27th; it was the opening lecture of a course before the Lyceum. The first public entertainment was on the evening of Jan. 20th, 1853; it was a concert of instrumental music. James Y. McClintock, Esq., erected two three-story brick blocks on High and Springs streets each block containing four tenements. --The construction of Doctor Payne's villa, at the corner of Waldo Avenue and Cobbett's Lane, now Vine street, was completed this year. It was designed originally for a Water-cure establishment.

CHAPTER LI. (1853.)

The popular amusements of this year were inaugurated in January by the exhibition at City Hall for several days of the Seven Mile Mirror, a Panorama of the river St. Lawrence and the lakes. --There was a concert of instrumental music by W illiam H. Whedden and others at Pierce's Hall in the evening of the twentieth. --The Misses Macomber, assisted by Mr. Covert, gave a concert of vocal music at the same place on the 8th of June. --A theatrical company under the management of Mr. J. P. Addams gave a series of performances at City Hall in May.

Messrs. Baker and Edwards became landlords of the New England House, in January, succeeding Luther A. Coombs; and in June, Mr. N. W. Holmes withdrew from the American House and Mr. Baker assumed the sole management.

We had lively times with the steamers this year; competition at one time bringing the fare to Boston down to fifty cents. On the third of January the Boston, Capt. T. B. Sanford, commenced running to Boston, making one trip weekly, and touching at Portland; in April she began to make two trips per week direct to Boston. The Admiral, Capt. Wood, commenced running between Boston, Frankfort and Eastport early in April; her last trip to the west was on the 26th day of March. The Eastern State, Capt. Foster Harding, began early in April to make one trip per week to Boston; in July she was taken off the route and sold to parties in Philadelphia. The new steamer Daniel Webster, Capt. Joseph Farwell, made her first appearance here on the 21st of April. A list of her officers will not be without interest to parties residing here who had an interest in her at the time. They were Capt. Blanchard, previously of the Huntress, First Pilot, Capt. A. Spear of Rockland, Second, W. L. Pennell and P. Richardson, Engineers, Edward Cushing, Clerk, S. K. Lowell, Steward, and J. F. Gould, Baggage-master. The Penobscot, Capt. Flowers, came early in May and made her last trip on the 18th of November; she advertised as the New Outside Line, and as the Outside Opposition Line. The Governor, Capt. Rogers, came on the 4th of May, ran on the outside route, and advertised as the People's Line. In July the Lawrence, Capt. Deering, began to run between this place and Ellsworth. In December, the Ocean, Capt. E. H. Sanford, came on to run through the winter, Capt. Sanford died in 1865. This year for the first time, according to the recollection of the compiler, the appellation of Sanford's Independent Line was adopted.

The lecturers before the Lyceum during the winter were Dr. Ezra S. Gannett of Boston, on New England, Rev. John Pierpont of Medford, Mass., a poem entitled the Scholar's Hope, Rev. Henry Giles, of Bucksport, five lectures on the civilized man, embracing the Hebrew, the Greek, or man of culture, the Roman, or man of sway, the Mediaeval, or man of personal force, the man of the Age, or man of social power. The fourth annual course before the Lyceum commenced in December. The first lecture was by Hon. Josiah Quincy of Boston, on the Mormons. He was followed by William C. Williamson, Esq., of this place, now resident in Boston, with a poem the title of which was Past and Present. The only other lecture of the year, so far as remembered, was by Rev. E. H. Chapin of New York on Temperance; it was delivered in the evening of the 9th of September.

About the first of March there was a change in the proprietorship as well as the name of the State Signal. Mr. D. H. Prime became its proprietor by purchase from Mr. Avery, and continued its publication under the name of Belfast Signal until November following, when he sold out to Messrs. J. R. Stephens and Co. They published a few numbers and discontinued it. The Signal had been from its birth, in 1840, a staunch advocate of the principles of the Whig party. Its publishers became aware of the fact that the Whig party was a "very sick man," and withdrew just in time to escape attending the funeral. On the 2d of May the copartnership existing between Levi R. Wing and George B. Moore, publishers of the Journal, was dissolved, and Mr. Moore became sole proprietor and editor.

There was a Grand Ball at Pierce's Hall on the evening of March 4th--Inauguration Day. The prominent feature was the veteran Major Jack Douglass, who made music on the occasion for the grandchildren of those who nearly half a century before tripped it on "the light, fantastic toe," to the sound of his fiddle.

On the 14th the people met to elect officers for the new city. The wardroom of Ward 1 was the Academy; of Ward 2, at the brick school-house formerly the Town Hall; of Ward 3, at the Vestry of the North Church; of Ward 4, at the school-house in District No. 7, at the Head of the Tide; of Ward 5, at the school-house in District No. 14, on the East side of the river. Hon. Ralph C. Johnson was elected Mayor by a vote of 550 against 86. The Aldermen elected were Rowland Carlton, Stephen S. Lewis, Thomas Marshall, Ephraim K. Maddocks and William Rust. Mr. Carlton resigned soon afterwards and Hiram O. Alden was elected to fill the vacancy. The Common Councilmen for the year were Joseph Williamson, Abram N. Noyes, Samuel Edwards, Andrew T. Palmer, William H. Connor, George McDonald, Franklin Brier, Moses B. Ferguson, George Woods and Elijah Morrill.

The city Government was organized at Pierce's Hall on the 21st. Joseph Williamson was elected President of the Common Council and John H. Quimby, clerk. Joseph Wheeler was chosen City Clerk. At a subsequent session, Augustus Perry was chosen Treasurer and Collector, Woodbury Davis, afterwards a judge of the Supreme Court, City Solicitor, Dr. John G. Brooks, now Mayor of the city, City Physician, James W. Webster, School Supervisor, Timothy Chase, Freeman Tufts and Charles Moore, Road Commissioners, Charles Palmer, Chief Engineer of the Fire Department, Phineas Davis, City Sexton. Mr. Palmer declined to accept the office of Chief Engineer and Calvin Hervey was elected in his place. Daniel Haraden, Ephraim Swett and George Woods were elected Assessors; Messrs. Haraden and Swett declined, and James P. White and Salathiel C. Nickerson were elected. Joseph Williamson, Jr., Esq., had been appointed by the Governor, Judge of the Police Court.

The first rooms occupied by the City Council were at No. 4 Phoenix Row, at an annual rent of thirty dollars. The whole amount of the town's indebtedness at this time was less than one thousand dollars. Daniel Faunce was the first one who filed notice of intention to build; the building to be erected was his dwelling-house at the junction of Church and Peach streets. The monies raised were for Schools $3,600.00, for highways, $3,000.00, for paupers, $1,000.00, for city debt, $1,000.00, for salaries and incidental expenses, $1,000.00, for engines, $200.00.

The official guillotine was put in operation at Washington as soon as decency would admit after the inauguration of President Pierce. Joseph S. Noyes was appointed post-master in the place of Charles Giles removed. He held the office until 1857, when he was removed to make room for his successor, Samuel Edwards. He was the first occupant of the present post-office.

Mr. Noyes was a native of Castine but came here when he was quite young. He learned the hatter's trade with the old firm of Furber and Bean, but being of a studious turn of mind abandoned it and became a very successful school teacher. In 1849 he went to California, but health failed him and he returned early in 1850. At the annual election of that year he was elected to represent this town in the legislature. After the expiration of his official term as postmaster he studied law, was admitted to the Bar and opened an office here; at the time of his decease he had a large and lucrative practice. He continued during his life to take a deep interest in our public schools, and always sustained the reputation of being a worthy citizen and an exemplary member of society. He died Oct. 16, 1862, in the thirty-ninth year of his age.

About the time of Mr. Noyes' appointment as postmaster, Hon. Adams Treat of Frankfort was appointed Collector of the Customs at this Port in place of Maurice C. Blake, removed. The subordinate offices were filled by the appointment of Ansel Lennan and Henry W. Cunningham.

Mr. Treat resigned in August following and Hon. Ephraim K. Smart of Camden was appointed in his place. Mr. Smart held the office until his official term expired, when Jonathan G. Dickerson, Esq., now Judge Dickerson, was appointed to succeed him. He died at Camden in September, 1872, aged fifty-nine. General Cunningham died at Washington, D. C., in October, 1871, aged sixty-five. His remains were brought here for interment.

The day set apart annually for "Humiliation, Fasting and Prayer" occurred this year on the 14th of April. Instead of devoting the day to playing ball and shooting turkeys, as had been the custom of years before, our merchants and business men generally, by mutual agreement, refrained from their ordinary avocations, and the day was observed more in conformity to the original design of the institution.

Fourth of July was celebrated on a larger scale than ever before in this place, it being the first one occurring after our organization as a city, our patriotism was, of course, more than ever exuberant. A heavy rain in the morning prevented the display of the Procession announced in the programme, and interfered somewhat with the literary exercises of the day, which were held in a large canvas tent erected on the Common. Hon. Ralph C. Johnson, Mayor of the city, officiated as President of the day, Rev. Cazneau Palfrey as Chaplain, Hon. Nehemiah Abbott as Reader of the Declaration and Governor Crosby as Orator. At the conclusion of the exercises there was a public dinner at Pierce's Hall, at which Mr. William O. Poor officiated as Toast-master; the toast were drank in "Adam's Ale." Speeches were made at the table by several distinguished guests. There was a grand display of fireworks in the evening, followed by a ball at Pierce's Hall. The Fantastics and Cosumiers were out, of course, in full force and feather.

In the evening of the 8th the house, barn and workshop of Mr. Abial Pierce, situated on a cross-road leading from Belmont to the Lincolnville road, were destroyed by fire. It was supposed to have originated from a spark falling on the roof. The house of John J. Mahoney on the Northport road was burned soon afterwards. These are the only fires destructive of any considerable amount of property that occurred this year, so far as remembered.

The Bath City Grays a finely disciplined military company, made us a call on the 28th. As we had no military organization here to do the honors our citizens entertained them with a ball in the evening. They left the next morning on the Daniel Webster.

Rev. Samuel Cole was ordained pastor of the Baptist Church on the 27th; the exercises were as follows: Sermon by Rev. E. B. Eddy of Beverly, Mass., Ordaining prayer by Rev. W. O. Thomas, then of Rockland, Right hand of fellowship by Rev. I. S. Kalloch of Rockland, Charge to Pastor by Rev. S. L. Caldwell of Bangor, and Address to the church and congregation by Rev. C. G. Porter of Bangor. Mr. Cole died at the house of his father in Beverly, Mass. , in November of the year following, after a brief but painful sickness. The church and society over which he was ordained in losing him sustained a great loss. He was highly respected and esteemed by all in the community who had become acquainted with him during his brief ministry in this place.

The eighth of September was a grand day with our firemen; the occasion being a visit from the Pioneer Company of Biddeford, to Hydrant Company No. 2. The Pioneers arrived in the morning on the Daniel Webster, accompanied by the Saco Brass Band, were welcomed with a salvo of artillery at the wharf, and escorted to the American House by the Hydrants. Our principal streets and the engine houses were decorated with flags. There was a parade of the two companies in the forenoon, and at 2 o'clock the Pioneers were escorted to Pierce's Hall and partook of a dinner provided by Mr. Baker of the American House. There was a ball in the evening. The Pioneers left the next morning on the steamer.

The annual fall meeting was held on the 12th. There were again four candidates in the field for the office of governor.

Albert Pilsbury of Machias was the regularly nominated candidate of
the democratic party, Wm. G. Crosby of this place, the incumbent, was
the candidate for the whig party, Anson P. Morrill of Readfield, of
the party which was born this year and christened the Republican party,
and Ezekiel Holmes of Winthrop of the free-soil party.   The votes thrown
in this place were 187 for Pilsbury, 337 for Crosby, 117 for Morrill
and 41 for Holmes.   There was no choice by the people, and at the next
session of the legislature Crosby was elected.   Alfred W. Johnson was
re-elected town representative, and James B. Murch of Unity, now of
this city, was elected county attorney.
     The annual Agricultural Fair was here on the 12th and 13th of October.
     Among the vessels launched this year were the ships Ralph C. Johnson
of about 1279 tons and the Chapin of about 883; the brigs Henry Guild
of about 250, the Etolia 298, and the Tiberias of about 249; the schooners
Emma L. Cottrell of about 200, and John Pierce 200, the Dido 52, and
the Tyro of about 50.
     The project of a railroad to Moosehead Lake began this year, for
the first time, to assume a tangible form.   A large and enthusiastic
meeting was held on the 7th of February to adopt preliminary measures
for the construction of such road.   A committee was raised consisting
of Hon. Joseph Williamson, Hon. Albert G. Jewett and Hon. Nehemiah Abbott,
to procure a charter.   The resolutions adopted at the meeting contemplated
a pledge of the credit of the city in aid of the road to an amount not
exceeding $250,000.   A charter was obtained, approved March 31st, and
books were opened in May for the purpose of receiving subscriptions
for stock, in Boston, Waterville, Monson, Dexter and this city.   By
the terms of the charter the capital stock of the corporation was to
consist of not less than ten thousand nor more than fifty thousand shares
of one hundred dollars each, and the charter was to be null and void
unless the road was completed by the 31st of December, 1863.   The act
of incorporation embraced the names of twenty-two corporators, all of
whom save nine are still living.   The charter was forfeited by failure
to comply with its terms, and the project slumbered until it was awakened
by the passage of the Act, February 28th, 1867, under which the Belfast
and Moosehead Lake Railway Company was organized, and the road was built
as far as Burnham.
     Three of our oldest inhabitants, Benjamin Hartshorn, Samuel Walton
and James Langworthy, all upright worthy and exemplary citizens, died
this year.   Mr. Hartshorn died March 13th, in his eighty-fifth year.
He had resided here more than half a century and was the owner of the
Hartshorn Farm, so called, now owned by Mr. Josiah Mitchell, on which
stood the last of the log houses.   He had voted at every Presidential
election from the second election of Washington to the election of Pierce
in 1852, both included.
     Mr. Walton, father of our fellow-citizen Mr. Alfred Walton, died
April 12th, aged seventy-seven.   He was one of the builders and owners
of the Babel, of which mention has often been made in preceding chapters.
     Mr. Langworthy died November 22d aged seventy-five.   He did not
come here to reside until 1821; he built the brick tenement on Church
street opposite the Court-house.   He was one of the most earnest advocates
for the construction of the Moosehead Lake railroad, and the firmest
in the faith that the work, soon or late, would be accomplished; finding
"confirmation strong" of his faith in the predictions of the prophets
of the Old Testament.

CHAPTER LII. (1854.)

The lecturers before the Lyceum this winter were as follows: Rev. Charles Rockwell, of Castine, on Southern, Western, and New England life, Rev. Samuel Cole of this city, on Elements of Success, Rev. Charles Allen of Biddeford, on Cromwell, Hon. Henry P. Torsey of Redfield, on The Bible for the Purposes of Mental Culture, Hon. Edward Kent, of Bangor, on Brazil, Miss Lucy Stone, on Woman's Rights, and on The Political Disabilities of Women, and Rev. Theodore Parker. Charles Lowell, Esq., of Ellsworth, delivered two or three lectures in March.

Madam DeMark, "the mysterious lady," was here in January, and enlightened ladies and gentlemen as to their future--in other words, "told their fortunes"--at the moderate charge of fifty cents for gentlemen, ladies half price. "Hindoo Miracles" by J. D. Abournet, the "wonderful Eire-King, or Eastern Wizard," with laughing gas thrown in, constituted the entertainment at Pierce's Hall on the evening of the 2d of March. McAllister--not the one whose "ointment was good," but the "great European Magician,-- appeared at his "Palace of Enchantment"--Pierce's hall--and gave "a brilliant series of his wonders of magic on a scale of unequalled splendor" in July.

Daniel Putnam was appointed sheriff, and Bohan P. Field Register of Probate for this county in February. Mr. Putnam appointed Ruel Stanley his deputy in this place, and Samuel F. Miller jailer.

There were but few concerts this year. Miss M. J. Brett "interested the people once more," by a concert at City Hall on the 20th of February. Mr. William H. Whedden, assisted by the Belfast Sax-horn Band and others, gave a concert and ball at Pierce's Hall on the 14th of March; it was a "benefit" given to Mr. W.   Of the six managers on the occasion only one half are now living. In June two concerts were given at Pierce's Hall by Messrs. Covert and Hector, Miss Macomber, and the Misses Hall, four sisters.

Our second annual city election came off on the 13th of March. The officers elected were as follows: Mayor, Sherburn Sleeper, Aldermen, Nathaniel H. Bradbury, Andrew T. Palmer, Calvin Hervey, Joshua Towle, William Rust. Councilmen, Samuel G. Thurlow, William T. Colburn, Ephraim Swett, H. G. O. Washburn, George McDonald, David G. Vose, Orrin Cunningham, Charles Moore, Jonathan Durham, 2nd, and Joseph Kaler. William E. Colburn was chosen President, and John H. Quimby, Clerk of the Council.   Joseph Wheeler was re-elected City Clerk, Dr. John G. Brooks, City Physician, and Woodbury Davis, City Solicitor; Rev. Edward F. Cutter was elected School Supervisor, and Daniel Haraden City Treasurer; Mr. Haraden declined, and John S. Caldwell was elected in his stead. The moneys raised were $4000.00 for schools, $3000.00 for highways, $1000.00 for salaries and incidental expenses, $800.00 for support of the poor, and $250.00 for expenses of the fire department.

On the 28th of March the Post-Office was removed from its old stand, now occupied by Dr. Sylvester, to the store on Church Street now occupied by Owen G. White; its next removal was in 1857, to the building on Custom House Square, where it has ever since been.

On the last day of March and the day following the "Kinetopoloscope" was exhibited at Pierce's Hall. It was not a wild beast, but a series of Panoramas; concluding with a "Pantoscopic voyage to the Land of Gold."

Hon. Nathaniel H. Hubbard, having been appointed Judge of Probate for this county, held his first court here on the fourth day of April.

The first steamer of the season was the Penobscot, Captain Flowers; she came on the 14th of April; she sailed under the flag of the Peoples Line, and the Opposition Line, and plied between Bangor and Boston. About the same time came the Daniel Webster, Capt. Samuel Blanchard; she plied between Bangor and Portland, making three trips per week, and running in connection with the railroad from the latter place to Boston. The Boston, Capt. T. B. Sanford, commenced running on the outside route to Boston on the first of May. Capt. Sanford died in 1858.

The T. F. Secor, Captain Deering, came upon the route between this place and Machiasport early in June and left on the 22d of November. Early in December she began to run to Portland on the winter route. The Governor, Capt. Rogers, ran for a portion of the months of June and July on the outside route to Boston. A record of the ultimate fate of these boats, so far as known, will not be out of place here, as no further mention will be made of them in these annals. Subsequently to running on this route the Penobscot was lengthened and named the City of Norfolk. She broke in two and sunk near Norfolk, Va. The Boston grounded in Otter Sound, S. C., while in government service and was burned to prevent her capture by the rebels. The Secor was employed by government as a war-despatch-boat, and was burned off Charleston, S. C. The Daniel Webster, two years ago, was running on the Saguenay river. The Governor having been thoroughly repaired and fitted with new boilers, sailed from Portland, or Boston, for the south, and was abandoned in a gale off the Capes of Virginia.

Mr. John D. Rust, who now resides in Rockport, became landlord of the New England House in April, succeeding Messrs. Baker and Edwards.

The Bank of Commerce was incorporated on the 8th of March with a capital of $7500.00; of the twelve corporators five have deceased. The meeting for organization was held on the 13th of May. Hiram O. Alden, Alfred W. Johnson, James P. Furber, John W. White, Asa Faunce, Columbia P. Carter and William H. Hunt, were chosen Directors. Mr. Alden was elected president and Charles Palmer was appointed Cashier. Mr. Alden continued to be President until March 24, 1856, when he resigned and Mr. Johnson was elected; he held the office until October 12, 1857, when he resigned and Mr. Faunce was elected, who held the office until October 1, 1868, when the Bank ceased to exist. Mr. Palmer held the office of Cashier until October 29, 1864, when he resigned and John H. Quimby, now Treasurer of the Belfast Savings Bank, was appointed; Mr. Quimby held the office for the remainder of the lifetime of the Bank. During the whole term of its existence the banking-room was the chamber over the store of Furber and Bean.

The first number of the Maine Free Press, started in opposition to the Journal but claiming to be like that democratic in principle, made its appearance on the 15th of June. It was edited by Hon. Ephraim K. Smart, then Collector of Customs for this Port, and Levi R. Wing was its publisher. It was under the editorial charge of John Abbot for a few months in 1855. Mr. Smart then resumed the editorial chair and M. B. Stetson became its publisher. In 1857 the office was removed to Rockland and a union was effected with the United States Democrat, published at that place; the two thus united assumed the name of the Democrat and Free Press.

Early in the next month the Progressive Age, the organ of the newly formed Republican Party, made its appearance. It purported to be edited by "an association of gentlemen," and was printed by Thomas J. Burgess. It was started as a campaign paper to be published during the political canvass then pending. The success of the party and the favor with which it was received were such as to justify its continuance and it became a permanent organ under the proprietorship of William M. Rust and Co. Not long afterwards Mr. Rust became and has continued to be its sole proprietor and editor. Its first office of publication was in the brick building on Main street now occupied by Mr. M. E. Dodge.

The "American, German and French Circus" was here on the 23d. Spalding and Rogers, with their two circuses combined. Kendall's brass band, and "General Washington on a live war-horse" were here on the 20th of July. A dramatic company under the management of Lanergan, Sandford and Fiske gave several entertainments during the same month. In August we were visited by Yankee Hill's Opera Troupe who furnished some Ethiopian melody, and the Monasco Troupe, comprising the "Young chief Otalifta, Red Jacket and Co., seven in all" gave two or three "Grand Indian Exhibitions" at City Hall.

The Fourth of July was duly celebrated with salvos of artillery and the ringing of bells. A procession was formed, for which escort duty was performed by Hydrant Company No. 2, and music furnished by the Belfast Sax-horn Band. One of its most interesting features was a Floral Car in which rode a bevy of little girls arrayed in white, each one representing a State in the union. It was followed by the school girls from the several schools, dressed in white with white hats wreathed with flowers. The procession moved to the Unitarian Church where, after prayer by Rev. Mr. Cole of the Baptist Church and the reading of the Declaration by J. G. Dickerson, Esq., an instructive and brilliant Oration was delivered by William C. Williamson, Esq., of this city. After the exercises were concluded there was a public dinner at the American House at which Mayor Sleeper presided and Samuel G. Thurlow officiated as Toast-master. There was a ball at Pierce's Hall in the evening. Of the sixteen managers at the ball, eight are still living.

While the Hydrants were enjoying their dessert at Mr. Baker's table they were called off to duty at a fire which had broken out in a large pile of wood at the Board landing. This was the first fire alarm of the year. The next was in the morning of September 12th on board the new brig Selah, coal laden from Pictou. The fire was speedily extinguished, but the damage done by it was estimated at $2000. On the night of December 29th fire broke out in that portion of the old Nesmith building at the intersection of High and Main streets which was occupied by Henry H. Hass. The building was one of the old landmarks of the village. The fire communicated to a building on High street next adjoining, which was entirely consumed, and to the old Cunningham tavern house, which was so far consumed as not to be worth repairing. The stores now occupied by J. C. Thompson, David Lancaster, Charles H. Mitchell, Andrew D. Bean, Francis Whitmore and F. B. Knowlton stand on this burned district.

At the annual State election, September 11th, the gubernatorial votes were 119 for Parris, democrat; 121 for Reed, Whig; 382 for Morrill, republican; and 2 scattering. There was no choice by the people, and at the next session of the legislature Morrill was elected. Salathiel C. Nickerson, now residing in Bridgeport, Conn., was elected representative.

Among the vessels launched this year were the ships Coronet, of about 136 tons, Peucinia, 700, Wild Cat, 674, Mary McNear, 992, and the Ocean Traveller, 695; the brigs, Progressive Age, 300, Abby Ellen, 300, Selah, 212, Martha Hill, 173; schooners Fred Wording, 154, Wyona, 50, and Opal, 47.

Hon. Joseph Williamson, father of our fellow citizen Judge Williamson, died suddenly of ossification of the heart on the evening of September 30th, after having been engaged through the day as counsel in the trial of a case. He was born at Canterbury, Conn., August 17, 1789, graduated at the University of Vermont in the class of 1812, pursued his professional studies at the offices of Frederick Allen, Esq., at Gardiner and his brother Hon. William D. Williamson, the historian of Maine, at Bangor, was admitted to the Bar in January, 1816, and immediately thereafter came here and commenced the practice of his profession. In 1820 he was appointed County attorney for the County of Hancock, and held the office until the organization of the county of Waldo, in 1827, when he received the same appointment for the new county, and held it until 1832. He was a member of the Senate in 1833 and 1834, and for the last year President of that branch of the legislature. In 1839 he received from Brown University the honorary degree of Master of Arts. The brick buildings on the westerly side of Main street, from Church to High streets, known as the Fire-proof Block, the block on Church street now occupied by the office of the Republican Journal, and the dwelling-house on High street now occupied by Mrs. Timothy Thorndike, were all erected by him.

Mr. Williamson was one of our most public spirited men, always among the foremost to aid and encourage, by word and purse, every enterprise which had for its object the promotion of the public welfare. In his daily walk no man among us was more exemplary. His whole professional career was marked by untiring fidelity to his clients,--he died with the harness on--by uniform courtesy to his brethren of the Bar, by honorable and upright dealing with his fellow-men. In all his relations, public and private, he was truly an estimable man, and his death was sincerely regretted, not only by his immediate friends but by the community at large.

His funeral, on the 4th of October, was attended by the members of the Bar, and Judge Tenney who was holding a term of the Supreme Court at the time, as mourners. The following resolution passed at a meeting of the Bar is an indication of the respect and esteem entertained for him by his professional brethren. "Resolved, that in the decease of Hon. Joseph Williamson the members of this Bar have lost a much valued friend and brother; one who through a protracted professional life, by faithful and indefatigable devotion to his profession, and unvarying amenity of manners, deservedly enjoyed the fullest confidence of the public and the highest esteem and respect of his professional brethren."

This chapter concludes the Annals of Belfast for the half century commencing with 1805 and terminating with 1854. As stated in his opening chapter, it has been the object and aim of the annalist to rescue from the realm of tradition, perchance from the gulf of oblivion, and place on record, the local events of this half century. The annals of this town, embracing a record of the daily walks, trials, joys and sorrows of those who here struggled for their daily bread a century ago would be a treasure to us of this day; perhaps this imperfect record may be so to those who walk in our footsteps a century hence.

There was a time since the publication of these annals was commenced-- nearly fifteen months ago--when it was questionable whether life and strength to bring them to the proposed termination would be vouchsafed to their compiler; but he has lived to finish his work, however imperfectly that work has been done.

"What is writ is writ, Would it were worthier!"

The perusal of these Annals may have afforded amusement, at least, to the readers of the Journal. In the hereafter, when our now miniature city shall count its population by tens of thousands, when its broad acres, as yet untouched by the hand of the artisan, shall be covered with stately edifices or lowly dwellings, when our beautiful bay shall be whitened by the canvas of ships, from whose mast-heads stream the ensigns of all nations, when the whistle of locomotives, steamers, and manufactories shall mingle constantly with the busy hum of trade, some prowler among the mouldering relics of the dead past may extract from them material for a mirthful article in the columns of the Journal of 1954.

There is a pleasure in the anticipation of events such as are thus foreshadowed, even though the anticipation be only the dream of an Old Settler. Yet it is a dream which may become a living reality if we, and those who are to succeed us in the arena of active life, will only open our eyes to see what may be done to promote the growth and welfare of our city, and open our hearts to do it.

And here the Annalist lays down his pen; to be taken up, he hopes, at the close of the next half century by some abler hand, who will do for the future, and far more abundantly, than he has done for the past. To those who have followed him in his wanderings through the labyrinth of the first half of the nineteenth century, he can only add in the language of the poet.--

"Farewell!--a sound that must be,--and hath been--
A sound which makes us linger;--yet--farewell!
Ye, who have traced the pilgrim to the scene
Which is his last--if in your memories dwell
A thought which once was his, if on ye swell
A single recollection, not in vain
He wore his sandal-shoon and scallop-shell."

SKETCHES

of the

EARLY HISTORY

of

BELFAST

by

John Lymburner Locke

PICTON PRESS
CAMDEN, MAINE
1989

Annals of Belfast for Half a Century by William George Crosby (1805-1881) was originally published in fifty-two installments in the Belfast, Maine newspaper *The Republican Journal*, 1874-75

Sketches of the Early History of Belfast by John Lymburner Locke (1832-1876) was originally published in serialized form in the Belfast, Maine newspaper *The Progressive Age* in sixteen issues beginning 10 April 1856.

History of Belfast From its First Settlement to 1825 by Herman Abbot (1783-1825) remained in manuscript form at the time of his death and for many years was feared lost. When the manuscript was finally rediscovered it was published in serial form in four issues of *The Republican Journal* of Belfast beginning 25 Jan 1900, and was then published in Belfast, also in 1900, by Miss Grace E. Burgess.

A History of Belfast with Introductory Remarks on Acadia by William White (1783-1831) was first published in Belfast, Maine in 1827, and was the first bound book published in that town.

Transcription of all four histories above was done for this volume by Elizabeth M. Mosher, RFD 2 Box 825, City Point, Belfast, Maine 04915

Available from:

Picton Press
P. O. Box 1111
Camden, Maine 04843
Manufactured in the United States of America
using acid-free paper

SKETCHES OF THE EARLY HISTORY OF BELFAST

Number 1.

Introductory remarks--The early settlers of Belfast--Their Scotch-Irish progenitors--Their trans-Atlantic history--The province of Ulster--Londonderry settled--The Scotch emigrants--The great rebellion--Seige of Londonderry--Noble defense of the city--Their sufferings--Their deliverance--effects on Protestantism.

Like many other New England towns, the early history of Belfast presents not only incidents of local, but, in many cases, events of general interest. The most interesting portion lies in the traditional part, which, if not soon rescued from oblivion, will ere long be numbered with the forgotten past.

From materials in our possession, we propose to give a few familiar sketches of some of the more prominent points in the early history of this town.

In order to form a correct estimate of the character of the pioneers of this place, it may not be inappropriate to revert to the history of their progenitors from whom they derived many of their characteristics.

The early settlers of Belfast came from Londonderry, N. H., and were the descendants of a Presbyterian colony called the Scotch Irish, who, half a century before, migrated from Londonderry, Ireland, and settled the town of the same name in New Hampshire. As the times that have preceded them in their fatherland, have found an unfading record on the page of History, and are allied and blended with our own, we will here commence the epoch of our sketches.

Just before the death of Queen Elizabeth and upon the accession of James I to the throne of England, a rebellion of her Catholic subjects in the northern part of Ireland was expressed, and by the attainder of the rebels nearly the whole of the province of Ulster fell to the Crown. James, knowing the salutary effects of a purer religion and of a more enlightened civilization, and desirious of laying deep the foundations of civil government, hitherto disregarded, resolved to settle this fertile province with industrious and intelligent colonists, of the Protestant faith. About the year 1612 under his royal encouragement and furtherance, many of his Scotch and English subjects, embracing husbandmen and mechanics, and some of the professional callings including persons of high rank, were induced to leave their own country and migrate thither. A London company had rebuilt the ancient city of Derry, and given it the name of Londonderry. In this city many of the colony from Argyleshire, Scotland, settled, and were thenceforward called the Scotch-Irish. In a few years industry, thrift and intelligence, became the marked features of the six northern counties of Ireland. This prosperity, however, was regarded with a jealous eye and feelings of animosity by the natives of the soil who had been expelled their possessions, and this ripened feeling, together with their cherished hate of "the heretical Protestant," was the cause of the rebellion that occurred thirty years afterwards in the reign of Charles I, in which 150,000 Protestants were massacred by the Papists.

But we will not here recount the inhuman barbarities committed by the Catholics during that scene of atrocity, but cast a mantle of charity over it, and pass to an event to us of more importance, and which tended more fully to develop and exhibit the true character of our ancestors. It relates to the memorable seige of Londonderry. "The Protestants of Ireland who had generally acknowledged the Prince of Orange, being apprised that James II," who had abdicated his throne, "intended an appeal to arms, and that Tyrconnel was raising troops and issuing commissions, began to put themselves in a posture of defense.

This they were also induced to do by a report," that proved to be well founded, "of an intended rising of the Catholics throughout Ireland on the 9th of December 1688 to massacre the Protestants without regard to age or sex." * Early on the morning of the 7th of December, intelligence was received that two companies of the enemy were within two miles of the city, which they were coming to take possession of. This announcement spread alarm and confusion throughout the city, and the inhabitants were perplexed about what course to pursue. The treacherous deputy mayor, who was secretly a friend of James, was in favor of admitting them, but many were opposed to it. While in this state of doubt and indecision their enemies appeared on the opposite bank, and were preparing to cross the river. At this critical juncture of affairs, thirteen resolute young men of the city seized the keys, rushed to the guards, drew up the bridge, and locked the gate just as the soldiers were in the act of crossing it. The names of these young men are still sacredly preserved in the archives of the city.

This heroic and decisive act confirmed the inhabitants of the city of their determination to defend it at hazards. "The city was not properly circumstanced to sustain a siege, the defenders consisting of a body of raw and undisciplined Protestants who had fled thither for shelter, and half a regiment of lord Montjoy's disciplined soldiers, with the principle part of the inhabitants making in all only 7361 fighting men."-- The siege lasted 105 days, during which time the besiegers lost 9,000 men while the besieged's amounted to 3,000. They were at last reduced to the direst extremity and were compelled to subsist on dogs, cats, rats, mice, leather, hides, et cetera. The garrison were constantly assured by the venerable Rev. George Walker in a prophetic tone that God would soon relieve them. Reduced to the last day's extremity and having but nine half starved horses and a pint of meal per man they were still resolute. At this crisis relief came. Two provisioned vessels and a frigate drew near the city; one of them dashed against the boom which the besiegers had stretched across the river and broke it in two, but from the violence of the shock rebounded and grounded upon the shore. The enemy seeing her critical position came in crowds to the beach to board her, when she discharged a broadside, rebounded from the bank, and with the swelling tide floated into deep water and sailed nobly up to the city to the relief of the besieged. The enemy were soon after defeated in the decisive battle of the Boyne, and thus the day for Protestantism and religious freedom was won. Had not this city offered such a successful barrier to the arms of James, he would have been enabled by many of his adherents who were ready to join him in Scotland, "to contend perhaps successfully with William, regain his crown, re-estalish Papacy, kindle anew the fires of martyrdom and crush the spirit of civil and religious freedom which from that renowned revolution has been strengthening and extending its influence over the nations." **

J. L. L.

* Parker's Hist. of Londonderry, N. H. See also Gordon's Hist. of Ireland.

** Hist. of Londonderry.

Number 2.

Unexpected religious intolerance--Propose to migrate to New England--
The reasons assigned--The memorialists petition Gov. Shute of Mass.--
Their departure and arrival--A company sails for Casco Bay--Dentention--
Return--Settle Londonderry, N. H.--Their character, &c.

After the kingdom became established under the Prince of Orange,
his Presbyterian subjects, who had participated in zealously defending
Londonderry during the siege, naturally conceived themselves entitled
to the enjoyment of religious freedom. But, being dissenters from the
Established Church, their pastors were not thus legally recognized,
nor their places of worship regarded as churches. Beside paying their
own church taxes, tithes were exacted for the support of the Episcopal
clergy, which they deemed to be act of injustice. With christian forbearance
they endured the intolerance of those times, and abided with patience
the day of deliverance. About the year 1717, a young man, the son of
a Presbyterian clergyman, who had returned from a visit to the New England
colonies, flatteringly represented the inducements held forth to colonists
to move thither. To migrate to such a country would be the realization
of their long cherished ideal land of freedom. The proposition to emigrate
met with a hearty response and resolutions at once were adopted to that
effect, by several congregations. On the eve of embarkation the Rev.
James McGregor preached them a discourse appropriate for the occasion
from these words of Moses: "If thy presence go not with me, carry me
not up hence." In his sermon the following are the reasons assigned
for their removal: "1, to avoid oppression and cruel bondage; 2, to
shun persecution and designed ruin; 3, to withdraw from the communion
of idolators; 4, to have an opportunity of worshipping God according
to the dictates of conscience and the rules of His inspired word." *
In the year 1718 the Rev. Mr. Boyd was dispatched with an address
to Gov. Shute of Massachusetts, expressing strong desire in case of
his encouragement to remove to New England. Mr. Boyd was also empowered
to make all necessary arrangements for their reception by the civil
authorities. The memorial (which was written on parchment and is still
extant) contains two hundred and seventeen names, all of which save
seven were subscribed by the persons themselves. Nine of this company
were clergymen, and three others were graduates of the University of
Scotland. The fact that so large a proportion of them were able to
write their own names, is a proof quite conclusive that they were intellect-
ualy in advance of the common class of emigrants.
Receiving from Gov. Shute the desired encouragement, Mr. Boyd forthwith
communicated the desired intelligence to the memorialists, who at once
converted their property into money and embarked in five ships for Boston,
where they arrived the 4th of August, 1718. It being optional with
them where to settle, they dispersed through the country, formed distinct
communities, organized churches and introduced the Presbyterian form
of worship. A company of sixteen families, who had formerly been under
the pastoral care of Rev. Mr. McGregor, in Ireland, and wishing to continue
that relation, formed the purpose of commencing a new settlement, and
thus secure to themselves the privilege of worshipping God according
to their own cherished faith, which they found was obnoxious to the
Puritans. Gov. Shute informing them of unoccupied land in the vicinity
of Casco Bay from which they might make their selection, they accordingly
embarked in a vessel with that intent. Arriving at the bay late in
the season the vessel was frozen in. As many as could not find accommodations on the shore were obliged to pass the winter on board the ship.
Willis in his history of Portland in speaking of them says--"They suffered
severely during the winter here; their provisions failed and our inhabitants
had neither shelter nor food for so large an accession to the population.

* Hist. of Londonderry, p. 34

In December the inhabitants petitioned the General Court at Boston for relief." "On this application the Court ordered that one hundred bushels of Indian meal be allowed and paid out of the treasury for the relief of the poor Irish people mentioned in the petition." When spring opened they prepared to continue their unfinished exploration, under the direction of Jas. McKeen.* During their detention in Portland neither sickness nor death had visited one of their number. After exploring some miles to the eastward and finding no place that suited them, they retraced their course westward, and ascended the Merrimack river to Haverhill, where they arrived April 2, (old style) 1719. Hearing of a tract of land 15 miles distant called Nutfield, which was unoccupied, "they at once decided to take up the grant which they had obtained of the government of Massachusetts of a township 12 miles square of any of her unappropriated lands."+ They first erected a few temporary huts and then returned to bring their families from Haverhill, together with the necessary outfits. They commemorated the occasion by appropriate religious services. They subsequently gave the township the name of Londonderry.--The accession to their numbers was so rapid that by September following the colony numbered about seventy families. In 1720 they purchased the Indian title, and thus although it was a frontier town they were exempt from the incursions of the Indians. They soon introduced the art of manufacturing linen which was held in high repute throughout the colonies. They also introduced the culture of the potatoe, "till then unknown in New England." Dr. Belknap in his History of New Hampshire, says of them that "being peculiarly industrious, frugal, hardy, intelligent and well principled people, they proved a valuable acquisition to the province into which they had removed, contributing much by their acts and industry to its welfare." In every emergency of our country they always were found to be her loyal subjects. The Declaration of Independence received the signature of one of her sons--Dr. Mathew Thornton. Stark, the hero of the battle of Bennington, was also a Londonderrian; so was James McKeen, D. D., the first President of Bowdoin College; and also the Hon. Samuel D. and his brother, Hon. Luther V. Bell, as well as the Hon. Horace Greeley,** and many others whose names are known far and wide, and to mention them all would be superfluous.--Leaving this digression we will in the next number resume our subject.

                                                                    J. L. L.

* He was grandfather of the first President of Bowdoin College.

+ Parker's History

** See the "Life of Horace Greeley," Chap. II.

NUMBER 3.

John Mitchell--His survey--Originates the scheme of settling Belfast--
Execution of the deed--The thirty-one proprietors--James Miller precedes
them--Erects   a   hut--Returns--Preparations--Re-embarks--Saturday   Cove
and   Sabbaday   Point   names--Arrival--Fellow   pioneers   disheartened   and
return--Richard Stimson--A query solved--Others follow--Origin of
Passagassawakeag.

Londonderry from her earliest history has been the nucleus whence
has issued many of the pioneer settlers of New England.
John   Mitchell,   a   Londonderrian,   originated   the   idea   of   forming
a settlement in the township subsequently known as Belfast.
During the year 1764, whilst on his passage from Boston to Schoodiac,
to superintend a survey for Gov. Barnard of Massachusetts, "Mitchell
put into Penobscot Bay, and became informed of the natural advantages
which those might enjoy who would there establish a settlement."*   On
his return to Londonderry, he communicated this knowledge to his friends;
but the scheme of settlement was not carried into effect till sometime
after the completion of the survey.   In the year 1768, a deed was executed
by the heirs of Gen. Waldo, conveying the subsequent township of Belfast
to "thirty-one proprietors," at the rate of twenty cents the acre.
It was therein declared that they should be only such as were of "good
moral   character,"   and   orderly   conduct,   which   requisite   qualifications
they were evidently supposed to possess.
During the above year, James Miller, one of the proprietors, took
passage in the vessel probably which brought the materials for a saw
mill Mitchell was to erect on "Wescott stream."   Selecting his situation,
(on the now called Frothingham lot,) he at once commenced felling trees
and clearing away a spot on which to build his log cabin.   All being
completed but the roof, which he was to cover in the spring with boards,
he re-embarked for Londonderry.
In the following spring of the year 1769, with two other families
besides his own, he made preparations for his final leave.   Owing to
the badness of the travelling, it was with difficulty they removed their
goods from Londonderry to Haverhill, and thus the transportation of
boards, with which to roof his cabin, was found to be impracticable.
From Haverhill, their movables, including the cattle, were floated down
to Newburyport in a gondola, where a vessel was in readiness to receive
them.   After a few days' sail they arrived, in the evening, at a place
they supposed was their destination.   A nearer approach discovered to
them their mistake, and they called it "Saturday Cove," which appellation,
as is well known, it still retains.   The next day being the Sabbath,
they went ashore and held services on the spot, since known, as then
named, "Sabbaday Point."   On arriving at their destined harbor they
prepared to disembark.   The families that came with Miller's were so
disheartened at the dreariness of the wilderness before them, extending
on either hand as far as the eye could reach, that they returned with
the vessel without even stepping their feet upon the shore.
It was with heavy though with hopeful hearts that this pioneer
family consisting of Mr. Miller and wife, two sons and a daughter, landed
with their effects upon the beach.+   They covered the roof of their
hut with bark, but not being impervious to water, the children used
to shelter themselves beneath the table on rainy days, whilst their
parents would sit contentedly in the corner by the fire.   The Miller
family were here a year before any other settlers had arrived, during
which time they had not seen the face of a single white person.

---
* See White's History of Belfast.
+ For some years afterwards their children and their descendants
used to annually repair to the rock on which they landed, and duly celebrate
the occasion.

Dr. Herman Abbot, in his MS. as quoted by Mr. White, maintains that Richard Stimson had settled on the flat just across the "half-way creek," which was then the dividing line between Belfast and Prospect, (Searsport) "before the proprietors had come into possession."

As to whether his lot would fall within the present limits of Belfast we are not prepared to state. We were informed a few years since by the late Mrs. Tolford Durham, that Stimson first lived out back of Searsport on the place afterwards called "Stimsontown," but now known as Mount Ephraim, where he resided till several of the proprietors arrived here, when he settled on the "flat" by the "half-way creek". This position is sustained by several other concurrent witnesses, and leaves no doubt in our mind as to its truthfulness.

At the opening of the spring in the year 1770, Mr. Mitchell, accompanied by "Chambers, Wm. McLaughlin, Wm. Patterson, Nath'l Patterson, John Morrison and Thomas Steele,"* arrived, and after selecting their lots, began to build their cabins and "open the forest preparatory to husbandry."+

At this time the only vestige to be seen of any former adventurers was the hull of a shallop which was partly sunk in the sand a few rods this side of the lower bridge. At certain seasons of the year lights (ignes fatui) were to be seen issuing from the hulk, crossing the river and dancing in a tree on "Patterson's Point." As the Indians beheld them they used to point to the vessel and then to the lights and exclaim, "Passagassawakeag!" which meant as they said, "dead men walk!" which circumstance was supposed to have given this name to the river.** It was inferred by the early settlers that the crew had been murdered by the Indians, and that they superstitiously regarded the lights as their departed spirits. The hulk was to be seen as late as the year 1808, about which time it was destroyed.

J. L. L.

* White's Hist. +Ibid.

** Williamson in his History of Maine gives it the meaning of "the place of sights or ghosts!" which, although different, is somewhat analgous to the above interpretation.

[All that now remains to remind us of the race that once roamed where we now live, are a few specimens of their nomenclature. It is enough that the red man should be exterminated, without seeking to obliterate every vestige that remains of all they have bequeathed us. We regret to witness the desuetude of many of the rich flowing names they once attached to the rivers and towns now bearing the hackneyed and worn out names of foreign countries, or of the too common appellations of every day use. What names are more beautiful and rich than those of Orono, Katahdin, Penobscot, Ontario, Seneca, and Erie! The State of Michigan has very sensibly enacted a law, the intent of which is, to preserve the noble and harmonious names which the aborigines had given to her various rivers, lakes and forests. As many of the Indian names with which our State formerly abounded, have, owing to their polysyllables, fallen into disuse, could we not in some instances abridge them, so as not to materially injure their sense or sound?

The original name of this bay, and present name of our river, which has been spelled from sound only, with no other just authority, we think could be made properly more agreeable to modern ears, and with utility, be adopted as the name of a street, club, band, &c. Agreeably to its prounciation would not the name of Passagassawakeag sound more euphoneous by an apostrophe contraction, thus: "Sagassawakeag, or, as some orthoepists would pronounce it: "Sarawakeag? Thus by inference, the apostrophe would acknowledge the prefix; the same as is the case with the word Damariscotta, which utilitarians often contract to "Scotta. In this mode, we could thus bring into general use and virtually retain, the name of Passagassawakeag.]

NUMBER 4.

Motives in selecting their lots--First framed house--Rev. Murry--Town incorporated; named--Tranquility--Anecdote--Neighborly visits; example--First road--Ferry--Morrison's stream--Foot path.

In selecting their lots it was the policy of the early settlers to locate them as near as possible to the center of the town, where their value would be enhanced as the settlement increased.

Mitchell supposed the principal part would be built on the eastern side of the river, and accordingly selected the beautiful and commanding situation on the point of land at the mouth of Goose River, (where the remains of his cellar are still to be seen.) Said he to Miller, "The village will be situated on the east side of the river." "No," replied Miller, "it will be on the west side;" which position is now sustained by the fact itself.

In the following year, 1771, the first framed one story dwelling house was erected by Mr. Miller, the cellar of which was to be seen a few years since in Mr. Frothingham's field. After becoming fairly settled, they invited the Rev. Mr. Murry, a Presbyterian minister of Boothbay, to make them periodical visits and dispense to them the words of life. On his arrival, the news was gladly circulated throughout the settlement, and his little flock repaired to the house of Miller, where they listened with delight to the teachings of this pious and eloquent man.

"When this little colony had grown to no more than twenty-five families, their prospects so filled them with hope that they requested to be incorporated."* --Accordingly, pursuant to a call of the General Court held at Boston, John Mitchell was authorized to convene the inhabitants at his house on the 11th of November, 1773, where the corporation was organized by the choice of appropriate officers. Col. Goldthwait, then commander at Fort Point, served them as chairman.+ Some were in favor of naming the town Londonderry, but the more euphoneous name of Belfast was given "by request of an early settler, out of respect for the name of his native place in Ireland.**

At this period the early settlers were enjoying the bounties of a plentiful harvest, and pleasures of a contented community, without wrangling feuds to destroy their tranquility, or litigations to neutralize and alienate their feelings of fraternal love.--They were emphatically a "band united," which union was strengthened by their being isolated as it were from the world, and each depending on the others' aid. Illustrative of these feelings of friendly reciprocity, we will relate the following incident: The time was midnight, when a family on the east side of the river heard the lowing of cattle as if in distress, on the opposite side. They forthwith aroused their neighbors, crossed the river, gave the alarm, and their brethren with torches joined them, and flew to the rescue. Following the direction of the sound, they soon found that a bear had made prey of a cow, and on their approach had fled, and left her in hardly a recoverable condition.--They continued the pursuit for bruin, overtook him, and made him pay the penalty of death for his temerity.

----

 * White.
 + Being at this time subjects of Great Britain, under George III, they were taught to look to Fort Pownal for protection in case of danger or distress. On the commencement of actual hostilities with Britain, the Colonel forsook the colony and adhered falsely to the crown."
 ** Will. Hist. ii 398. We are not informed, but would conjecture that this "early settler" was Miller, from the fact that he was born in Belfast, Ireland, when he migrated to Londonderry, N. H.

Notwithstanding the distance that intervened between their dwellings, the female portion frequently interchanged visits. It was no unusual thing, and it was considered by them a pleasure, for our grandmothers to row a skiff cross handed across the river, to see their neighbors; a thing, which now-a-days, would be heralded abroad as an exploit extraordinary. Their afternoon "calls" were not a la Lady Partington's of the present day, where for lack of work they dilated upon their neighbors' foibles, and retailed the unimportant gossip of the day; but you would almost invariably see them either with their knitting or needle work, and thus prudently and sweetly enjoying the social hour.--Those who received the visit would be either plying the needle or weaving at the loom, thus being worthy exemplars for their posterity.

At this time, the only road in town was the one Stimson had surveyed, which was defined by notched trees, and extended from St. George to Sandy Point. A skiff, which was hollowed out of a log, served as a ferry boat, between the east and west side of the river. Before a ferryman was appointed, persons were ferried from the west side by James Miller, and from the east side by Tolford Durham, generally without compensation. The "Morrison brook," which has since dwindled to a small stream,* was crossed by large pine tree being felled across it. Frequent travel soon traced out a foot path, and thus superceded the necessity of being guided by "spotted" trees.

J. L. L.

* It is situated just this side of Mr. Jos. Wight's farm.

NUMBER 5.

Revolutionary times--Committee of safety and censor appointed--State constitution adopted--English garrison at Castine--Fleet dispatched to destroy it--Mitchell's counsel disregarded--Gen. Lovell's attack--A council of war held--Com. Saltonstall's obstinacy--British fleet appears--Lovell's retreat--American fleet destroyed--Evacuation of Belfast--Dispersion of the inhabitants.

We now approach "the times that tried men's souls"--the stirring days of the American revolution.   When the Declaration of Independence was received, it met the hearty approval of the inhabitants of Belfast. They at once "adopted such precautionary measures as were best calculated to secure the independence of the country."   "In addition to a committee of safety, the inhabitants in 1777 elected a censor, whose duty, as appears on the record of the meeting, was "to lay before the general court the misconduct of any person by word or action against the United States," and Solon Stevenson was appointed to this distinguished office.* In 1778, with entire unanimity, the town adopted the constitution Massachusetts had prepared for her government.   In 1779 the cloud of war began to lower over the colony; report after report followed each other in succession of the havoc of war.   Neighboring settlements were being plundered and the inhabitants in many instances compelled to flee their homes or become prisoners of war.   With these facts before them, our settlers were still determined to remain legal to the colonial government.

On the 12th of June 1779, the enemy took possession of Biguyduce, (Castine) where, under Gen. McLean, they established a post and garrisoned it with 650 men.   Massachusetts formed the scheme of dislodging them, and accordingly with great celerity dispatched a fleet of "19 armed vessels and 24 transports," mounting in all 344 guns, and carrying nearly one thousand marines and soldiers.   The command of the fleet was entrusted to Commodore Saltonstall, and the land forces to Generals Lovell and Wadsworth.   They arrived in Penobscot Bay the 25th of July.   On their arrival, "Mitchell and others were requested to visit the fleet and communicate their knowledge of the position and strength of the enemy. These strenuously advised Gen. Lovell to an immediate assault.   They saw no formidable obstacle to entering the harbor, securing the three English vessels that were there, landing the troops and marching into the fort.   This counsel was not relished.   It was then advised that a portion might land in the harbor and the residue at Perkin's cove, which was taking the enemy in front and in rear at the same time; this advice was also disregarded."+   Disregarding this judicious advice, Lovell landed his troops and made his attack in the most disadvantageous place, at the base of a steep cliff 200 feet high, which was almost inaccessible.   In climbing the precipice our force lost 100 our of 400 men from the fire of the enemy, but succeeded in gaining the summit. Instead of following up their success, they threw up a slight breastwork within about 125 rods of the enemy, and made preparations for a regular siege.   The land and naval forces next held a council of war.   "The former," says Williamson, "were for summoning the garrison to surrender, offering them honorable terms, but the Commodore and most of his officers were opposed to the measure."   Various plans of attack were suggested, but the obstinate and self-willed Commodore frustrated them all.   After fruitlessly spending a fortnight in throwing up intrenchments and reconnoitering the enemy's works, and in occasional skirmishes, word was received that a British fleet of seven sail was approaching the peninsula.   Gen. Lovell immediately ordered a retreat, and conducted it in the night "with so much silence and skill, that the whole of the American troops were embarked undiscovered."**

---
*   White's Hist. of Belfast
+   Ibid.

As Sir George Collier with his fleet, carrying 200 guns and 1500 men, approached, Saltonstall ran his ships ashore and destroyed the greater part of them by burning or blowing them up, while those that escaped destruction were taken as prizes by the enemy.*

We will now return to the colony. The inhabitants had been watching with great anxiety the manoevuring of the two fleets, and when they saw in the distance the lurid flames belching from our exploded ships, they took it for granted the enemy had won the day. They were aware that by taking the oath of allegiance they could remain secure in their dwellings, but they spurned with contempt the thought of swearing fealty to a power they so much detested. They chose rather the alternative of fleeing their homes, and remaining loyal to their country. Preparatory to flight, many hid their dishes under logs concealed by brakes, and some they sunk in wells, and in various ways secreted such articles as they chose not to carry with them. All the gondolas and batteaux in town were brought into requisition to convey the inhabitants and their effects to a place of safety. They numbered in all about sixty persons. "To the last man they abandoned their homes, leaving their flocks in the pastures and the corn in the fields ready for harvest. Not one remained to tell a passing stranger of the cause of the entire desolation that ensued."+ They started the 14th of August, at sunset, and arrived at Camden the next morning. A few families remained at Clam Cove, whilst others went to Warren, Saco, Bristol and other towns, and many returned to New Hampshire. Among the latter number was Mr. Mitchell, who went to Chesire, where he remained till his death.

J. L. L.

----

* Com. Saltonstall's course was almost universally disapproved of, and on the following September he was cashiered by the General Court.

+
White's History, p. 42

NUMBER 6.

Miller returns to Belfast--Majorbiguduce expedition--Tragedy at Moose
Point--A marauder killed--Interred--Disinterred--House and barn burned
in revenge--Severe winter--Gen. Wadsworth and Major Burton's imprisonment
at Castine--Their escape--Arrive at Miller's--Secreted in the woods--Arrive
at Thomaston.

After remaining at Clam Cove, Camden, a short time, Miller returned
to Belfast to harvest his corn, and then returned to Camden.
The Durham and Miller families found accommodations at the house
of Samuel Tollman, who, being a "tory," was then absent on a predatory
excursion.   After tarrying at Clam Cove a month, Miller determined to
return to the settlement with his family and effects. The Durham, and
other families, remained in Camden for nearly a year before they returned.
Many of the marine and land forces of our ill-fated Majorbiguduce
expedition, retreating westward by way of Belfast, halted in town a
short time to relieve their exhaustion, and satisfy their hunger. A
barrel of Alewives Miller had left in his cellar, together with a quarter
of an acre of potatoes they dug, were used by them, and all such edibles
as they could elsewhere find.   Our settlers residing on the western
side of the river suffered no very material loss during their absence
up to this time.
The Houston family being in Bristol, Richard Stimson occupied their
house in the meantime, and was the foremost of those that returned on
the eastern side of the river.   It was while Stimson was living in Mr.
H.'s house (in 1779) that the following tragic event occurred.
Owing to the depredations committed by the English on the settlers'
live stock, a posse of twelve men was dispatched from Camden under Sergeant
David Jenks, to accompany Stimson thither, and drive the cattle to Camden,
where there was an American encampment, to be secure from the incursions
of the enemy.   Arrived in Belfast, this force quartered at Stimson's
house.   Stimson, being adept of a marksman, arose early in the morning,
shouldered his gun and went down towards the shore in search of game.
As he was descending the bank in front of his house, he was surprised
by a barge full of British marauders from Castine, who were just landing
to make plunder of cattle, sheep and poultry, as usual.   The leader,
whose name was Armstrong, was from the Provinces, and was of a corpulent
frame, and six feet in height, withal a formidable foe to cope with,
single handed.   Approaching Stimson, he disarmed him of his gun, and
ordered him "to right about face," and pilot them to his house.   When
S. had got within about twenty rods of his house, he saw Jenks sallying
out of the door, and in an instant he turned about, clenched Armstrong,
threw him down, and there held him until Jenks arrived.   Meanwhile,
seeing their leader in such an unexpected situation, one of the clan
tried to bayonet S. in the abdomen, but the thrust was warded off by
coming in contact with his wallet in his vest pocket.   Seeing Jenks
rushing upon them, they forsook their leader and fled for the barge.
In an instant Jenks discharged his gun at his head killing him instantly.
A rough wooden box was constructed, and he was buried near the place
of his death--at "Moose Point."   A few days after this, the British
sent a barge from the peninsular after his body.   Arriving at about
dark, they ordered Stimson's daughters to conduct them to the grave,
and hold a lantern wnilst they disinterred him.   He was carried to Castine
and there buried.   They shortly came again to avenge the death of their
comrade, by burning Mr. Houston's house and barn, which contained many
of the neighbors' goods.*

———— * Jos. Houston, Esq.

The winter of 1779-80 was one of unusual severity. Persons travelled on the ice from Belfast to Camden, and Castine.--"For forty-eight days the sun had no power to melt the snow, even on the roofs of the houses."*
The snow averaged four feet in depth in February, and on the 9th of April it was three feet deep; yet the year opened with an early spring.

The year 1781 is remembered as the year in which Gen. Peleg Wadsworth and Major Benj. Burton made their escape as prisoners of war from Castine. It will be recollected by the general reader, that Wadsworth was captured, after a noble defence, at his headquarters in Thomaston, on the night of the 18th of February, by a detachment of twenty-five men sent from Castine, under Lieut. Stockton; and that Burton was taken prisoner while on his passage from Boston to St. George, in the following April. They were both confined in the same room in the barracks at Castine. On the night of the 18th of June, when the rain was pouring in torrents, they issued from an aperture they had made, and by a well contrived plan, eluded detection and made their escape. By design, they separated, expecting to meet at a certain place, but, missing each other, pursued their course alone. Fording the cove, which was about three feet deep and a mile in breadth, Wadsworth pursued his course, and when within seven or eight miles from the fort, he was overtaken by Burton, to their mutual great joy, each supposing the other lost. By sunrise, the weather clearing up, they reached the house of Talford Durham, on the eastern bank of the river. Considering that Durham might suffer for the act if detected, they paddled themselves across in his canoe, and went to the house of James Miller. Fearing to accept the proffered hospitality of his roof, they went into the depths of the forest with his two sons, James and Robert, where they constructed a hut, and covered it with fir boughs, and made a bed of evergreens, and carried blankets to it, and supplied them with food until the sharpness of the pursuit was over; when, with a pocket compass the Millers gave them, they pursued their way to Mt. Pleasant, and thence to Thomaston, and finally to Portland.+

---

* Annals of Warren.

+ Vide Williamson's History of Maine, Willis' Hist. of Portland, Annals of Warren, Hist. of Belfast, in loco.

NUMBER 7.

Peace declared--Arrival of settlers--"Lord" Timo. Dexter's speculation--Grist
mill erected--Mode of occupying long evenings--"Way houses"--Hospitality
to strangers--A "tavern" opened--Miller's hotel--Michael Davis the hunter--
Described--Peculiarities--Anecdotes, of his hunger, turtle--His death.

Nothing further worthy of note transpired until peace was declared.
The treaty was signed September 3, 1783, and was received by our colonists
with acclamations of joy. Quite a number had returned to the settlement
prior to the cessation of hostilities, but, when the storm of war was
hushed, it was considered as the general precursor of their return.

On the first of May 1784, a vessel arrived, Captain Tufts master,
containing eight families, some of whom were former settlers, and others
were new. We have the names of sixteen families besides these who had
arrived up to this date.

The eccentric "Lord" Timothy Dexter, of Newburyport, made quite
a profitable speculation by buying up the claims of several proprietors,
who had left Belfast during the evacuation, and selling or mortgaging
them to new settlers. Among these claims was the lot of Thomas Morrow,
which he bought for a trifle and sold at a good bargain. From this
point of time we will take a glance at the past.

From the earliest times of the colony, our settlers used to carry
their grist to Camden to the mill of Maj. Wm. Minot, situated at the
foot of Megunticook stream. Two men would carry down in a boat all
the grist of the town, and thus the settlers done alternately, until
John Tufts erected a mill on the site where Gannet's mill now stands.

During the long winter evenings, the family all at home, they would
be seated around the ample fire place, reading by its blazing light
the well worn family bible, or the oft-used Scottish Psalter, or the
poems of Burns, or perhaps be listening to hear an aged sire recount
the siege of Londonderry in which their fathers participated, and tell
over the sufferings of the pious Covenanters, or the scenes through
which they had passed, that their children might profit by the examples
of the past, and be true to their country and their God. These oft
repeated stories never wearied but always were listened to with profit
and delight.

The main road, which (as before stated) was indicated by spotted
trees, had by this time become a well worn path, and was occasionally
travelled by persons from a distance. The cabins situated on the road
were called "way houses," and as night overtook the traveller with one
of these houses in view he was sure not to be compelled to sleep in
the woods, (as was the case when they could not reach them,) but was
always readily welcomed to the hospitalities of the roof and the sociality
of the home circle. At times the number was so large they were necessitated
to find accommodations on the floor, which they covered with evergreens
and fir boughs. Considering their company as an ample compensation,
new faces being so few and far between, they seldom charged the stranger
anything for his lodging or breakfast. When travelling became quite
frequent, a "tavern" was opened by an Irishman named Owen Kallerhen.
It was a rude log cabin, and was situated on the place now occupied
by Mr. Bloomfield White's house. He was a jolly old soul, kept plenty
of such drinkables as produced jollity, and was one of those characters
of whom readible anecdotes are told. We would here diverge, by saying,
that in late times when it became more of an object, James Miller opened
his large two story house for a hotel, (Frothingham's.) which was, more
strictly speaking, the first tavern kept in town.

At about this time, (1784-85,) the settlement began to be visited
by a man by the name of Michael Davis, who formerly lived in Concord,
N. H. His faithful dog was his only companion. Whenever in his unfrequent-
ed visits he sought shelter beneath the roof of the settler, the children
would gather around him and listen with interest to his tales and personal

adventures. He is well described in the following graphic account by the author of the Annals of Warren.* He says that he was "one of those singular characters that sometimes vary the picture of life; a sort of 'Leather Stocking' of the wilderness, hovering on the borders between civilized and savage life. He lived a solitary life in the woods, clad in skins and subsisting on the products of the chase, which formed his sole occupation. He had no intercourse with the settlers, except an occasional visit for the purpose of exchanging his fur for ammunition and other necessaries; but his path was frequently crossed by the hunter, who was oftentimes entertained by him with such refreshment as his camp afforded.--On these occasions he was hospital and social, talked of his dangers and accidents by 'flood and field, his hair breadth 'scapes,' and causeless frights, with apparent satisfaction; but it was evident his heart was not with his guests--he sighed not at their departure, and returned with pleasure to the society of his own feelings. His grotesque appearance, his hairy costume, his beard descending to his breast, and his white locks streaming to the wind excited the curiosity of children and rendered his coming a memorable event. Nor was his behavior more free from whimsical peculiarities than his dress. One of these was that of bowing with great reverence when favored with the sight of bread. Whether this proceeded from religious or other notions, his distant and taciturn manner rendered it difficult to determine. He shifted his quarters to various places as convenience required and followed hunting from the Kennebec to the Penobscot. From his long residence in the present town of Montville, that place, before its incorporation, was called Davistown. Of his early history and the time of coming hither, nothing was known. Rumor ascribed his eccentricity to disappointment in love, and it was said he had one daughter in the western country to whom he contrived to remit the proceeds of his hunting." At one time, owing to the scarcity of game, he had been for nearly a week without food, and began to feel the terrible pangs of hunger. Recollecting of a bear he had killed a fortnight before, he directed his steps accordingly. On finding the skinless carcass it was in a state of putrefaction; but, by dextrously using his hunting knife, he soon came to the edible part, and commenced with a relish and ended with a satisfaction. He often said it was the most delicious repast he had ever partaken of.

"On one occasion," continues Mr. Eaton, "after a hunting tour of some days, he returned to his camp, kindled a fire, and sat down to his lonely musings; when he was suddenly startled by the most piercing cries proceeding from his fire. At first he could ascribe it to nothing but the foul fiend himself, but a huge tortoise, crawling out from the ashes in which he had made his bed, soon relieved his apprehensions and afforded him a delicious meal." "He continued this kind of life for a long time, when his hunting range being gradually curtailed by the settlement of the country, and his natural powers abating, he was at last compelled to receive support from his fellowmen, and is said to have died a pauper, in one of the towns that had sprung up beneath his eye on the borders of the Penobscot."

J. L. L.

------ * Page 208

NUMBER 8.

First mail carrier--Post office established--Home made fabrics--Abundance
of game--Goose river named--Anecdote of a wolf--Bears--Moose--Cougar
killed by a squaw--Women as helpmates--Educational privileges--The first
school house--Religious matters--Tythingman appointed--Preaching--Rev.
Messrs. Murray, Powers, True, Ely--His death--Lining hymns--An old psalm
book.

The first mail carrier of whom we have any account was Samuel Russel
of Castine. At its incipience the mail was carried in a handkerchief,
but as the number of letters began to augment, they were carried in
a leather bag on his back. The journey was performed once a week by
him between Wiscasset and Castine. When the road became passable for
a horse, the post rode horseback with his mail in saddle bags.--When
within a mile of the village, he gave the premonition of his approach
by sounding his post horn, until within a short distance of the post
office. "The post office was first established July 1, 1786"*

Quite a number of our settlers being practical weavers, used to
weave their own linen, from home raised flax; make their own clothes
from home-made woolen, and linsey woolsey cloth, and thus for years
supplied their own demand for wearing apparel, esteeming foreign fabrics
as useless extravagances.

An abundance of different kinds of game was to be found in this
section at this period. "Goose River" derived its name from the great
number of wild geese that used to frequent it. So numerous were their
eggs, that before incubation settlers would go and gather baskets full
of them.

Wolves, though not very numerous, were occasionally seen in the
woods on the outskirts of the settlement. At one time while Mrs. M___
was driving some cattle which went astray, to their owner, who lived
near the "Spring farm," a wolf made his appearance in the path, a short
distance ahead. In her fear thinking to frighten him away, she picked
up the detached limb of a tree, and began to smite against a stump and
to halloo at the top of her voice. After looking at her awhile with
indifference, he quietly walked away.

Bears were more numerous, and whenever killed, as they afforded
quite a dainty food, were divided among the neighbors. Many anecdotes
might be told about their being trapped and killed, but space forbids
it now. Moose and deer were often forced to yield to the fleetness
of the hardy settler, who pursued them often for miles on snow shoes
in the winter. We have on record a few instances of catamounts or cougars
being seen. While an Indian squaw was once passing through the woods
in the present vicinity of McClintock's large block she espied on a
limb overhead a catamount in the act of springing upon her. She instantly
levelled her gun and brought him at her feet.

The skill of the marksmen was not exclusively confined to the men,
but we have instances in which the women have illustrated their skill
with the musket. In passing, we would observe, that in most all things
incident to the hardships of pioneer life, and pertaining to husbandry,
our grandmothers were emphatically help-mates.

In regard to education in those times, it was quite limited, yet
the town was possessed of a few who were persons of decided abilities,
and quite extensive acquirements. The educational privileges of many
for a lifetime, were often crowded into the space, at longest of a year,
presenting a great contrast in comparison with the present advantages
of their descendants. We know of one whose early schooling was comprised
in the space of a month, in which time she learned to read, write and
worked a sampler, but with this foundation she was able to pursue other
branches at home. The method then adopted, was similar to that pursued

----
* Williamson's History of Maine, vol. ii. p. 398.

by our own seminaries at the present day. Some scholars boarded in the families of Samuel Houston and John Cochran, who were men of good education, and were instructed in common with their children; and others were instructed by their own parents, around the home fireside. The first school house of which we hear, was a duplicate of "Killerhen's tavern," and was situated on the east side of the river, about fifty rods south of Amasa Patterson's house. It was probably not erected by the "town authorities," but by a "devoted few," who had the interests of the children of their district truly at heart. There is still one survivor who attended that school, and, a few years since pointed us to where it stood.

The first settlers of Belfast were christians of the Presbyterian order. From the associations connected with the persecutions, and deprivations of their fathers for adhering to their cherished faith, their children were firm in the adoption of the belief in which they were nurtured.

As a few heedless persons were disposed to desecrate the Sabbath, the attention of the corporation was called to the fact, and a meeting was held in Oct. 1775, at which a tythingman was appointed to enforce the observance of that day. In the above meeting, it was voted, that "Whosoever shall make any unnecessary visit on the Sabbath, shall be held in contempt by the people, until atonement shall be made by a public confession."*

From the time the Rev. Mr. Murray ceased visiting them, till the day the Rev. Mr. Price was ordained, they were supplied with preaching by the following preachers: Rev. Mr. Powers of Deer Isle, who was a Congregationalist; Rev. Mr. True, [Congregationalist] who preached one summer, and the Rev. Mr. Ely, one summer, who was a Socinian in his belief.

It was alleged that he was one of the malcontents in the "Shay's Rebellion," which insurrection found no favor with the inhabitants of Belfast. Mr. Ely moved to Northport, where he was drowned. Before the erection of a church, the meetings were held in Mr. Miller's house. In singing, it was then customary for the preacher to "line the hymn," which the congregation would repeat in a sing-song way. We have in our possession one of the psalm books then used, said to be the first one ever used in town. It has the date of MDCCLIII, and was printed in Glasgow.

J. L. L.

———— * White's History of Belfast, p. 66.

NUMBER 9.

Size of lots--The Weeks' lot--Weeks' vessel--Price of wood--Indians'
camping ground--First vessels built--First house of worship erected--Another
erected--Rev. Eb'r Price ordained--Remonstance presented--Petition refused
to be granted--The minister's lot--Cause of opposition--Vote ratified--
Juvenile partizans--Mr. Price dismissed--Compromise--He removes to New
Hampshire--Succeeded by Rev. Mr. Blood.

There are oftentimes, seemingly trivial incidents connected with
the history of a place, unimportant in themselves, yet, of such a character,
as to give additional interest to more important events, with which
they are inseparably blended. With these remarks, we ask the reader's
indulgence for some of our past, and also, our future, dry details.
The "first division lots" on the west side of the river, were 40
rods wide by one mile and a quarter in length, from the shore; or, otherwise
extending as far as the "Campbell farm" if a direct line were drawn
from the shore. Until the year 1791, the wild forest trees, where now
stands "Phoenix Row," were undisturbed by the woodman's axe. It was
on the first of January of the above year, when the first load of cord
wood was cut, on this "the Weeks' lot," to load the first vessel owned
in town. It belonged to Capt. Lemuel Weeks. Wood was then worth, before
transportation, 80 cents per cord, including cutting, which was 25 cents.
This locality, before and after it was cleared up, was occupied by the
Indians as a camping ground. At the intersection of Main and High streets,
usually known as "the corner," were there to be seen at the camping
season of the year, generally between five and ten wigwams.
The first vessel built in town was by the McKeens in 1791. The
next was by the Millers in 1793, and was named the "Jenny Miller."
The former, a sloop, was built on McKeen's point, between the upper
and lower bridge. The latter, a schooner, was built in the present
vicinity of Miller's wharf.
As the grantors of the township had included in the grant "150
acres above the quantity purchased for the use of the ministry,"* an
attempt was made in 1789 to erect a house of worship; but as the minority
on the western side were opposed to locating it on the eastern side,
and formally protested against it, the subject was postponed. Three
years afterwards, a proposition for each section to build a house without
charge to the other met with no opposition.+ The site of the one on
the eastern side was nearly contiguous to the burying ground. The one
on the western side was framed in 1791 adjoining the old "grave yard,"
then but just laid out; but, owing to the locality being a swampy place,
it was shortly taken down and erected on the spot where the house of
Joseph Williamson stands. In 1796 by a vote of the majority, but against
the formal remonstrance of a minority of twenty-four, the town decided
to extend the invitation to the Rev. Ebenezer Price, to become their
settled minister. He was ordained "December 29th, 1796, when there
were only 90 families and 12 framed houses."** "In the following year,"
says Mr. White, "twenty of those malcontents remonstrated with the majority
against the vote, to confirm the title of Mr. Price to the lot of land
before appropriated to the first settled minister. This remonstrance
being disregarded, served no other purpose than to embitter the sentiments
of an opposition already exasperated. The minority did not permit themselves
to slumber. Solon Stevenson, a man memorable for his sincerity of heart,
sound judgment and constancy of purpose, and twenty-two others with
him carried the subject before the Legislature, and as a relief, they
pray to be incorporated as a separate religious society.--Here also

----- * White's History. +Ibid.

** Will. Hist. of Maine.

the friends of Mr. P. procured a majority, and the prayer of the petitioners was refused to be granted."

In probing the subject thoroughly, we are inclined to the belief of Sir Rodger de Coverly, "that much might be said on both sides." It appears that one of the principal objections of the remonstrants, was the tenor of the deed, as it unqualifiedly deeded the land to the first settled minister, instead of making it transmissible as a parsonage, as the following vote taken at a proprietors' meeting, March 10, 1798, declares: "Voted, To confirm and ratify a former vote of said proprietors in granting and appropriating lot No. 26 first division, to the first settled gospel minister in said town of Belfast." At a subsequent meeting, a committee of three was appointed, "to give Rev. Eben'r Price a deed of lot No. 26 first division, agreeably to a vote of the town." It was averred, however, by his friends, that the opposition was more on account of some of his particular tenets of belief, than the reason alleged.

The children entering into the censorious spirit of their parents, would manifest their virulence by rudely hailing, and setting the dogs on Mr. Price as he passed by.

Mr. White continues: "New subjects of complaint were found, true or false, and old ones urged with more zeal, so that in April, 1801, the town voted to withhold from Mr. Price his salary, and also that as a teacher of religion they had for him no further employment. In May, 1802, the civil contract between Mr. Price and the town was closed by a compromise," by which Mr. Price came into possession of "the minister's lot," now known as the Thomas Reed farm. Mr. Price then went to Bucksport where he remained but a short time, and thence removed to New Hampshire. Two years since he was still living in Hopkinton, N. H. We believe he was succeeded by the Rev. Mr. Blood, before the Rev. Mr. Johnson was employed.

J. L. L.

NUMBER 10.

The first vehicle--Produces a sensation--Visit of the Duke de la Rochefoucault
--His description of the town. [NOTE: Result of the confiscation act--Title
bought in by Gen. Knox.] The first store--Washington's death commemorated--
New streets laid out--First framed school house--Representative elected--
Aquaduct laid--Rev. Alfred Johnson installed.

We will here resume the period of 1796. We know not the year,
but the incident itself will give us the time when the following occurred.
When the first vehicle, a chaise, was brought into town, it created
a great sensation. It was introduced by a lady from Massachusetts,
who came here on a visit.--Before landing she doubtless anticipated
riding through the town on graded or passable roads. It was a novel
sight to many of the juveniles, who had never before seen a chaise,
and a ludicrous one to their seniors, to see its zig-zag operations
in shunning the stumps that obstructed the road. In passing the houses,
every 7 x 9 of the lower sash had a staring occupant. When past the
house, the boys would mount the fence, whilst their more coy sisters
would peep around the corner of the house, and watch the spectacle till
out of sight. For days the sight was the chief topic of conversation
throughout the town, until by its repetition it ceased to be a novelty.

In 1797 the Duke de la Rechefoucault, who was evidentally a French
nobleman, in traveling through this town with Gen. Knox, thus speaks
of Belfast in the book of his travels:*

"The township of Belfast, adjoining that of Little River, is better
settled than that through which we last passed. The houses are better,
and even in some instances painted; the lands have been brought into
a better condition.

"This territory was sold thirty years ago by the family of Waldo,
and its present state of superior improvements seem to evince that the
uncertainty of the possession of those who have settled other townships +
must be the chief reason that induces them to leave their lands so destitute
of culture.

"A river that is at the mouth about a mile broad but navigable
for only three miles upwards, here falls into a creek, much larger than
any other we had hitherto seen. We were to pass this river at a place
where the access is extremely difficult. The ferry boat is small, and
for horses very inconvenient. We were waiting for it a whole hour,
and thought ourselves fortunate in reaching the opposite bank; when
the wind became boisterous, the tide rose higher in the river, and our
horses became unruly. The General's negro conducted over two of the
horses swimming. Considerable mountains arise immediately adjacent

----

* As quoted by the Rep. Journal, March 25, 1853.

+ By a law passed by Congress in Sept. 1778, all the estates of
tories were declared confiscated.--Among these tories were all the heirs
of the Waldo patent, except Gen. Knox's wife. These proprietors, forsaking
the Colonies, and adhering to the Crown, were called "absentees," and
their estates confiscated, and the Judges of Probate empowered to appoint
agents to administer upon them as though the late possessors were in
fact dead. Thus, by the enforcement of this act, the proprietors could
not give valid titles to lands within the patent, now generally considered
as forfeited. Regarding them as public lands, it was an inducement
to the practice of "squatting" upon them, which custom prevailed for
several years. The titles of the former joint proprietors of the Waldo
patent were bought in by Gen. Knox, and by his application, were confirmed.

Owing to the early purchase of their titles, the settlers of Belfast
were exempt from the litigations suffered by many other towns in Maine
in consequence of the invalidity of their claims.--L.

to the bank of the river. These mountains were the highest I had ever seen in this tract of the country. The ground interjacent between them and the river's edge is cleared: not a stump remained, and the trees lay scattered on the surface. I thought the meadows to be the best I had seen for a long time.

"In the township of Belfast is a church, the only one in all the Waldo Patent. The roads become here better, because the soil is firmer, and because they are more carefully repaired than elsewhere."

The first store opened in town was kept by James Nesmith, in 1799, on the site now occupied by S. & E. Edwards, then called "Nesmith's corner." At the commencement, his entire stock consisted of two cotton handkerchiefs, valued at $1,00 each, and a barrel of rum. At his death he was estimated to be worth $15,000.

On the 22d of February, in the year 1800, on the birth day, and in commemoration of the death of Washington, a large concourse of the citizens of this town marched in a procession through the streets, with a badge of black crape on the arm, and then repaired to the meeting house on this (the west) side of the river, and listened to an appropriate discourse from the Rev. Mr. Price.

In that procession were to be seen veterans who had fought under Wolf at Quebec, members of the famous "Tea Party," and patriots who had served through the Revolution under the leadership of Washington himself.

Up to this year the houses were built mostly on one street, and as the inhabitants began to increase new situations were demanded. Accordingly a Mr. Varnum was chosen to lay out the town in squares for a village. He moved to Ohio in 1801.

In 1802, after unsuccessfully agitating the subject for several years, the town voted to appropriate $600 for building a school house. It cost when completed $591,36. It was erected just in front of the meeting house, or within the present boundary of Mr. Williamson's front yard. Just prior to the war the district was divided (on this side of the river,) and this school house was moved where Mrs. Landworthy's house now stands,* and another erected just below Mr. Salmond's house.

In 1803 the town for the first time was represented in the State (Mass.) legislature by Jona. Wilson.

It was during this year that an aquaduct was laid by Kirk Patridge, under the direction of Jas. Nesmith. The water was conducted from a well just back of the "Leach house," in cedar conduits, to the houses of such as were willing to pay their proportionate part of the expense. These wooden pipes are occasionally exumed by the laborer in digging cellars and in making culverts, whilst they are as ignorant of their history as many of those who question concerning them.

In Sept. 1805 the Rev. Alfred Johnson, of Freeport, was chosen by the town as the installed successor the Rev. Mr. Price. His ministry continued eight years.

J. L. L.

———— * This house is still to be seen at the foot of Spring street, and was occupied until recently by Mr. Murch as a block-maker's shop.

NUMBER 11.

Squatter troubles in Greene--Writs of Ejectment issued--The Green Indians--
Col. Cunningham's treatment--His horse shot--Troubles in Montville--Bridge
built; rebuilt--Lynch Law incident.

Before relating an incident connected with this period of our sketches,
it may not be inopportune nor uninteresting to take a summorary view
of connecting events.

It was about the year 1804 and '05 that troublesome times began
to be experienced by the "squatters" of Greene plantation,* now known
as Belmont. As those who had unlawfully squat upon these lands refused
to recognize the claims of the proprietors, writs of ejectment were
accordingly issued against them. Thos. Cunningham, then deputy sheriff,
was ordered to serve these writs, and dispossess them of their assumed
and invalid titles. Before his arrival, word was received, and the
alarm quickly spread throughout the plantation. At this signal, they
disguised themselves, and with weapons of defence awaited the appearance
of the sheriff. On his arrival, they surrounded him, and inquired the
intent of his errand. On informing them, he drew forth his precept,
and began to read it to them. The chief, advanced towards him, feigned
ignorance of the language, and said, "Me no summing."--The sheriff then
produced another writ, and commenced to read in personation of the Indian.
The chief then wished to examine the document to see if it was genuine
and was what it purported to be. On receiving it, he immediately destroyed
it before the sheriff's face. Resistance was useless under such circumstances.
At another time sheriff Cunningham went with a posse comitutus, when
a melee ensued, and his horse was shot from under him. At another time,
the proprietors' agent, Maj. Joseph Pierce of Boston, was sent to make
an amicable settlement with the squatters of Greene plantation and Montville;
he was forcibly seized in the night, while at Mr. Everett's house in
Montville, his portmanteau, supposed to contain his papers, burned,
and he rode on a rail and dragged through the streets, when he was released
under promise of quitting the place. He immediately left for Belfast.
Several of the perpetrators were arrested and brought to Belfast, where
they were held in custody in the Whittier house. This was about the
year 1809.

Belfast, being in proximity to Greene and Montville, was always
alive during these turmoils. During the time the above prisoners were
in close quarters, the inhabitants of Belfast were aroused from their
slumbers by the report of musketry on "Wilson's hill." The whole village
was alarmed, supposing the "Greene Indians" were engaged in an affray,
and marching into town to rescue their comrades and commit acts of retalia-
tion. In a short time the village was in commotion, preparing to meet
the most extreme exigency. Part of the military company was mustered,
and others were prepared to assist them.

The Rev. M. ___, entering with patriotic zeal into the spirit
of the time, collared a man, and in a mandatory style exclaimed with
animation, at the same time giving him a sudden jerk, "In these perilous
times don't be standing here, sir!"

The company were soon in readiness for an encounter with the enemy,
and directed their course accordingly, under the command of Capt. Ephm.
McFarland. On arriving at the summit of the hill, the firing had ceased,
and the Indians had decamped.

------

*Thus called in honor of Gen. Greene, of Revolutionary memory.

The fact soon became known that these "threatening sounds of bloody strife" were produced by some fun-loving young men, who, taking advantage of the excited state of the public mind, quite effectually feigned an alarm by firing among the stumps, and making hideous Indian noises.

The joke was too rich to be lost, and so was commemorated by doggerel verse, commencing as follows:

> "Tell Mac to rise,
> And wipe his eyes,
> That he can see more clear:
> Tell him to run,
> Get out great gun,
> And turn out volunteer!"

Notwithstanding a bridge was erected in 1801, the ferry was used until 1806, at which time a bridge was built one mile below it. This bridge became almost impassable by decay, and during a heavy wind was blown down about the year 1832, and the present one erected in 1833. Its position may be traced by the position of the spiles, which are to be seen at low water.

About the year 1809, there being no "Maine Law" in force, and as moral suasion was unavailing, a company clubbed together, determined to try the effects or Lynch law upon the offender, who, when under the influence of liquor, used to shamefully abuse his wife, as her screams often indicated. One night when he was unmercifully beating her, this mob forced open the door, rushed in, and seized him from his bed, and sitting him bestride a rail, rode him through the streets, while he was hallooing at the top of his voice, imploring them to release him, and he would promise better fashions. After deeming him sufficiently chastised, they rode him home on the rail and put him to bed again. The next day the (fence) rail was found in front of his house, with this distic inscribed upon it.

> "Old Hamilton's horse is both long and slim,
> If he whips his wife he'll ride it again."

It laid him up for a fortnight, and proved an effectual antedote for his mad spasms, from which his wife was never again known to suffer.

J. L. L.

———— * Jos. Doliff, who is still living, in Belmont, was the author of this burlesque poetry. It soon became as popular in this vicinity as are familiar melodies with us at the present day.

NUMBER 12.

Ecclesiastical affairs--Merging of the Presbyterian into the Congregational church--A schism--Its cause--Rise of the Baptist society--Methodist society formed--Chapel erected--First Universalist sermon--Church organized --An unsuccessful compromise--Academy erected--Its grant of land--[NOTE: The first school house again]--Extraordinary appearance of Aurora Borealis-- Supposed precursor (?) of war.

We have now approached a period which is somewhat of an epoch in the ecclesiastical history of the town.   Until this time there was but one sect recognized in the place.

At the earliest history, the Presbyterian form of worship was the acknowledged faith of our colony. As its tenits of belief were substantially those of the Congregationalist order, and differed mainly in matters pertaining to church polity, it was but a slight transition from one to the other; and as preachers of the latter faith were more obtainable than those of the former, their procurement met with the general concurrence of the inhabitants.

There was a combination of causes that created the schism which occurred in the vicinity of the year 1809.   Prominent among the reasons of dissent was the practice, although sanctioned by law, of exacting church taxes from even non-conformists against their will.   Another alledged ground for complaint was the inexemplary life of the one they were taught to regard as their shepherd.   There were others, however, who conscienciously differed from the majority in their religious views, holding those of Arminus, while others, who conformed mostly to the "Saybrook platform," differed principally on the article of baptism.

It was about the year 1809 that the Baptists became identified as such.   John Merriam was one of their most active members, and as a man of influence, did much to establish the society, which was incorporated in 1811.   They did not worship in a house of their own until 1821 or '22, of which, more hereafter.

The same year (1809) the Methodist society was formed by Rev. John Williamson, an itinerant preacher, who organized a "class," and appointed Robert Miller as leader.*   They held their preaching meetings in school houses, until, being molested in the exercise of their privileges, they were obliged to repair to private houses, where alone they could enjoy the right "of worshipping God according to the dictates of their own consciences." In 1823 they erected their chapel at a cost of $1,300.

It was during this year (1809) also, that the first Universalist sermon was preached,--in the house of Benjamin Joy, better known as the "Cunningham house," which has recently been destroyed by fire. The preacher (whose name to us is unknown) merely tarried for a day, and then departed.   We are not aware of any fruit resulting from his transient visit, as a society was not organized until some years afterwards. In 1822 Rev. W. Frost of Framingham preached a few times, to whom, we think, the incipience of the church may be attributed. Two years afterwards in 1824, a society was formed, and Rev. Wm. A. Drew removed here and became its first pastor.

------ *   The first Methodist sermon ever preached in town, was delivered by the Rev. Joshua Hall, about the year 1796, in the Frothingham house, then owned by the Millers.   Mr. Hall is still living,--in Frankfort,--and by his robustness bids fair to attain the age of a centinarian.   He is now 88 years old, we think.

Mr. White, in speaking of the period under review, says that "Mr. Johnson, in a letter to the assessors on the 5th of January, 1809, exempted from any additional taxation, persons who should continue to fulfill their contract with him; assuming himself to sustain the loss of that portion of his salary which the seceders, had they remained faithful, would have been required to pay." Consciencious dissent, however, was beyond the power of compromise, and was destined to be an eventful epoch in the history of sister churches.

Until the year 1811 there was but two school houses in the village on the west side of the river, and as one of a higher grade was demanded, an academy, (a wooden structure,) was built by the "munificence of individual inhabitants." It being an incorporated body of trust, the State donated it 11,520 acres of land in Aroostook county, valued (in 1845) at $3,840. About a dozen years since the academy was accidentally burned down, and the present brick edifice erected in its stead.+

In the fall of the year 1811, an unusual and somewhat extraordinary phenomenon was seen in the heavens. As it was witnessed by many of our inhabitants, and attracted general attention throughout the province of Maine, it may not be out of place to mention it here.

Throughout the night the Aurora Borealis assumed the appearance of armies marching in platoons, entering into engagements, and then retreating, and going through various military evolutions. Such attention did it attract, that large groups of persons collected on different eminences, and viewed for hours, with interest, the exciting scene. As it was unlike the ordinary appearance of the northern lights, it was considered by many as the certain precursor of war.

The present accumulated memorabilia of auroral observations, however, divests it of its marvelousness, and teaches us to class it among the varied phenominal phases of the Aurora Borealis.

J. L. L.

+ In a former number we spoke about the first known (log) school house in town, as being "situated about 50 rods south of Amasa Patterson's house." Since penning the above assertion we have learned that the precedence is not to be thus awarded, but belongs to the one, not dissimilar in appearance to the before mentioned one, which was situated on the present site of Capt. John C. Blanchard's house in Searsport, then included in Belfast. The two were contemporaneous, but the latter was the first one erected: the former one, however, may be considered as the first one built within the present limits of the town.

NUMBER 13.

The war of 1812--An avidity for the news--Examples--The British fleet--The corvette Adams--Fort at Castine blown up--The Hampden skirmish--Lieut. Barnwell--Precaution--Belfast visited--Field pieces and guns secreted-- Companies mustered--Their enthusiasm.

The year 1812 marks a memorable epoch in American history. Most every sea-board place, as well as many interior cities and towns, in our country, have connected with their history some memorials of "the last war" with Great Britain. Among these places of historic claims may be included the town of Belfast.

We have nothing eventful to record, however, until towards the close of the war. During the hostility, our inhabitants were informed of the progress of events by every arrival of the mail, when some letters or newspapers would be received, detailing the exciting news. As the horn sounded at the approach of the mail carrier, it sent an unwonted and peculiar thrill through every heart, for the pending struggle was one in which every loyal citizen was deeply interested. As the carrier arrived, a crowd would eagerly gather around him, to learn the summary of news he had gathered on his way.

As soon as the mail was opened, squads of persons would cluster on the corner, and as auditors listen to hear some more favored ones read from their gazettes the latest intelligence of the war. At night a privileged circle of friends would spend the evening at the house of some neighbor, who "took the paper," and by turns the best readers would read aloud the details of the battles, skirmishes, and the other accompaniaments incidents to warfare. On the morrow, those who had either read or heard the news, became the mediums of imparting the informa- tion to others, and thus, in lieu of the multiciplicity of newspapers with which we are favored at the present day, our inhabitants then became generally versed in the accounts of the stirring scenes of those times. By thus dwelling upon and becoming familiarized to the threatening state of belligerous affairs, our citizens more readily anticipated a visit from the enemy.

On the 26th of August, 1814, a British fleet was despatched from Halifax station, under command of Gen. Pilkington, to subdue Castine. On their way they reduced Eastport and Machias, and arrived in Penobscot Bay in the morning of the 1st of September.

A few days before the arrival of the fleet, the U. S. sloop-of-war Adams, mounting 24 guns, made her appearance in the Bay, and proceeded up to Hampden to undergo repairs. Her first appearance created somewhat of an alarm here, but on ascertaining her character all fears were allayed. On Thursday morning, Sept. 1st, the above-mentioned fleet made its appear- ance in our Bay. So numerous were their masts that the fleet is described by an eye witness as having "looked like a spruce swamp." So formidable was the appearance presented, that Lieut. Lewis, without offering any resistance, blew up the fort at Castine and retreated across the Neck. Part of this garrison proceeded up the river, to render assistance to our force at Hampden in checking the further progress of the enemy. In the afternoon, when about six miles north of Bucksport, they heard of the defeat of Gen. Blake, and sent word to him for directions how to proceed. He advised them to go to Wiscasset and report themselves to Capt. Perry of the regular service; which they accordingly did in due time.

Lieut. Barnwell,* who was commander of one of the garrisons, as soon as our troops left Castine, immediately mounted his horse, and started for Belfast, where he arrived at about four o'clock, took a carriage, and with his wife, who was at Col. Cunningham's house, started for the Kennebec.

As soon as the fort at Castine was blown up, (it being distinctly seen here,) many began to remove their furniture and other movables out into the country, to places of safety, as they expected the enemy would visit and destroy the town.

Soon after Castine was surrendered, a brig and two seventy-fours shaped their course for Belfast, where they arrived at about 4 o'clock P. M., and anchored off abreast Judge Reed's shore.

In the meantime, the town was all astir with excitement. Capt. Alfred Johnson, hearing we were to be disarmed, ordered the two brass field pieces to be conveyed away, to prevent them falling into the hands of the English, as our defenceless situation forbid resistance.

Jonathan Durham, Annis Campbell, and Peter Rowe, being entrusted with the sake-keeping of the two guns, took them, together with the baggage wagon and about thirty stand of arms they collected, and carried them out to Peter Rowe's. Making a hole in the underpinning of his barn, they then deposited the muskets, whilst the cannons, and wagon, we think, were carried over Park's hill and there secreted. Quite a number of guns were also secreted in the Avery house (on Wilson's hill) whilst private individuals hid their pieces about their premises. At this time, the most of the regular troops of this district had left for the frontier of Canada. A detachment of about thirty of our militia company, were in the garrison at Castine, whilst a few were engaged in the skirmish at Hampden. Nathan Swan was captain of our militia, and Alfred Johnson was captain of the artillery, but we believe that Col. Thos. Cunningham, and Jacob Ulmer, were chief in command of the company that was mustered at this time. On the approach of the English, many companies from the surrounding towns were collected, and under their respective leaders assembled at the Simon Watson farm, (Hayford's) about three miles from the village. It was said, that this force, which consisted mostly of raw recruits, numbered 1200 men, but, not having the official account, we cannot determine its correctness. They anticipated having an engagement with the British, and in case the enemy committed any act of violence, or depredations, or did not render obedience to the honors of war, they were determined to resent it at all hazards. Many of the more sanguine recruits were impatient of restraint, and were unduly anxious to pitch into the Britishers, and give them a trial of their valor," but as a collision could not be expected without just provocation, they were compelled to await the developement of events.

J. L. L.

───── * Some say it was him who applied the torch to the magazine, but others who were present, attribute the act to Lieut. Lewis, as before stated.

NUMBER 14.

Arrival of the English ships--A flag of truce sent ashore--Reasons for landing--Gen. Gosselin and officers conducted to the hotel--A mnemonic couplet--Debarkation of the troops--Described--Quartered--Houses and meeting house occupied--Guards stationed--Pound converted into a fort--Strictness of discipline--Illustration--Civilities--John Bull illustrated--A desertion--Permission granted to leave town--A surmise.

As before stated, the English man-of-war ships anchored in our Bay about 4 o'clock in the afternoon. Soon after their arrival, a barge was despatched to the shore, containing several officers with a flag of truce. A crowd had gathered on the beach to witness their reception. Before they landed, Asa Edmunds, the 1st selectman, waded into the water to accept the flag.* Before it was tendered to him, the spokesman, (we believe it was Gen. Gerard Gosselin,) briefly stated that their object was to land their troops, and remain here four days to allow them to recruit their strength, after which they would peaceably depart; but if during their stay a gun was fired they would burn the town. With these assurances the flag was accepted.

Gen. Gosselin, and several officers, were then accompanied to the tavern, (the present building occupied by S. A. Howes' store,) by Wm. Moody, Esq., where, we believe, they tarried till after supper, and then returned to their ships.

The date of their landing is retained in the memory of some by the following couplet, which was afterwards familiar to the mouth of every youngster:

> "On the first of September,
> The English we'll remember."

At the dusk of evening, the troops began to disembark in barges. They landed in the present vicinity of Farrow's wharf, just back of the foundry. As soon as they were all debarked, they began to march up Main street, under command of Gen. Gosselin.

They were attired in a gray fatigue dress, in place of their red uniform, which they wore when on parade. On their caps was the number of the regiment. They were lately from Spain, and were picked men, equally of a height. Half of the 29th regiment landed, which numbered about 600 strong.+ As "in slow and measured tread," they silently marched through the streets, preceded by black musicians, not Gen. Gosselin, was gracefully mounted upon a beautiful chestnut colored Spanish pony, on whose left hip was brandid D.L.O. They halted abreast of Capt. Ephraim McFarland's house, when they proceeded to take up their quarters in the places their officers assigned them. They were quartered in most of the principal houses on the outskirts of the village. The meeting house was taken possession of, and the pews bedded with straw, and occupied by the soldiers as a barrack.** On Friday morning our staid citizens were somewhat surprised to find that guards had been stationed during the night around the entire village, and they prohibited from passing the circumscribed bounds without a proper permit.

---
* Some say that the act of reception was performed by Wm. Moody, but others assert the contrary, that it devolved upon, and was done by the 1st selectman.

+ There is a diversity of opinion as to the number landed. Williamson says there were 600; White, "about 700;" and some of our citizens assert that it was 1200. As it was half a regiment, we think the medium of between 600 and 700 would embrace the aggregate.

** As this house was neglected to be cleaned after the English left, the rotted straw emitted such an odor that we believe it was not again used until purchased by the Baptists in 1821, when they removed it to the place now occupied by Benj. Brown's house. It was used by them as a place of worship until they built their present church. When Mr. Brown erected his house, he set it back a few rods, (where it now stands,) and converted it to the use of a barn.

"The old pound" was converted into a sort of a fortification, by raising a parapet inside high enough to make the outer wall serve as a breastwork.

In their military discipline they were most strict: every improper or unsoldier-like act was subjected to rigid account, as the following incident will illustrate:--

While standing guard, a soldier observed some clothes blow over a fence near at hand, when he unsuspectingly jumped over to get them. He was immediately seized by an officer, court-martialed, and castigated for his imprudence.

Our citizens were treated with the utmost respect, and their rights honorably regarded. Without demurring the "enemy" paid the full price for whatever provisions or articles they obtained, thus making their visit withal an agreeable occurrence to many of our farmers, merchants, and mechanics.

It is an undeniable fact, that wherever or under whatever circumstances John Bull may be placed, he will gratify his inherent desire of boasting. A soldier came to the house of Capt. Lymeburner to purchase some poultry, and soon entered into conversation. In speaking of the expedition, he assumed a pompous position and vauntingly said: "England! that little garden, has conquered most of the whole world, and we have now come over to conquer America, after which we are going to return home to live in peace!" These taunting remarks were heard with suppressed indignation, and treated with silent contempt.

To dissuade the soldiers from deserting, the officers represented to them that Belfast was situated on an island, some distance from the main land; which idea had the effect of deterring many from desertion. One of the guards stationed on Wilson's hill conceived the idea of exploring the western extremity of the island, and so one night he suddenly left his post for the direction of the setting sun. When his comrades departed, he was in the vicinity of Montville, where, as a respected citizen, he resided until his death.

On Sunday morning Gen. Gosselin granted our inhabitants permission to leave town and carry with them such articles as they felt disposed to. A worthy citizen soberly remarked to a neighbor the day before, in the words of Scripture, "Let not your flight be on the Sabbath," yet when the permit was given, his oxen were hauling his best furniture over the hill to a place of safety.

It was somewhat of a ludicrous sight to see two women mounted on a horse in taking their flight, yet, such a mode of riding was not then unusual. As many thought there might be an engagement between our troops and the English force, they anticipated that the town would be laid in ashes, and thus the motive many assigned, in removing their goods and families.

J. L. L.

NUMBER 15.

Sociability of the English officers--Dr. Hall's ruse--Its effect--Precautions taken--A toper's advice to a soldier--Taken prisoner--Carried to Halifax--Returns--Evacuation of the English--Incident--Sail for Halifax--The American force march to Belfast--Their conduct--Anecdote of a bragadocia--March to Northport--Return to Belfast--A British seventy-four--Our troops repair to Prospect--Retrace their course--A furlough granted--Ordered to Wiscassett--Discharged--The treaty of peace received.

But a small part of the male portion of our inhabitants quitted the village on the day permission was granted them; but the major part remained until the British left.

As before intimated, many of the English officers were quite intimate in their social familiarity with certain of our citizens, but there was quite a strict surveillace exercised over the private soldier.

Dr. Charles Hall, (who was one of our physicians,) in conversing with an officer, gravely told him that the inhabitants in the adjoining settlements were as savage as Cossacks, and that the Green Indians were perfect barbarians, and treated their enemies with brutal cruelty: and in speaking of the American force assembled "out back," that they were desperate foes to cope with, and so advised him in a friendly manner to warn his fellow officers to be on the alert. It appears that notwithstanding the extravagance of the doctor's assertions, they were not regarded as altogether exaggerated by the British officers, for additional precautions were soon after taken to prevent a surprise, or be in readiness for any emergency. Gen. Gosselin took the extra pains to keep his pony by him, in Capt. McFarland's front entry, (where the prints of his hoofs were to be seen a few years since.) during the night, to be in readiness for any sudden exigency.

As we have alluded to the surveillance to which the private soldier was subjected, we will relate in substantiation the following humorous incident: Wm. D.___ of Northport, a man of about 50 years of age, came up to Belfast after his usual dram, and after imbibing to excess, shaped his course for home. Falling in with one of the sentinels who was on guard, he soon began to indulge in his accustomed loquacity. In this "freedom of speech," and agreeably to his surcharged feeling of benevolence, he began to advise the soldier to desert, and become a free man, promising to secrete him in his house, and aid and protect him to the extent of his power. An officer, observing his intimacy, approached within hearing distance, and overheard the conversation. Marching up to D___, he said, "Sir, you are a prisoner!" Despite of his apologies and entreaties, he was carried on board of one of the British ships, and kept in close confinement. When the English sailed, his children came down to the shore, and seeing him on deck they affectingly bade him farewell. On his voyage to Halifax, D___ afforded the company much merriment when under the influence of liquor; but he was well treated, and a few months before peace was proclaimed, he was dressed up like a gentleman, and sent home rejoicing.

On Monday morning, on the 5th of Sept., the enemy began to re-embark. An officer, who had unceremoniously appropriated the horse of Sheriff Saml. Burkmar to his use during their stay, rode down to the shore upon it, followed by its owner, who little expected to gain possession of it. Arriving at the beach, the officer dismounted, and tendered the horse to Mr. B. with a guinea as a compensation.

At about 8 o'clock in the morning the British ships weighed anchor, and sailed for Halifax.

At the expiration of the time the enemy set for their departure, our American force, stationed at Hayford's, took up their march for the village, expecting to have an encounter with the English if they had not left at the appointed time. Our troops arrived here about noon, by which time Col. Cunningham, with a small company, had arrived from the Hampden skirmish. As our undisciplined recruits reached here about dinner time, many of them began to relieve their hunger by indiscriminately entering such gardens as contained esculents, and eating to satiety; thus giving occasion for the oft-repeated declaration that our own soldiers were more rapacious than the enemy they came to expel. Most of our force, however, acted with decorum, and acquitted themselves becomingly.

They learned that the British, (who were apprised of their coming,) had left four hours previous, and so after dinner they started for Camden, thinking the enemy might land to commit depredations.

We will here interweave the following anecdote; In the Montville company, (which was under the command of Capt. James Wallace,) was a man by the name of D____ H____, who, previous to leaving home, was boasting of his bravery, and telling how ready he was to "have a brush with the red coats," at the same time, suiting his gestures to his words, while he was quietly listened to by his interlocutor, (who was a corporal,) when he replied, that perhaps he (H.) might prove to be a hero, but for himself, he thought he should be likely to act the part of a coward. To be brief: when a British 74 hove in sight, H____ began to grow pale, and feigned sickness, and as soon as a furlough was granted his company, he hired another to act as his substitute, when he gladly returned home, doubtless satisfied that all braggarts are not actual heroes.

Our force marched as far as the Northport bluff on its reconnoitering expedition, but seeing no signs of the enemy, they started for Lewis Pitcher's, (Batchelder's mills,) where they dined, and then returned to Belfast. They arrived here in the latter part of the afternoon, and quartered for the night. Soon after they halted here, a British 74 sailed up the Turtle head, came in sight, and anchored a few miles this side of long Island. At night our soldiers found accommodations in houses and barns on either side of the river. The next morning the 74 went out of the Western Bay.

Hearing that the English were going to cross the river from Bucksport to Prospect, our force immediately started for Prospect to repel them. Arriving at Prospect, (now Searsport,) they found that the English, hearing of their approach, had abandoned their design. Retracing their steps, they again reached this place, where the several companies were granted a four days' furlough, which was improved in recreating, and in visiting their families and friends. They were again mustered, and marched to Wiscassett, which was the place of general rendezvous, and at this time was filled with American soldiery, who were ordered there to resist the enemy's making conquest of the Kennebec. One company of this section remained there until the 24 days of service was completed, when they were inspected, discharged, and disbanded.

The news of the treaty of peace, which was signed at Ghent on the 24th of Dec., was brought here by the driver of the western mail, on the 15th of February, 1815, which tidings were received by our inhabitants with acclamations and demonstrations of joy.

                                                        J. L. L.

NUMBER 16.

CONCLUDED.

Remarks--A controversal pamphlet--influence arising from it--note--Preaching
--Rev. Messrs. Piper and Frothingham--New Church erected--Dedicated--Invita-
tion extended to Rev. Mr. Frothingham--Installed.   A disagreement--An
anecdote--Mr. F.'s position defined--A schism--Conference building erected--
The first Steamboat.   An excursion--Phoenix Row built--Origin of the
name--Eagle Hotel built--First Newspaper--Conclusion.

The war being concluded, attention was now directed to the pursuits
of agriculture, trade and commerce.

The fluctuating and unsettled state of affairs consequent upon
a state of war, was not so sensibly felt in this town as it was in other
places on the sea-board, Penobscot river, and many of the more inland
settlements.   The minds of our inhabitants being diverted from belligerent
topics, was now directed to moral and religious subjects.   Between the
years 1815 and '18, politics engaged, much less swayed but little, the
minds of our staid citizens.

About this time, a few copies of a pamphlet were brought into town
which treated on theodicy, or metaphysical theology, which treatise
discussed the question as to whence eminated original sin, or whether
god himself was the author of sin.   The pamphlet was read and re-read,
borrowed and lent, until every person of an investigating mind had threaded
its mazes of thought.   The subject soon attracted general attention,
by its being discussed in houses by neighbors, and becoming the chief
topic of conversation in the streets, where knots of persons might have
been seen arguing as earnestly and as tenaciously upon the question,
as may be seen their sons or descendants, disputing upon the political
issues of the day.   To such an extent did the discussion lead that it
caused sides to be taken even in church, where its deacons took the
negative or affirmative sides of the controversy, and gave their grave
sanction, or disapproval, of the doctrine set forth.

[Since the above was written, we have found that the period of
the religious controversy, belongs to the vicinity of the year 1800
instead of 1815 and '18, which mistake the reader may accordingly rectify.
The author of the aforesaid treatise was Loano Jennings.   In passing
we will here correct another error.   In a preceding number we spoke
of the first store being kept on Nesmith's corner.   Whereas, before
keeping there, he had a store down by Little River and afterwards removed
here, and kept in a building on the spot now occupied by Mr. McClintock's
"City Block," of stores and subsequently removed into the building which
formerly stood on the site of S. & E. Edwards.   We were misled by Mr.
Whites "History of Belfast."]

Notwithstanding the earnest probings, we believe our fathers did
not give a final quietus to the question, for even now it engages the
thought of astute metaphysicians as a vexata qucestio.

From the time of the Rev. Mr. Johnson's resignation (1813) to the
year 1818, there was no regular preaching in town by the Congregationalists.
The desk was supplied the principal part of the time by the Rev. Mr.
Piper, of Lynn, and a few times by the Rev. William Frothingham, then
of Dixmont but more formerly of Lynn.   As a unity of feeling prevailed
in the church at this time, it was decided to build a new and commodious
house of worship, which was undertaken with zeal, and liberality, and
completed to satisfaction.   It was dedicated on the 15th of Nov. 1818.
As the Rev. Mr. Frothingham met the esteem of a majority an invitation
was extended to him to become their pastor.   At a council called, a

number thought he was not explicit enough on certain fundamental points of doctrine, whilst others took it for granted that he was "sound in the faith." Mr. F. was accordingly installed on the 21st July, 1819, in the presence of a large audience. As he advanced ideas which were deemed by some as hoterodox, a part of the church summoned another council to pass their consideration upon the subject. A humorous anecdote is related of an old lady--Mrs. L---h, who, having lived in the family of a D. D. in Massachusetts, flattered herself that her smattering of theology obtained from him, was sufficient to test Mr. F.'s orthodoxy was determined to call upon, and ask him one particular question, which, to her mind, was paramount to all others, and if he was sound on that one point his evangelicanism was undoubted. Said she, "Mr. F. do you believe in total depravity?" "Well, madam," replied he, "It is my belief that man is sadly depraved." The answer was sufficient for her. She returned home perfectly satisfied, and always asserted that Mr. F. was a staunch Orthodox, and always afterwards attended his ministry. It was not long, however, before Mr. F. plainly defined his position giving his parishoners to understand that he was not a Trinitarian, but unequivocally a Unitarian. The plain avowal of his belief created a schism, and resulted in the withdrawal of a large portion of his society, and the formation of a new church. The seceders built the so-called "Conference room," which was situated just above the Hon. R. C. Johnson's house. We believe the Congregationalists worshipped in it until they erected their present church.* Hence the reason why the Unitarian church is denominated the 1st Parish Congregationalists Unitarian church, and the Orthodox church distinguished as the 2d Parish Cong. Church.

Time forbids our entering further into the details of the succeeding history of these churches, as we only designed to note the period of their incipiency. The other churches which began to flourish about this period, we have noticed in another place.

The first steamboat that ever greeted the sight of the people of Belfast, was called the Maine, and was commanded by Capt. Daniel Lunt, (who is still living in Lincolnville) in the year 1823. She then plied between Portland and St. Johns. She was also the first boat that ever visited St. Johns. On her arrival here, every window which was in sight was crowded, as was also the wharf at which she landed. There being a few passengers on board, bound for Castine, and as it would not pay to go on purpose for them only, it was determined to make an excursion to Castine if a sufficient number could be obtained. In a short time 200 of our citizens availed themselves of the opportunity of gratifying their novelty to the fullest extent. Her appearance also created a great sensation in Castine, as it did in every other place.

In the year 1824 the brick block known as Phoenix Row, was built, and under one of its north corners was deposited a box, containing, we believe, a bottle of brandy, the first newspaper printed in town, and several coins, besides several other things, as is customary in the erection of distinguished buildings. It derived the name of Phoenix, from the circumstance that several buildings were previously destroyed on its site, and like the fabled bird arose from their ashes, figuratively speaking. Among the buildings there destroyed was the house of Samuel Jackson, whose daughter, being asleep at the time, was suffocated, and burned to death.

———— * The old conference building was removed down by the shore on Josiah Farrow's Wharf, where it remained until destroyed by the fire that consumed the foundery a few years since.

In 1825 the Eagle Hotel, now known as the American House, was built by Doty Little, of Castine, and Thomas Pickard.

The first newspaper printed in town was called the Hancock Gazette and was published by Simpson & Fellows, and edited by "school-master" Wm. Bigelow, who used to edit it when not engaged in his school. The first number appeared July 6, 1820.

Having thus traced out the early history of Belfast we will here terminate our "Sketches," leaving its recent history for some future pen to describe. Much more might have been written, but for the present we will let this suffice, for fear of wearying the patience of the reader.

J. L. LOCKE.

EDITOR'S NOTE

The following two early histories of Belfast, Herman Abbot's *History of Belfast From its First Settlement to 1825* and William White's *A History of Belfast with Introductory Remarks on Acadia*, serve together to round out the story of Belfast's development, supplying details not found in the preceding works by Crosby and Locke. The compilers Abbot and White were both born the same year and both in New Hampshire. Like the authors of the first two histories given earlier in this book, both were professional men who had early cast their lots with the new settlement beside Penobscot Bay.

Herman Abbot was born 13 August 1783 at Wilton, New Hampshire, the son of William of Phebe (Ballard) Abbot. William Abbot could trace his patrilineal line back to the immigrant, George Abbot, who about 1640 was one of the first settlers of Andover, Massachusetts. Herman Abbot was only ten when his father died, leaving a widow with nine children to raise. Perhaps this circumstance explains why the young man could spend only two years at Harvard College as he prepared himself to practice medicine. Coming to Belfast in 1810, his fellow townsmen elected him Town Clerk in 1822 and he served in that office until his death 24 July 1825, shortly before his forty-second birthday. Probably it was while Abbot was Town Clerk that he began collecting materials for a history of Belfast; he did not live to see it published and for some years his manuscript was lost. An obituary in the *Hancock Gazette* not only recognized his "scientific research" and "professional skill" but went on to eulogize Dr. Abbot as a man of "unbending integrity" and "unaffected piety."

Abbot's manuscript was rediscovered late in the 19th century, and was then serialized in four issues of the pages of *The Republican Journal* beginning with 25 Jan 1900. Later that year it was published in Belfast in book form by Miss Grace E. Burgess. It is from the latter that this copy was transcribed by Elizabeth M. Mosher.

William White was born 13 May 1783 at Chester, New Hampshire, the son of William and Elisabeth (Mitchell) White. He graduated from Dartmouth College in 1806 with the highest honors in his class, a distinction that won him election to Phi Betta Kappa. After reading law with Hon. Amos Kent, of Chester, and Hon. John Wilson, of Belfast, he began practice at Union, Maine and for two years served that town as Postmaster. White moved to Thomaston in 1812 and the next year he moved on to Belfast where he was to live the rest of his life. In 1813 the young lawyer married Maria A. Ashman, and they were the parents of one daughter, Lydia. In 1818 his adopted town elected him as its Representative to the General Court of Massachusetts. Death claimed him on 17 June 1831 at the age of forty-eight. His thorough education in the law, added to his attainments as a scholar, not only made him an attorney of the first rank but earned him a reputation as a graceful and eloquent public speaker. A contemporary at Dartmouth described White's style as a writer as "easy and glowing and marked with a classical elegance."

When in 1827 White produced *A History of Belfast with Introductory Remarks on Acadia* it was the first bound book to be published in Belfast.

Abbot's and White's books, taken together with the works of Crosby and Locke given earlier in this volume, and with the perhaps much better known *History of the City of Belfast in the State of Maine* by Joseph Williamson (1877), present the reader with an unusually comprehensive account of the founding and growth of this much-loved town on the Penobscot River. Picton Press is pleased to have been able to bring all four works to the historical and genealogical public, with the aid of the meticulous transcription of the originals done by Elizabeth M. Mosher. It was at her suggestion, and and as a result of her hard work, that Abbot's and Whtie's books were added to this volume.

HISTORY OF BELFAST

From its First Settlement

to 1825

by

Herman Abbot

PICTON PRESS

CAMDEN, MAINE

1989

Annals of Belfast for Half a Century by William George Crosby (1805-1881) was originally published in fifty-two installments in the Belfast, Maine newspaper *The Republican Journal*, 1874-75

Sketches of the Early History of Belfast by John Lymburner Locke (1832-1876) was originally published in serialized form in the Belfast, Maine newspaper *The Progressive Age* in sixteen issues beginning 10 April 1856.

History of Belfast From its First Settlement to 1825 by Herman Abbot (1783-1825) remained in manuscript form at the time of his death and for many years was feared lost. When the manuscript was finally rediscovered it was published in serial form in four issues of *The Republican Journal* of Belfast beginning 25 Jan 1900, and was then published in Belfast, also in 1900, by Miss Grace E. Burgess.

A History of Belfast with Introductory Remarks on Acadia by William White (1783-1831) was first published in Belfast, Maine in 1827, and was the first bound book published in that town.

Transcription of all four histories above was done for this volume by Elizabeth M. Mosher, RFD 2 Box 825, City Point, Belfast, Maine 04915

Available from:

Picton Press
P. O. Box 1111
Camden, Maine 04843
Manufactured in the United States of America
using acid-free paper

HISTORY OF BELFAST

From its First Settlement to the Year 1825.

BY HERMAN ABBOT.

PREFACE.

To collect and preserve a few facts relating to the early history and settlement of this town; the leading traits in the character of its first inhabitants, together with their privations and hardships; to notice our litary and religious institutions; our growing wealth and population; to mark the course of events and to describe the improvements which have taken place here in the period of little more than half a century may be thought an object worthy of some attention. The proprietors and town records furnish much valuable information respecting the days which have long since passed away. These sources alone abound in too few materials to answer the purpose, and treat of topics too general in their nature to embrace a copious and useful variety. A more detailed account therefore appeared indispensable; and it has become necessary by consulting the aged inhabitants and the descendants of the proprietors and first settlers to arrest valuable matter in its slow but steady march to oblivion. The knowledge of many little incidents of former times has by these means been sought out, arranged and committed to writing, which with the addition of more recent occurrences contain, as I trust, an interesting compilation. Considering, however, the manner of procuring some portion of the materials for this sketch of Belfast, I am sensible that slight inaccuracies will be found; at the same time the public may be assured that no pains have been spared to obtain the most authentic information.

To those who have kindly assisted me in this undertaking, and particularby to Mr. John Cochran, the only surviving original proprietor resident in this town, through whose politeness I have had access to the proprietars' deed and records, I tender my grateful acknowledgments.

HISTORY OF BELFAST.

In the year 1768 a number of young men belonging principally to Londonderry, N. H., began to adopt measures for the purchase of Belfast Township in the Province of Maine.

The straitened circumstances of some and the strong local attachments of many more, who were unwilling to remove the distance of two hundred miles to endure hardships in a wilderness inhabited only by Indians and wild beasts, presented prospects truly formidable. A spirit of enterprise, however, overcame all obstacles and the plan was so far matured that a meeting was notified and held at Londonderry on the fourth day of October, when the intended purchasers divided the township into shares, subscribed for the number of shares each would take, and appointed a clerk to record their proceedings.

In June following, Joseph Chadwick made a survey of the township, which contained, according to his estimate, 19,359 acres. This was divided into fifty-one shares, and a deed bearing date August 29, 1769, was made in consideration of fifteen hundred pounds by the heirs of Brigadier General Samuel Waldo, viz.: Samuel Waldo, Esq., Francis Waldo, Esq., and Sarah Waldo, wife of said Samuel, (her right of dower) of Falmouth, in the County of Cumberland, Maine; Isaac Winslow, Esq., of Roxbury, Massachusetts; Thomas Flucker, Esq., and Hannah Flucker, his wife, (daughter of Brig.-Gen. Waldo) of Boston, Massachusetts, (1) to John Mitchel, six shares; John Gilmore, five shares; John Steel, three shares, Samuel Houston and James McGregore, each two shares; Moses Barnet, John Moor, John Durham, Joseph Morrison, John Brown, James McGregore,

---
1. Winslow derived an interest through his deceased wife, a daughter of General Waldo. Thomas and Hannah Flucker were the parents of the wife of General Knox.

231

Jr., John Morrison, Alexander Stewart, James Miller, William Clendinen, Matthew Reed, Samuel Marsh, Nathaniel Martin, and Joseph Gregg, each one share; William Patterson, Matthew Chambers and William McLaughlin, each half a share; all of Londonderry, N. H. John Tufts and James Gilmore, each two shares; Robert Macklewane, Alexander Wilson and John Davidson, each one share; all of Windham, N. H. Robert Patterson of Pepperellboro, Maine, three shares; Alexander Little and John Cochran, both of Boston, each one share; David Hemphill of Newburyport, one share; James McLaughlin of Pembroke, N. H., half a share; and the remaining four shares in equal proportions to the afore named John Mitchel, John Gilmore, Moses Barnet, John Tufts, Samuel Houston, John Moor and James McGregore, Jr.

Previous to executing the deed the grantors of this township employed Richard Stimson to survey a suitable location for a road from Thomaston to Fort Point, for which service he was to have one hundred acres of land at some place on the route. He accepted the proposal and selected a spot near a small creek (2) which is the dividing line between this town and Prospect. Thither his father, Ephraim Stimson, removed, whose family, the first ever settled here, consisted of himself and wife, two sons, Ephraim and Richard, and several daughters.

In 1769, James Patterson and Nathaniel his brother, both young men, came to this town from Pepperellboro (3) and commenced the business of felling trees and clearing land. They spent the ensuing winter here, at which time there was but one family in the place, the Stimson's, above mentioned.

The next year, 1770, several of the town proprietors arrived and took possession of their newly acquired purchase, with the view of converting the lonely forest into fruitful fields for the support of themselves and families. It was to be expected that they would bring with them the religion, manners, habits and customs of the places they had left. Twenty-seven our of thirty-two purchasers belonged to Londonderry or Windham, whose inhabitants were principally of Scottish or Irish descent. In the former of these towns there were two societies of Presbyterians with each a clergyman of the first respectability, Rev. William Davidson and Rev. David McGregore, who had been settled there no less than thirty years. In the latter was the Rev. Simon Williams, a highly useful Presbyterian minister. To exchange these religious privileges, therefore, for a situation where they could enjoy no stated preaching of the word and but very seldom hear a prayer or a sermon from those who are called to labour in the vineyard of the Lord and whose business it is more particularly to watch for souls as those who are to give account, must have been matter of deep regret to them and their friends. Many domestic and social ties implanted in man for wise and beneficient purposes, and which form necessary links in the great chain which connects the human species, were severed by their removal. Taking the final leave of father and mother, brothers and sisters with the express design of seeking a residence in the wilds of Maine awakened the tenderest sensibilities and gave impulse to the most affecting emotions of which kindred hearts are susceptible.

These few adventurers were fully persuaded that patient labour and rigid economy were necessary to success in a new country. Industry, temperance and frugality were virtues on which they set a high value; by the practice of which they acquired a hardy constitution and saved their earnings for useful purposes.

---

2. The stream in the western part of Searsport village, called Half-way creek, Stimson's father first settled on the hill named for him Mount Ephraim.

3. Now Saco. James Patterson settled upon the Stock Farm, on the east side, long the homestead of his nephew, the late Robert Patterson 5th. Nathaniel resided on lot No. 32, also on the east side.

In their manners they exhibited a model of perfect plainness and simplicity indicative of contentment and a cheerful disposition, and so cordial was their reception of those who visited them that with very limited means it might be truly said they were given to hospitality. The Scottish dialect was understood and spoken by several of them; and some traces of it are retained to the present day. Those of the first settlers who remain and their immediate descendants, read the poems of Burns with a keen relish and are enthusiastic admirers of the language of the Scottish Bard.

Nothing memorable happened after the settlement began until December 1770, when John Morrison and Thomas Steel were drowned by the upsetting of a boat in Belfast bay.

The Proprietors held their first meeting here June 25th, 1771, the land was laid out into lots, and partition was made of so much of it as became necessary for the convenience of the settlers.

The first white child born here was Ann, the second daughter of William Patterson, and afterwards the wife of Enos West. Her birth happened May 9th, 1772. The same year William Patterson 2nd was married to Mary Mitchel by Dr. Crawford of Frankfort, a justice of the peace. This was the first marriage that took place in town.

In 1773 the Town was incorporated and the warrant for calling the first meeting of the inhabitants was issued by Thomas Goldthwait, Esq., of Frankfort, of which the following is a copy.

To Mr. John Mitchel of Belfast, Gentleman,--Greeting.

Whereas the great and general Court at their sessions began and held at Boston upon Wednesday, the twenty-ninth day of May last, passed an act for incorporating a certain tract of land lying on the westerly side of Penobscot Bay into a town by the name of Belfast in the County of Lincoln, and the said General Court having impowered me, the subscriber, to issue a warrant directed to some principal inhabitant in said town to notify and warn the Inhabitants thereof qualified by law to vote in Town affairs to meet at such time and place as shall be therein set forth to choose such officers as may be necessary to manage the affairs of said Town, at which first meeting all the then male inhabitants that be at the age of twenty-one years shall be admitted to vote.

These are, therefore, in his majesty's name to require you, the said John Mitchel, to notify the said Inhabitants of Belfast to meet at your dwelling house in said Town on Thursday the eleventh day of November, at ten of the clock in the forenoon, then and there to choose a Town Clerk, Selectmen and all other Town Officers according to law and make return of this warrant with your doings as soon after the same is carried into execution as may be.

Given under my hand and seal at Frankfort, October 1773.

THOMAS GOLDTHWAIT.

In obedience to the above warrant I have warned the Inhabitants of Belfast to attend their first meeting as appointed in said warrant.

JOHN MITCHEL.

At this meeting Thomas Goldthwait was chosen Moderabor; John Mitchel, Clerk; John Brown, Benjamin Nesmith and James Patterson, Selectmen; John Barnet, Treasurer; William Patterson, 1st, Constable; John Durham Jr., Alexander Clark, and James Miller, Surveyors of Highways; John Durham and James Morrow, Wardens.

In 1774 the Town voted to send a petition to the General Court at Boston to have non-resident lands taxes; that John Tufts carry the petition; and that he be allowed, as wages, three shillings a day; he finding vituals and drink for himself.

Mr. John Barnet and Miss Isabella Durham were joined in marriage Sept. 27th, 1774 by Daniel Little.

The Town Clerk entered on the records a certificate bearing date Nov. 8th, 1774, stating that he had lawfully published Mr. James Morrow to Miss Elizabeth Durham, both of this Town.

In 1775 the Town voted to raise one hundred dollars for the highways, and fifty dollars for preaching. John Tufts, John Brown, Solon Stephenson, James Patterson, and Samuel Houston were appointed committee of safety. John Tufts was recommended by vote of the Town for a Justice of the peace, and was soon after commissioned.

The Town also voted, that if any person makes unnecessary visits on the Sabbath, he shall be looked on with contempt, until he make acknowledgment to the public. The inhabitants, at this time, felt great inconvenience, in being obliged to go fifteen miles, or more to mill; and an article was inserted in one of the Town warrants this year, 'To see if they could lay any plan to have a grist mill in town.' It does not appear that anything was done to remedy the evil complained of, except that the laying out certain roads to mill streams might be considered, as holding out to individuals encouragement to build mills. The Selectmen warned Joseph Dow June 10th, 1775, to withdraw from this Town forthwith; for they would not accept him, as a Town inhabitant.

1776.   The committee of safety was composed of the same persons, as last year.   Mr. James McCurdy was married to Miss Ann Mitchel Nov. 30th, 1776.

1777.   Committee of safety, inspection and correspondence; Alexander Clark, Solon Stephenson, John Mitchel, James Patterson, Robert Patterson, Samuel Houston, and Benjamin Nesmith.   The Town appointed Solon Stephenson to lay before the General Court the misconduct of any person, either by word, or action against the United States.

1778.   The Town voted unanimously to approve of the constitution, or form of Government, as agreed on by the honorable Convention of this State.   Yeas 19.

Messrs.   John Tufts, Solon Stephenson, John Brown, Committee of safety, &c. and were re-elected next year.

1779.   The Town voted to raise twenty-five pounds for its own use, or in a more modern style, for incidental expenses.

This year Castine was taken by the British and the Inhabitants of Belfast to their inexpressible mortification were required to come forward and swear allegiance to the King of Great Britain or be treated as enemies.   To the arbitrary measures of this monarch they were violently opposed; and refusing to bind themselves by the solemnities of an oath to engage in a cause which they so heartily despised and finding themselves in danger they quitted their farms and made good their retreat to places out of the reach of persecution. (4)

1785.   No sooner had the war between this country and Great Britain come to a happy termination and the enemy had withdrawn from our borders than the settlers scattered in all directions, began one after another to return and occupy their farms.   Some, however, were so well situated elsewhere that they did not wish to revisit the place where they had met so much trouble and vexation.   There had been no town meetings since 1779 and Jonathan Buck, Esq., of Penobscot, agreeably to a resolve of the General Court, issued a warrant to John Tufts, Esq., directing him to call a meeting of the inhabitants on the twenty-ninth day of March for the purpose of choosing town officers and transacting town business.

----

4.   This is an error.   Ten of the eighteen heads of families then here, took the oath "under the compulsion," as they afterwards admitted.

1788.   The town sent a petition to the General Court that they might be empowered to lay a tax of two pence per acre on all the lands in town to raise money in order to build a meeting house, settle a minister, make bridges and repair roads.

1790.   Number of inhabitants in town 245.

1792.   Forty three votes were given for the separation of the District of Maine from Massachusetts & two against it.

The town voted to build two meeting houses one on each side of the river to be erected at the expense of the inhabitants of each side separately.   In the autumn town meetings were held in both of these houses.

1794.   A demand was made by government of ten soldiers from the Belfast Company. (5) The town voted them a liberal allowance in addition to their regular pay in case they should be called into actual service. Mr. James Miller died Jan. 11th, aged 82.

1795.   Mr. John Steel died June 14th, aged 84.

1796.   At the commencement of this year there were only twelve framed dwelling houses in town and but one of them two stories high. (6)

A committee was chosen by the town to treat with Mr. Ebenezer Price on terms of settlement as a minister composed of the following persons, John Tufts, Solon Stephenson, Samuel McKeen, Samuel Houston, John Cochran, James Patterson, Benjamin Nesmith, Robert Steel, Tolford Durham, John Cochran 2nd and Alexander Clark.

The town voted to give Mr. Price two hundred dollars a year as a salary and to add ten dollars each year until it shall amount to three hundred dollars; also a parsonage lot reserved for the first settled minister except one acre for a meeting house to stand on and a sufficient quantity of land for a burying ground.

A protest against the settlement of Mr. Price is on the records of the town signed by Solon Stephenson, Zenas Stephenson, Caleb Stephenson, William Patterson, William Patterson, James Patterson, Nathaniel Patterson, Robert Patterson, Jerome Stephenson, George Cochran, Robert Cochran, Peter Cochran, John Cochran, John Young, Job Young, John Osborn, Josiah Dillingham, Ichabod Clark, Elisha Clark, Nathaniel Eells, Robert Miller, James Gammon, Robert Steel and Jonathan White.

The following is a copy of the Letter of the Committee appointed by the town to wait on Mr. Ebenezer Price and notify him of his call to the ministry dated Belfast Sept. 19th, 1796.

To Ebenezer Price, A. B.
Preacher of the Gospel.
The People of the Town of Belfast wish health, grace and peace.

We being fully sensible of our disconsolate and unhappy situation as a people while destitute of a spiritual guide, feeling ourselves and offspring deprived of rich and peculiar blessings so long as we are destitute of a regular church of Christ, the stated dispensation of the word and the administration of the ordinances of the gospel, and viewing ourselves candidates for immortality, duty calls on us to use our ability and exert our most zealous endeavors to obtain those spiritual blessing and privileges which Christ our Saviour hath provided in the gospel. We, therefore, make known to you, dear sir, our situation.

It is now a considerable time that you have laboured with us in word and doctrine and we view it the smiles of providence that you have been led to this part of the vineyard of our Lord to us who are scattered like sheep upon the mountains without a shepherd. You have by your public labours, private walk, doctrine, example and by the testimonials

------

5.   This call was occasioned by Indian hostilities in the western country, and anticipated difficulties with England.

6.   The two story house was built by James Miller in 1791. It was afterwards occupied by Rev. William Frothingham, and perished in the great fire of 1873.

of others recommended yourself to us as a faithful ambassador of Christ which demand our affection, respect and reverence. Ever since our first acquaintance the eyes of the people have been upon you that you should set over them in the Lord; and 'tis the general voice and united desire and prayer that should there be a church gathered here according to the rules of Christ you should take the pastoral care of this church and people, to be ordained over them and spend your days for their spiritual interest in the high and holy calling of a gospel minister, that we may no longer be as sheep going astray subject to be devoured by wolves, but that in you we may find a faithful shepherd, a spirirtual guide, one who will naturally care for us, who will deliver to us the doctrines of the gospel with plainness and simplicity, whose talents may be improved for our edification, whose words a balm for the wounded in spirit, whose example our pattern and whose seasonable admonitions our preservation from error, that we may walk together while here on earth in love enjoying the ordinances of the gospel and be prepared to sit in Christ's kingdom forever.

That you dear sir, may see your way clear to manifest your acceptance of this call to the pastoral care of this church when gathered and congrega- tion in the town of Belfast is our general, fervent and humble prayer to Almighty God.   But as we expect of you spiritual things we would in like manner minister to your wants in carnal things.   (Then follows the offer of the town in respect to settlement and salary)

We submit this call and these proposals to your serious and solemn consideration, beseeching God to direct you in the path of duty particularly in this most important matter and that he would grant that whatever be your determination we may acquiesce in the dispensation of his providence.

Signed by Samuel McKeen, John Cochran, Tolford Durham and Alexander McMillan.

Mr. Price's answer.
TO THE SOCIETY AND PEOPLE OF BELFAST:--
DEAR AND BELOVED:

'Tis now a considerable time since I received by the hand of your committee a call and proposals to settle with you in the gospel ministry. Sensible of your situation I feel myself under obligation as soon as possible to make known to you the result of my reflections on the solemn and important subject.   It is a subject of the greatest moment both to you and me because in it each of our soul's eternal interest is material- ly concerned.-- On the decision I am called to give, much is depending, as it must be attended with endless consequences and because from it the glory and honor of Christ's kingdom are inseparable.   Therefore, with what reverence, caution and assurance of duty ought I to decide, lest I wrong my own soul and mar the divine glory. --According to the clearest light and helps I have been able to obtain from a prayerful enquiry and the most mature deliberation providence directs to receive the call of the Society of Belfast as the call of God. --I do therefore, relying on God in obedience to what appears duty, publicly and cordially accept your invitation and proposals to be ordained over you in the work of the gospel ministry, and that as soon an Ecclesiastical council may be convened and a Church of Christ gathered should the present appearanc continue.

I am not insensible that this decision is attended with things at present disagreable and self-denying.   There is an opposition to my settlement.   No ministers at hand with whom I might advise on emergent occasions and I am far removed from my kindred and friends, but the cross must be borne by the followers of Christ.   I would feel submissive to God who disposeth all things according to infinite wisdom.--

The reasons influencing me to this my answer are, the peculiar operations of providence relative to you as a Society since my first acquaintance with you; the repeated instances of your unanimity and apparent engagedness in the cause of the Redeemer and especially your last general public act. These, taking into view your critical situation should your endeavors prove ineffectual with the Council of my reverend fathers and brethren in the ministry are reasons which leave me no room to doubt the propriety of my decision notwithstanding what has appeared to the contrary. --But when I consider my unworthiness of so high and holy a calling, my youth, inexperience, liableness to err and to be drawn aside by temptation, to have the care of immortal souls, how terrifying the idea! Nothing but the desire of promoting the cause of the Redeemer in this place would influence me to settle with you. Should this proposed union take place much will depend on you as a church and people not only to make my life comfortable but to ease the burden of my ministerial labours. Those of you who profess to be the children of God will I trust feel it a duty constantly to bear me to the throne of grace, to strengthen my hands and encourage my heart. May I ever enjoy your counsel and since I am a man subject to like passions with other men, when occasion calls do not withhold your seasonable and friendly admonitions. I shall expect from you moderation, candour and charity in your conduct towards me, and may I toward you discharge the duty of the ministerial character, watching over the Lord's flock like a faithful shepherd, ministering to your spiritual wants teaching the commandments of God, preserve my garments unspotted from the world and by soul free from the blood of all men. --And may I increase in grace, knowledge, wisdom, prudence and humility that you may be profited by my labours and example. --Should we unite as Minister and People, O that it might be for your mutual edification comfort and joy. May I go out and in before you in the fear of God, not counting my life dear to me but manifesting a willing mind to spend the days God shall give me in the service of Christ for your sakes. --And may you in me receive a rich blessing. May there be many souls from among you edified, comforted and brought to the saving knowledge of Christ thro' my instrumentality.

The God of grace grant that we may walk together as minister and people enjoying the ordinances of the gospel in love, union and Christian fellowship until God in his own time shall call us from this scene of trial to spend an eternity with the spirits of the just made perfect.

EBENEZER PRICE.

You have doubtless anticipated that as my parents and friends live at a great distance a few Sabbaths yearly will be necessarily taken in visiting them.

A Council was convened on the twenty-eighth day of December consisting of Rev. E. Gillet, Rev. Jona. Powers, Rev. Jona. Huse and Rev. W. Riddel, with their delegates. The next day a church was organized and Mr. Price was ordained. The original associates who composed the Rev. Mr. Price's church were John Tufts, Samuel McKeen, Samuel Houston, John Brown, John Cochran and John Alexander, the two first of whom were afterwards appointed deacons.

1797. Mr. William McLaughlin died March 27th aged 90. Mr. Nathaniel French died July 1st aged 50. Mr. Enos West was married to Miss Ann Patterson, the first born child of Belfast Dec. 5th.

1798. Solon Stephenson and twenty-two others petitioned the General Court to be incorporated with such others as might join them, their polls and estates, into a distinct Parish by the name of the Religious Society in the town of Belfast. In the petition they assert 'that there is settled within said town of Belfast a minister who tho' approved by a majority of the Inhabitants of said town hold tenets and preaches doctrines which your petitioners cannot conscientiously receive.' Also, 'we sincerely and honestly believe that the principles approved and doctrines inculcated by the Minister of the Town are unscriptural, immoral and distructive to the order and interest of Society.'

The General Court ordered the petitioners to notify the Town of Belfast by serving the Clerk thereof with an attested copy of this petition

& their order thereon thirty days before the second tuesday of their next session that they may appear and shew cause if any they have who the prayer of said petition should not be granted. In November the Town appointed Robert Houston, Esq., John Cochran 2nd and Tolford Durham a committee to present a memorial in behalf of the town against this petition. This memorial which appears at full length on the town records is ably and ingeniously written & it met with a favourable reception for at the next session of the Legislature the petitioners had leave to withdraw their petition.

1799. Mr. John Cochran died January 1st aged 59.

1800. Mrs. M. H. Cochran died March 8th aged 85. Mr. Samuel Eells died Aug. 3d aged 41. Mr. Benjamin Nesmith died Sept. 18th aged 66.

1801. William Cunningham, Jonathan Wilson, William Patterson, Ephraim McFarland, Samuel Russell, Robert Patterson 2nd, Abner G. McKeen, Nathaniel Patterson, Ephraim McKeen, Jacob Eames, Robert B. Cochran and John S. Osborn were incorporated Feb. 10th, by the name of the Belfast Bridge Company to build a toll bridge over Belfast River. This commonly called the Upper Bridge was completed the same year at the expense of about $6000.

1802. Deacon John Tufts died March 3rd aged 78. Mrs. Grisel Jameson died March 18th aged 96. Mr. Robert Steel died October 25th aged 43.

Forty-one deaths happened in town this year a list of which is preserved on the church records.

The town appointed a committee to wait on the Rev. Mr. Price to see on what condition he would have his connexions as minister of the town dissolved. The terms that he proposed were that they should pay up the arrearages of his salary give him two hundred and fifty dollars and procure for him a warrantee deed of the parsonage lot from the propriet-ors. On his part he would give a deed to the town of one acre of the same lot where the East meeting house stands and moreover would lay out a sufficient quantity of land for a burying ground. His offer was accepted and his dismission took place Sept. 22nd.

1803. The town voted 500 dollars for the support of schools and 2000 for the repairs of highways. A company of Artillery was organized within the bounds of this Regiment and its officers were Jonathan Wilson Capt., Ephraim McFarland 1st Lieut.; Thomas Cunningham 2nd Lieut. Jonathan Wilson Esq. was chosen Representative to the Legislature the first ever sent by this town.

1804. This town gave 102 votes for Governor. A company of Cavalry was organized here, and John Wilson was commissioned its captain, Robert White 1st Lieut., Joseph Houston 2nd Lieut.; & Abel Baker Cornet. --Jenny Patterson daughter of James Patterson and Elizabeth his wife and the youngest of their twelve children was born April 11th. Her eldest brother was at this time 28 years 4 months and twenty six days old and the mother a little rising of forty six years.

1805. Jonathan Wilson Esq. and his associates were incorporated for the purpose of building a toll bridge over Belfast river at the village called Belfast East Bridge March 14.

Lemuel Weeks Esq. died May 20th aged 50.

Rev. Alfred Johnson was installed minister of this town Sept. 25th salary $700 per ann.

1806. Belfast East Bridge was completed at the expense of $18,500. Its length was 122 rods.

1807. Mr. Solon Stephenson died Feb. 14th aged 73.

1808. Belfast Academy was incorporated Feb. 29th and the following gentlemen constituted the Board of Trustees, George Ulmer and Samuel A. Whitney Esqrs.; Rev. Alfred Johnson, Phineas Ashmun, Bohan P. Field, Thomas Whittier, James Nesmith, Nathan Read, John Wilson & Jonathan Wilson Esqrs.; Doct. Thaddeus Hubbard, Doct. Oliver Mann, Rev. William Mason, Rev. Mighill Blood and Caleb B. Hall Esq.--Votes for Governor 186.

1809.   Abel Baker Constable and Collector of taxes for the years 1806, 1807, and 1808 having absconded with considerable of the Towns money a meeting of the Inhabitants was notifed and held Feb. 9th to make choice of a Collector to complete the collection of taxes in the bills committed to the said Baker.   This arrant rogue never afterwards appeared here and the town after making the necessary abatements recovered the deficit on the bonds. --Mr. James Gilmore died Nov. 28th.

Rev. Alfred Johnson addressed a letter to the Assessors of the town stating in substance that he understood several persons liable to ministerial taxes in this town had joined others in a petition to be incorporated into a Baptist Society whereby the burden of his support might be greater on those who continued members of his society he therefore thro' them would declare that those who remain faithful to the covenants of the town with him their taxes should not be increased by the apostacy of others.

1810.   The town contains 1,274 inhabitants.   Mrs. Brown died aged 90.   John Merriam and twenty-eight others, petitioners to be incorporated by the name of the first Baptist Society in Belfast had an order of notice granted on their petition which was duly served and the Town at a meeting Dec. 13th did not think proper to remonstrate.--

1811.   The Baptist Society was incorporated.

James Nesmith Esq. doed March 4th aged 47.

Belfast Academy was opened May 17th and an address was delivered by Mr. James Porter the first Preceptor. --A ship of 490 tons was built here called the Belfast of New York.

1812.   Number of Polls in Belfast 319.   Mr. James Gordon died aged 86.

Rev. Alfred Johnson gave the first Congregational Parish a bond relinquishing his salary during the present war with Great Britain & not long after one extending the time indefinitely.

1813.   John Wilson Esq. of this town was elected member of Congress two years from March 4th.

Benjamin Poor Esq. died Aug. 10th aged 52.--

Rev. Alfred Johnson. took his dismission Oct. 3rd 1814.   The British landed a body of troops in this Town amounting to about six hundred Sept. 1st who embarked on the 5th.

1815.   Messrs. Nathan Cram, Parker Brown and Daniel Toward of this town and Mr. Joseph Woodward of Islesboro' were drowned by the upsetting of a boat in Belfast Bay Oct. 23rd.

William Lowney A. M., a graduate of Dublin College died Nov. 8th aged 76.

1816.   This was a remarkably cold season.   Apple trees were in blossom July 1st, and the crops were very scanty.

A Town meeting was held Sept. 2nd to consider the question of separating the District of Maine from Massachusetts on certain prescribed terms. The votes stood thus, yeas 95, nays 65, and Alfred Johnson & John Merriam Esqrs. were appointed Delegates.--

1817.   John Wilson Esq. was again elected member Congress.   Mr. Francis Anderson died Feb. 22nd aged 39.

Mr. Patrick Gilbreth died April 4th aged 78.

Mr. John Brown died in May aged 86.

1818.   A Custom House was established here and Col. Daniel Lane appointed Collector.--

Rev. William Frothingham received a call from the first Congregational Parish April 27th & from the Church May 7th to settle with them in the work of the Gospel ministry.

Mrs. West, wife of Enos West died at Monroe, May 7th aged 46. (7)

The frame of the first Congregational Meeting house was raised June 10th and 11th.

_____
7. She was the first child born here.

The new Meeting house was solemnly dedicated Nov. 15th.

The cost of it including the bell purchased afterwards by the Parish was about $7,500; the expense of which was defrayed by the sale of the pews.

Rev. William Frothingham made a communication in answer to the call given him to settle here as follows:

(See original letter).

1819.   The small pox made its appearance and one hundred and fifty persons were the subjects of the disease in this town between the middle of April & the end of June.   It was first introduced here by picking up and washing some infected clothes which had drifted ashore.   To nine persons it proved fatal.

On the return of Rev. Mr. Frothingham in May some disagreement being found to exist between him and a majority of the Church in respect to religious tenets and a church covenant, the parish unwilling to entrust the church with the making arrangements to settle Rev. Mr. F. under present circumstances assumed the right of selecting the council and a committee of eight was chosen with power to choose a council and provide suitable accommodations for them at the expense of the Parish.   The Parish Committee and Rev. Mr. F. having chosen an equal number to compose an Ecclesiastical Council, the day was fixed on and the council appeared. A few weeks before his installation the church informed Rev. Mr. F. that the calling of the council according to ecclestical usage belonged exclusively to themselves and not to the Parish; they had voted, that the council should consist of nine ministers and their delegates of which they had chosen six & he might elect three.   This proposal was rejected by Rev. Mr. F. and he was settled July 21st without a church. The Clergy who officiated at the installation of Rev. Mr. Frothingham were Rev. Dr. Ripley of Concord, Rev. Dr. Allyn of Duxbury, Rev. Mr. Lowell of Boston, Rev. Dr. Packard of Wiscasset, Rev. Mr. Mason of Castine and Rev. Mr. Warren of Jackson.   His salary is $600. per annum.--

On Thursday August 12th Rev. William Frothingham, Samuel Cunningham, Nathan Read, William Poor, Nicholas Coffin & Herman Abbot formed themselves into a Church by adopting a platform and covenant & at the end of this year it consisted of eighteen members.

Alfred Johnson Esq. was chosen by the town Sept. 20th a Delegate to the Convention for framing a Constitution for the State of Maine.--

1820.   This town contains 2026 inhabitants of which 402 are ratable polls.   A number of the inhabitants seceded from the first & formed a second Congregational Parish in May. (8)

1821.   Rev. Mr. Frothingham's church having increased to twenty seven members, two Deacons were appointed on the fourth day of June.--

Mr. Laughlin McDonald died July 24th.   His age was not accurately known, but supposed to exceed one hundred years.

1822.   A company of Light Infantry was organized, and its officers were Joel Hills Captain, Dudley Griffin Lieutenant, and Loring Varney Ensign.   The town has 485 ratable polls.

The First Baptist Society purchased the old West meeting house, removed it to a central part of the village and put it in good repair. It is a one story building 36 feet square and has 49 pews. (9)

The conference meeting house (10) 40 feet by 32 was built for the Second Congregational parish.

----
8.   The present Congregational Society.

9.   The place of removal was Bridge street, between High and Washington streets.   In 1838 it was converted into a stable, and existed as such until 1895.

10.   It stood on Primrose Hill, just above the house of Ralph C. Johnson.   After the erection of the North church, it was removed to Front street and was destroyed by fire in 1851.

1823.   Number of ratable polls 525.   In one year ending Sept. 1st
the Selectman granted forty-eight Store, four Tavern, and two victualling
Licenses, which yielded an income to the town amounting to two hundred
and eighty-five dollars.
1824.   The town voted to give Col. Nathan Stanley Six hundred and
seventy dollars to free the town one year from all expense on account
of paupers.   Three thousand dollars were raised for repairs of highways
and fifteen hundred for the support of schools.   Number of polls 574,
and of School Districts 14.
The Town house, a handsome brick building was begun. (11)
Rev. Charles Soule was ordained over the Second Congregational
Parish & church, or as they style themselves the Society associated
with the first Congregational Church June 30th.--
The officiating Clergy were Rev. Messrs. Gillett of Hallowell,
Tappan of Augusta, Blood of Bucksport, Cummings of North Yarmouth, Mitchel
of Waldoboro, Merrill of Freeport and Ingraham of Thomaston.
--Rev. Mr. Soules salary is $ per annum. (12).   The number of
legal voters whose names were on the list in November was 555.--
The Methodist Meeting House was built and solemnly dedicated December
31st. (13)
Fifty seven deaths happened in town this year.   Fever combined
with Dysentery was the prevailing epidemic which proved very fatal to
children.--
List of persons who have died in Belfast from 1819 to 1824, including
some belonging here whose deaths happened abroad.

1819.	1820.
Capt. Samuel Houston 92.	Mr. Jerome Stephenson 82
Dr. Charles Hall 41.	Mr. Archibald York's wife
Mr. Ziba Hall Jr.	Mr. John Thurston's wife
Mr. John Sargents wife	Mr. Andrew Leach
Mr. Abraham Clark	Mr. Nathaniel Johnson
Mr. James Gilbreth	Mr. John Houston
Mr. James Read	Mr. Issachar Thistle's wife
Mr. Soloman Hamilton	Mrs. Sarah Knowlton
Miss Lydia Quin	Mr. Daniel Batchelder's wife
Maj. Wm. Cunningham's wife	Miss Esther Gilbreth
Capt. James Doyle's wife	Mr. John Huse
Mr. John Brown's wife	Mr. Alexander Clark's wife, 49.
Mr. Andrew Patterson's child	Mr. George Barter.
Mr. Jesse Basford	Mr. John Winkley +
Mr. Robbins	Mr. William Davis' child
Mr. Caleb Stevenson's child	Mr. Zacheus Porter's child
Capt. John Wales' child	Mr. Peter Rowe's child
Mr. Samuel Buckmar's child	Maj. John Russ' child
Mr. Elijah Patterson's wife	Mr. Otho Abbot's child
The eight last named died of the Small	Mr. Benjamin Cunningham's child
Pox.	Mr. Paul wentworth's child
Mr. Jones	Mr. Daniel Batchelder's child
Miss Clemenia Toward	Mr. Jeremiah Swan's child.
Mr. William Mayhew	1821
Capt. Samuel Bird *	Mrs. McCrillis
Mr. Samuel Brown's child	Miss Betsey Gilmore
Mr. Hugh Ross' child	Mr. Josiah Twitchel's wife
Mr. William Mayhew's child	Miss Miriam A. Cross
Col. Philip Morrill's child	Capt. Benj. Hazeltine's wife
Capt. James Doyle's child	Capt. William White *
Mr. Samuel Tyler's child	Capt. Phineas Kellam *

---
11. Now the High schoolhouse.
12. He was promised $500, besides aid from abroad.
13. At the corner of Miller and Cross streets.

[List of persons who have died in Belfast - continued]

[1821]
Mr. Elisha Small*
Mr. William C. Kimball *
Mr. James Smith
Mr. Martin Patterson *
Mr. Paul Giles *
Capt. David Pierce's wife
Capt. Thomas Stewart
Mrs.   Jones 84
Mr. Daniel Thurston *
Capt. James Cunningham's wife
Mr. Simon D. McDonald's wife
Mr. Henry Burk's son *
Mr. Ephraim Coulson's son
Mr. Ebenezer Burgess' wife
Mr. Laughlin McDonald
Mr. Joseph P. Ladd's child
Mr. Peter Rowe's child
Mr. Charles Bran's child
Mr. George P. Day's child
Mr. William Pitcher's child
Mr. Jeremiah Walker's child
Mr. Eleazer Davis' child
Mr. David Goddard's child
Mr. Issachar Thistle's child
Mr. Thomas Pickard's child
Mr. Alexander C. Todd's child
Mr. Silvanus Gallison's child
    1822
Mr. George Cochran 85
Mr. James Shirley 57
Mr. William Patterson
Col. Thomas Cunningham 42
Benjamin Whittier, Esq. 39
Mr. Abel B. Eastman
Mr. William Davis
Mr. Joseph Williamson's wife
Mr. David Elliot's wife
Mr. Samuel Walton's wife
Mr. William Wording's wife
Mr. Hiram Emery
Mr. John Pace's wife
Miss Lavina Thompson +
Miss Abigail West
Miss Jane Patterson
Mr. Franklin M. McKeen
Mr. Noah Matthews +
Mr. John Merriam's son
Mr. John Hopkins' son
Capt. Harvey B. Eells' child
Mr. Caleb Stephenson's child
Mr. John Roberts' child
Mr. William Frederick's child
Col. Philip Morrill's child
Mr. Nicholas Phillip's child
Mr. Josiah Twitchel's child
Mr. Thomas Clark's child

    1823
Mr. John Durham 74
Mr. Greenleaf Porter *
Mr. Moses Prescott
Mrs. Martha True
Mrs.   Woodward
Mrs. Hannah Huse *
Miss Nancy Kidder
Miss Margaret Lymburner
Miss Mary E. Jackson
Mr. Zaccheus Porter's child
Mr. Joshua Adams' child
Mr. Nicholas Phillips child
Capt. Nathan Swan's child
Capt. Josiah Simpson's son
Mr. Peter Holmes' son
Mr. James Durham's child
Mr. William Quimby's child
Mr. Samuel Jacksons Jr. child
Young man at Capt. N. Eells +
    1824
Capt. Soloman Kimball 73
Mr. Samuel Huse
Mr. James Patterson 80
Mr. Milton Patterson
Hezekiah Torrey Esq.
Mr. Nathaniel Holden
Mr. Andrew McFarland *
Mr. Caleb Smith 58
Robert Houston Esq. 60
Mr. Jonathan Clark 78 +
Mr. Henry Pendleton *
Mrs. Starret P. White
Mr. Ralph Matthews +
Mr. Michael Nortol * [Norton]
Mr. Daniel Davis
Mr. John Brown
Zaccheus Porter Esq. 44
Capt. William Furber's son *
Mr. Oliver Lane +
Mr. Leonard Crosby's wife
Mr. Samuel Jackson's wife
Mrs. Sturtivant
Mr. Gershom F.Cox's wife
Mr. Thomas Pickard's wife
Mrs.   Houston
Mrs. Harriet Smith *
Mr. Abraham Libby's wife
Miss Julia Longfellow
Miss Hannah Rowe +
Miss Mary Stanley
Miss Emeline Stanley
Mr. Nathan Stanley Jr.
Capt. Miller's Sailor +
Mrs. Giles child
Mr. John Thurston's child
Mr. John P. Kimball's child

[1824]
Mr. Soloman Cunningham's child
Mr. William Torrey's child *
Mr. Thomas Houston's child
Mr. Edward Wight's child
Mr. Josiah Hall's child
Mr. Cyrus Hall's child
Mr. Benjamin Eells' child
Mr. Dennis Emery's child
Mr. Thomas Flagner's child
Mr. Benjamin Monro's child
Mr. Isaac Dunham's child
William Ryan's child
Mr. William Ryan's child
Mr. Robert Smart's child
Mr. Josiah D.Hinds' child
Mr. Josiah D. Hinds' child
Mr. James Kelloch's child
Mr. James Kellock's child
Mr. William White's Jr. child
Mr. Lewis Bean's Jr. child
Mr. Nathaniel Patterson's 2nd child
Mr. John B. Durham's child
Mr. Jacob Cunningham's child
Mr. Benjamin Brown
Mr. Elijah Torrey's child
Mr. Andrew W. Park's child
Mr. James Morrice *

*denotes died abroad. + belonged abroad.
Figures denote the age.

List of Moderators presiding at meetings for the choice of Town Officers
in Belfast. Also Clerks, Selectmen,
Treasurers, Constables & Representatives.
1773 to 1825.

MODERATORS

1773	Thomas Goldthwait *	1773
1774	John Brown *	1774
1775	John Tufts *	1777
1778	John Mitchel *	1778
1779	John Brown *	1779
1785	John Tufts *	1786
1787	James Patterson *	1787
1788	Samuel McKeen *	1788
1789	John Brown *	1789
1790	Jerome Stephenson *	1790
1791	John Brown *	1792
1793	Lemuel Weeks *	1794
1795	Jerome Stephenson *	1796
1797	Tolford Durham	1797
1798	Jonathan Wilson	1798
1799	Robert Steel *	1799
1800	Jonathan Wilson	1800
1801	Thomas Cunningham	1804
1805	William Crosby	1811
1812	Oakes Angier	1812
1813	Thomas Cunningham	1813
1814	Jonathan Wilson	1814

1815	William Crosby	1815
1816	Jonathan Wilson	1816
1817	Bohan P. Field	1818
1819	William Crosby	1819
1820	Bohan P. Field	1823
1824	William White	

CLERKS

1773	John Mitchell *	1775
1775	Samuel Houston *	1780
1785	Samuel Houston *	1791
1791	Alexander Clark	1800
1800	Jonathan Wilson	1813
1813	William Moody	1814
1814	Benjamin Whittier *	1815
1815	William Moody	1816
1816	Benjamin Whittier *	1822
1822	Herman Abbot.	

SELECTMEN

1773	John Brown *	1777
1773	Benjamin Nesmith *	1776
1773	James Patterson *	1777
1776	John Tufts *	1777
1777	Solon Stephenson *	1780
1777	Robert Patterson	1780
1777	Alexander Clark	1780
1785	Samuel Houston	1788
1785	James Patterson *	1787
1785	John Cochran *	1791
1787	Solon Stephenson *	1790
1788	Tolford Durham	1790 .
1790	Jonathan Wilson	1791
1790	Robert Steel *	1792
1791	Samuel McKeen *	1793
1791	Alexander Clark	1792
1792	Samuel Houston	1797
1792	Jonathan Wilson	1794
1793	James Miller	1794
1794	James Nesmith *	1795
1794	Robert Steel *	1797
1795	James Miller	1796
1796	Alexander McMillan	1799
1797	Henry True *	1798
1797	Nathaniel Patterson	1798
1798	Robert Houston *	1802
1798	Daniel Clary	1800
1799	Ephraim McFarland	1800
1800	James Nesmith	1803
1800	James Miller	1801
1801	Thaddeus Spring *	1802
1802	Samuel Houston	1803
1802	John Cochran	1805
1803	Robert Houston *	1805
1803	James Miller	1804
1804	Thomas Cunningham	1805
1805	William Crosby	1806
1805	Reuben Derby *	1806
1805	Tolford Durham	1806
1806	William Moody	1810

[Selectmen - Contd.]

1806	Bohan P. Field	1808
1806	Samuel Houston	1809
1808	Isaac Senter	1809
1809	Henry Goddard	1811
1809	George Watson	1810
1810	Samuel Houston	1813
1810	John Merriam	1811
1811	George Watson	1814
1811	Benjamin Poor *	1812
1812	Benjamin Whittier *	1813
1813	Jonathan White	1814
1813	Joseph Houston	1814
1814	Asa Edmunds	1815
1814	Nathaniel Eells	1815
1814	Robert Patterson	1815
1815	George Watson	1817
1815	Jonathan White	1817
1815	Joseph Houston	1816
1816	Robert Patterson	1817
1817	Manasseh Sleeper	1820
1817	Nathaniel Eells	1818
1817	John Merriam	1819
1818	James McCrillis	1825
1819	John S. Kimball	1820
1820	John Merriam	1823
1820	Nathan Swan	1822
1822	Manasseh Sleeper	1823
1823	Philip Morrill	1824
1823	William Avery	1824
1824	George Watson	1825
1824	Salathiel Nickerson	1825
1825	Rufus B. Allyn	
1825	Joseph Smith	
1825	Samuel Gordon	

TREASURERS

1773	John Barnet	1779
1779	John Cochran	1780
1785	John Tufts	1786
1786	Tolford Durham	1796
1796	Jonathan Wilson	1797
1797	Solon Stephenson	1798
1798	Tolford Durham	1802
1802	James Nesmith	1805
1805	Bohan P. Field	1806
1806	James Nesmith *	1809
1809	John Wilson	1812
1812	John Huse	1813
1813	John Angier	1814
1814	John Merriam	1815
1815	John Cochran	1817
1817	Asa Edmunds	1818
1818	John S. Kimball	1820
1820	Zacheus Porter	1821
1821	Rufus B. Allyn	1822
1822	John S. Kimball	1823
1823	Samuel French	1824
1824	Thomas Marshall	

CONSTABLES

1773	William Patterson	1775
1775	Nathaniel Patterson	1776
1776	John Durham *	1777
1777	John Davidson	1778
1778	James Miller *	1779
1779	John Brown *	1780
1785	John Brown	1786
1786	John Tufts	1787
1787	James Patterson	1788
1788	Samuel Houston	1789
1789	Benjamin Nesmith	1790
1790	Solon Stephenson	1791
1791	William Patterson	1792
1792	James Miller	1793
1793	John Cochran	1794
1794	Robert Patterson	1795
1795	Jonathan Wilson	1796
1796	John Brown *	1797
1797	Robert Steel *	1798
1798	John Cochran	1799
1799	William Houston	1800
1800	John Brown *	1801
1801	Nathaniel Eells	1802
1802	Jeremiah Bean	1803
1803	Paul Giles *	1804
1804	Thomas Reed	1805
1805	John Russ	1806
1806	Abel Baker	1809
1809	John Merriam	1810
1810	Thomas Cunningham *	1815
1815	John Merriam	1817
1817	Stephen Longfellow	1821
1821	Samuel Cunningham	1821
1821	Robert Patterson	1822
1822	Nathaniel M. Lowney	1823
1823	Thomas Cunningham	1824
1824	Stephen Longfellow	1825
1825	John Wagg	
1825	John T. Poor	
1825	Isaac B. Ulmer	

REPRESENTATIVES

1803	Jonathan Wilson	1805
1806	John Wilson	1807
1807	Thomas Whittier *	1808
1808	Jonathan Wilson	1810
1810	Thomas Whittier *	1812
1812	George Watson	1814
1812	Jonathan Wilson	1813
1816	John Merriam	1817
1818	William White	1819
1819	Alfred Johnson	1821
1819	John S. Kimball	1820
1821	Ralph C. Johnson	1822
1822	James McCrillis	1824
1824	George Watson	1825
1825	James McCrillis	

FINIS

A

HISTORY OF BELFAST

With Introductory Remarks

on Acadia

by

William White

PICTON PRESS

CAMDEN, MAINE
1989

Annals of Belfast for Half a Century by William George Crosby (1805-1881) was originally published in fifty-two installments in the Belfast, Maine newspaper *The Republican Journal*, 1874-75

Sketches of the Early History of Belfast by John Lymburner Locke (1832-1876) was originally published in serialized form in the Belfast, Maine newspaper *The Progressive Age* in sixteen issues beginning 10 April 1856.

History of Belfast From its First Settlement to 1825 by Herman Abbot (1783-1825) remained in manuscript form at the time of his death and for many years was feared lost. When the manuscript was finally rediscovered it was published in serial form in four issues of *The Republican Journal* of Belfast beginning 25 Jan 1900, and was then published in Belfast, also in 1900, by Miss Grace E. Burgess.

A History of Belfast with Introductory Remarks on Acadia by William White (1783-1831) was first published in Belfast, Maine in 1827, and was the first bound book published in that town.

Transcription of all four histories above was done for this volume by Elizabeth M. Mosher, RFD 2 Box 825, City Point, Belfast, Maine 04915

Available from:

Picton Press
P. O. Box 1111
Camden, Maine 04843
Manufactured in the United States of America
using acid-free paper

A
HISTORY OF BELFAST
WITH
INTRODUCTORY REMARKS
ON
ACADIA

BY WILLIAM WHITE

BELFAST: PUBLISHED BY E. FELLOWES.   1827

DEDICATION.

These pages have been prepared for the inhabitants of Belfast, and to them they are respectfully inscribed by their fellow citizen

THE AUTHOR

March, 1827

ADVERTISEMENT

Doctor HERMAN ABBOT had collected many facts, with the view of compiling a history of the town of Belfast. All the good purposes and labours of that worthy man were ended in his death, which occurred in the midst of his great usefulness, and filled society with grief. His memoranda, by his administrator were placed in the possession of the author, who has found them accurate and useful. And that no part of them should be lost to the public, the manuscript is lodged in the Town Clerk's office.

The manuscripts of Chadwicke and of Mitchell, and the books of the proprietors of the township; the town records, and the records in the land office and the office of Secretary of State of Massachusetts have been carefully consulted. The aim was a compilation of facts; so far as opportunity and talent has permitted, in both which the author is much restricted, they are faithfully collected and recorded. Should this sketch preserve a single incident, or material, suitable to be used hereafter when the history of the State shall be written, this essay will not have been altogether in vain.

PREFACE

History has the advantage of addressing itself to the strongest of the human passions, self-love; therefore, man in every condition in life from the rudest to the most polished, regards it with peculiar interest. Who is there that has not a strong desire to know what passed among his ancestors? And who is there that does not believe that posterity will be equally desirous to know the fortunes of their ancestors? In this manner we are made to enjoy the past and the future as well as the present; we are brought to a knowledge of generations that are gone by; and seem also to have a being with those that are yet to be born.

Nations so rude as to have no knowledge of letters or arts, indulge this passion for history in raising mounds of earth, or heaps of stone, or other monuments, and rehearse songs and ballads, to perpetuate the deeds of ages past; and to them it is a pleasure superior to all others, excepting that of recounting their own exploits. Among civilized nations this passion grows in proportion to the means of gratifying it; and it is well, if it excite, as nature intended, the industry of the mind to improvement in virtue; and make better men, and better citizens, by teaching them philosophy in the school of example. In the following pages the author has cautiously avoided any impeachment of the actions, opinions, or motives of the living; and of the dead he has been no less careful that nothing but the truth be spoken.

PART FIRST

This memoir, assuming to be the history of a town only, will go
first into a brief detail of the political occurrences connected with
the discovery and early history of the ancient province in which Belfast
is situated.

If any apology were required for this course, it might be found,
in the consideration, that no condensed view of this subject is a present
to be had. The incidents of interest connected with that portion of
Acadia, included in the present Commonwealth of Maine, are scattered
through many books, some of which have become rare; and many records
and manuscripts to which access is with difficulty obtained.

Cabot [1497], Casper de Cortereal [1500], Verrassano [1524], Horn [1536],
Whitborn [1579], Humphrey Gilbert [1583], Bernard Drake [1586], George
Weymouth [1593], Anthony Shirley [1597], Charles Leigh [1597], LaRoche
[1598], Goswold [1602], and Martin Pring [1603] in the order they are
mentioned, and in the several years noted, on voyages of discovery had
visited the eastern frontier of North America; but discovered no intention
of effecting any permanent settlement. The French took some fish on
the banks in 1504, and seventeen years afterwards fifty vessels of the
several European nations were engaged in that employment (1).   In 1522,
fifty houses had been erected on Newfoundland (2). The number of fishing
vessels had increased by 1578 to three hundred and fifty (3).

Pierre du Gast (4), a servant in great favour with majesty, and
one of the bed chamber of Henry IV, was appointed Lieutenant General
of Acadia and the adjoining country, with an authority, civil as well
as military, unrestricted.

The Lettres (5), gave him all that portion of America between 40^0
and 46^0 of north latitude, from the atlantic ocean westward to the western
ocean (6).

Early in the following year du Gast embarked for America. He entered
upon the expedition with all the zeal, that a well founded hope of becoming
the sole prince of so wide a dominion, might be supposed to excite.
His fleet arrived on the coast at a harbour now called Liverpool (7). On
doubling the Cape Sable and entering the bay of Funday they discovered
the harbour of Port Royal; with which, Poutrincourt, a friend of du
Gast, was so delighted, that no less could be done, than to make it
his by formal assignment (8).

After surveying the Bay, du Gast ran down the coast as far at least
as Kinnibekei; and returning he passed the winter in a fort which he
built on an island in a river by him named St. Croix, which was the
first settlement of Europeans in Arcadia.

At this period, the public mind became generally awakened in Europe,
and making discoveries and planting colonies in America, was the most
fashionable of princely employments.

In England, the Earl of Southhampton with his associates, was deeply
interested in the subject; and George Weymouth, who twelve years before
had been on the Labrador coast, was by them equipped and commissioned
to cross the Atlantic in search of a north west passage to China.

------

1.   Anderson's history of commerce, 2d. 9-34.
2.   American Annals, 1, 67.
3.   Anderson, 2, 144.
4.   Sieur de Monts; Sullivan in his history has it De Motte.
5.   L'Escarbot, 417. See appendix No. 1.
6.   Hazard Coll. page 45, the letters are dated Nov. 8th, 1603.
7.   Belknap's Biog. 1,324.
8.   American Annals, page 148, note 5.

This distinguished naval officer has the reputation of commanding the first European ship, that is known to have entered the Penobscot river (9).   It was in early summer that Weymouth entered the river, when the forest trees are the richest and the proudest of all the trees, and the scenery was new and bold and imposing. He was lost in solemn delight.   On his return to England he published a history of his voyage; and his imagination communicated to his story the spirit and coloring of romance.   At first his book gave to the friends of colonization a more extended and animated support (10); afterwards it was condemend as a collection of fables.

The abode for one winter, of Popham and Gilbert (11), with 43 others on Parker's Island at the mouth of Kennebec river, cannot be considered a settlement [1607-8], but Aaldworth and Elbridge who twenty one years afterwards planted themselves at Bristol, made their patent effectual by an uninterrupted occupation of the teritory, and in 1631 received a grant from the Plymouth Company of Devon, investing them severally of 6000 acres, each of their people or servants of 100 acres; and fifty acres for each child that should be born to the individuals of the company within seven years next after the Grant.   In some instances the lineal descendants of these grantees are now, the possessors.   In the same year that Bristol was settle Charles 1st of England made letters patent, (12) to Beauchamp and Leverett investing them of the title to a tract of land east of the Muscongus river and bounded upon it,--and from the Atlantic ocean extending ten leagues into the land.

The description in this grant implies an intention of conveying a teritory ten leagues square (13); but the language adopted is full of uncertainty, and much perplexity ensued in settling its limits.

France in the mean time had made great progress in fortifying her positions on and near the Bay of Funday, and the right of sovereignty over that portion of Maine which has the Kennebec and Androscoggin rivers for its western boundary was claimed by both kingdoms.   For a century and a half the question remained unsettled; although it was repeatedly made the subject to treaty between the two nations; and not until Quebeck came into the possession of England, was France willing entirely to relinquish all hope of holding a footing upon this part of the new continent.

During this stormy period, whenever the animosity of these rival nations, for any cause was about to discover itself in action, some transaction by authority in Acadia could readily be found to furnish a plausible pretext for war.   And these nations, polished as they are, have been, perhaps more than most others, accustomed to enforce their doubtful claims when resisted, by the last argument of kings.

In these conflicts contrary to all humanity the savage was enlisted; an enemy so ferocious as to make it his amusement to torment his captive. To the sudden invasions of these merciless butchers (14), the provincials were continually exposed.   So long as the settlements were few and weak they were made to suffer. Those, having been planted under the countenance of one nation, were not to expect in the character of the other any thing but enmity. They preyed upon each other. The inducements the country offered to emigrants were greatly diminished in value by this unsettled and turbulent state of the province. And the melancholy fate

---

9.   1605, Belknap's Biog. vol. 2, page 149. American Ann. 151.

10.   In the next year 1606 the grants of North Virginia and South Virginia were made. Sullivan, 272.

11.   "The place was occupied soon after by the French" Sir Samuel Argal removed them in 1613 Sullivan (Hubbard) 170.

12.   Hazard Coll. page 315 vol. 1st.

13.   John Gleason Esq. has the original charter.   See Appendix, No. 2.

14.   Smollett's England, vol. 2, page 575. Phila. ed. 1822.

that awaited those, or many of them, who had the hardihood to encounter
the sufferings connected with the attempt to effect a settlement within
the contested territory, was made a standing theme of popular lamentation.

For reasons like these, Acadia continued an almost unbroken wilderness,
after villages had been planted on the northern and western borders,
and had grown into comparative importance.

Sir Samuel Argal of Virginia, in 1613 (15), found some French families
at Penobscot, and also at Mount Mansel (16), now Mount Desert, and dislodged
them;   and proceeding eastward, seized the forts of St. John, Port Royal,
and La Have, and made prize of the goods and effects they contained.
He took with him on his return to Virginia the French settled at the
mouth of the Kennebec.   The English had not, as yet, extended their
views beyond the Penobscot; and the French returned to their more eastern
positions.   Sulivan says, the Plymouth Colony first visited the Penobscot
in 1621 (17); this is probably in error, for in three other instances,
(18) the same historian dates the building of the fort or trading-house
at Castine in 1626, and Hutchinson fixes the year to be 1627 (19); and
Bristol we have seen was settled in the following year.

The settlement at Castine paid no regard to agriculture; the sole
object of that little community was peace and trade with the savages.

James I of England had made a compliment of Nova Scotia, the English
name for Acadia, to Sir William Alexander (20), and Sir William had
sold it to France; and the fort at Castine with the property appurtenant
was claimed by the French under the conveyance (21).   In 1632 a French
vessel visited the Penobscot, "having a false Scot aboard;" (22), they
seized the fortress, pillaged it of 500₤ in property, and departed.
The post remained with the English until 1635, when Rossillan, Governor
of La Have, despatched D'Aulney to take and hold the possession.   Let
not France be hastily censured for these measures.   Her subjects, as
we have seen, had purchased the country of England, and in the treaty
of St. Germains, 1632, "the frenchified court of king Charles," (23)
confirmed the sovereignty of Acadia in the French throne (24).

Girling, commanding an English armed ship, at the instigation of
the Plymouth colony, immediately attempted to regain the fort at Penobscot,
but without success, and France was left in actual possession until
1654 (25).

D'Aulney was made Governor of Pentagoet (26), and died in that
office in 1651 (27).   At this time Cromwell was at war with Holland,
and send Col. Sedgwick against New-York, the strong hold of the Dutch
in America.--Peace was made before Sedgwick had an opportunity to bring
his armament into action, and he turned his attention upon Acadia.--First
he possessed himself of the fort at Penobscot, and afterwards every
other fortress or settlement on the Acadian frontier.

If the Protector did not in his general commission direct the expedition, he made no public disavowal of the conduct of Sedgwick, and could

----

15.   Hutchinson, 1, 32.
16.   Sullivan, 274, 275.
17.   Page 274.
18.   Pages 275, 157 and 158.
19.   Page 32
20.   1621, Sept. 10.   Confirmed 1625, July 12.   Sir William conveyed
1620, April 30, to French gentlemen named, on condition that they are
and will be faithful to Scotland.   Jefferson's notes, 244 and onward.
21.   Hutchinson, 33.
22.   Gov. Bradford's report in Hutchinson, page 34.
23.   Hutchinson's expression, page 34, vol. 1.
24.   American Annals, 265.
25.   Am. annals, 284.
26.   The original French name of Castine, &c.
27.   Sullivan, 282.

never be persuaded to restore (28), the conquered territory. But his successor in 1667 was more complaisant, while a Dutch fleet was carrying war and terror up the Thames, and to free England under such circumstances a peace was purchased of the "allies" upon the best terms to be obtained; and France recovered the possession of her favorite Acadia.

During the past time, the Indians, under various provocations, by them alleged, manifested an increasing bitterness of enmity towards the English settlements. That their complaints had no foundation, is not to be readily admitted. In the fur trade they were liable to be duped; and if afterwards they discovered the imposition it was considered an affront not to be forgotten. In attempting to avenge it they sometimes shed blood.--Themselves sometimes suffered--in either result the contest was food for their implacable resentment.

In the year 1665, Charles II granted to the Duke of York the section of country lying between Pemaquid on the west and the river St. Croix; and, in 1677, the Duke directed his Governor, resident at New-York, to enter upon the patent and hold it in possession. Andros accordingly sent a force to Pemaquid, and erected a fort, and established a garrison; and the settlements in that vicinity were joined by many Dutch families from New-York (29).

This fort for some years served to hold the neighboring savages in awe; especially those upon the Penobscot.

Soon after the peace of Breda, the French regiment of Carignan was disbanded in Canada; and the commander the excentric St. Castiens came to Penobscot, and took possession of the plantation which Col. Temple had recently abandoned. The Baron, for so Castiens is called, greatly enlarged the gardens, and renewed and strengthened the fort; his object was trade with the savages; he had learned their language in Canada, and although a "gentleman of fortune," was not averse to their solitary habits of life.

The Baron opened a large trade in fish and furs, which he received in exchange for European merchandize. Naturally artful and insinuating, and being well informed, he soon rendered himself the idol and oracle of the indian tribes. Madocawando, the Sachem of Penobscot, gave to the Baron his favorite daughter, to grace the circle of his indian wives; and whenever the interests of the tribe were at hazard, the father-in-law took council with his son, whose secret influence was felt throughout all the settlements in New England. In some instances the Baron led the tribe to battle (30).

When Acadia, as far as St. Croix, became a part of the Massachusetts by charter [1692], this already powerful colony began the needful work of protecting the interests of the settlements within that territory. The fort built by Andros at Pemaquid had fallen and decayed. The General Court authorized Gov. Phipps to rebuild it with stone; and with all possible expedition the work was executed.

Nor was this all that Massachusetts conceived for the good of their new subjects; a statute was enacted and published, prohibiting under penalty any subject of France from Entering any port in the new portion of the province, without license first obtained from the Governor and council.

Measures less imperious in their bearing would probably, by France, have been deemed a sufficient provocation for renewing the war.

Massachusetts was to be taught, that legislation alone could not prove a sufficient security for her, of the newly acquired territory.

---

28. Cromwell granted Acadia to Etienne, Crown and Temple in 1656. Making the river St. George the western boundary.--Hazard coll. 1, 616. Col. Temple lived at Penobscot some years.--Sullivan, 158.

29. Belknap's N. H. 1, 158. Sullivan's M. 160. Am. Annals, 442.

30. Abbe Raynal, 7, 219. LaHouton's voyages.

Officers of merit, Iberville and Bonaventure, were commissioned for the service; and with a sufficient fleet arrived in Penobscot bay. Here Castiens joined them with a force of two hundred indians of Penobscot. Of savages, he was a worthy chief. The united force appeared at Pemaquid, on the fourteenth day of August, and beseiged the fort.

No declaration of war had preceded this movement; nothing had transpired to put the garrison on their guard. They were suitably equipped, and sufficiently strong in numbers, to resist the assaults of the tribes of savages that surrounded them. The summons from this great force to surrender the fortress, received an answer of defiance, and the battle began.

An attempt was made to storm the fortress, which proved unsuccessful; and Castiens foresaw that much time would be required to secure their object, if sought through the ordinary modes of warfare; and that what could be done, must be done, before knowledge of the expedition should reach Boston. He formed his purpose, that if they continued to resist, but without final success, they should be given up to the rage of his savages; that in prompt submission alone they were to hope for safety. Such information was appalling to the soldiery to whom Castiens contrived to communicate it in a letter under his own hand; and they constrained their commander to capitulate. No time was lost in demolishing the fort; and after a stay of some days at Penobscot the armament returned to the Bay of Fundy (31).

The surrender was deemed by the government of Massachusetts to have been precipitate, and the commander of the fort was deprived of his commission. The treaty of Ryswick in the following year, was altogether illusory, so far as it concerned the American Colonies.

M. Villabon, in 1698, renewed the war by exciting the savages; and his views were promoted by Ralle, a French Jesuit, who had taken a residence with the Indians at Norridgwog. In him the French had found another Castiens; as a priest, he had secured the confidence of the natives, and moved them as he was instructed by the government of Quebec.

The English settlements had long been greatly annoyed by this tribe; and Capt. Harmon and Capt. Moulton were despatched from York [1724] to destroy them. The expedition was managed with energy; eighty of the tribe, with their priest, were slain; their altar broken down, and their dwellings demolished (32). It was a check so severe, that savage courage never after recovered its accustomed tone in the province.

The treaty of Utrecht (1713) it was expected would forever quiet French claims to Acadia. That instrument in the twelfth particular provision, confirmed the province to England, as the same was described in the treaty of St. Germains, or as ancient Acadia (33).

The Island of Cape Bretton only remained to France. The ancient Acadia was bounded by Henry IV. in this grant to De Monts. The treaty had in some respects restricted it.--The French ministry intended to restrict it much more. They were indignantly opposed; and the colonies still found themselves at war, notwithstanding the declaration of peace.

Beauchamp and Leverett, before mentioned, had not entered upon their patent; and in 1719, John Leverett, at that time Governor of Massachusetts, representing himself sole heir of Thomas Leverett, who as the survivor of Beauchamp, became the sole proprietor, prefered his claim to the estate.

Mr. Leverett found many impediments to the establishment of his title; and made it convenient, in order to overcome them, to associate with him nine other persons of great consideration; one of whom was

31. Hutchinson, 2d, 89, 133, 286.
32. Belknap's N. H. 2d, page 60.
33. See Appendix No. 3.

Sir William Phipps, who in his right, brought into the company the Indian deed of Madocawando, conveying the interest the tribe had claimed in the territory. These were afterwards called "the ten proprietors." Subsequently, and in the same year, 1719, twenty other persons were made to share an interest in the patent. By this time, so much of the nobility of Massachusetts had become personally interested in the claim, that its merits were easily made manifest.

But under the treaty of Utretcht the British Crown prefered claim, by right of conquest and cession, to the whole province of Acadia, nothwithstanding it had been, by the same crown, before granted. This was not to have been expected. As subjects of Great Britain, the company had supposed that the benefit of the cession from France to England would belong to them; as England, at a previous period, when their right was not in dispute, with consideration, had bestowed it upon those from whom the claim of the company was derived.

The pertinacity of ministers so alarmed the thirty proprietors, that in 1732 they joined in a deed of one entire half of the patent to Gen. Samuel Waldo, in consideration that he would obtain from the crown a relinquishment of this arbitrary claim.

After many years of untiring application at court, Waldo procured a reference of the question to the "law officers of the crown," who found but little difficulty in forming an opinion in favor of the company.

It was afterwards agreed by the company to dissolve the partnership, and divide the estate. The ten proprietors took to their share Frankfort and that vicinity. The twenty before named, had Camden, Hope, Appleton, Montville and Montville Plantation set to them; and the residue of the patent appertained to Waldo. When the boundaries of the patent came to be ascertained by actual inspection, it was found that Waldoborough river, and a line from the head thereof to the northwest corner of Thorndike thence on the north line of Thorndike, Jackson, Monroe and Frankfort to the river, and thence by the river and bay of Penobscot to the sea shore, and thence by the sea shore to the mouth of Waldoborough river, embraced the territory granted.

The necessary surveys were effected by Waldo in 1759, and in September of that year he died at fort Pownal in Prospect.--The general court of Massachusetts Bay in 1762, confirmed the title of the respective claimants to the territory described; and the state legislature in 1785 repeated the same act of confirmation. Two fifths of the Waldo claim having however been sequestered by the state, in the interval, was purchased by Gen. Knox, who had acquired the other portions also, two fifths by purchase, and one by marriage.

After the peace of Utrecht, British power in Acadia began to assume an imposing attitude. The indians, becoming sensible of their growing weakness, began to be more pacific. Massachusetts was already formidable, and entertained no kindness towards France. French influence was rapidly declining in all the northern provinces, add the loss of Louisburg, in 1745, the founding of Halifax, in 1748, and the capture of Quebec in 1759 (34), extingushed her last hope.

---

34.   In this year Gov. Pownall built the fort in Prospect, at the cost of 4969 ₤; 17s: 2d. and placed in it a garrison consisting of one hundred men. The year previous, the Indians had made an assault upon fort George and the settlements on Georges' river. After fort Pownal was built nothing more is heard of their ravages. Amer. Annals.

PART SECOND.

The province of Ulster in Ireland, having fallen into the crown by attainder of rebels, James I. of England, introduced companies of farmers from England and Scotland, to improve and enjoy that fertile section of the United Kingdom.

A society of Presbyterians from Scotland, were among them. In the reign of Charles I. and that of James II. protestantism was not favored in London; in Ireland it was persecuted. These presbyterians had become numerous; an hundred families of them adopted the resolution of removing to America. They embarked, and with ministers of religion, according to their own forms and faith in the performance and efficacy of worship, arrived at Boston in the autumn of 1718. Early in the following year, a portion of these adventurers planted themselves in Nutfield, a plantation in the province of New Hampshire.--Their first care was to place over their religious interests James McGregore, who had accompanied them from Ireland. This little colony were industrious, frugal and pious; and necessarily become populous, and accumulated property.

Of the Israelites it was said, that the land in which they were strangers could not bear them because of their cattle; these presbyterians found it necessary to seek some Mount Seir for their accommodation.

In every direction rich land was open to purchasers; and a company was formed, who examined, and afterwards selected and purchased the site of Belfast.

The heirs of General Waldo conveyed the tract to John Mitchell and thirty one others, in shares, according to the interest of each proprietor.

[The following is a list of the names of the original proprietors, with their respective number of shares annexed. The whole number being fifty-one.

John Mitchell, 6 shares--John Gilmore, 5--Robert Patterson, 3--John Steele, 3--Samuel Houston, 2--James McGregore, 2--John Tufts, 2--John Moor, 1 --Joseph Morrison, 1--John Durham, 1--William McLaughlin and William Patterson, 1--James McGregore, Jr., 1--John Brown, 1--William Clendinen, 1--John Morrison, 1--Matthew Reed, 1--Robert McElvane, 1--Alexander Wilson, 1--Alexander Stewart, 1--Alex. Little, 1--James Miller, 1--Samuel Marsh, 1--Moses Barnet, 1--John Davidson, 1--David Hemphill, 1--Matthew Chambers and James McLaughlin, 1--Nathaniel Martin, 1--Joseph Greg, 1--John Cochran, 1--Mitchell, Gilmore, Barnett, Tufts, Houston, Moor, and M'Gregore, Jr. as proprietors committee, four shares--James Gilmore, 2 shares.

Mr. John Cochran is the only surviving original proprietor, and resides in Belfast, enjoying a large circle of relatives, and possession the confidence of very many devoted friends. The evening of life is pleasant to him, and he is closing it in the enjoyment of all its substantial comforts.

The facts which Mr. Cochran has communicated, belonging to this memoir of Belfast, require and receive the acknowledgment of the compiler.]

This early purchase exempted the inhabitants of Belfast from the great evil, which the want of title, inflicted upon many other towns in Maine after the revolution; yet the entire devotion of Belfast, to the cause of freedom on that occasion, lost them all else but the bare title to their lands.

[Belfast, by the Waldo deed, is bounded from half-way creek, (being the westerly boundary of Frankfort) westerly round the harbour called Passagawassakeag to little river; 2dly, from thence upward by sundry turns in little river, about as far as salt water flows, and crossing the river to a black birch tree, computed thirty-seven chains; 3dly,

from thence south 60 degrees west 223 chains to a birch tree; 4thly,
from thence north 22 degrees west 372 chains, equal to 4 miles 203 rods
to a rock-maple tree, one rod westerly of a quarry of stones; 5thly,
from thence north 68 degrees east 602 chains, equal to seven miles and
three quarters, to the westerly line of Frankfort; 6thly, from thence
south thirty-seven chains to the largest of half-way creek ponds; 7thly,
from thence downwards by the stream, called half-way creek, to the first
mentioned place.]

In 1770, Mitchell,* Miller,+ Chambers,E Wm. McLaughlin, Wm. Patterson,
and John Cochran, of the original proprietors, and Jas. Patterson, Nathaniel
Patterson, John Morrison, and Thomas Steele,# the representatives of
others, began to open the forest preparatory to husbandry. One continued
wilderness now extended from Georges' river to the Penobscot; and until
this time, over this now busy field, the noise of labour had never distrubed
the silence of ages. When this little colony had grown to no more than
twenty-five families,** their prospects so filled them with hope, that
they requested to be incorporated; and the general court of George III.
gave their habitation a name, with the usual municipal attributes.

"Previous to executing the deed of Belfast, the grantors had employed
Richard Stimson to survey and make a suitable location for a road from
Georges' river in Thomaston to fort point in Prospect; and Stimson having
rendered the service, was to be entitled to one hundred acres of land
on any part of the route he should select. The work was performed,
and Stimson made choice of a plat on the west and adjoining to the "half-way
creek," which is the line between Belfast and Prospect. Here Stimson
with his family had arrived before the Belfast proprietors had come
into possession; and by Chadwick's survey Stimson's location is within
the town, and he may therefore be called the first settler, although
not connected with the proprietors."--Dr. Abbot's Ms.

At Mitchell's house by the shore, eastward and near the mouth of
Goose river, on the eleventh day of November, 1773, the corporation
was organized. The following is a copy of the warrant.

"To John Mitchell of Belfast, Gentleman,
GREETING.

Whereas the great and general Court at their sessions begun and
held at Boston, upon Wednesday the 26th day of May last, passed an act
for incorporating a certain tract of land, on the westerly side of Penobscot
bay into a Town by the name of Belfast in the county of Lincoln; and
the said general Court having empowered me the subscriber to issue a
warrant directed to some principal inhabitant in said town to notify
and warn, the inhabitants thereof qualified by law to vote in town affairs,
to meet at such time and place as shall be therein set forth; to choose
such officers as may be necessary to manage the affairs of said town.
At the which first meeting all the male inhabitants that become at the
age of twenty-one years, shall be admitted to vote.

These are therefore in his majesty's name to require you the said
John Mitchell to notify the said inhabitants of Belfast to meet at your
dwelling house in said town, on Thursday the 11th day of November, at
ten of the clock in the forenoon. Then and there to choose a town Clerk,
Selectmen, and all other town officers according to law. And make return

---

*   Mitchell settled upon now Thomas Reed's farm.
+   Miller where Mr. Frothingham now resides.
E   Chambers upon Judge Reed's lands.
]   McLaughlin and Patterson on Mr. Sargent's lot.
Morrison and Steele were drowned in Dec. 1770 in attempting
to return from Penobscot river, where they had been in a canoe to a
corn mill.
**   William Patterson, 2d. and Mary Mitchell were the first to
be joined in marriage. Ann Patterson was the first white child born
in the town. She was the wife of Enos West.

of this warrant, with your doings, as soon after the same is carried into execution as may be.
Given under my hand and seal at Frankfort, October, 1773.
(Signed)   THO: GOLDTHWAIT."

The inhabitants when assembled made choice of Coll Goldthwait for moderator;   4
John Mitchell, Town Clerk*; John Brown, Benjamin Nesmith, James Patterson, Selectmen; John Barnet, Treasurer; John Durham, jr. Alexander Clark, James Miller, Surveyors of highways; William Patterson, sen. Constable; John Durham, sen. James Morrow, Wardens; and thus the town became an organized body. Col. Goldthwait here mentioned is the same who at this time commanded the fort on Fort Point; to this fortress the inhabitants of Belfast were taught to look for succour in a season of distress; but on the commencement of actual hostilities with Britain, the Colonel forsook the colony and adhered closely to the crown.

This little company were immersed in a wilderness, far from the capitol of New-England, the nursery of the spirit of human freedom, then about to be developed; first to the admiration, and afterwards the applause of the civilized world; but while yet in Britain their fathers had entertained similar sentiments, and the half century they, as a people, had already passed in America only served to enlighten the views and strengthen the hopes they had inherited. Their feelings were entirely in unison with the friends of the people; and in 1776 they adopted those precautionary measures,** best calculated to secure the independence of the country.

In addition to a committee of safety, the inhabitants in 1777 elected a censor; whose duty as appears on the record of the meeting was "to lay before the General Court the misconduct of any person, by word or action against the United States;" and Solon Stevenson was appointed to this distinguished office. In 1778 the town voted unanimously to approve and adopt the constitution of government, which the Massachusetts colony had prepared for their acceptance.

The period was fast approaching when the principles of those few patriots were made to undergo the severest test. They were required to deny their professions or sacrifice their property.

General McLean+ with a force of six hundred and fifty men had established a post at Bigaduce for the protection of Nova Scotia against the incursions of the patriots. In the summer of 1779, an expedition was fitted out and despatched from Boston to make a conquest of this fortress. Seventeen ships, of all descriptions, having aboard, fifteen hundred troops, Saltonstall commodore, and Gen. Lovell commanding the army, in July arrived in the Penobscot Bay. Three small armed British vessels only were then in the harbour of Bigaduce.

Saltonstall's largest ship carried thirty-six guns. On his arrival, Mitchell and others were requested to visit the fleet and communicate their knowledge of the position and strength of the enemy; these strenuously advised Gen. Lovell to an immediate assault. They saw no formidable obstacle to entering the harbor, securing the three vessels that were there, landing the toops and marching into the fort. This counsel was not relished. It was then advised that a portion might land in the harbour, and the residue at Perkin's cove, which was taking the enemy in front and in rear at the same time; this advice was also disregarded.

---

*   The Town Clerks that have succeeded Mitchell are seven. Samuel Houston, Alexander Clark, Jonathan Wilson, William Moody, Benjamin Whittier, Herman Abbot, Nathaniel H. Bradbury.
    **   John Tufts, John Brown, Solon Stevenson, James Patterson, and Samuel Houston Committee of Safety. John Tufts Representative. John Tufts to be Justice of the Peace.
    + Bissett's England, vol. 1, page 612.

But, in his own time, Lovell landed his men in one body, at Dice's head, a bank so bold and so elevated, as to be ascended by any army only with great difficulty, when no opposition should be offered!   McLean had posted a detachment on the summit and disputed the ground.   A landing was effected, with the loss of thirteen patriots killed and a number wounded.

Lovell now had his foe in his grasp.   But he sets himself down before the fortress, and makes dispositions for a regular siege.   The breast work of the enemy was a fence of rails slatted perpendicularly with pipe staves.   Weeks were consumed in this indecisive warfare; when Admiral Collier, despatched from New York, arrived in the Bay with a respectable squadron, in aid of McLean.   At once all was confusion. 4* Lovell broke up his camp and evacuated it in the night of the thirteenth of August.   Saltonstall pushed his ships aground wherever he was able; and they were burned.   The sailors and soldiers took themselves to flight. Defeat was never more absolute.   And the inhabitants of Belfast found themselves left at the mercy of a conquering enemy.   The first care of the British was to enlarge the fortress and render it more permanent, and add to the strength of the garrison.

The inhabitants were then offered the privilege of British protection if they would merit it by an oath of allegiance and fidelity to the British king.   The proposition filled them with disgust.   The spirit of freedom which had for so many generations warmed the blood of their ancestors was theirs by inheritance; and the profer was rejected, and such intrepidity left them no choice; to the last man they abandoned their homes, leaving their flocks in the pastures and the corn in the fields ready for harvest.   Not one remained to tell a passing stranger the cause of the entire desolation that ensued.

The war filled the country with marauders, who in small parties visited the coast in search of plunder.   A clan of these freebooters landed on the eastern shore of the town, near Moose Point, where it happened they were met by some patriots.   They attempted to make a prisoner of Richard Stimson and were resisted.   One of the marauders was killed, but Stimson escaped.   On the next day a boat came from the fort on the peninsula,* and burned the house and barn of Samuel Houston, on the ground where his son, Joseph Houston, now resides.

After the peace many of the first settlers returned, and the town began to attract public attention.   New-England, as yet, was not populous and new settlements made progress but slowly.   It was not before March, 1785, that population had so much increased as to need municipal restraint and directions.   Jonathan Buck, Esq. of Buckstown, was then authorized to issue a warrant for the inhabitants to assemble and choose whom they would have to serve them as municipal officers.

------   *   In the progress of the revolution, General Wadsworth and Major Barton were taken prisoners in fort George and carried to Castine. They broke from the fort soon after they were confined, and by wading to their mouths for half a mile through the tide, they eluded the guard and effected an escape.   By a canoe they crossed the Penobscot at Prospect, and by a circuit through the deepest woodlands they arrived finally at Belfast, exhausted.   At this time the Miller family had returned. Miller was their friend, but they dared not accept his hospitality at his house--His sons, James and Robert, went into the depths of the forest, a mile from any settlement, erected a hut and covered it with the boughs of the fir tree, made a bed of evergreens, and carried blankets to it, and food for the inmates; and there these patriots were thus hid and thus fed, until the sharpness of the search for them was done, when with a pocket compass and provisions to help them on, they pursued their course across the country and arrived at a post of safety.

At this point of time may be dated the permanent settlement of Belfast. And here a topographical notice of the subject may be taken. In this immediate region the work of creation was prosecuted on the sublimest scale.

The town is situate in latitude 44 deg. 25m. 30 sec. on the west angle of the bay of Penobscot, where the river Pasagasawakeag comes into the bay. By this river the town is nearly equally divided. The bay making round White Head, its southern angle, comes up forty miles into the country to meet the river at the town, and their confluence there forms a harbour not excelled in the world. The British navy might float in it commodiously. The town extends two miles on the west and four miles on the east side of this harbour, and Long Island and Sears' Island guard it at the entrance. On the west side and at the head of this harbour the village of Belfast is built. The bay embosoms other islands of sufficient territory for townships, and some of them are now to be numbered among the most flourishing corporations in the county. The shores of Belfast may be called beautiful. When the tide is out there is no extensive flat to disgust the eye; and the land on either side of the harbour or river rises gradually and easily for a great distance from the water. Thus the prospect is made extensive. A finer site for building a large city could not be desired. Vessels go but three miles above the town, where they have a water of eight feet.

Goose river, a small stream coming into the harbour on the east, with the surplus water of a large pond of the same name, is worthy of notice on account of the numerous opportunities it affords of applying water power to useful purposes. A large number of mills are already built upon it, and other privileges are still open.

The Penobscot river comes into the bay at the north angle, twelve miles from Belfast harbour. This noble river, for thirty miles in a direction nearly north, has a water sufficient for the safe navigation of ships of the line. Frigates have visited Bangor. Large boats and rafts find a sufficient water an hundred miles higher.

The choice arable lands in Maine it is known are not on the Atlantic border; but of all the lands upon the tide waters of New-England, it is not known that any are to be prefered to the shores of the Penobscot.

It requires the time of one life to remove the trees of a forest, and prepare the earth for cultivation. The age of Belfast therefore precludes the posibility of great advancement having been made in agriculture. Yet the town comphrehends many good farms; and the farmer of New-England, of all men, is the most happy; his comforts are mingled with no anxiety, the continuance of them does not depend on a vigilance, both painful and unwearied.

The soil and climate are suited to the growth of wheat, barley, oats and rye; the potatoe is raised in abundance and of a fine quality; and is an essentual article of food in almost every family.

In some season indian corn grows to great perfection, but is not a safe crop on the banks of the Penobscot. Grass is easily raised; consequently it is easy to make good butter and pork and feef; lambs in July are large and fat; stall fed mutton is excellent; wool is plenty; and hay is one article of export.

The cultivation of fruit has been by many neglected. In some instances apple orchards were set as soon as the ground was cleared of the forest; these now afford cider. In other cases where the work was commenced a succession of unpropitious summers discouraged the planters entirely; and in truth 1816* was nearly fatal to every thing vegetable that could

————— * Apple trees did not blossom till late in June of this year. On the tenth of that month snow fell with the wind at N. W. and the frost was quite severe. Still the crops of wheat were never better.

be destroyed by frost. Since that year the farmer has been more flattered by the seasons, and orchards now receive a very general and skilful attention. Currants are grown in great plenty. And so are cherries, and all the small stone fruit. But the peach, it is at present considered, cannot survive a Penobscot winter. The town has been greatly negligent in planting ornamental trees; and the performance of this pleasant duty in individual instances, only shows how much has been lost by the general inexcusable omission.

The citizens, in building their houses, have not like the citizens of some commercial villages, consulted their taste and their fancy, but have confined themselves to more economical views. The places of principal business are built of brick. The dwelling houses more generally are of wood. There is a prevailing appearance of neatness and durability.-- The streets in some instances are injudiciously located; but the general wish to repair the inconvenience is daily correcting the evil.--Church-street may be mentioned as a street well built, extending more than half a mile in a direct line, being four rods wide, and terminating at the south on a public square of four acres, the site of the academy. It may be called a handsome street.

On the west side of church-street, near midway of its length, in an open space of near three acres inclusive of adjacent streets, stand the new Church and the Town Hall, large and well finished buildings; the last is constructed of brick. The courts of the county of Waldo are to be held in the hall; and the county offices also are to be there kept.

The whole number of houses and stores in the town is four hundred and fifty. The first house of two floors erected in the town, is the Rev. Wm. Frothingham's: and the first house erected on Main-street was built in 1795, by Doctor John Osborn, it was raised upon the ground now covered by the Eagle Hotel.   5

James Nesmith commenced the business of a merchant at Nesmith's corner in 1799; and his was the first shop in the village. The east bridge thrown over the river at the village is 122 rods in length; it rests on framed wooden piers, and was erected at an expense of $18,484. It was built in 1806. A mile above this bridge one was built in 1801 at an expense of $6000; the last has been rebuilt. Nine commodious wharves are built for the uses of commerce. Boards and cord-wood, shingles and timber cut to dimentions, are among the articles of export. Ship-building is becoming an extensive employment. In 1818, the town was made a port of entry for an extensive district.

But Belfast had no more than a name in the hey-day of New England's peculiar commercial prosperity. From the close of the revolution to the close of the commercial warfare afterwards waged in Europe, it contained a small population. Two hundred and forty-five was the census of 1790; and in 1800, the number had increased only to 674; and the season of great profits was now rapidly coming to a close. No part of the wealth therefore which, in so many instances, during that extra-ordinary period was fortuitously acquired, came to Belfast. And the town also is without some of the evils, which a sudden influx of property, that comes without judgment or labour, and before expectation, is calculated to create.--Econom as a characteristic of the people, is therefore, to be expected as the necessary result of moderate earnings.

In 1810 the number of inhabitants was 1259, and in 1820, two thousand and twenty six. The population is rapidly increasing, as well as the employment of the useful classes.

[The village affords,
Apothecaries   3--Booksellers   2--Bookbinder   1--Butchers   3--Brick-masons
6--Brick-makers   2--Block-maker   1--Barbers   2--Clock-makers   2--Clothiers
2--Cabinet-makers   3--Chair-maker   1--Counsellors   and   Attorneys   at   law
10--Candle   Chandler   1--Grocers   8--Housewrights   11--House-carpenters
4--Inn-holders 5--Jeweller 1--Milliners 5--Meat shopmen 2--Meat cartman 1--

Milk cartman 1--Ministers resident 3--Merchants 42--Printers 2--Painters
2--Physicians and Surgeons 6--Smiths 8--Saddle and Harness makers 3--Shoe-
makers 10--Sheriff's officers 3--Shipmasters 7--Ship carpenters 15--Sail
maker 1--School teachers 3--Tailors 3--Tanners and Curriers 3--Truckmen
2--Wharfingers 7--Wheelwright 1. The number of inhabitants is now estimated
at 3000.]

The civil history of the corporation is soon recited.   In 1803
the town for the first time was actually represented in the state legislature.*

It has since been the privilege of the town to furnish three+ senators
of state, and twice a representative** in the congress of the United
States. The judge# of probate; a formerE and the present county solicitor];
a former chief judge++ of common pleas; and a former chief justice of
sessions.[]

Mitchell had been appointed to a captaincy in the militia before
the commencement of the revolution. He declined exercising any authority
under the king, after the war began, and no company was organized in
Belfast until the colony of Massachusetts under the declaration of Independence had formed a constitution, for their own government. Samuel Houston
was Mitchell's successor in the office, and Tolford Durham and Benjamin
Nesmith were his subalterns. Durham% had charge of the company at Castine
under Lovell in 1779.

Samuel Houston, Jr. who had served during the war in Washington's
guard, succeeded his father in the command of the Belfast militia.
In 1803, a company of artillery was formed, and the year following a
company of light horse, and in 1822 a company of light infantry. These,
with two infantry companies, compose the military() strength of the town.

Preparatory to the war of 1812, a small fort had been erected at
Castine, and in 1814 was defended by a lieutenant and a part of one
regular company. On the first of September in that year, Gen.Pilkington[][]
from the Halifax station, after reducing Eastport and Machias, arrived
in the Bay of Penobscot, and finding no force to resist him, possession
of the fort at Castine was immediately taken; and on the following day
a detachment of about seven hundred men were landed at Belfast, under
the immediate protection of a frigate and two sloops of war. The regular
American troops had all left the district for the frontier of Canada;
and Pilkington's strength was not to be resisted by the few companies
of militia that could be brought into action. The enemy shew the utmost
respect for the persons and property of the citizens; and after four
days returned to Castine.

Schools for the education of youth, have been fostered by the town
from the beginning with that solicitude so common for that interest
throughout New England.   Fourteen district schools are maintained each

_____

*   Deacon Tufts in 1778 did not take his seat.   In 1803 Jonathan
Wilson was the member.
+   Wm. Crosby, Eben. Poor and John S. Kimball.
**   John Wilson.
#   Alfred Johnson, Jr.
E   Wm. Crosby.
]   Joseph Williamson.
++   Wm. Crosby.
[]   John Merriam.
%   Lieutenant Durham is in his eighty-second year, enjoys good
health, and all the native energies of his mind. He speaks of the conduct
of Lovell with great animation; and refuses to accord to him both the
merit of a good officer and of a true patriot. The General's management,
in the mind of Mr. Durham, stands directly opposed to the one, or the
other.
()   Present commanders, Paul Richard Hazeltine, artilery; David
Gillman Ames, horse; Joel Hills, light infantry; Jonathan Towle Quimby,
1st infantry; Benjamin Houston, 2d infantry.   5*
[][] Bissett's England, 3d, 283

a portion of the year, and in the village a number of subscription schools are constantly open. The number of children between 4 and 21 years of age, which by the law of the State are made the objects of instruction, in 1826 was 1183, as appears on the town record. The number actually schooled may be estimated to exceed one thousand. And during the summer months one hundred at least of those under four years of age enjoy the privilege of public instruction. Two Sabbath schools have been kept, in summer, for some years past; and with the happy success which so sensibly gratifies the friends of religion and virtue.

In the last year, a society called "The Infant School Society," was established. The following extracts from the constitution will discover the objects of the institution.

"The object of this society shall be to establish and constantly maintain in this village, a school on the monitorial system of instruction, for children, principally between the ages of 3 and 7 years." "It shall be one of the duties of this society, and one not to be overlooked, to furnish instruction gratis, to all children whose parents are unable to pay tuition; and to see that they avail themselves of the privilege thus afforded them." "It shall not be necessary in order to become a member to render any pecuniary aid to the society."

This society with a zeal suited to the liberality of the principles disclosed in their constitution immediately put in operation the school they had designed. They procured an able instructer, and upwards of one hundred pupils were immediately collected and the success of the school surpasses the expectations of its warmest friends.*

Sixteen years since, the munificence of individual inhabitants, caused an edifice to be erected suitable for a public Academy. They were incorporated as a body of trust, and eighteen square miles of land in the county of Washington, granted to them as an endowment. The trustees+ have not met all the encouragement they could have desired; but the institution has been useful and promises to be greatly so.

The present preceptor, with the approbation of the trustees, has adopted in part, the monitorial system of instruction. The number of pupils at present is upwards of eighty. The building was not located entirely to public satisfaction. To some it seemed remote from the village. The opening of new streets has in a great measure removed this objection, and the future usefulness of the institution will unquestionably reward the efforts of its friends.

One place is, for natural causes, considered more healthy than, some other places. No opinion of Belfast here can be offered; and any opinion upon the subject is valuable, only so far as it is formed upon facts which time alone developes. A young settlement has no character established, in this respect. Belfast has grown to that importance which may make the point a subject of enquiry; and it should not be entirely overlooked. The climate is to be estimated. Cold and heat, rain and sun, are very unequally distributed in the same latitude; the

---

* The officers of the Infant School Society, are,
David Whittier, Chairman.
William Poor, Clerk.
Daniel Lane, Treasurer and Collector.
Philip Morrill, Peter Osgood, Thomas Marshall, William A. Drew, William Barnes, Standing Committee

+ The statute board of trust, embraced George Ulmer, S. A. Whitney, Alfred Johnson, Phineas Ashmun, Bohan P. Field, Thomas Whittier, James Nesmith, Nathan Read, John Wilson, Jonathan Wilson, Thaddeus Hubbard, Oliver Mann, William Mason, Mighill Blood, and Caleb B. Hall.

average temperature of atmosphere in one place is not decisive of the degree of heat or cold in another place on the same parallel. Montpelier, Vermont, and Kingston, Upper Canada, experience a greater extreme of heat and cold than is suffered at Belfast. At the falls of St. Anthony, in the Mississippi river, the heat and cold are both less in degree than they are at Belfast; yet all these places are nearly in one line of latitude. It is not so warm or so cold, either, at Belfast, as report makes it in towns on the Kennebec river, nearly in the same latitude. Ten degrees of Farenheit, below zero, is seldom known at Belfast, and eighty-six above, is the very extreme of summer heat. If it have risen to ninety, accidental circumstances probably operated. The greatest heat is usually before noon; about meridian a light breeze in summer usually comes up on the bay from the south, and the heat is allayed.

In other places where the mercury is raised to one hundred, the heat of the day does not reach its maximum usually until three or four of the clock in the afternoon. There is less sun at Belfast than on the high lands twenty miles westward; and fog and mist is more frequent. But the fog comes from the bay, and so great a body of tide water may have a great agency in tempering the atmosphere about it.

The township is principally opened to the sun. The soil is a blue clay mixed with loam and a coarse dark gravel. The quality of a soil by some, is most satisfactorily estimated, by noting the trees that grow upon it naturally. The maple, the birch, and the beech were the prevailing forest trees; the spruce, the hemlock, and the pine were sparingly interspersed.

The prevailing winds are from northwest and from southwest. The formation of the river and bay favors these courses. When the wind is up, ice does not make in the bay, however cold the atmosphere may be; but in extreme cold, attended by the accidents of a calm and a snow, which are seldom united, ice has been made in the bay so that persons have passed on foot, over a reach of twelve miles. The first instance was in the memorable winter of 1780, and the other in the winter of 1815. Rains in winter have been frequent in late years; snow necessarily falls less frequently, and is often followed closely by rain. The changes from cold to heat and the reverse, are sudden and great, especially in the spring season. For Dec. 1826, and January and February 1827, the greatest depression of the mercury in a northern exposure, protected from the wind, was nine below zero; and the greatest elevation, in the same time and same position, was thirty-six above. The greatest variation in one full day was twenty-four degrees. So much for the data on which to estimate climate, and the probabilities of health. Some other facts may be added from experience.

Persons born in Belfast cannot be old, the town is not old; but many persons who were early settlers have lived to a great age.--Twenty-three persons have died in this town of a great age.

[The names of these persons, their respective ages and the years of their deaths, are seen in the following table.

"In their manners they exhibited a model of perfect plainness and simplicity, indicative of contentment and a cheerful disposition; and so cordial was their reception of those who visited them, that with truth it might be said, they were given to hospitality. Their descendants read the poems of Burns' with a keen relish, and are enthusiastic admirers of the Scotch bard."--Dr. Abbot's Ms.

1794 James Miller, aged 82 years.
1795 John Steele, 84.
1797 William McLaughlin, 90.
1800 Margaret Cochran, 85.
1802 John Tufts, 78.
"   Grissel Jameson, 96.

1807 Solon Stevenson, 73.
1810 Mary Brown, 90.
1812 James Gordon, 86.
1815 William Lowney,* 76.
1817 Patrick Gilbert, 78.
  "   John Brown, 86.
1819 Samuel Houston, 92.
1820 Jerome Stevenson, 82.
1821 Elizabeth Jones, 84.
1821 Laughlin M'Donald,+ aged 110 years.
1822 George Cochran, 85.
1823 John Durham, 74.
1824 James Patterson, 80.
  "   Jonathan Clark, 78.
  "   Susan Sturtevant, 84.
1826 Nathaniel Patterson, 79
  "   Agnes Robinson, 89.

* Mr. Lowney was graduated at Dublin College   6
+ McDonald was born in Scotland, and entered the army while a boy; his age is not positively ascertained. He remembered to have seen the Duke of Marlborough who died ninety-nine years before him; he came to American in General Wolfe's army in 1759, and after Quebeck was reduced, came to Bucksport, and from thence to Belfast. The lowest estimate of his age, made by his relatives, has been taken.]

Thirteen persons are now living in Belfast, whose average age is eighty-two years seven months and eleven days.

[Their respective names and ages follow,
Samuel Cunningham 88 years old; Wm. Cunningham, 86; Robert Patterson, 85; Jane Patterson, 77; John Cochran, 78, the surviving original proprietor; Sarah West, 80; John Burgess, 92; Nathaniel Stanley, 82; Alexander Clark, 81; Elisha Clark, 81; Tolford Durham, 81; Annis Cochran, 80; Elizabeth Campbell, 82.]

But our work is not finished. In 1802, when the population of the town did not exceed eight hundred, there happened forty-one deaths. In 1824, fifty-seven persons died in the town, and the population was then estimated at twenty-five hundred. In 1825, seventy-six deaths occured; and for these reasons these years are memorable. In 1802, the fever irrupting in measels, destroyed children generally, but the exact number of their deaths is not known.

In 1824 and 1825, a flux and fever with measles prevailed; in 1826 the alarm had not subsided, but the deaths were only fifty.--Children suffered 28 of the deaths of 1824, and 45 of the deaths of 1825. Philosophy will make her deductions.

The commerce of the town is at present comparatively inconsiderable. Heretofore there has been too generally entertained, an aversion to foreign adventure. The coasting trade has not been at any time retrograde, and perhaps the same may be said of the commerce called foreign; but all branches of maritime concern have felt the fluctuations that have been common to the whole country. Mr. Bradbury, of the Custom House, informs, that in 1825 "twenty-five vessels, mostly brigs, loaded at the port of Belfast, for foreign ports, nearly all for the West India Islands; their tonnage amounted to three thousand seven hundred and forty. Their cargoes were generally the productions of the industry and soil of this and the neighboring towns. The following were some of the principal articles of export--2,168,000 feet boards and scantling-- 744,000 shingles--63,000 staves--20,500 feet of oars--3,390 sugar box shooks--1,736 hhd. shooks--295 spars--478 boxes soap--160 bbls. pickled fish--46 hhds. and 480 boxes dried cod-fish--261 bbls. potatoes--

150 boxes candles, &c. valued at twenty-six thousand dollars."

Of the coasting interest, no custom-house record is to be had. James McCrillis, Esq. has had charge of the east bridge for five years last in succession. By his books he discloses, that an average of two hundred vessels pass through the draw in each year. Merchants in the village may disagree in judgment, but a quarter of the vessels clearing coastwise from the town, it is believed do not pass above the bridge. If then eight hundred cargoes coastwise in a year are now exported, the trade of the town is not behind the trade of the neighboring villages.

The first inhabitants of Belfast were christians of a straight sect. They were born and nurtured in the faith and pious forms and ceremonies, their fathers, from James 1st had received and cherished. Not more perfect however than the "pilgrims" as they increased in numbers and the means of leisure and enjoyment, they became involved in religious feuds.

In the broken traces of their proceedings leading to the purchase of the township, it is to be discovered that they kept a steady eye upon the object of a distinct provision for the church. Their solicitude was so apparent, and seemed so commendable, to the grantors themsleves, that they included in the grant one hundred and fifty acres, above the quantity purchased, "for the use of the ministry."* In the first summer of their coming to their estates, and when no more than five families had arrived, Mr. Murray, then of Boothbay, was induced to make them a visit, and in the language of the time, give them a sabbath, and administer to them the consolations of his office.

In each succeeding year, to the time of their dispersion by the British army, this little flock made liberal provision for religious instruction. If teachers were not always had, no effort was spared on the part of the society to obtain them. Nevertheless all was not perfect. Some members it seems were not conformed to duty in some things. To the more cautious and heedful this made occasion for offences; and in Oct. 1775, the attention of the whole corporation is called to the subject of the observance of the sabbath, in an article annexed to a warrant for holding a town meeting; and a vote was taken, and is recorded, that whoever shall make an unnecessary visit on the sabbath, shall be held in contempt by the people until attonement shall be made by a public confession. When the peace of seventeen hundred eighty three permitted them to return to their homes they brought with them the same warm zeal for the church. Now now content with liberal appropriations for the support of the gospel, in 1789 a vigorous attempt was made to erect a house for public worship.

Those, and all those, then westward of the river, although a small minority were opposed to erecting a house on the eastern side of the harbour, formally protested against it, and the subject was postponed. Three years afterwards a proposition for each section to build a house for themselves, without charge to the other, met with no opposition.

The house now to be seen on the east side of the river, was accordingly built, and also that house now so commodiously repaired, and by the Baptist society occupied in the village. The Baptist purchased the house in 1822, and removed it to the place where it now stands.

Until 1796, the man, among the many persons, who had appeared as candidates, whom the citizens prefered as a religious guide had not been found. In this year the Rev. Ebenezer Price conciliated the esteem of a majority, and against the remonstrance of 24 members of the society, who represented in a formal manner their objections, pledging themselves to each other and to the town to withhold all aid to his support, and to resist to the last any tax that might be assessed, for the accomplishment and maintainance of the object, Mr. Price was ordained.

───── * Chadwick's minutes.

6*

In the following year twenty of those non-contents remonstrated with the majority of the town against the vote, to confirm the title of Mr. Price to the lot of land before appropriated to the first settled minister. This remonstrance being disregarded served no other purpose than to embitter the sentiments of an opposition already exasperated. The minority did not permit themselves to slumber. Solon Stevenson a man, memorable for his sincerity of heart, sound judgment and constancy of purpose, and twenty two others with him, carried the subject before the Legislature, and as a relief, they pray to be incorporated as a separate religious society. Here also the friends of Mr. Price procured a majority, and the prayer of the petitioners was refused to be granted. The opposition remained undismayed. New subjects of complaint were found, true or false, and old ones urged with new zeal; so that in April 1801, the town voted to withhold from Mr. Price his salary, and also that as a teacher of religion, they had for him no further employment.

In May 1802 the civil contract between Mr. Price and the town was closed by a compromise. And Mr. Price received a liberal compensation for his labors.

The town still continued to make annual appropriations of money for the support of religious instruction; and in 1805 the Rev. Alfred Johnson passed a season with them, at the close of which, the town, five members only dissenting, offered Mr. Johnson a salary of 700 dollars per annum to become their minister.

The invitation was accepted and Mr. Johnson was duly installed. The strife of the church, for a season, was hushed. The town was now making considerable acquisitions in population, by emigrants; among whom many Baptists were to be found. So numerous had that class of christians become by 1809, that it was deemed by them expedient to be made a corporate body. This stirred the embers of the fire that had been covered since Mr. Price was dismissed.

Some professed to believe that religious instruction could not be good if bought with money; and the town was now much indebted to Mr. Johnson. Those who should become Baptists, expected probably, to free themselves from this inconvenience; and when interest and religious impression coincide, there is not much doubt of perseverance. Mr. Johnson in a letter to the assessors on the fifth of January, 1809, exempted from any additional taxation, persons who should continue to fulfil their contract with him; assuming himself to sustain the loss of that portion of his salary which the seceders had they remained faithful, would have been required to pay. Yet the Baptist society increased daily, and in 1811 was incorporated.

Mr. Johnson's partial relinquishment of salary was not entirely satisfactory, and in 1812 Mr. Johnson relinquished it entirely during the war with England then commenced.--Two years later, Mr. Johnson dissolved his connection with the parish.

The population of the village was increasing, and in 1818, it was thought a house of worship was wanted within it.

Before the time now spoken of, the Rev. Wm. Frothingham had been made acquainted with the parish. The attendance of the people at religious exercises had become an agreeable performance of duty. All were desirous to become interested in the erection of a building that should afford them a suitable accommodation. Under these commendable feelings the house on Church-street was built. The work was originated, prosecuted and finished in great harmony, and is, and will be a strong bond of religious connection. On the 15th of Nov. 1818, the house was opened and dedicated; on the 21st day of the following July Mr. Frothingham was installed.

A majority of the early church, having found occasion of disagreement with Mr. Frothingham, relative to certain subjects of christian faith, refused their assistance at his installation, and a new church was organized.

The early church resolutely maintained their distinctions, and their countenance of Mr. Frothingham being withheld, they continued to be a society separate from the parish. This society has built a house for worship; and have enjoyed the privileges of an ordained minister; but are now without a pastor.

The society of Baptists, has continued to prosper, and is at present supplied with a teacher, the Rev. Noah Hooper.

The society of Methodists is also a large and devotional congregation; having built for themselves a house; and in the manner presecribed by that denomination of christians, this branch of the great Methodist family, is continually supplied with instructers, who are anxious for the safety of man.

The fifth and last religious association is that denominated Universalists. For two years past they were taught from scripture by Mr. Drew. They now have no teacher.

Thus under the salutary influence of entire freedom of thought and opinion, in what is alone personal, five different forms of christian worship are seen to be peaceably and profitably instituted in the bosom of a little community, composed of three thousand people.

====

JOHN MITCHELL.

John Mitchell did not return to Belfast, to become a resident, after the war of the revolution; but as he was so greatly active and efficient in acquiring the grant, and effecting the first settlement of the town, its history requires that some notice of him should be taken.

He was born in 1714, in the town of Londonderry, Ireland; and, when his parents, who were of the Ulster emigrants to Londonderry, New-Hampshire, came to America, was five years of age. He served an apprenticeship to a housewright; but he soon forsook that employment, and became a 7 well known practical surveyor, and a teacher of the higher branches of mathematicks.

Barnard, Governor of Massachusetts, appointed him to superintend a survey of the Scoodic river, and the bay of Passamaquoddy. In 1764 and 1765 this service was performed to the entire satisfaction of the Governor, who, having heard Mitchell's report of the expedition, and of the inducements the country offered to emigrants, became greatly desirous of obtaining a grant of land south of that bay and river; and Mitchell it appears, had inspired Barnard with a confidence, which disposed him to make the former a partner in interest.

It was on his passage from Boston to Scoodic, that Mitchell put into Penobscot bay, and became informed of the natural advantages which those might enjoy who would there establish a settlement. This knowledge he carried to his friends in Londonderry, New-Hampshire, and it has been seen, that his opinions were respected. But the settlement of Belfast was postponed to the prosecution of the scheme of Gov. Barnard. Many obstacles were found in the way of their success. Since the charter of 1692 from the crown to Massachusetts, neither the crown, nor the general court of the colony, deemed themselves to be endowed with the requisite powers separately to make a valid grant of land in Acadia; and a concurrent act of cession, by the two authorities, at this period of feverish jealousy, was not to be expected.--It was therefore proposed to treat for a title with the province of Nova Scotia. A stipulation was accordingly entered into with that government for a tract of 100,000 acres, and Morris, the provincial surveyor,* set off that quantity by measure to Francis Barnard, Thomas Pownall, John Mitchell, Thomas Thornton,

—— * A copy of Morris' map is in the possession of the author.

and Richard Jackson.   The Scoodic river northerly, and the Cobescook, or Denny's river, southerly, were made the boundaries of the patent. At this time, Morris marked the Cobescook as the St. Croix, which circumstance, gave rise in all probability, to the perplexity which afterwards attended the adjustment, by the English and American governments, of the eastern boundary of the states.

When the war of the revolution opened, no settlement, by the patentees, had been made within their territory; and the treaty following the peace, placed the grant within the State of Massachusetts; and, Mitchell being the only grantee remaining, neglected to obtain, or to attempt to obtain, from Massachusetts, a confirmation of his title.

In the mean time, as has been seen, however, the purchase and settlement of Belfast had been effected.   Mitchell was foremost in the enterprise; and with great cost of workmen and materials from Boston, built a saw mill on the Westcot brook, before a house had been erected in the town. To his management the proprietors entrusted their concerns; and he kept the records after the town was incorporated.   Of his six sons, five went early into the war, in the service of the colonies; four of them went, not to return.--Robert only, after the peace, being released from prison in Europe, where he had been for a long time confined, returned to his family. John first served with McNeal as a sailing master, afterwards with Manly as lieutenant.   George was a midshipman.   Samuel and joshua were seamen.

After the defeat suffered by Lovell, Mitchell lot no time in removing himself beyond the reach of British authority.   In the night following that disaster, he put what of his effects he was able so to manage, into a gondola, and with his family, and such others as chose to share his fortunes floated down the bay to a cove in Thomaston; where they landed, and crossed over the peninsula to fort George; and afterwards proceeded to New-Hampshire, where he resided until his death in 1801. His age was eighty-seven years.   7

MISCELLANY
====

There is a general impression among the people, that the trade of the town, has been in a decline, for the last two or three years. Taking the fact as granted, they are at no loss to find a cause of this change, but it seems all have not charged it upon the same circumstances.

One finds sufficient reason, for a diminution in business, in the scarcity of money; and attributes this scarcity of circulating capital, to the management of the monied institutions of Boston. Another, says that trade is decaying in most other places in the Union, and that nothing but the universal peace that has been so happily maintained, for so long a time, could produce an effect, at once, so uniform and extensive. The mass of retail trade in the American sea ports, it is conceded, has been, much diminished, by the almost entire suspension of commerce with England. But the town of Belfast has not, at any time, maintained that intimate connection, with British commerce; nor been brought into that collision with the Boston Banks, that the suspension of the one, or the rigid exactions of justice in the other, could produce a general sensation. If trade be falling away, the accident is chargeable to other causes.

Belfast is situate, in the midst of a country that has, continually, and steadily, though not rapidly, grown in population. The people collectively, from year to year have considerably increased the mass of means for their support and their comfort; and with this people, increasing in numbers, and improving in estate, the principal traffick of the town is maintained. Neither the peace, nor the want of British commerce, nor the Boston Bank management, supplies the necessities of these people; and still they are supplied--they are as well fed, and better clothed than formerly. How then has trade, in the aggregate, diminished? That trade has fallen into many more hands, than controled it in time past, is very true. And that many modern traders are neither serving themselves, nor the public beneficially is true also; but still it remains to be proved that the amount of business is decreased.

It is believed, however, that the open trade of the country does not grow, in equal degree, with the population. The experiment, which the Legislature has been trying, for the benefit of "poor debtors," has operated to put a portion of trade under cover. How the honest poor are ultimately to be affected by the experiment, can only be ascertained by the trial. They, at present, are utterly without credit--for the reason that they are raised above all personal responsibility. The statutes, having placed it at their option, to pay, have done them the infinite mischief, of robbing them of all their ambition to make an effort. These persons, deserving confidence, and who, under the policy of the past time, found it reposed in them, are now entirely excluded from the books of the professed trader. But in every neighborhood, some individual of credit for money, is found; and one too, who is ready to stand between his poor neighbor and his necessities, upon stipulated terms. By pledging his own credit, he procures for his neighbor the supply of his wants, at a price enhanced by an intermediate profit. Whether this system will make slaves of the honest poor, the experiment alone can test. That it will build up a few individuals in each town with the sweat and the labor of the poor is already more than probable. Yet no one can doubt that the best interests of the poor were supposed to be consulted, in adopting the legislation, that leads to these results.

A single glance at the future may here be admissible. In estimating the chances of Belfast to take precedence, at some future day, of the other towns upon the Penobscot, there is wide room for difference of opinion. The subject presents itself to different persons in very different aspects. Partiality insensibly operates with some, and the want of

a knowledge of the whole ground, is a source of error in others.   And
none may presume to pronounce a final opinion without hesitation.
     It is doubted perhaps by no one, that some town on the Penobscot
waters, by common consent, will ere long become the principal mart upon
these waters--Camden, Belfast, Prospect, Frankfort, and Bangor, have
each had their pretentions to this distinction.   We will consider them
according to the information we have obtained,--after premising that
two circumstances, must be kept in view--a common centre and a good
harbor.   Camden has the advantage of being nearest to sea, but consequently
is removed from the centre; and the town environed by hills which forbid
easy roads to reach it from the interior.   The site of the town is a
pleasant one; the harbour is small, and not easy of access.   Bangor
has claims to great consideration.   It stands at the head of summer
navigation, about fifty miles above Camden.   The river is safely navigated
to Bangor, and will shortly be settled to its sources but the ice in
the river suspends navigation four months in the year, and time will
produce as many clusters of houses and stores as there may be found
mill seats on the river.   Frankfort, at the head of winter navigation,
might be considered as the natural rival to Bangor, but the map shows
its location, in relation to the interior, to be unfavorable, calculating
that trade is to come principally from the north and the west, both
Frankfort and Prospect, are in some respect, insulated; and the formation
of the country makes the approach to them any thing but easy and direct.
And if at no time the ince below Frankfort is impenetrable it is often
found to be greatly embarrassing and injurious to navigation.--Belfast
holds the intermediate ground among the aspirants.   Within the knowledge
of. man, its harbour has been twice only seriously blockaded by ice,
(1780, and 1815,) in that respect therefore it is greatly more eligible
than the harbor of Portland or Boston, being at all times as accessible
as either of them, and when entered, is found more commodious and safe.
In the discussion of this subject it is not remembered, if the strongest
argument in its support have ever been urged.   Belfast is the natural
seaport of the northern and western Kennebeck; and it is no strength
of fancy to imagine that nature once thought of bringing that river
to the ocean at this place.   From Winslow to Belfast the distance is
twenty-eight miles over a champaigne country.   It is more than two thirds
the same distance from Winslow to Hallowell.   Four months of the year,
the difference in the cost of transportation between Winslow and these
towns would not be material.   By taking an early, and employing a late
hour, horses will perform the journey to Belfast and return the same
day.
     But the difference in distance is more than compensated by difference
in market.   The one is open to the world; from the other all competition
is excluded by ice.   This circumstance in winter operates as a tax of
a whole tithe upon the farmer who shall frequent the Hallowell market.
But the winter is the farmers market season.   He cannot wait for the
ice to disappear that he may transport his products by boat to Hallowell;
when that time arrives he is employed in preparing to raise another
crop.   In fine, Belfast is forty miles up into the heart of a country
as suitable for agriculture as any portion of New-England, and is the
centre of Maine.   With capital and enterprize at any moment she may
take the trade of the vale of the Kennebeck with mutual profit.   The
remotest angle of the county of Somerset is nearer to Belfast than to
Portland.   And if by many the idea may be reckoned among the chimeras
of the day--yet it must be admitted as possible that Belfast one day
shall have become the largest town in the State.   One thing is already
certain, that many circumstances, powerful as nature can make them,
are now conspiring to bring to pass, if possible, that event.

The County of Waldo, of which Belfast is the court town, is constituted of twenty-three towns and two plantations.

The following is a list of them, with the census of 1820; and also that of 1810, so far as it was taken is annexed.

Towns	Census of 1820	Census of 1810.
Belfast	2026	1274
Belmont	743	----
Brooks	318	----
Burnham	202	----
Camden	1825	1607
Frankfort	2127	1493
Freedom	788	----
Hope	1179	787
Islesboro'	639	583
Jackson	375	----
Knox	560	----
Lincolnville	1294	1013
Liberty	409	----
Monroe	630	----
Montville	1266	864
Northport	939	780
Palermo	1056	761
Prospect	1771	1300
Searsmont	675	----
Swanville	503	----
Thorndike	438	----
Troy	505	----
Unity	978	793
Appleton Plantation	511	----
Waldo "	245	----
	22,002	11,255

APPENDIX
====
[No. 1.]

The author is indebted to his friend, GEORGE WATSON, Esq. for the
following accurate, and only perfect translation of the Patent to De
Monts that has been made. Some of the language of the original, has
become obsolete; in other instances it is technical.--Mr. Watson has
overcome all these embarrassments, and whoever will compare this version
with that published in London in 1654, can have no hesitation in determining
to which of them, the preference should be given.

LETTERS PATENT for the Sieur de Monts, lieutenant-general of Acadia,
and the adjoining countries; November 8, 1603.
HENRY, by the grace of God, king of France, and Navarre,--to our
dear and well beloved Sieur de Monts, gentleman in ordinary of our bed-cham-
ber, greeting.
As our greatest care and labor, since our accession to this crown,
is, and always has been, to maintain and preserve it in its ancient
dignity, greatness, and splendor; and to extend, and enlarge, as far
as lawfully may be done, its boundaries and limits: *8
WE, being of a long time informed of the situation, and condition of
the countries and territory of Acadia; moved, above all things, by a
peculiar zeal, and a devout and firm resolution, which we have taken,
with the aid and assistance of God, the author, distributor, and protector
of all kingdoms and states,--to cause to be converted, brought over,
and instructed in christianity, and in the belief and profession of
our faith and religion, the people who inhabit that country, at present
a barbarous race,--atheists, without faith or religion; and to draw
them from the ignorance and infidelity in which they now are. Having
also for a long time understood, by the reports of masters of vessels,
pilots, merchants, and others, who a long time ago visited, frequented
and traded with the people of these parts, how profitable, convenient
and useful would be to us, our states and subjects, the residence, possession
and settlement of those places, by the great and apparent profit which
may be drawn from the great frequency and connection with the people
there; and the trade and commerce, which by these means may be safely
entered into, and carried on: WE, for these causes fully confiding
in your great prudence, and in the knowledge and experience which you
have of the quality, condition, and situation of Acadia,--from the divers
voyages, travels, and repeated visits which you have made in those parts,
and others near thereto,--assuring ourselves that this our resolution
and intention being to you committed, you will know how to execute it
attentively, diligently, and not less courageously and valorously, and
bring it to the perfection we dsire;--we have expressly appointed, and
established,--and by these presents, signed by our own hand,--we do
appoint, ordain, make, constitute, and establish you our lieutenant-general
to represent our person in the country, territory, coasts and confines
of Acadia; beginning at the fortieth degree, to the forty-sixth degreee
[of north latitude]; and within the said extent, or part thereof, as
far inland as may be done, to establish, extend, and cause to be made
known, our name, power, and authority; and unto the same, to subject,
cause to submit, and to obey, all the people of the said land and parts
adjacent and by the means thereof, and by all other lawful ways and
means, to call upon, instruct, urge and excite them to the knowledge
of God, and to the light of the faith, and the christian religion;--to
establish it there,--and in the exercise and profession thereof, to
maintain, keep and preserve the said people, and all others inhabiting
the said places; and in peace, repose, and tranquillity, to command
there, as well by sea as by land; to ordain, decide, and cause to be
executed all that you will judge necessary, and be able to do, to maintain,

keep, and preserve the said places under our power and authority,--by the forms, ways and means prescribed by our ordinances; And to aid and assist you in the premises,--to appoint establish and constitute all needful officers, as well in concerns of war, as of justice and policy,--in the first instance,--and from thence afterward to be nominated by you, and presented to us for our approbation and confirmation,--and to give such commissions, titles and grants as may be necessary.

And as circumstances may required yourself, with the advice of prudent and capable men, to prescribe, under our good pleasure, laws, statutes and ordinances, (as conformable to ours as may be) especially in such matters and things as are not provided for by these presents;-- effectually to negotiate treaties of peace, alliance and confederation. good friendship, correspondence and communication with the said people, and their princes, and others having power and command over them;--to maintain, keep, and carefully observe the treaties and alliances which you shall enter into with them:--provided they do the same on their part; and in default thereof to make open war, to compel them, and bring them back to such reason as you shall judge necessary, for the honor obedience and service of God,--and the establishing, maintaining and preserving our authority among them; at least to visit and frequent there by yourself and by all our subjects, in all safety liberty, intercourse and communication; to negotiate and trade there amicably and peaceably; to give and grant them favors and privileges, employments and honors.

Which said entire authority, we will, and ordain that you have over all our said subjects, and others who may go to inhabit, trade, negotiate and reside in those parts;--to hold, take, reserve and appropriate to yourself what you may wish and find to be most suitable to your rank, quality and use;--to parcel out such parts and portions of the said lands,--to attribute to them such titles, honors, rights, authorities and faculties as you will see needful, according to the quality, condition and merits of the persons of the country and others; above all things to people, cultivate and cause to be settled the said lands, as speedily, carefully and skilfully as time, places and conveniences will permit. And for this purpose to make, or cause to be made, such discovery and knowledge of the extent of the sea coasts, and other countries of the main land, as you will direct and prescribe to be done within the said fortieth and forty-sixth degrees; or otherwise as far as may be, along the said coasts and in the main land;--to search after and carefully find out, all mines of gold and silver, copper and other metals and minerals; to cause them to be wrought, purified and refined, to be converted into use; and (as we have prescribed by the edicts and regulations which we have made in our kingdom) to dispose of the profits and emoluments thereof, by yourself, or by those you shall authorize for this purpose; only reserving to us the tenth part of the proceeds of the gold, silver and copper; taking to yourself our portion of the other metals and minerals, towards relieving you in the great expences which the above said charge will occasion you.

In the mean time desiring your safety and convenience, and that of all those of our subjects who shall go to inhabit and trade in the said places,--as, also, generally all others who shall place themselves there under our power and authority,--we authorize you to build and to construct one, or more forts, fortified places, cities and all other houses, dwellings and habitations, ports, havens, retiring places and quarters, as you shall judge proper, useful and necessary in the execution of the said enterprize; to establish garrisons, and soldiers to keep them.

And to enable you to do this more effectually, you may take with you and employ the vagrant, idle and dissolute persons, as well from the cities as from the country,--and also those condemned to perpetual banishment, or for three years at least, beyond our realm;--provided this be done by the advice, consent and authority of our officers.

Besides the before mentioned (and what is otherwise prescribed and ordered by the commissions and authorities given you by our dear cousin the Sieur Damville,* admiral of France, in what relates to the charge of the admiralty, in the achievement, expedition and execution of the above said things) to do generally for the conquest, peopling, settlement and preservation of the said land of Acadia, the circumjacent territories, their appertenancies and dependancies under our name and authority, as we ourselves could do if we were there present in person, even in cases requiring more special direction than we have given in these presents;--To the contents of which we command, order and very expressly enjoin all our judges, officers and subjects to conform themselves, to obey you, and give attention to you in all and each of the abovesaid things, their circumstances and dependancies. Also to afford you in the execution thereof all the comfort, aid and assistance of which you may have need and be by you required,--all under the pain and penalty of rebellion and disobedience.

And in order that no person may pretend ignorance of this our intention and thereby wish to interfere in whole, or in part with the charge, dignity and authority which we have given you by these presents; we have, of our certain knowledge, full power and royal authority, revoked, suppressed and declared null and of no effect, hereafter and from the present time,--all other powers and commissions, letters and dispatches given and delivered to any person whomsoever to discover, and inhabit within the above said limits of the people aforesaid lands, situated between the said fortieth and forty-sixth degree, whatsoever they may be.

Moreover, we direct and order all our said officers of whatever quality or condition they may be,--that these presents, (or the certification thereof duly made by one of our belov- and faithful counsellors, notaries and secretaries,--or by other royal Notary,) they, the said officers, at your request, application or suit, or that of our attornies,-- cause to be read, published and registered in the registers of their respective jurisdictions, authorities and districts; preventing as much as belongs to them to do, all trouble and hindrance contrary hereunto; for such is our pleasure. Given at Fantainbleu, the eighth day of November, in the year of our Lord one thousand, six hundred and three,--and of our reign the fifteenth.

[Signed]   HENRY.
        By the King--POTIER.

NOTE. This peculiar and interesting document was first published in Paris in 1609, in the Histoire du Neuvelle France, by Mare Lescarbot; and the English translation, by Erondelles, was published in London in 1864.   9

----
    * In the French copy, in Hazard's Collection of State papers it is Sieur D'Anville--and in other copies Ampuille; both which appear to be erroneous, as Charles Montmorenci Duc de Damville, was, at that time, Admiral of France.   Translator.

APPENDIX.

[No. 2.]

To all to whom these presentes shall come greetinge Knowe yee that the counsell established att Plimouth in the countie of Devon for the plantinge rulinge orderinge and governinge of New-Englande in America for divers good causes and considerations them thereunto especially moovinge Have given granted bargained soulde enffeoffed allotted and

set over and by these presentes doe hereby and absolutely give grannte
bargaine sell alien enffeoffe allott assigne and confirme unto John
Beauchamp of London gent. and Thomas Leverett of Boston in the countie
of Lincolne gent. their heires associats and assignes--All and singular
those Lands Tenements and hereditaments whatsoever with thappurtenances
thereof in New-Englande aforesaide which are situate lyinge and beinge
within or betweene a place there commonly called or knowne by the name
of Muscongus towards the south or southwest and a straight line extendinge
from thence tenn leagues up into the maine Lande and continent there
towards the greate sea commonly called the South Sea and the utmost
limitts of the space of tenn Leagues on the north and north-easte of
a river in New-Englande aforesaid commonly called Penobscott towards
the north and northeaste and the greate Sea commonly called the westerne
ocean towards the easte and a straight line extendinge from the most
westerne parte and pointe of the said straight line which extendes from
Muscongus aforesaid towards the South sea to the uttermost northerne
limitte of the said tenn leagues on the north side of the said river
of Penobscott towards the weste--And all Landes groundes woods soiles
divers waters fishings hereditaments proffitts commodities privileges
ffrannchises and emoluments whatsoever situated lyinge and beinge ariseinge
and happeninge or renneinge of shall arise happen or renne within the
limittes and boundes aforesaide or any of them togeather with all Islandes
that lie and be within the space of three miles of the said Lands or
premisses or any of them.

    To have and to holde all and singular the said landes tenements
and hereditaments and premises whatsoever with thappurtenances and every
parte and parcell thereof unto the said John Beauchamp and Thomas Leverett
their heires associatts and assignes forever to the only proper and
absolute use and behoofe of the said John Beauchamp and Thomas Leverett
their heires associatts and assignes for ever more. To be holden of
the Kinges most excellent. Ma. tie. his heires and successors as of
his mannor. of East-Greenwich by ffealtie and not in capite nor by Knigtes
service yeelding and payinge unto his ma. tie, his heires and successors
the ffifte parte of all such share of gold and silver as shall be gotten
and obtained in or uppon the premisses or any parte thereof In Witness
whereof the said counsell established att Plimouth in the countie of
Devon for the plantinge rulinge orderinge and governinge of New-Englande
in America have hereunto putt their common seal the thirteenth day of
march in the ffifte year of the raigne of our Soveraign Lord--Charles
by the grace of God King of Englande Scotlande ffrannce, and Irelande
defender of the faithe &c. &c.--Anno Domini 1629
    [Seal]   WARWICKE

                            ====

                         [No. 3.]

    The ancient limits of Acadia are thus described in the treaty of
St. Germains. "Extending on the west towards New-England by the river
Penobscot or Pentagoet, that is to say, beginning at its mouth and from
thence drawing a right line on the north side as far as the river St.
Lawrence, or the great river of Canada, on the north by the said river
St. Lawrence along its southern shore as far as Cape Rosiers, situate
at its entrance; its eastern limits extend through the gulf of St. Lawrence,
from said Cape Rosiers on the south east side by the Islands of Baccalaos,
or Cape Breton, leaving these Islands to the right and the gulf of St.
Lawrence and Newfoundland, with the Islands thereto belonging to the
left, as far as the cape or promonitory called Cape Breton; and its
southern limits extend through the great Atlantic Ocean, drawing a line
on the southwest side from the said Cape Breton through Cape Sable,

comprehedning the island of the same name in the entrance of the Bay of Fundy, which rises on the east side within the country, as far as the mouth of said river Penobscot or Pentagoet."*   The French claimed however to Sagadahoc, which is the Androscogin.+

───── *   Intercepted French papers translated and published New-York, 1759. Smollett's England, vol. 2, page 120.
    + Turner's map of Nova Scotia.
                    *9

APPENDIX

[No. 4.]

Boston in New England, 20th October, 1654.

May it please this honored court,
    Providence having soe disposed it as to bring the province of Acadia under the power and government of his highness Oliver, lord protector of England, Scotland and Ireland, we well knowing what greate respect you owe unto the state of England, and not doubting of your readiness in any thing you can to manifest the same to them, are, therefore encouraged to make these few propositions in the name of his highness and the state of England.
    1. That you would be pleased to declare that if the English inhabiting in the country of Acadia be at any time assaulted with an enemy, or in any occasion of needing helpe from this government, you will assist us with such men as we may stand in neede of we paying for them according to the custom of paying soldiers in this country in any service you employ them in.
    2.   That as its well knowne, that at present there is noe wayes to maintaine the vast expence of the garrison but by trade with the salvages, as its now a settled law in that province that not any should trade with them but such as are deputed by those in authority in that province, that accordingly you would assent and consent that law and order, soe as when any shall be convicted of the breach thereof they may suffer as if they had been taken in the province of Acadia.
    Many reasons we might give and shall if desired, why there might be a compliance with us in this our request but we hope that respect and compliance with England will be argument enough to admit this favour, in which we hope we attend much the good of these plantations, and be confident you shall find us readie to our power to serve you either here or in any place God shall caste us in, and remain your humble servants.
        (Signed,)   ROBERT SEDGWICK.
                            JOHN LEVERETT.
                            WM. HATHORNE.
                            ROBERT FEARM.
                            MARK HARRISON.
                            ROBERT MARSTIN.*

*State papers, printed by T. & J. Fleet: Boston, 1769, page 254.

REGISTER.

A register of the Legislative Officers, within the County
of Waldo for the political year 1827.

COUNSELLORS.

SAMUEL WHITNEY, of Brooks.
JONATHAN THAYER, of Castine.

SENATOR.

JOHN S. KIMBALL, of Belfast.

REPRESENTATIVES.

Belfast--Ralph C. Johnson.
Burnham, &c.--Martin Edmonds.
Camden--Ephraim Wood.
Frankfort--Thomas Snow.
Hope, &c.--James Weed.
Knox, &c.--James Lamson.
Lincolnville, &c.--Samuel A. Whitney.
Monroe, &c.--Hosea Emery.
Montville, &c.--Joseph Gowen.
Northport, &c.--David Alden, Jr.
Prospect--Ephraim K. Smart.

COUNTY REGISTER

As the COUNTY OF WALDO is composed of a portion of Hancock, Lincoln
and Kennebeck, its register can be found in detached parts--and these
parts need some correction. These considerations have raised a belief,
that a register of the county could not fail to be acceptable; and it
has been prepared accordingly, and many errors that occur in the State
register are here corrected.

COURT OF SESSIONS.

Bohan P. Field, of Belfast, Chief Justice.

Joseph Shaw, Thorndike,   ]Associate Jus-
Thomas Eastman, Palermo   ] tices.

Committee on Roads.

Paul H. Stevens, Lincolnville.
Stephen Ide,Frankfort.
Philip Greely, Knox.

Judge of Probate--Alfred Johnson, Jun. Belfast.
Register of Probate--Nath'l M. Lowney, Frankfort.
Register of Deeds--(not yet chosen.)
County Treasurer--   do
Clerk of Courts--Hugh J. Anderson, Belfast.
County Attorney--Joseph Williamson, Belfast.

APPENDIX.

APPOINTED TO QUALIFY CIVIL OFFICERS.

Belfast--Alfred Johnson, Jun.; Daniel Lane.
Brooks--Samuel Whitney.
Camden--Jonathan Thayer.
Frankfort--Alexander Milliken; Joshua Hall.
Lincolnville--Ephraim Fletcher; Nath'l Milliken.
Munroe--Azariah Edwards.
Montville--Joseph Chandler; Joseph Gowen.
Palermo--Moses Burley; Thomas Eastman.
Swanville--Ebenezer Williams.
Unity--Rufus Burnham.

JUSTICES OF THE PEACE AND QUORUM.

Belfast--Bohan P. Field; Wm. Crosby; John Wilson; John Merriam; Alfred
      Johnson, Jr.; Daniel Lane; Joseph Williamson; John S. Kimball.
Brooks--Phineas Ashmun.
Camden--William Parkman; Jonathan Thayer; Benjamin Cushing.
Frankfort--Joshua Hall.
Lincolnville--Ephraim Fletcher, Nathaniel Milliken.
Montville--Joseph Chandler; Joseph Gowen; Ebenezer Everett.
Northport--David Alden.
Palermo--Thomas Eastman; Eli Ayer.
Searsmont--Harry Hazeltine.
Swanville--Ebenezer Williams.
Unity--Rufus Burnham.

Justices of the Peace.

   Belfast--George Watson; Samuel Gordon; Arvida Hayford; William
Moody; Asa Edmunds; Manasseh Sleeper; Ralph C. Johnson; James M'Crillis;
William White; Joseph Eayres; Rufus B. Allyn; James White; Peter Rowe;
S. W. Eells; John Brown; James Poor; Nath'l H. Bradbury; John Clark;
Hugh J. Anderson.
   Belmont--Joseph Drew; James Weymouth; James Bicknell; William White
2d.; Abiel Cushman.
   Brooks--Samuel Whitney; William Huxford; Joshua Perry; Jacob Roberts;
Thomas Sawyer; Luther Fogg.
   Burnham--Ebenezer Williams; Martin Edmonds.
   Camden--Samuel Jacobs; Job Ingraham, Jun.; Richard Wilson; Jesse
Cushing; Ephraim Wood; David Tolman; Robert Chase; Daniel Packard; Edward
Haniford; Charles R. Porter; Stephen Barrows; William Carlton.
   Frankfort--William McGlathry; Archibald Jones; Abner Bicknell;
Samuel Merrill; Tisdale Deane; Simeon Kenney; Bailey Pierce; Thomas
Snow; Joseph Thompson; Elijah P. Pike; Oliver Parker; James B. Chick;
Nathaniel M. Lowney.
   Freedom--William Sibley; Peter Ayer; Ithamar Bellows; Nathan W.
Chase; Matthew Randall; Robert Thompson; Jason Wood; Daniel Ricker.
   Hope--Fergus McLane; Matthew Beveridge; Almond Gushee; Wade Sweetland;
Micah Hobbs; Thaddeus Hastings; Frye Hall; Boyce Crane; Robert Jacobs;
William Battie; James Weed.
   Islesborough--Josiah Farrow.
   Jackson--Bordman Johnson; Thomas Morton; Ezra Abbot; Silas Warren;
Isaac Abbot; Timothy Thorndike.
   Knox--Philip Greely; James Lamson; John Kelsey; John Haskell.
   Liberty--Jonathan Fogg.

APPENDIX

Lincolnville--Sam'l A. Whitney; Hezekiah French; Jonathan Fletcher; Paul H. Stevens; Sam'l D. Reed.

Monroe--Joseph Neally; Ezra Thistle; Hosea Emery; Luther Parker; Winthrop Frost.

Montville--Timothy Copp; Cyrus Davis; Nathaniel Emery; Moses True; Richard Small; Sam'l Atkinson; Robie Frye.

Northport--Jones Shaw; Phineas Billings; Henry Brown; Jonathan Holbrook; Patrick Mahoney; David Alden, Jun.

Palermo--Moses Burley; Christopher Erskine; Samuel Buffum; Elijah Grant; Jonathan Greely.

Prospect--Andrew Leach; Joseph P. Martin; Jonathan Dow; Josiah Lane; Zetham French, Jun.; John Clifford; Ezra Treat; Samuel Shute; James Blanchard; Nathaniel Kidder; Green Pendleton; Stephen Ellis; Ephraim K. Smart; Benjamin Houston.

Searsmont--Noah Prescott; Ansel Lothrop; Waterman Maxcy; James Mahoney; John Moody.

Swanville--James Leach; Ebenezer Williams, jr.; Samuel Eames.

Thorndike--Joseph Shaw; Joseph Blethen; Josiah Moulton; Peter Harmon; Thomas Holbrook.

Troy--James Parker; Dennis Fairbanks; Charles Hillman; Hanson Whitehouse.

Unity--Henry Farwell; Daniel Whitmore; Thomas Broadstreet; Hezekiah Chase; Isaac Adams; Abner Knowles; John Stevens; James Fowler; Elijah Winslow.

Appleton Plantation--William Meservey; Benja. P. Keene; Abraham Ripley; George Pease.

Waldo Plantation--Henry Davidson; Hall Clements.

Notaries Public

BELFAST--Alfred Johnson, jr.; Manasseh Sleeper.
CAMDEN--Jonathan Thayer.
FRANKFORT--Archibald Jones.
LINCOLNVILLE--Samuel D. Reed.

Counsellors at Law.

BELFAST--Bohan P. Field; William Crosby; John Wilson; William White; Alfred Johnson, jr.; Joseph Williamson; R. B. Allyn; James White.
BROOKS--Phineas Ashmun.
CAMDEN--Jonathan thayer; Charles R. Porter.
FRANKFORT--Archibald Jones.

Attorneys at the Common Pleas.

BELFAST--William Stevens; Hiram O. Alden.
FRANKFORT--Nathaniel M. Lowney; Albert L. Kelley.
MONTVILLE--John Emerson.

Sheriff.

CAMDEN--Joseph Hall.

Deputy Sheriffs.

Coroners.

BELFAST--Joseph Houston; Stephen Longfellow.
BROOKS--Joseph Freeman.
CAMDEN--Ephraim Wood; Alden Bass.
FRANKFORT--Daniel Toby; Tisdale Deane; Henry H. Trevett; Elisha Chick; Nathan Weed.
HOPE--William Arnold; John Jones; William Hasty.
ISLESBORO"--Elisha Eames.
JACKSON--Jonathan Wright.
KNOX--Scolly Baker.
LINCOLNVILLE--Solomon Brooks; Josiah Stetson; Israel Miller.
MONTVILLE--Stephen Barker.
NORTHPORT--Benjamin Stevens.
PALERMO--Jacob Greely, jr.; Chase Robinson, jr.
PROSPECT--Paul Hitchborn.
SEARSMONT--Bailey Moore.
SWANVILLE--Samuel Eames.
THORNDIKE--Silas Whitcomb.
TROY--Joseph Green.
UNITY--Daniel Whitmore; Hezekiah Chase; John Stevens.

Inspectors of Fish.

BELFAST--William Becket; Robert Emery.
CAMDEN--Tilson Gould; Robert Ogier.
FRANKFORT--Tisdale Deane; John Lindsey; Abner Twining.
ISLESBORO'--Job Philbrook
PROSPECT--Daniel Putnam.

Inspectors of Lime.

CAMDEN--Job Ingraham, jr.
HOPE--Thomas Bartlett.
LINCOLNVILLE--Abner Milliken, jr.

10*

BELFAST TOWN OFFICERS for 1827

Nathaniel H. Bradbury, Town Clerk

Bohan P. Field,   ]
Robert Patterson, 2d [Selectmen, Assessors and
John Palmer   ] Overseers of the Poor.

Thomas Marshall, Treasurer and Collector of Taxes.

Auditors of Accounts.

Rufus B. Allyn; R. C. Johnson; William Grinnel.

Police Officers.

Philip Morrill; John S. Kimball; Samuel A. Moulton; Joel Hills; James Langworthy.

APPENDIX.

Surveyors of Highways.

District No. 1--Alexander Houston.
    "   "   2--Joseph Houston.
    "   "   3-- George Patterson.
    "   "   4--James Durham.
    "   "   5--Hiram Holmes.
    "   "   6--Robert White.
    "   "   7--Joseph P. Ladd, Stephen Longfellow.
    "   "   8--Robert Patterson, 2d.
    "   "   9--David Otis; John T. Poor.
    "   " 10--Samuel W. Miller.
    "   " 11--Calvin Pitcher, Benjamin Dillingham.

Constables.

William Salmond--John W. Shepherd.

Firewards.

George Watson.	Philip Morrill
Daniel Lane	John S. Kimball
Joseph Smith	Bohan P. Field
Benjamin Hazeltine	Benjamin Cunningham
Ralph C. Johnson	Salathiel Nickerson, jr.

Tithingmen.

Thomas Pickard; Peter Osgood; William Durham

Surveyors of Lumber and Measurers of Wood.

Nathan B. Foster	James Gammans
Samuel French	John Groos
Benjamin Eells	Jonas Emery
John Haraden	John T. Poor
Samuel Jackson, jr.	Shepherd B. Blanchard
William Becket.	Joseph Treat
Samuel Jackson	James McCrillis
Samuel B. Hanson	Peter Winslow
Salathial Nickerson, jr.	Josiah D. Hinds
Thomas Cunningham	Otho Abbot
Samuel Gilbreth	

Culler of Hoops and Staves.

J. L. Moor.

General School Committee.

Rev. William Frothingham; Rev. Nathaniel Wales; Hiram O. Alden; William Poor; Zebah Washburn.

Law Agent.

Bohan P. Field

APPENDIX

School Agents.

District No. 1--Mark Blaisdel.
    "   " 2--Lewis Bean, 2d.
    "   " 3--Robert Patterson, 3d.
    "   " 4 and 5--Philip Morrill.
    "   " 6--C. C. Chandler.
    "   " 7--John W. Wilder.
    "   " 8--Benjamin Monroe
    "   " 9--Nahum Hunt.
    "   " 10--John T. Poor.
    "   " 11--Robert Hills
    "   " 12--Nathaniel Gilmore
    "   " 13--Dennis Emery
    "   " 14--James McCrillis

BELFAST DEBATING CLUB

Present officers.

Alfred Johnson, jr. President.
Joseph Williamson, 1st Vice President.
James White,   2d   do
Hiram O. Alden, Secretary.
John S. Kimball, William Crosby, Bohan P. Field, R. C. Johnson,
Daniel Lane, Standing Committee.

Insurance Offices.

The following offices have agents in Belfast.

Manufacturers and Mechanics, Boston--James White.
Commonwealth, Boston--G. F. Cox.
Protection, Hartford, Conn.--H. O. Alden.
New-England, Concord, N. H.--William Stevens.

====

CUSTOM HOUSE.

Daniel Lane, Collector of the Customs.
Nathaniel H. Bradbury, Deputy Collector, Inspector, Gauger, &c.
James Douglass, Inspector, employed in revenue boat.

Camden.

Calvin Curtis, Inspector.

Frankfort.

Aaron Holbrook, Inspector.

Bangor.

Joseph Carr, Inspector.

This ends the rare *Early
Histories of Belfast Maine*,
originally written in 1825,
1827, 1856 and 1874. Tak-
en together they give an unusually complete picture of
the development of this
Maine waterfront town. We
hope that you have found
the book both enjoyable
and useful.

Picton Press

The following Every-Name index includes all personal names found anywhere in this book. Additionally the names of houses, farms, blocks, etc. which include a surname (such as Williamson's block, etc.) are indexed. In all there are a total of just over 5,000 entries in the index.

Names are indexed only once per page, except when it seems likely that two different individuals of identical names have been referred to on one page. In the latter case the name indexed will be followed by a number in parentheses which indicates the number of times it is found on that page. "Wilson, John, 237 (2)" thus indicates that at least two occurances of the name John Wilson will be found on page 237, and that at least two different individuals seem to be included. Hence you must check each referenced page carefully to see if the name you are seeking appears more than once.

As is common in historical and genealogical works, names appear is a wide variety of spellings. Use your imagination, and check all possible spellings in this index.

Lewis Bunker Rohrbach, C.G.   19 July 1989   Rockport, Maine

Uriah, 127
Ballard,
  Phebe, 229
Banks,
  Franklin, 5, 170
Barker,
  Benjamin F., 153, 173
  Dr. -, 85
  George, 99
  Stephen, 277
  Thomas C., 88
Barnard,
  Francis, 264
  Governor -, 199, 264
Barnekoy,
  and Company, 156
Barnes,
  Elizabeth A., 150
  William, 142, 259
Barnet,
  Isabella (Durham), 233
  John, 233(2), 244, 254
  Moses, 231, 232, 252
Barns,
  William, 59, 72, 73
Barnwell,
  Lieut. -, 220
  Mrs. -, 220
Barrett,
  Jonas S., 129, 136
Barrows,
  Stephen, 275
Barter,
  George, 241
Bartless,
  A., 136
Bartlett,
  Dr. -, 114
  Thomas, 14, 68, 110, 120,
    167, 169, 277
Barton,
  Marjor -, 255
  William, 113
Basford,
  Jesse, 241
  Jonathan, 14
Bass,
  Alden, 277
Batchelder,
  Daniel, 241(2)
  Daniel's child, 241
  Mrs. Daniel, 241
Batchelder's,
  mills, 224
Bates,
  Daniel, 98
Battie,
  William, 275
Beal,
  Professor -, 153
Beaman,
  and Perry, 147
Bean,
  and Derby block, 58, 59
  Andrew D., 100, 153, 193
  Jeremiah, 244
  Joseph, 59, 98, 100, 137,
    141
  Joseph 2d, 137, 139
  Josiah, 100
  L. and J., 100
  Lewis, 59(2), 100(2), 173
  Lewis 2d, 279
  Lewis Jr., 243
  Lewis Jr.'s child, 243
  see Furber and Bean, 98,
    137, 143, 188, 192

Beauchamp,
  -, 247, 250
  John, 272
Becket,
  William, 277, 278
Beckett,
  William, 139
Bell,
  Luther V., 198
  Samuel D., 198
Bellows,
  Ithamar, 275
Berry,
  Abigail (Marshall), 136
  F. W., 136
  Franklin W., 131
  Jeremiah, 80
  Joseph, 80
  Watson, 131, 132, 148
Beveridge,
  Matthew, 275
Bibb,
  Henry, 165
Bicknell,
  Abner, 275
  James, 14, 275
  Stephen G., 14
Bigelow,
  William, 227
Billings,
  Amos H., 158
  Phineas, 276
Bingham,
  Albert, 85, 86, 92, 105, 123
Bird,
  Mr. -, 153, 176
  Samuel, 241
Birney,
  -, 144
Bishop,
  and Wright, 79
  Cony, 76
  house, 60
  Hutson, 58, 100
  Jane (--), 54
  Mrs. Nathaniel C., 76
  Nathaniel C., 76, 88
Bishop's,
  wharf, 75, 88
Bissell,
  Simon B., 128
Bite,
  tavern, 158
Black,
  Hayford, 92
  Jesse, 165
Black's,
  corner, 119, 141
Blackstone,
  B. F., 116
  Benjamin F., 117, 120, 125,
    129, 133, 140, 143, 145,
    149, 180
Blaisdel,
  Mark, 279
Blake,
  General -, 219
  M. C., 120
  Maurice C., 167, 188
Blanchard,
  Capt. -, 187
  D., 148
  James, 276
  John C., 218
  Samuel, 191
  Shepherd B., 78, 278
Blethen,

Joseph, 276
Blisse,
  Carl, 89
Blodgett,
  and Co., 47
  S. A., 24
  Samuel A., 158
Blood,
  Mighil, 71
  Mighill, 238, 259
  Rev. Mr. -, 60, 86, 95,
    212, 241
Bonabenture,
  -, 250
Bond,
  Benjamin F., 78
Bowen,
  Mr. -, 136
Bowers,
  Francis A., 63
Bowker,
  Rev. Mr. -, 150
Boyd,
  Rev. Mr. -, 197
Boynton,
  Amos R., 139, 178
Bradbury,
  A. H., 40, 105, 148
  Mr. -, 86, 261
  Mrs. Nathaniel H., 58
  N. H., 81
  Nathaniel B., 105
  Nathaniel H., 39, 40, 58,
    64, 67, 70, 77, 113, 117,
    155, 191, 254, 275, 277,
    279
  see Hendrie and Bradbury,
    148
Bran,
  Charles, 242
  Charles' child, 242
Brannigan,
  W. S., 149
  William S., 143, 173
Bray,
  Joseph, 66
Brett,
  Miss M. J., 191
Bridgham,
  Derrick, 48
Brier,
  Franklin, 176, 180, 188
Briggs,
  Frances (Towne), 136
  Jesse, 66
  Richard, 136
British royalty,
  King James I, 195
  King James II, 195, 196
  Prince William, 196, 197
  Queen Elizabeth, 195
Broadstreet,
  Thomas, 276
Bronson,
  -, 150, 154
Brooks,
  John G., 188, 191
  Rev. Mr. -, 186
  Solomon, 277
Brown,
  and Nickerson, 109
  Benjamin, 9, 131, 221, 243
  Benjamin's child, 243
  Caroline M. (Kimball), 129
  Charles P., 129
  Edmund, 4, 13, 14
  Edmund P., 158

CONSOLIDATED INDEX

Trevett,
  Henry H., 277
True,
  Henry, 243
  John K., 143, 147
  Moses, 276
  Mrs. Martha (--), 242
  Rev. Mr. -, 210
Tufts,
  Capt. -, 207
  Deacon -, 258
  Freeman, 188
  John, 207, 232, 233, 234,
    235, 237, 238, 243, 244,
    252, 254, 260
  see Waring, Tufts and Co.,
    99
Turner,
  A. and Sons, 114
Twining,
  Abner, 277
Twist,
  Oliver, 127
Twitchel,
  Josiah, 241, 242
  Josiah's child, 242
  Josiah's wife, 241
Tyler,
  John, 150
  President -, 123, 135, 144
  Samuel, 55, 66, 241
  Samuel's child, 241
Tyrconnel,
  -, 195

-U-

Ulmer,
  General -, 19
  George, 171, 238, 259
  Isaac B., 244
  Jacob, 220
  Miss -, 171
unknown,
  British deserter, 222
  Dr. - [liar], 162
  Harry, 84
  man, 120
  man [Millerite], 128
  man [Mormon], 128
  Mr. D- H-, 224
  Mrs. L--h, 226
  negro, 213
  preacher, 217
  sailor, d. 1824, 242
  young man, d. 1823, 242
unknown [Hamilton?],
  drunk & wife, 216
Upton,
  Charles H., 88
  Francis H., 85, 88
  Helen A., 184
  Samuel, 51, 59, 81, 85, 86,
    87, 89, 97

-V-

Van Amburgh,
  Mr. -, 149
Van Buren,
  -, 120, 159
Varney,
  Loring, 48, 240
Varnum,
  Mr. -, 214
Verrassano,
  -, 246

Very,
  Edward D., 183
Villabon,
  -, 250
Vose,
  David G., 191

-W-

W.,
  Madam -, 7
Wadlin,
  and Merrill, 174
  John B., 140, 168, 174
Wadsworth,
  General -, 69, 203, 255
  Peleg, 206
Wagg,
  John, 244
Wakefield,
  Mr. -, 157
Waldo,
  family, 213
  Francis, 231
  Gen. -, 252
  General -, 199
  Hannah, 231
  heirs, vii, 213, 252
  Samuel, 231(2), 251
  Sarah (--), 231
Wales,
  John, 241
  John W., 90
  John's child, 241
  Mr. -, 66
  Nathaniel, 71, 278
Walker,
  George, 196
  Jeremiah, 242
  Jeremiah's child, 242
Wallace,
  James, 224
Walton,
  Alfred, 190
  Messr. -, 75
  Mrs. Samuel, 242
  Samuel, 148, 190, 242
Ware,
  William, 176
Waring,
  Tufts and Co., 99
Warren,
  Mr. -, 158
  Rev. Mr. -, 240
  Silas, 41, 46, 275
  William, 158
Washburn,
  and Eastman, 59
  H. G. O., 99, 191
  Mr. -, 155
  Mrs. H. G. O., 37
  Oliver A., 85
  Zebah, 278
Washington,
  General [George], 214
  G[eorge], 110
  hotel, 54
Waters,
  Joseph G., 87
Watson,
  - (Leach), 42
  George, 42, 48(2), 56, 57,
    61, 62, 72, 73, 244(4),
    269, 275, 278
  Simon, 24, 33, 220
Watts,
  Dr. -, 46

Webster,
  - (Moody), 117
  Daniel, 102, 115, 116, 163,
    183
  General -, 117
  George W., 14, 39, 68
  James W., 80, 88, 90(2),
    91, 92, 96, 97, 99, 101,
    105, 123, 156, 188
  Washington, 11
Weed,
  James, 274, 275
  Nathan, 277
Weeks,
  house, 5
  Lemuel, 211, 238, 243
  William H., 146, 164
Wells,
  Captain -, 148
  George G., 56
Wentworth,
  Paul, 241
  Paul's child, 241
West,
  - [painter], 158
  Abigail, 242
  Ann (Patterson), 233, 237,
    253
  Enos, 233, 237, 239, 253
  Mrs. Enos, 239
  Sarah, 261
  William, vi
Wetherbee,
  John E., 93
  L. B. and J. E., 93
  Liberty B., 71, 93
  Miss -, 58
Wetherbee's,
  store, 87
Weymouth,
  George, 246, 247
  James, 275
Whedden,
  William H., 187, 191
Wheeler,
  Joseph, 145, 149(2), 173,
    176, 180, 188, 191
  N., 157
  Rev. Mr. -, 154
Wheelock,
  Mr. and Miss, 179
Whitborn,
  -, 246
Whitcomb,
  Silas, 277
White,
  - (Ashmun), 89
  - (Gordon), 89
  - (Hazeltine), 58
  - (Patterson), 62(2), 104(2)
  - (Sleeper), 161
  --, 14
  and Connor, 152
  and Kimball's foundry, 178
  and Rowe, 78
  Bloomfield, 207
  Elisabeth (Mitchell), 229
  George F., 58, 62
  James, 78, 89, 91, 95, 96,
    105, 107, 108, 110, 127,
    161, 166, 173, 275, 276,
    279(2)
  James P., 38, 62, 104(2),
    105, 176, 188
  Job, 42, 55, 155
  John W., 62, 139, 192
  Jonathan, 16, 62(2),